The Story
of Leisure

Context, Concepts,
and Current Controversy

Jay S. Shivers
University of Connecticut

Lee J. deLisle
Director of Parks and Recreation
Groton, Connecticut

Human Kinetics

Library of Congress Cataloging-in-Publication Data

Shivers, Jay Sanford, 1930-
    The story of leisure : context, concepts, and current controversy
/ Jay S. Shivers, Lee J. deLisle.
      p. cm.
    Includes bibliographical references and index.
    ISBN 0-87322-996-7
    1. Leisure--History.   2. Leisure--Sociological aspects.
    3. Leisure--Political aspects.   4. Leisure--Economic aspects.
    I. DeLisle, Lee J., 1954- . II. Title.
    GV15.S533   1997
    790--dc21   96-48339
                                      CIP

ISBN: 0-87322-996-7

Acquisitions Editors: Richard D. Frey, PhD and Scott Wikgren; **Developmental Editor:** Holly Gilly; **Assistant Editors:** Chad Johnson, Andy Smith, and Henry Woolsey; **Editorial Assistant:** Amy Carnes; **Copyeditor:** Judy Gallagher; **Proofreader:** Karen Bojda; **Indexer:** Theresa Schaefer; **Graphic Designer:** Robert Reuther; **Graphic Artist:** Julie Overholt; **Photo Manager:** Boyd LaFoon; **Cover Designer:** Jack Davis; **Printer:** Braun-Brumfield

Printed in the United States of America   10 9 8 7 6 5 4 3 2 1

Human Kinetics

Web site: http://www.humankinetics.com/

United States: Human Kinetics, P.O. Box 5076, Champaign, IL 61825-5076
1-800-747-4457
e-mail: humank@hkusa.com

Canada: Human Kinetics, Box 24040, Windsor, ON N8Y 4Y9
1-800-465-7301 (in Canada only)
e-mail: humank@hkcanada.com

Europe: Human Kinetics, P.O. Box IW14, Leeds LS16 6TR, United Kingdom
(44) 1132 781708
e-mail: humank@hkeurope.com

Australia: Human Kinetics, 57A Price Avenue, Lower Mitcham, South Australia 5062
(08) 277 1555
e-mail: humank@hkaustralia.com

New Zealand: Human Kinetics, P.O. Box 105-231, Auckland 1
(09) 523 3462
e-mail: humank@hknewz.com

CONTENTS

Preface   v

Part I   Leisure and Human Development   1

Chapter 1   The Dawn of Leisure   3

Leisure and Human Development   5
Early Divisions of Labor   5
Life Course and Survival   6
Security and Leisure   6
Tool Manufacture and Leisure   7
Diversification and Social Organization   8
Pebble Culture   8
The Advent of Humans   9
Fire, Order, and Communication   9
Fire and Leisure   9
Breaking the Circadian Rhythm   10
Homo Sapiens and Leisure Development   10
Specialization and Leisure   12
Aesthetic Forms and Leisure   12
The Mesolithic Era   13
From Hunting to Farming   13
Settlement and Community   14
The Waning of the Mesolithic   14
The Neolithic Era   14
Cultural Diversification   15
Cultural Accretion and Civilization   15
Cooperation, Survival, Leisure, and Conquest   16
Leisure and Evolution   17

Chapter 2   Ancient Near Eastern Civilizations and Leisure   19

Social Association and Effectiveness   21
Near Eastern Contributions to Western Culture and Leisure   23

Chapter 3   Ancient Western Civilizations and Leisure   33

The Hellenic Age   36
The Romans   42

Chapter 4   Leisure During the Middle Ages   49

The Dark Ages   51
Work and Leisure in Medieval Europe   52
Days of Toil and Holidays   54
Town Air Is Free and Provides Leisure   56
The Burgher's Leisure   59
Aristocratic Life and Leisure   60
The Influence of the Renaissance on Culture and Leisure   63
The Reformation, Calvinism, and Leisure   68
Leisure Activities of the Masses in the 16th Century   70
Leisure Activities of the Aristocrats in the 16th Century   71

Chapter 5   The American Experiment   75

Leisure in Colonial America   77
The Enlightenment   79
Invention and Humanism   79
Leisure and Recreational Activity After the Revolution   80
Moving Toward Part II   83

Part II   Leisure in Social Context   91

Chapter 6   Understanding Leisure and the Recreational Experience   93

The Free-Time Definition of Leisure   94
The Nature and Functions of Leisure   98

Work and Leisure 100
The Nature of the Recreational Experience 102
Recreational Activity and Self-Fulfillment 104
The New Behavioral Concept 106

Chapter 7 Community Coordination for Leisure Service 107

Community Coordination and Organization 108
Coordinating Councils 108
Neighborhood Advisory Councils 111
Coordination Through Other Efforts 114
Coordination and Cooperation 118

Chapter 8 The Economics of Leisure 119

Indirect Expenditures on Leisure 120
Direct Expenditures on Leisure 122
Popular Recreational Activities 123
Recreational Service 130
Economic Impacts on
Recreational Activity and Service 132
Economic Priorities 135

Chapter 9 Leisure Threats to the Environment 137

Finite Resources 138
Environmental Damage and Pollution 141
Recreational Impact on the Environment 148
Environmental Goals 149

Chapter 10 Social Pressures and Leisure 151

Human Relations and Social Development 152
The Influence of Social Institutions 153

Social Institutions and Recreational Experience 156
Social Disorganization and Its Effects 159
Attempts to Solve Social Problems 163

Chapter 11 Leisure and the Market 167

Historical Foundations 168
Leisure and Marketing 174

Chapter 12 Leisure and Popular Culture 181

Cultural Levels 181
Change and Popular Culture 182
Materialism and Popular Culture 184
Consumerism and Popular Culture 184
Popular Culture and Taste 185
Recreational Service: *Quo Vadis?* 188
Communication, Leisure, and Popular Culture 188

Chapter 13 Trends in Leisure 191

Classical Leisure 191
Modern Definitions 192
Trends in Leisure Service 195
Leisure and Aging 198
Summary 200

Endnotes 201
Index 209
About the Authors 217

PREFACE

This text offers a detailed examination of leisure as a significant aspect of human life from the beginnings of free time in prehistory to the present. The authors have attempted to pull together all the concerns that relate to leisure. Thus, we discuss historical importance, sociological constructs, political implications, economic impacts, and trends in academic perspective. All this material provides a framework on which leisure may be understood in context.

It is our position that leisure can be defined only as free time. Other scholars sometimes embellish that definition, but in our opinion, no other definition is logical. Those scholars feel as strongly about the precision of their definitions as we feel about ours, so this book may invite controversy as we deconstruct their definitions.

While all efforts dealing with leisure theory can help to move students toward a better understanding, it is vital to begin at the beginning. We need to explain what leisure really is, rather than loading the concept with extraneous values in terms of what actions or behaviors occur during this time. We have attempted to place the concept of leisure in its historical settings while noting the philosophical orientations that have influenced much of the thinking about this subject. We have been careful to avoid defining leisure as activity or as a psychological state; although we have named many of the uses to which leisure may be put.

This text covers concepts and eras that have been largely overlooked by students of leisure. It is designed to enlighten and strengthen readers' understanding of a topic that has had a long history of mythic interpretations and nonfactual reporting. We hope that this production will alleviate those errors.

Otium Opportunitas Est

PART I

Leisure and Human Development

Humans are set apart from animals in their ability to accumulate, assimilate, and record information about themselves. We may share sentience, communicative capability, and even physiology with other creatures, but only humans build on what they know, and thereby develop culture. History, a collection of fact, opinion, bias, and balance, reveals both the general and specific acts and interrelationships that offer a glimpse into the human condition.

Humanity's salient characteristic and extraordinary accomplishment is its unusually zealous level of function and inventiveness, its pyramiding aptitude to innovate change. Human culture uniquely moves onward (and, one hopes, upward). It has been multiplied by self-aware choices and options as much as by chance and natural stresses, by the amassment of a trove of experience and knowledge.

The beginning of human history is pure speculation. Biological changes internally and climatic changes externally radically altered the precursor animals into hominids and finally, after millions of years, into Homo sapiens. During these millennia, tools were crafted, fire was used, social organization came into being, and the accumulated knowledge that had been amassed pointed toward the need for cooperative efforts to achieve security. Hunters brought to a home base their prey for division and distribution. Since hunters could not be burdened by children when tracking or stalking prey, it fell to the females to provide child care at an easily defensible location and perform gathering or other domestic chores. The nature of the hunt required strength, speed, and stamina that was beyond the capacity of those females; hence the likelihood of early division of labor based on gender.[1]

At some undiscernible point, when security and fire combined to overcome the remorseless circadian rhythms, the shadowy prospect of leisure probably appeared. No precise date can be given for these events, but cooperative hunts and the taking of meat to a central place surely released time that was previously used to forage for food.

Time is the great ingredient. The developing human brain produced dwellings, fire, and manufactured objects with an incipient aesthetic touch only with much forethought. Free time was needed to contemplate such projects. Thus, leisure came to be.

Chapter 1

THE DAWN OF LEISURE

Objectives

After reading this chapter, the student will be able to do the following:

Understand the development of human beings from infrahuman animals.

Discuss the origins of the divisions of labor.

Describe how security led to leisure.

Indicate why tool manufacture proves leisure availability.

Explain how diversification produced a social order.

Discuss how fire increased leisure.

Explain why leisure permitted art to flourish.

FRUH

THE HOMINID, WHO CALLED HIMSELF FRUH BECAUSE OF the grunt he emitted when startled, awoke from his burrow within the treeline bordering on the savannah. He had slept fitfully. The night was a fearful time, with prey and predator sharing a common habitat.

Fruh looked toward the river flowing through the gorge. Every so often he would see others of his kind, but as yet no contact had been made. Orphaned early, he was fortunate to have survived. He could no longer remember who had first nourished him. It seemed that he had been alone all of his nine years.

The first order was to fill his belly. Because Fruh was bipedal and walked upright, he could peer over the tall grass that covered the plain. He sniffed the warm air, trying to catch the scent of game or at least the aroma of a carcass that might have some meat left on it. He could always eat grubs, grass, roots, or anything else that came to hand. Water was not a problem. But the urge for food was compelling and incessant, as was the need for alertness. The threat of death was a constant companion. When his hunger was assuaged, he would explore the immediate area.

Late in the morning he found remnants of a carcass. When his hunger pangs abated, he had time to think and remain idle for a while. He trotted to a cliff face, where the brassy sun reflected on some stones that attracted him. He picked up two. His opposable thumbs permitted a powerful grip. The stones were round and fitted easily into his hands. He rubbed them together and then, by chance, struck them against each other. The sound appealed to Fruh and he repeated the action. One rock split slightly and left a sharpened edge. Fruh did not realize what he had done, but this quality of the rock would have great significance when his descendants deliberately tried to shape rock shards to produce a sharp edge.

About 2.4 million years later, a paleontologist would unearth a fragment of Fruh's skull near Lake Baringo in Kenya and claim it as the earliest corroborated fossil of our own genus. Fruh's tale (and the time between the first exploratory experiences and the evolution of modern humans) is also the story of leisure.

Millions of Years Before the Common Era

10.0—*Ramapithecus* (Europe, Asia) ■ **6.0**—Split between apes and hominid line ■ **5.0-2.0**—Pliocene ■ **4.4**—*Australopithicus ramidus*

Almost a million years ago, a group of hominids sat around a well-tended fire in what would become Beijing, China. They were ensconced in a cave that had been the home of a bear. They had set up stone slabs at the entrance, thrown a few animal skins on the cave floor, and started a fire to provide heat and light. After finishing their evening meal, these humanlike creatures took the time to split the long bones of the animal they had hunted and to suck out the marrow. Enjoying this dessert was a leisure activity for them. How they got where they did, the artifacts they left, and the probability that they had leisure are the core of the story. The change from hominid to human and the parallel origin and growth of leisure contribute to the cultural (in its full meaning) development of the human race.

Most cultural advances have been made in ages when people have had and used leisure positively. The arts and sciences, particularly the humanities, developed out of the creative use of leisure. Free time, constructively used, advances society, enriches individual life, and produces massive cultural development over time.

One of the most illuminating methods for understanding the present is to view it from a historical perspective in order to appreciate its progression from distant origins to contemporary form. Leisure was a part of culture before civilization developed, before our ancestors learned how to speak.

LEISURE AND HUMAN DEVELOPMENT

Leisure became integral to culture when the human brain conceived the difference between survival activities and activities that developed without compulsion. In the beginning there was only survival, the struggle to stay alive. The nascent human beings of 5 million years ago must have learned to adapt to their environment. In the process they acquired certain skills and traits that permanently separated their descendants from other animals. However, when hominids were diverging from their infrahuman contemporaries, there was no escape from incessant survival pressure. Of course these protohumans could think, but that is no evidence of leisure. It was probably not until they had evolved to a point where they better

understood their habitat and achieved some degree of safety that they could relax their constant vigil. At that point, whenever it was, leisure was created.

The procreative act of these early hominids was a survival tactic in much the same manner as natural selection drives animals to pass along their genes. Sex would have been performed furtively, hurriedly, and with a wary eye for intruders. It was hardly a manifestation of leisure. As their brains evolved, these hominids acquired the prefrontal enlarged brain area associated with speech production. Probably real speech developed over the next million years, so oral communication likely occurred between 1 and 2 million years ago.

Australopithecus afarensis is the oldest known direct lineal ancestor of modern humans. *Afarensis* was probably well adapted to arboreal dwelling as protection against attack. However, over the millennia, changes in habitat, sexual reproduction, and the need to forage for meat protein may have caused them to begin the tricky business of learning to walk upright about 3.75 million years ago, or 2 million years before tools were made.[1] Bipedalism was an adaptation for survival.[2] The initial findings in the Afars region, beginning with Lucy (the name given to the female skeletal remains of *afarensis* by Donald C. Johanson, president of the Institute of Human Origins in Berkeley, California) waited 20 years for confirmation. The discovery of a complete skull in 1994 did much to corroborate Johanson's speculations.[3]

Afarensis was eventually replaced by *Homo habilis,* the earliest human ancestor. Olduvai Gorge in East Africa was one of its homes. Threatened by predators and scavenging for a living, *habilis* scratched out a living—just barely.

EARLY DIVISIONS OF LABOR

These antecedents of modern humans ate plants as well as huge quantities of meat when they could get it. Meat had as much nutrient value as plants, but in a more available form. It was present during the dry seasons, when many plants could no longer be found. The dietary change from vegetarianism to omnivorousness led to a new social order. From a large piece of meat, either scavenged from the kills of other carnivores or hunted, a hominid could obtain

Millions of Years Before the Common Era

(Middle Awash, Ethiopia) ■ **4.0**—Hominid (Kanapor) ■ **3.6**—*Australopithecus afarensis* (Laetoli) ■ **3.2**—*Australopithecus afarensis* (Hadar)

required nourishment and have enough left over to share with others not directly involved in the catch. This may have been one of the factors that made possible a division of labor within the residential group.

More significantly, the game that fed *habilis* was difficult to trap and kill, so some coordination of effort was needed. Planning a cooperative hunt meant a quantum leap in communication and social organization skills. Such development took enormous lengths of time to occur. The hominid brain, unlike the brains of infrahuman species, had the potential for growth and reorganization that made *habilis* and its descendants capable of planning for the future.

The size of the brain and its organization enabled hominids to survive in their fiercely competitive habitat. Until human beings learned how to make fire at their own discretion, preserve whatever food they could find or kill, ensure an adequate water supply, and build or locate a home easily defensible against marauding foreign groups of the infrahuman species and savage animals, their every thought focused on just staying alive. Until they had the luxury of ideas not concerned with survival, these animals knew no such thing as free time.

LIFE COURSE AND SURVIVAL

Critics of this scenario say that hunter-gatherer cultures at subsistence levels actually have more leisure than do technologically advanced societies.[4] This presumes that while hunting and gathering, such hominids interspersed leisure with their chief occupation—finding food. The business of survival would have precluded unessential use of limited time. It must be remembered that subsistence creatures were as much prey as they were hunters. Only during daylight could they hunt or scavenge. This left precious little time for leisure. Where there is technological advancement, security is relatively available and leisure flows from that source.

But according to the most recent and enlightening paleoanthropological finds, early hunter-gatherers were dependent on scavenged kills and, more often than not, were prey themselves. Then the habitat of *Homo habilis* changed radically, making survival even more difficult.[5] Continuous tectonic plate movement caused extended global cooling, which increased aridity at the equator. The rapid change in climate gradually produced open plains and a decided loss of tropical rain forest. *Homo habilis* had to adapt greatly to the altered environment.

Any comparison between early hominids and contemporary food collectors is unlikely, from both an anatomical and an environmental point of view. Life for *habilis* was short and brutal. Early hominids would have been adults by age 12, parents at 13, and dead shortly thereafter. True, some few members of *Homo erectus* may have reached 30 years of age, but the mean life span was 18. In terms of what we now know about the radically changing environment, shortages of food, carnivore enemies, and other features inimical to survival, 18 years on average seems accurate for creatures who lived 1 to 3 million years ago.

It is beyond the realm of sound logic to ascribe any leisure to an animal whose every waking moment is concentrated on survival and scrounging for food. The contrarian view insists that hunter-gatherers rarely experience famine but farmers often do. This opinion is flawed on several important points. Agriculture developed several million years after *Homo habilis* and *Homo erectus* eked out a mean existence from their habitats. The hunter-gatherer techniques then contended with animal ferocity and scarce edibles. Agriculture became the preferred method of food supply after *Homo* became modern humans, sometime between 40,000 and 200,000 years ago. The two systems neither competed nor nourished the same mammals.

Furthermore, modern hunter-gatherers, usually found in tropical climates, have merely to stretch out their hands to obtain food in abundance. Unlike their ancestors, they do not have to expend tremendous effort to survive. Aside from interpreting paleontological findings inaccurately, mixing cultural epochs, and spuriously attributing food sources to the wrong hominid group, proponents of early leisure overlook the short lifespans of *Homo habilis* and *erectus* in contrast to *Homo neanderthalensis,* who was, in fact, distinctly human.[6]

SECURITY AND LEISURE

Eventually, however, free time could have become available as the *habilis* brain developed and as generational experience led to social structure, which offered a little security. With less risk to survival, not all time was given over

Millions of Years Before the Common Era

2.5—*Australopithecus africanus* (South Africa); emergence of genus *Homo* ■ 2.0-0.01—Pleistocene ■ 2.0—*Australopithecus robustus*

to the incessant search for food, protection, and other needs. Free time (leisure) would have been used to make life easier and more secure, in part through the invention of tools.

We now know that human beings have been on earth at least 2 million years longer than was previously thought.[7] Recent anthropological discoveries prove that our immediate precursors probably existed 3.7 million years ago and the *Homo* line was separate and distinct from those of other primitive primates for approximately 5 million years.[8] This simply means that human beings and other hominid forms evolved along parallel, but not the same, tracks. Humans' larger brain capacity probably offered greater opportunity to think abstractly and to comprehend cause-effect relationships more quickly than other species.

TOOL MANUFACTURE AND LEISURE

While there is no solid scientific evidence of when prehistoric hominids first possessed lei-

sure, certain speculations can be made about the effects of free time on human development. During the time of *Homo habilis,* free time was available and tools came into being.

Tools are artificially and purposefully manufactured implements from natural or created sources designed to accomplish some objective. Simple stone tools are dated as early as 2.5 million years ago. As Johanson states:

We are still, of course, in the very embryonic stages of understanding the transition from Australopithecus *to* Homo habilis *and how this might have been influenced by environmental change which prompted changes in diet and behavior. As is so often said, necessity is the mother of invention; it is very possible that early hominids, observing carnivores, took advantage of a niche (perhaps scavenging), allowing them to procure some of their leftovers. Without the requisite dental and masticatory adaptations, they would have had to resort to another means of obtaining, in this case, bone marrow. I don't think they necessarily sat down and had a*

Ancient ax.

© Corbis-Bettmann

Millions of Years Before the Common Era

(Olduvai, South Africa) ■ **1.9**—Global migration out of Africa ■ **1.6**—*H. habilis* (Olduvai) ■ **1.1**—*H. erectus* (Olduvai)

deep introspective thought about what to use. But, it would have taken the idiosyncratic behavior of perhaps only a single individual to demonstrate the tremendous potential and impact of using an implement. There is documented evidence of chimpanzees, in West Africa, using stones to break open wild nuts. So there certainly is a tendency among our closest relatives to use tools in various ways.[9]

Stone tools made to a standard pattern first appeared around 2 million years ago. The Olduvai Gorge has produced a trove of these artifacts. Half a million years later, the sophistication of tool construction showed that the manufacturers were clearly more intelligent than modern chimpanzees (the cleverest of the primates other than humans). The tools are proof of some refinement of those portions of the brain that control manipulative skills, as well as some degree of foresight or planning. *Habilis* had cognitive powers beyond anything else in their world.

It must be recognized that evolution is not a continuous series of improvement up to the present. Rather, it is a discontinuous series of development or extinction. Evolution is a process of success through natural selection, environmental adaptation, mutation, and survival. If a species cannot adjust to its habitat, it perishes. If mutations by trial and error cannot find a happy genetic combination that promotes survival, the species dies out.

The same is true of cultural development. Tool-making did not develop from crude object to a sophisticated standard without a great deal of time investment and trial and error. It is one thing to learn that a large enough stone will crack a bone; it is quite another to invent a scraper, cutter, or hand ax. Getting marrow from a bone by splitting it would have been accidental, but chipping flakes from a rounded stone to produce a sharp edge would have occurred only with thinking, planning, and experimenting with materials at hand. Therefore, free time had to be available to early hominids for tools to evolve.

DIVERSIFICATION AND SOCIAL ORGANIZATION

Habilis needed tools to butcher the animals they found dead or hunted. The tools uncovered at Olduvai suggest the human characteristic of a brain separated into left and right hemispheres with particular functions of performance. No tool is merely a natural object; it is a specialized article deliberately invented to enable or enhance activity. Again, it no doubt took thousands of years to understand the need to get under animals' thick hide for the meat and to invent tools. For all that time, just keeping the species alive was an incredible effort. Therefore, society must have been organized based on the hunt, division of labor, and cooperative enterprise. By creating a new social order, *habilis* incidently freed some time from the all-consuming struggle to survive.[10] It was this free time that provided the opportunity for sophisticated invention.

The initial event that resulted in tool creation may have been pure accident, perhaps a foot cut on a rock shard. It probably took more than one such incident. Eventually, *habilis* must have discerned that sharp edges that could cut skin might also cut an animal's tougher hide. They may have searched for sharpened rocks. When none were found, they realized they had to fabricate a sharp edge on demand. They must have tried and failed many times until at last they found a way to hold a large stone in one hand while striking off flakes from it with a stone held in the other hand. These rather sharp flakes were the first tools. Once butchering could be accomplished, a new social organization was possible. None of this occurred rapidly. Hundreds of generations may have passed before social reorganization took place, but with it more leisure also occurred.

PEBBLE CULTURE

The hominids who lived around the lake that became Olduvai Gorge some 3 million years ago learned that certain rocks could be fractured to produce sharpened flakes. These flakes and other handheld stones gave rise to the name by which they are known today: the pebble culture people.

The pebble culture people must have had leisure to conceive of tools and actually manufacture them from pebbles and rock shards some 2.5 million years ago.[11] Although necessity may force an individual to acquire new skills, adapt to a habitat, or invent tools, leisure is an essential factor in any such invention. Without the time to think about a given

Millions of Years Before the Common Era

■ **1.0**—*Australopithecus robustus* (South Africa)   ■ **0.03**—*Homo neanderthals'* ancestors migrate from Africa to Eurasia   ■ **0.025**—*Homo*

problem and its possible solution, to play with ideas, it seems unlikely that tools could have been created and shaped for specific use.

Perils and disease were endemic in primitive childhood, and mortality rates were high. Youth was short, adulthood began early, and soon the individual was absorbed in the never-diminishing labor of defending and maintaining the group. Females were consumed with child care, males with provisioning. There was as little time for childhood as there was for adulthood. Nearly all of their time was taken up in survival behavior. Only with security through community were enough humans freed from the burden of survival to use the intangible values of leisure to create culture and, much later, art.

THE ADVENT OF HUMANS

The transition from *Homo habilis* to *Homo erectus,* the direct lineal ancestor of modern human beings, occurred during the lower Pleistocene period. *Homo erectus* spans a period of more than 1.1 million years, to approximately 100,000 years ago. These prehistoric humans wandered over what are today the central plains of Europe. Because they had learned to create and use fire, they could do what no other animal had ever done—adapt the environment to accommodate their needs instead of adjusting themselves to the environment. The dwelling places of *Homo erectus* could now be warmed and somewhat illuminated. In these caves they constructed a zone of safety. They did not have to fear a sneak attack and could more easily defend against prowlers.

FIRE, ORDER, AND COMMUNICATION

Beyond providing new opportunities for living, fire may have been even more important in human intellectual evolution. Some theorists suggest that by changing humans' habits, the use of fire modified their brain structure and improved their ability to learn and communicate.[12]

When humans took to the caves, they had to dispossess bears, lions, and other carnivores. They could penetrate caves to the deepest recesses with the light and warmth that fire provided. Unusual evidence suggests that fire was used in hunting.[13] The cooking of meat is assumed to have originated during the time of *erectus*. The ability to consume softer, cooked foods may have reduced the musculature of the jaw and its skeletal composition, enabling morphological changes that resulted in a skull with more space for cranial expansion and a larger brain.[14]

The psychological changes, which probably developed along with physical modifications, could have come from the use of fire. Less impulsive behavior would occur when food was cooked. Instead of eating raw food on the spot, people began to take it to their dwelling places to be allocated, cooked, and eaten. This was more enjoyable and required formalized constraint or regulation. It must have led to an advance in the ability to communicate.

Fire surely played an important part in changing one of life's basic rhythms. Instead of being directed by an internal biological clock, which produced a twelve-hour cycle of waking and sleeping, *Homo erectus* was required to awaken often to tend the fire. This biological adjustment produced an artificial environment that other animals did not have. Humans no longer depended on the sun for light and heat. The evening hours could now be illuminated, at least to some extent, and activities that ordinarily would be postponed until daylight could be expanded.

FIRE AND LEISURE

Domesticated fire brought a new leisure into the lives of *Homo erectus*. Now there was time to think about activities that were increasingly complicated—coordinated hunting, animal and tribal migration patterns, and cultic or ritualistic ceremonies that were forerunners of religious experiences. With fire, human beings gained time that was free of danger, insecurity, and environmental pressure. They could use this time and their developing minds to plan imaginative activities, attempt enlarged communication with peers, enjoy eating cooked foods, and perform activities that offered the physical pleasure of mental stimulation. Incremental leisure was one outgrowth of the ability to handle fire.[15]

The shift away from full-time engagement in survival techniques brought about a measurable increase in absolute free time. Surely this occurred over a long period, since brain

Thousands of Years Before the Common Era

development took place simultaneously. The biological clock, directed by a cluster of nerve cells buried deep within the hypothalamus, no longer held sway.

BREAKING THE CIRCADIAN RHYTHM

Writers who theorize that prehistoric humans continued to dote upon circadian time as the natural order of events fail to consider that the biological cycle was broken long before the appearance of *Homo sapiens*. If anything, the nomadic existence of paleolithic hunters was freely chosen in comparison to alternative lifestyles like farming, but they could enjoy their leisure only when survival needs had been met. It was not until fire became a tool that something of a settled leisure condition could be counted upon.

The statement that "the governance of cyclical, natural time was inherently leisurely" is questionable.[16] More likely, it was hurried, troubled, and stressful. Those unfortunate enough to belong to this cultural epoch rarely lived beyond 30 years of age. Individuals who achieved the age of 40 were looked upon as ancient sages of the community.

The nomadic way of life still prevails in modern times, and the nomads gear their days to the herds and the seasons they follow. However, these nomads have habitual settlements, artificial illumination, and other creature comforts that take them a long way from mere survival techniques. That they have leisure is unmistakable, but it is no more guided by cyclical or circadian time than the leisure of any other people who have fire or other artificial illumination. In short, any attempt to conceptualize leisure as an attitude or as indistinguishable from either work or survival activities must be considered suspect.

Homo erectus roamed the earth for approximately 900,000 years. During those millennia, certain physiological changes must have appeared. Toward the end of the middle Pleistocene, new evolutionary hominids began to appear. Some scientists have suggested that because of varying environmental conditions, the origin of modern racial groups can be dated to this middle Pleistocene hominid expansion. The later *erectus* and early *sapiens* populations evolved contemporaneously. Whatever future

discoveries disclose, there is substantial evidence that the humans of this era were craft-making individuals, and the tools they fashioned as well as the sites of their dwellings became the names by which they were known.

During the late third glacial period, the first modern humans appeared. With their greater intellectual capacity, they either competed for the same survival resources more successfully or eradicated their contemporary competitors. Traces of modern humans may go back several million years, but their evolution to the present form took place only 100,000 years ago. The upper Pleistocene hunters of Europe displayed cultural acceleration and technological progress to an extent that dwarfed all preceding *Homo* forms.

Additionally, their aesthetic senses came to fruition, allowing subsequent generations to mark their passage with cave paintings, sculpture, and the like. Such artifacts are the reason we know about *sapiens'* leisure.

HOMO SAPIENS AND LEISURE DEVELOPMENT

The remains found in the grotto of Cro-Magnon in Dordogne, France, show that these late Paleolithic people brought the human race a matchless step forward. They were artists who drew and painted on any smooth surface that could take their materials, as their drawings on cave walls and cliff faces attest. They carved as well. Quite a bit is known about some of the populations residing in European regions, particularly in France, where many artifacts, habitations, tools, and cave art have been uncovered.

Late Paleolithic humans traveled into North and South America and Australia as human development continued in Asia and Africa. During the 30,000 years of the late Paleolithic, *Homo sapiens* lived in small groups as hunters and gleaners. To all outward appearances, they looked very much like contemporary humans.

Art and Leisure

In diversity, taste, and style, Cro-Magnon culture far surpassed its predecessors. These people probably did not fear attack by other hominids or animals, at least not as much as their ancestors had. Upper Paleolithic people hunted the hairy mammoth as well as bison, reindeer, horses, and aurochs. Their greater

Thousands of Years Before the Common Era

neanderthals' predecessor and *H. erectus* diverge into evolutionary tracks ■ **135**—*H. neanderthal* appears ■ **120**—*H. neanderthal* uses

intelligence and the moderate environment in which they lived permitted a more secure life. When the urgency of the hunt was over, they had leisure.

What they did with it has been recorded for posterity. The cave dwellings and assembly places of the Cro-Magnards were alive with pictorial representations of the animals they hunted, tamed, or ate. Ivory, bone, and clay carvings and statuary also attest to their artistry. Although their drawings preserved in the caves of Spain, France, and Croatia show neither depth perception nor frontal views of any image, they display a high degree of skill and vividness.[17] These people used a variety of pigments to make different hues, as both the cave paintings and opened graves show. Color was a primary medium they used in life and death. Body decorations were painted on, and evidence suggests that the females of this species were well coiffed.

Upper Paleolithic people inherited many of the Neanderthal tool techniques, but they refined them to produce fine stone tools and delicately worked bone articles. The most striking change was the manufacture of blade tools used to work bone and wood. Among the various tool types were burins, chisel-shaped blades used to engrave bone, wood, or antler. Another functional tool was the borer, which was worked to a sharp point and used as a drill. Different scrapers were employed to hollow out wood or bone, scrape hides, remove bark from wood, and plane workable objects.

Notched blades were probably used to shave the wood of arrow or spear shafts. Among the implements recovered are projectile points that could be fitted to a wooden shaft and used as a hunting tool or combat weapon. These people even shaped daggers.

Upper Paleolithic tool kits are sharply differentiated by the inclusion of such items as polished pins or awls made of bone or antler. Between 17,000 and 12,000 years ago, during the period known as the Magdalenian, hooked rods for spear throwing, barbed points, harpoons, fishhooks, needles with eyes, bodkins, belt fasteners, and other assorted tools were common. They were often highly decorated with hunting scenes, animals, and lines. All of this suggests that elaborate wearing apparel, probably made of tanned hides, was a part of life.

Art and Magic

The numerous traces of artistic work the Cro-Magnon people left behind tell us much about their daily life, ceremonial practices, and stresses. The upper Paleolithic hunters continued to worship animals, particularly the cave bear. To attempt to gain control of a world that, despite their intelligence, they could not quite understand, they sought supernatural and magical explanations. The cave art they created

© W. Lynn Seldon

Cave drawing.

Thousands of Years Before the Common Era

has aesthetic merits, but it was likely designed to obtain control over natural forces by sympathetic magic.[18]

Upper Paleolithic man made dramas out of his rituals. To ensure a plentiful supply of bears, reindeer, horses, and bison, he made images of them in clay or paint within his deeply recessed caves. He then danced in front or around these images while praying to their spirits not to be hostile or angry with men, but to provide them with food as good parents should. At the end he symbolically killed the animals, either by sticking spears into the soft clay or perhaps by throwing weapons at those that were painted. The reality of the dance and the rituals thus became a cause-effect relationship that would create a future supply of food. Bison and herds of deer and horses were painted as if early man were driving them off the tops of cliffs or trapping them in marshes or within narrow, high-banked streams. By depicting what had taken place in the past, man hoped to ensure the duplication of it in the future.[19]

SPECIALIZATION AND LEISURE

Another indication that the paintings were functional rather than aesthetic is the fact that many pictures are superimposed on top of each other. At the Lascaux cave in France, some paintings are four layers deep.

In addition to painting, Cro-Magnon people sculpted. They wrought relief outlines on cave walls and engraved animal outlines. Some statuettes are fertility symbols depicting the female figure in ivory, bone, fire-hardened clay, or stone.[20] The prime discovery is the Venus of Willendorf, a four-inch high limestone statuette with wavy hair and exaggerated curves. If there was time to paint, draw, and establish some system of burial, and to wear elaborate hairstyles, there must have been much leisure. If women who had so many time-consuming domestic chores to perform for survival had the time to sit patiently and do up their hair in elegant ways, they must have lived comparatively secure lives and had social customs that allowed for free time.

Well-defined specializations probably required certain activities to be accomplished by certain family members or by one gender. Certainly some activities may have been combined—for example, hunter/crafter or shaman/artist. But it is more likely that clan or tribal members with artistic skills and talent were encouraged to work full-time at recording group activities, rites, and seasonal changes.

As in more modern times, specialization permitted specific periods of work coupled with periods of rest and relaxation. The late Paleolithic people were specialized enough to have time for tremendous cultural advances, as seen from their technical progress in tools, dress, habitation, and social customs. Another indicator is the secure position they attained in the various dwelling places they controlled throughout their 30,000-year history. The permanent habitations were strongholds with good water supplies, located along the migration routes of herd animals. Some groups lived in parasitic relationship to migrating herds of reindeer and wandered with the animals through their seasonal pasturing cycles.

AESTHETIC FORMS AND LEISURE

Security, specialization, and social custom all helped to free these populations from spending every moment on survival needs. Out of this arrangement, leisure developed. A culture that could spare highly skilled group members from finding food so that they could paint, draw, or sculpt was richly equipped to function in its environment. Some researchers claim the artists were not enjoying leisure but actually working for the welfare of the group through the functional use of art (art as magic). However, nonfunctional art forms, designed purely for the enjoyment of their makers and users, were also manifest. These may be called chattel art.

Chattel art forms are aesthetic devices not associated with cave or ritual art, but used as decorations on utensils and clothing, fasteners, or other bodily adornments. They are forms of self-expression rather than essential means for coping with daily life.

Whether art is functional or self-fulfilling, the aesthetic force does not spring full-blown into the world from a vacuum. Even genius requires nurturing. Upper Paleolithic artists must have had some apprenticeship before they could perform at the skill levels preserved in some of the caves and on artifacts that have been discovered. Such practice requires leisure.

Thousands of Years Before the Common Era

hunts deer and other game; Homo sapiens evolves its modern physical form ■ 50—Symbolic artwork appears in the world; H. sapiens

Without free time, the original artists and their disciples could not have developed their abilities of painting with various colors, carving, engraving, and sculpting.

If the chattel art view is correct in any respect, it illustrates the role of leisure in the advancement of culture. One might even say that the degree of leisure any culture has attained is revealed in its social institutions, its technology, and the art it produces.

The upper Paleolithic people were great travelers. They moved across the various land bridges then connecting the continents, thereby spreading very early to all parts of the old and new worlds. There is not yet sufficient evidence to date their movements and settlements precisely. Some scientists believe hominids trailed animals into the Americas through an unbroken land bridge joining Asia and Alaska as recently as 15,000 to 30,000 years ago. Others argue that these excursions may have occurred 40,000 or 50,000 years ago. Some New World artifacts have been carbon dated at 37,000 years old. In any case, early humans covered the earth through successive waves of migration.

THE MESOLITHIC ERA

The nomadic hunters' way of life lasted for many centuries in some parts of the world. In other parts, the human race changed significantly about 10,000 years ago, when the final glacial period came to an end and the modern climate began to develop. This period of change at the end of the last Ice Age is known as the Mesolithic or middle Stone Age. The people of the upper Paleolithic age, the precursors of modern humans, carried hominids far beyond what had been attained up to then. More importantly, they bequeathed to their descendants an anatomy that permitted articulate speech. The brain of these talented artists, crafters, and hunters was that of modern people. From them stretches an unbroken genetic line through all the succeeding human epochs.

The Mesolithic period was brief. It lasted from one thousand to several thousand years, depending on the people and the region they inhabited. It was a time of more efficient food organization, the invention of many tools, and the development of fishing as a supplement and substitute for meat. Some populations had long eaten shellfish, but shore dwellers now began

to eat them as a staple. People learned how to spear fish. They then developed hooks, nets, and weirs to catch them. They began smoking fish, both to preserve it and to enhance the taste.

As people began to learn about obtaining foods from the sea, they exploited new regions for settlement. They invented the dugout canoe, which helped them catch more fish and provided transportation over formerly impassable rivers and large inland lakes. They began to settle woodlands, with all of their natural resources for constructing shelter and hunting.

Among the inventions created by Mesolithic humans were the bow and arrow. They also fabricated stone axes, adzes, and mattocks so they could cut down trees to furnish housing materials as well as implements and fuel for heat, light, and cooking. All of these advances gave the Mesolithic people greater control over their environment. The bow assisted greatly in hunting the kinds of animals that provided their protein staple. Domesticating the dog made it easier to track, corner, and retrieve game. Dogs also served as guardians and pets.

FROM HUNTING TO FARMING

Despite innovations in tool manufacture and habitation, these people continued to rely on hunting as their major means of obtaining food. Wood, stone, and bone remained the basic materials for implements. The world's population grew relentlessly and the seemingly inexhaustible supply of open space and animals waned. Another food source was needed as a growing population placed increasing strain on both the herds and the territorial range of each group's hunters. Tribes could no longer move on to new regions when they depleted the local animal supply. Famine became a real threat.

For the first time, a new method of obtaining food would have to be attempted. People had long known where and when certain grains grew best. The cause-effect relationship between planting and harvesting had been observed and used to supplement diets during the late Paleolithic period. This information had been transmitted to Mesolithic peoples through graphic records on cave walls and bone carvings, as well as the spoken word. But it was not until hunting lost its ability to provide enough food that agriculture became a primary

Thousands of Years Before the Common Era

colonizes Australia ■ **40**—Cave art is created in Koonaldo Cave, Australia ■ **35**—*H. neanderthal* becomes extinct; H. sapiens appears in

source of nutrients. The agricultural revolution radically changed human existence. As John Pfeiffer states:

> Man's first major food crisis occurred before written records, before the coming of crowds and mass production and cities. It began 10,000 to 15,000 years ago, when there were fewer people in the whole world than there are today in New York City. It produced man's first and in many ways most drastic revolution, the shift from hunting and gathering to agriculture, from a nomadic life to a settled farming existence.[21]

The people of the Mesolithic era grew wild barley and wheat; in time they also cultivated many wild vegetables and fruits. With this first attempt at large-scale farming came the invention of tools adapted for plowing, cultivating, and reaping a variety of grains and other plants. Initially, the lack of prey forced people to adapt to farming for food. However, once nomadic existence died out, arable places were settled. With settlement came the need to farm intensively, because population increased much faster than it had when the nomadic lifestyle prevailed. Irrigation was needed as larger settlements used all of the available space to produce more and more food.

SETTLEMENT AND COMMUNITY

Farming ties the population to a specific place. No longer did the nomadic life influence the majority, although it was and still is followed by a number of people roaming through various parts of the globe. The cultivation of crops permitted the establishment of villages, which itself required the adoption of new customs, codes, and innovative techniques if people were to survive the stress of living in close proximity.

The Mesolithic was a short-lived period linking the upper Paleolithic with the Neolithic. There was an upsurge in sexual taboos and ritual as the establishment of a steady food source provided more time for nurturing social behavior and speculating about a spirit world or life after death. With settlement, housing became very important. Many types of residences, from mud-daubed huts to tepees and longhouses, were developed. The first permanent community was settled 9,000 years ago in Jericho, in what is today Israel. The establishment of Jericho changed the world forever.

THE WANING OF THE MESOLITHIC

In southwestern Asia and the Middle East, the Mesolithic ended sometime between 5000 and 7000 B.C., when a new life force came into being with the development of farming and the village settlement. The Mesolithic lasted until about 3000 B.C. in western Europe. To the north it continued for at least another 600 years.

The Mesolithic gave way to the Neolithic, in which most of the world's inhabitants remained until nearly the 20th century. That is, 95 percent of the world's population were farmers (peasants, serfs, sharecroppers, or tenants) until about 1850. Even at the beginning of the 20th century, some Europeans were still living as their Neolithic ancestors had.

The Mesolithic was a transitional period that retained many of the mores from the upper Paleolithic. But the farming ethic, together with village existence, did much to change the time schedule by which people lived and the amount of leisure they had. Now the pressures of limited space called another problem into being. The passage of time and increasing population spawned a desire for annexation; this can be seen from the ossified remains of Mesolithic people killed by arrows as marauders attempted to cope with the pressures of survival in a rapidly receding nomadic existence. The cyclical relationship among survival, threat, cooperation, security, and ensuing leisure began.

THE NEOLITHIC ERA

In the beginning was the need to survive. Survival usually required cooperation from at least one other person. Such cooperation led to trust and a better chance of performing those activities that ensured basic survival. Group living started with the family and spread to clan, tribe, and eventually community. Living in collectives produced greater cooperation and coordination, which required communication. Communication and enlarged groups required some codes of governance or sharing, which

Thousands of Years Before the Common Era

central Europe; Cro-Magnons migrate to Europe   ■   30—Chauvet cave art is created in Ardeche Valley, France; organized hunts occur in

became a force for developing a social contract. As soon as survival was ensured, a minute amount of leisure became available. Cooperation, coordination, and communication facilitated the lot of early humans; more leisure enhanced their lives and led to innovations in materials and ideas.

The heritage of human life continued to be passed along over the millennia and was radically changed during the latter Mesolithic. In all subsequent history, there has been the added ingredient of the ultimate human atrocity—subjugation by war. Approximately 8,000 years ago, a new race of people began to develop whose distinguishing trait was farming. The Neolithic era began.

The Neolithic age is characterized by five distinct features: (1) polished stone implements; (2) agriculture; (3) pottery and weaving; (4) domesticated animals; and (5) cookery. As with preceding periods, the term *Neolithic* refers to the tools made by the people of this era. But the Neolithic culture included other developments. Jericho, the first permanent community, now became the first walled town. Some people built houses with roofs, hearths, and food storage sections. Religion also played a role in this ancient culture; special rooms were cordoned off for gods and rituals. The people practiced both farming and animal husbandry.

CULTURAL DIVERSIFICATION

In their settlements along rivers and lakes, people were learning how to shape new materials. The accidental discovery of fire-hardened clay led to the making of pottery. Before long, people were making pots of different shapes and sizes and decorating them with carvings and paints. Neolithic people also invented the loom, which enabled the fashioning of woven garments and has remained relatively unchanged these thousands of years. In time they learned to spin flax, cotton, and later wool for clothing. Agriculture, village life, domesticated animals, pottery, weaving, spinning, and polished tools—these comprised Neolithic culture for the peoples of the Near East. This culture soon spread via migrant groups and individual travelers and traders.

Neolithic culture was not universally adopted. Some communities resisted it violently as a challenge to their traditions. Others simply never took it up. Nevertheless, the Neolithic culture was absorbed by much of humankind, especially those around the Mediterranean basin and in central Asia, India, Western Europe, and the Far East.

The chief tool of the Neolithic era was the hand ax, which also made an excellent weapon. Neolithic people used bows and arrows in hunting and fighting. Perhaps it was to protect against bands of archers that the inhabitants of Jericho built their surrounding walls. A people who had the bow probably also had some form of stringed instrument. There is little doubt that if they carved whistles from bone, then they used hollow reeds as pipes. They knew how to stretch skins over hollow tree trunks and over drum bases made of pottery. There is no evidence of when people began to sing, but since they had musical instruments and verbal communication, songs must have been sung. That people always had some leisure cannot be challenged. How they used that leisure is quite another question.

CULTURAL ACCRETION AND CIVILIZATION

During the Neolithic age, stone and then metal became part of life. Copper was probably discovered by accident some 5,000 years ago when copper-bearing rocks were used to encircle a campfire or cooking fire. First it and then the alloys of bronze and brass were smelted. Trade in preservatives (like salt), bronze weapons, tanned skins, and a variety of ornamental minerals (jade, silver, gold) was carried on over great distances.

The passing of several millennia led to discoveries of other energy sources. People in primary culture knew only the energy of their own muscle power. In the Neolithic age, they hitched animals to plows and sledges. Animals domesticated for this drudgery included asses, camels, reindeer, and horses. Even with these animal helpers, people continued to supply the muscle to accomplish everyday tasks. In the late Neolithic era, the invention of the wheel and of sails for small craft revolutionized the moving of goods and people over land and over the waterways that bound the world together.

Before the advent of the wheel and the use of metals, a more distinctive change took place

Thousands of Years Before the Common Era

© Corbis-Bettmann

Prehistoric drum made from scalps.

COOPERATION, SURVIVAL, LEISURE, AND CONQUEST

When people first tamed fire and could tell somebody else how to build a blaze from pyrites and tinder materials, when the older generation was able to pass on instructions concerning the handling of sharpened stones, wooden implements, pottery, and eventually metals, when food could be cultivated instead of chased, then people had leisure and culture progressed rapidly. But the cycle, once begun, was repeated over and over again.

Initially, survival was uppermost. Survival required cooperation. Cooperation permitted planning and coordinated activities, which provided some respite and, therefore, leisure. With leisure there was time to think, invent, and innovate. Eventually, such activities produced land exploitation, population increases, and the need to expand the food supply. When people began cultivating crops, they established permanent settlements from which sprang the stirrings of civilization. At each step, because of specialization and tools that made work easier and less time-consuming, leisure increased.

Unfortunately, settlement and social contracts had negative consequences too. The land space diminished, paving the way for raiders who sought to take over the rewards that hard work had earned. In response, each settlement created a warrior class to protect it. But this class eventually sought to expand the boundaries of its own settlement at the expense of other communities. These raids and retaliations returned the community to survival activities, closing the circle.

We have seen that throughout the development of human culture, some leisure has been present. Anthropologists believe that recreational experiences were a direct outgrowth of the possession of leisure.[22] Preliterate societies seem to have used leisure and recreational activity as both an instructional vehicle and a monument to human beings' aesthetic and creative tendencies.[23] When people began to gain some control over their environment and, by chance, learned to use found materials as utensils, they fashioned vessels of clay to hold their food and water. They decorated these purely utilitarian products with ocher and other col-

in the Neolithic. Agriculture brought the first of the surplus food supplies that supported specialized laborers who did not farm. People in settlements where goods and labor were exchanged or bartered learned how to maintain records and to account for transactions.

That Neolithic people had time to think and invent is self-evident, for only when individuals can relax their intensive preoccupation with survival can a culture flourish. Neolithic people possessed a great deal more leisure than had any of their predecessors. With it they developed primitive writing, some art, metal tools, agriculture, religious rituals, symbolism, and tribal taboos. The Caucasian age in Europe, of which the Neolithic period was the first phase, continued until the modern era of power-driven machinery. In fact, remnants of the Mesolithic period could still be observed in several parts of the world where culture resisted modern infringement or was isolated.

Thousands of Years Before the Common Era

Willendorf statuette is made in Austria ■ 18—Spotted-horse frieze is made at Pech-Merle, France ■ 13—Salar Noir of Niaux, France,

oring substances. We can see the results in museums of natural history. As human personality became more sophisticated over thousands of years, people expressed their feelings on the walls of caves as well as on pottery, thus symbolizing and transmitting their ideas concerning the creatures they met and the lives they lived.

LEISURE AND EVOLUTION

Early people could not control their environment mechanically, but they had human strength at their disposal. Gathering of families or clans into tribal groups and tribes into communities produced the first step in social organization, which ultimately led to the development of law. Tribal customs, based on taboos, superstitions, and the like, served to guide and formulate what would later become the political, martial, economic, religious, educational, and family institutions of the social order. While there was no differentiation among these activities during humanity's preliterate stage, they were the basis for the civilized complexity of more highly developed social structures. The ethos of civilization and culture finds its earliest seeds in the leisure that was first attained as evolution changed an animal into a human being.

The origins of leisure are as shrouded as the origins of humankind. In whatever era of human evolution leisure first came to light, it offered the unbounded time for individuals to strive for self-realization and personal enhancement. It has always been this way. Leisure is free time. Of course, there are many other theories of leisure, but this one has the virtue of simplicity. Whether leisure is used for personal indulgence, expression, creation, or indolence is immaterial; the point is that it is an element of discretionary time, limited only in terms of how it will be used or allowed to pass.

Thus, leisure is both a personal choice and a bridge between prehistoric and modern human behaviors. It has affected culture and social development. Contemporary leisure has antecedents in all previous times. What we do today (except for the added variables of technology) draws from past cultures and experiences that we can discover by the careful analysis of human origins, evolution, and development.

SELECTED REFERENCES

Ben-David, Joseph, and Terry N. Clark. *Culture and Its Creators*. Chicago: University of Chicago Press, 1977.

Foley, Robert, ed. *Hominid Evolution and Community Ecology*. London: Academic Press, 1984.

Friedle, J., and J. E. Pfeiffer. *Anthropology: The Study of People*. New York: Harper & Row, 1977.

Haviland, W. A. *Anthropology*. 2d ed. New York: Holt, Rinehart & Winston, 1978.

Knudson, S. J. *Culture in Retrospect: An Introduction to Archaeology*. Chicago: Rand McNally, 1978.

Kottack, Conrad P. *Anthropology: The Exploration of Human Diversity*. 2d ed. Westminster, Md.: Random House, 1978.

_____. *People of the Lake*. Garden City, N.Y.: Doubleday, 1978.

Lewin, Roger. *Bones of Contention*. New York: Simon & Schuster, 1987.

Lewin, Roger. "The Origin of the Human Mind." *Science* 236 (May 9, 1987), 668-69.

Pfeiffer, John. *The Emergence of Humankind*. 4th ed. New York: Harper & Row, 1985.

REVIEW QUESTIONS

1. Does the appearance of tools signify leisure or work?
2. What impact did the use of fire have on early hominids and subsequent leisure?
3. What effect did bipedalism have on early hominids?
4. How did the cave drawings of 50,000 years ago change *Homo sapiens'* behavior?
5. What does the early home base indicate about the presence of leisure?

Thousands of Years Before the Common Era

depicts a bison ■ **10**—End of last Ice Age; tip of South America is colonized ■ **9**—Walls of Jericho are built; Fertile Crescent of

GLOSSARY

Australopithecus afarensis: (southern ape) A genus of fossil found in Tanzania and Ethiopia that is a distinct species separate from previously discovered *Australopithecus*.

Deconstructionism: A theoretical viewpoint that seeks to remove the implied powers or interpretations previously held or employed by a government or an agency. Literally it means to take something apart.

Hominid: Any creature of the family *Hominidae;* while there were many species throughout the evolutionary periods, only *Homo sapiens* exists today. The closest family related to the hominid is the pongid, associated with the gorilla, chimpanzee, and orangutan.

Homo habilis: Remains of this species of hominid were first discovered in 1959-60 in the Olduvai Gorge in Tanzania. They roamed sub-Saharan Africa about 1.5 to 2 million years ago.

Homo neanderthalensis: A hominid living in close association with *Homo sapiens*. Remains have been found in the Neander Valley of Germany.

Homo sapiens: The genus and species of modern humans, distinguished from earlier hominid by its bipedal stance, brain capacity, high forehead, small teeth and jaw, defined jaw, use of tools, and ability to create and use language and other symbols. *Homo sapiens* can be traced back some 400,000 years.

Magdalenian period: An era typified by the creation of tools and artistic traditions approximately 11,000 to 17,000 years ago. The abundant artifacts of a utilitarian and artistic nature are sure indications that these people had leisure.

Chapter 2

ANCIENT NEAR EASTERN CIVILIZATIONS AND LEISURE

Objectives

After reading this chapter, the student will be able to do the following:

Discuss how early civilizations arose.

◼

Explain how a leisured class developed.

◼

Tell how we know that the masses had some leisure.

◼

Understand why conquest might lead to assimilation.

◼

Discuss the types of activity that occupied leisure.

◼

Explain why Egyptian laborers had leisure.

◼

Discuss why leisure was important during Hammurabi's dynasty.

◼

Explain the Sabbath as a day of leisure.

◼

Recognize the Hanging Gardens of Babylon.

◼

Discuss the idea that leisure is the mother of invention.

GLATH

Glath was an artisan who lived in the city of Erech in Sumer around 3100 B.C. He belonged to the burgher (middle) class and was a free person. Glath was a copperware maker of great skill whose products were marketed both at home and for the export trade throughout the Middle East. Trade was carried on for barter, of either grain or precious metal of a certain weight, since there was no coined money. By all accounts, Glath was a successful worker and businessman.

His day began with sunrise and morning prayers to both the local god-king and Innini, the mother goddess. His morning meal consisted of uncooked barley and beer. His house also served as his shop and retail outlet. He either worked to order or created utensils and plaques, knives, armbands, rings, seals, or other decorative objects. After working all morning, he might either deliver his wares or take them to the central market in his quarter of the city. He took lunch at midday, eating cheese and drinking goat's milk.

In the early afternoon, Glath might return to his house, walk in the public gardens, seek solace at the temple, view artworks of various types, read poetry or prose written in cuneiform at the city library, or go swimming, fishing, or hunting. Or he might visit the temple priestesses, whose religious rites would be considered unusual today: The Sumerians did not separate the sacred from the profane, and the priestesses had sex with worshippers to honor the gods.

Glath lived in a culture that was old when Egypt was first being united. It provided him with a good life, secure behind the walls of the city and protected by the local *patesi*, or priest-king. He had whatever leisure he wanted because he was free and self-employed. The middle and upper classes had a great deal of comfort and their style of living could be considered luxurious. Glath's circumstances gave him ample opportunity to participate in a variety of recreational experiences, ranging from intellectual and aesthetic stimulation to invigorating physical activity. But not all Sumerians were as fortunate. Peasants had little leisure and less substance.

Thousands of Years Before the Common Era

Why would anyone want to build a botanical garden 70 feet above ground? When did agricultural surplus thicken into the more elaborate urban life that we call civilization? Although leisure was prevalent during the slow rise to civilization, only a few individuals had a great deal of it; the masses had very little. Yet leisure was a part of the daily lives of people of all classes. How leisure came into existence and how it was used are no longer a Middle Eastern mystery.

Civilization occurs when a culture attains a great concern for human welfare. It is brought about by invention and sustained by the need for organization, cooperation, and communication. All civilizations have developed institutional forms of government, economics, religion, and symbolic devices for language. Where a flowering of intellectualism and incremental cultural achievement is coupled with the stabilizing influence of science and technology, civilization develops. Through technological invention comes the need to regulate or guide conduct, which permits the rise of standardized action and organization. Out of organization grow governance, specialization of labor, and social thought.

For the most part, civilization is nurtured in an environment where individuals may interrelate, feel protected from hostile forces, exchange ideas, engage in reciprocal practices, and promote the common good. It is an atmosphere in which aesthetic creations are indulged, trade is promoted, and the cultural heritage is transmitted through formal methods (for example, literature). Throughout its history, civilization has been closely associated with city life. From farming village to trading center and then to the home of social intercourse, cultural achievement, and technological facilitation, the city has been most congenial to the advance of civilization.

SOCIAL ASSOCIATION AND EFFECTIVENESS

Humans are not voluntarily political beings. We join with our peers less from want than from routine, mimicry, and the force of environment. We do not so much love society as we hate being alone. We associate with others because isolation jeopardizes us and because many activities can be performed more effectively in concert than singularly. Nevertheless, in our innermost being we are each alone and battling valiantly against the universe.

It is likely that the average person could have been far happier without any state. Even modern humans fear and resent the state and assure themselves that the only certainties are death and taxes. Perhaps there is some truth to the Jeffersonian ideal that "that government is best which governs least." Despite the fact that many laws are enacted at our or our representatives' behest, it is merely to answer the immediate needs of others. In our mind's eye, the law is unnecessary for us personally. Anarchists have always felt this way.

The Rise of the State

In the simplest cultures, government barely exists. Primates accepted some strictures on individual behavior only when survival in hunting groups required them. In time, common association in families led to clan formation and, over millennia, to tribal organization. The jump from tribe to state required war, which liquidates the weak and rewards heroism, brutality, intelligence, skill, and violence. More significantly, war erased primitive communism and individuality, substituting organization and conformity. Eventually, it led to slavery, class distinctions, and the institution of government. The parents of the state were possessions and war. "Everywhere we find some warlike tribe breaking through the boundaries of some less warlike people, settling down as nobility, and founding its state," wrote Franz Oppenheimer.[1]

Force alone cannot sustain a state for very long. Many calming procedures had to be created and introduced into human affairs. The societal institutions of church and school were formulated to transmit the culture and build a sense of national pride and loyalty. The family unit was sustained and legalized by the state. Overall, the masters transformed their force into a code of law that, while stabilizing their rule, offered security and tranquility to their subjects. Indeed, the rights of subjects were sufficiently recognized to ensure their acceptance of the law and devotion to the state. Once the idea of state, government, law, and other institutional forms that bind humans together become commonplace, the real civilizing forces of education and religion propelled all races in their respective development.

Thousands of Years Before the Common Era

With education, the mythology of origin was transformed into historical legend. Overlords traced their heritage back to the gods, which gave them the divine right to rule. Religion, in its turn, fostered a reverence for fidelity to the ruler and the state. It also created fear of disobedience in terms of eternal punishment and encouraged conformity with promises of everlasting bliss. Out of these mental essences the birth of civilization was accomplished. In the process, so complex and time-consuming, the hard-won security of communal living provided opportunities for embellishing life through the various arts.[2]

Some of the earliest and greatest human achievements occurred in the Mediterranean basin and the Near East, which are very ancient homelands for the human race. The upper Paleolithic era is well represented in this region. Most importantly, one of the earliest agricultural sites lies at the eastern end of the Mediterranean. The modern climate, which appeared about 11,000 years ago, saw increased cultural advancement and the abandonment of nomadic ways for the settled life that food cultivation made possible.

This text focuses on the beginning of town-dwelling and farming ways of life around 9000 B.C. in the Middle East. Out of this developed city-state civilization and, relatively quickly, kingdoms and dynasties. By 4500 B.C., Mesopotamia was well on the path to civilization; Egypt followed 500 years later. From these centers of notable achievement, ideas rippled outward to adjacent lands.

The Rise of Civilization

By 4000 B.C., many groups of people were leading their lives in diverse ways. Neolithic peoples had migrated in a great arc from the eastern end of the Mediterranean, across the Turkish plains, and through the highlands of what are now Iraq and Iran. They were now farming, trading, building communities, and learning to weave, paint, make pottery, and smelt metal. While some nomadic tribes still lived by hunting, the greater part of humanity had settled into the domestication of animals and the stability of an agricultural existence. Populations grew rapidly, and competition for fertile areas became serious. Not for the first time (or the last), there was strife between groups who controlled food resources and those who were perpetually hungry.

The Fertile Crescent. One of the regions that would be fought over continuously was situated at the very heart of the various groups who peopled the land. It was only about 150 miles wide and 600 miles long and extended from the foothills of northwestern Iraq to the Persian Gulf. This Fertile Crescent, the land between the Tigris and Euphrates rivers, was called Mesopotamia. For the next 3,500 years, Mesopotamia would witness the ascent and destruction of many kingdoms, cultures, and empires: Sumerian, Akkadian, Babylonian, Assyrian, and Chaldean. By 4000 B.C., the earliest farming communities existed in the upper reaches of the Tigris. From these rude settlements were born the civilizations of the Middle East.

These civilizations contained continuously inhabited structures and some codes of law by which the people abided. Mesopotamia's southern section flowed through broad plains that, when irrigated, became ideal for farming. The most ancient communities of these civilizations were formed when Eridu, a town in Sumer in the delta near the Euphrates River, was founded. Within a few hundred years, many new towns and cities were established. The city-states of Sumer—Eridu, Ur, Uruk, Kish, Susa, Larsa, Lagash, and Nippur—have been described as the beginning of civilization.

The growing complexity of life along these riverbanks required some form of government organization and farsighted leadership to forestall chaotic uprisings and natural calamities. Over time, the war chief was transformed into a governor (king) who also performed certain rituals (priest). The emerging king-priest class commanded the respect of their followers, first by prowess in warfare and later as the administrators of the city. From this combined function, the king-priests and then the aristocracy emerged to reign over the great masses who populated the cities.

The First Leisure Class. The king-priest's duties included officiating at all ritual occasions, and there is good evidence that recreational activity was part of religious festivals and rites.[3, 4] The king-priests came to be endowed with divine stature and were considered descendants of the gods. Since they ordinarily could not participate in the typical activities of their subjects, they had more and more leisure, which they used for planning social development. Kings were enjoined from performing menial

music is played in Egypt ■ **2.7**—Stonehenge is built in England; masons and smiths become crafters ■ **2.5**—Pyramids are built in Egypt;

Ancient priests belonged to the leisure class.

the rise of institutions helped organize all of the people, facilitating the job of daily living. Agricultural, political, religious, martial, and other tasks were performed cooperatively; division would mean dissolution and probably destruction by invaders.

The priests were now the kings' councillors, and much that the priestly class ordained had the sanction of the king's authority. The priests were probably more intelligent than the average person and passed much of their time in contemplation. This gave them a chance to develop rituals dealing with metaphysical concepts, originate many taboos based on seasonal cycles or other natural occurrences, and instigate mystical signs and symbols to give them apparent command of the occult and supernatural world. In this way they were not very different from their Paleolithic forebears.

The priestly order of ancient Sumer (circa 4000 B.C.) used games, dance, and other recreational activities in their rituals.[5] The games held a deadly significance. Human sacrifices were made to propitiate the gods, and it was all done in play-acting form.[6]

Art and Toys. Artifacts from Sumer indicate that children played with dolls. Art was used to express creativity as well as to record significant happenings on scrolls, tablets, walls, and utensils. Dancing, in the ritual of temple ceremonies, was also used to express emotion, depict events, and explain traditional activities carried on as part of the people's daily lives.[7]

Dancing has become an activity practiced by all cultures, which have contributed their own symbolic steps, movements, or physical attitudes.[8] Rhythmical movement probably developed out of boredom. Dancing presumably became established as a result of individual leisure and has almost universally become associated with leisure activity. However, the dancing that accompanied religious ritual was obligatory rather than recreational. The ceremony could not proceed without its performance.

NEAR EASTERN CONTRIBUTIONS TO WESTERN CULTURE AND LEISURE

In the Mesopotamian and Egyptian societies, social complexity evolved into a distinct separation of classes around 3600 B.C. Political and

tasks and were limited to governing, leading troops in war, and hunting for sport. Even the arduous requirements of governance were turned over to priest-ministers and scribes, who saw to the daily administration of the city-state.

We may discern the development of a leisured class from these earliest aristocracies. The nobles' restricted employment left a great deal of free time, which had to be filled lest boredom overtake them. Sports, games, entertainment, and other diversions became a way of life for the well-to-do.

From this communal development, with its social structure and division of labor, developed a separate social classification, which led to institutions oriented toward maintaining life. External and internal pressures reinforced the tradition of king-priest and establishment of the first aristocracy and leisure class.

As the community became more complex, the king-priest combination was separated into two distinct functions. A class system based on occupation developed. Social stratification and

Thousands of Years Before the Common Era

libraries are built in Egypt ■ **2.0**—Minoan civilization dominates Mediterranean; Abraham leaves Ur ■ **1.9**—Mycenaean culture develops

military power was given into the hands of a central figure, the king. Mystical rites were handed to priests; these rites included most, if not all, of the arts and sciences of the day, not just religion. The rest of the populace was left with the burden of cultivating crops, engaging in commercial and trade enterprises, and generally increasing the material wealth of the state.

Briefly, there arose a series of societies ruled by an individual accorded divine-right powers. Among these were the Babylonian, Hittite, Assyrian, and Persian empires. Several books could be written on every aspect of these kingdoms' cultural importance, but we concentrate on the leisure and recreational elements.

Sumer and Akkad

During the age of Sumerian unification, in which the city-state of Sumer rose to power over the southern Fertile Crescent communities, the area between the Tigris and Euphrates rivers constituted a most prized possession. For a thousand years, beginning in 3600 B.C., countless struggles and periodic wars were waged between the mountain-dwelling and plains-dwelling peoples. Internecine warfare was endemic as were periodic incursions by other warrior societies. This condition lasted until 1900 B.C. The state of Akkad held sway over the northern section of the Plain of Shiner, which became known as Akkadia.

These two hostile states were decidedly different. The Sumerians had a well-disciplined agrarian civilization; the Akkadians were desert nomads without the military training or organization to confront the heavy infantry of the southerners. During the centuries when the two states engaged in border wars against one another, there was comparative internal peace. However, sometime around 2630 B.C. the Semitic chieftain Sargon, known to history as "the Great," led his lean archers against the Sumerian host and defeated them in a conclusive battle. He swiftly consolidated his conquest by invading the entire land and pushing his claims from Elam in the east to the Mediterranean Sea in the west and the two rivers in the north. Despite unification, warfare was a constant for another 300 years.

Although the Akkadians had conquered in battle, they were gradually assimilated by their victims. They adopted Sumerian ways, including a calendar, a numbering system, the technique of measurement, arts and crafts, commercial organization, and metal smelting. Sargon's forced union of Akkadia with Sumer changed the Akkadian standard of living, and it was the Sumerian civilization that prevailed over the simpler Semitic culture. The Semites left their desert life for town living. They married Sumerians and adopted their spoken language as well as their cuneiform writing style.

With the civilizing influence of the towns, the Akkadians settled the land, and it became the Sumerian-Akkadian empire. When the vigorous, warlike Semitics began to acquire the cultural attributes Sumer had developed over 2,000 years, they ceased to be have-nots and became the leisured aristocracy. They hunted and participated in many outdoor sports and games, including chariot racing. But they regarded manual labor, especially agriculture, as the province of inferiors. In a few generations, the conquerors became an integral part of the civilization they had overthrown. There was an exchange of religious, political, and social ideas. In the process of refinement, the conquerors lost some of the hardy pioneering spirit that had impelled them to fight. The Semites turned aristocrat and came to rely on mercenaries and hirelings to enforce their rule, thus laying themselves open to invasion by other lean and hungry societies.

Sumerian civilization was a combination of crude origins and spasmodic but consummate skill. History began at Sumer: the first agricultural centers, the first irrigation projects, the first use of precious metals for currency, the first transaction contracts, the first credit system, the first law code, the first widespread use of writing (and with it poetry and literature). To house and teach these cultural advancements, the first schools and libraries were created. Architectural development proceeded apace, along with sculpture and bas-relief. The arch, vault, column, and dome were used in palaces and temples. Ornamentation of things and self produced cosmetics and jewelry.

It was a culture diffuse and nuanced, overflowing and intricate. Out of this differentiated society a selection process developed that produced a higher standard of comfort, luxury, and leisure for the aristocracy and relegated the proletariat to a routine of hard and stringent

Thousands of Years Before the Common Era

in the Peloponnesus, Greece ■ **1.8**—Hammurabi is king of Babylonia ■ **1**—Knossos in Crete is destroyed; Shang dynasty is founded in

labor. It was from this model that history would write its multiple variations.

Training for war and fighting were the chief occupations of the leisured class. As a sport and a valiant exercise to maintain physical prowess, hunting was the preferred recreational activity of kings, aristocrats, and the moneyed. The lower classes hunted too, but more for food than for fun. Hunting became the badge of nobility. The leisure class might hunt in the prey's natural habitat, or animals might be brought to special preserves or hunting parks (paradises), where the king and his invited guests could indulge themselves. Big game—particularly lions and tigers—was the sport of choice.

Javelin throwing, archery, horseback riding, chariot driving, fishing, swimming, boating, and horse racing were among the recreational activities of these early people.[9] Even the masses had some free time due to public celebrations or aristocratic largess, so they too could enjoy dancing, hunting, fishing, and other simple pleasures. Music certainly graced noble occasions, and lesser folk must have played or listened to it as well. A clay seal from Bronze Age Sumer depicts a harpist. Leisure provided the opportunity for such diversion as an adornment of society.

The Sargonid dynasty lasted less than two centuries, but it is an era filled with artistic works. Among them are the Sargonid seals, cut from stone and depicting men and animals in violent action.[10] The art of sculpting was raised to its highest form in terms of human development at that stage.

As the Akkadians lost their hardiness, fresh incursions of warlike people took place. The Sumerian-Akkadian empire was overthrown in 2470 B.C. under the direction of the city-state of Ur.

The Kingdoms of Egypt

During the late Paleolithic era, about 10,000 years ago, people began to settle in the Nile Valley. They assimilated the cultural development of nearby Mesopotamia. They began to farm, and the land prospered. Until 6,000 years ago, Egypt was only a series of towns bordering the Nile River. As the towns grew, headmen or chiefs emerged who consolidated the communities so that two countries were born—Upper and Lower Egypt. Because the Nile flows north, Upper Egypt is below Lower Egypt on a map.

In 3200 B.C., Egypt was united by Menes and burst into the splendor that it sustained for the next 27 centuries. Egypt was one of the earliest ancient lands to develop the strains of culture into an impressive civilization. More significantly, it maintained its achievements without flagging for 2,700 years. Few cultures can make that claim.

Trade and Culture. Certain aspects of Egyptian culture came from the sea trade between Mesopotamia and Egypt. Because the great western desert and the Nile cataracts blocked cultural contact with Africa, such contacts were made with lands to the east. The primitive culture of Egypt contained many Mesopotamian elements (such as pictographic writing, a Sumerian development). The cylindrical seal, of Mesopotamian origin, appears early in Egyptian history. The chariot, finely worked copper, statuettes, pottery, and the potter's wheel itself were adopted or adapted from Mesopotamian states. When Egypt emerged from its learning period, it flowered into one of the greatest cultures in history.

Egypt's social order can be compared to the pyramid. At the apex was the pharaoh. In descending order came the high officers of the state, the government bureaucracy, and the masses who labored to maintain the kingdom in every known form of trade, agriculture, or service.

With all power centralized, labor could be directed to harness the Nile. Irrigation projects were continually expanded to bring life-giving water to the parched fields beyond the riverfront. Dike systems were constructed to reclaim thousands of arable acres. As agriculture became more productive, the material wealth of Egypt increased. By 2600 B.C., Egyptian trading vessels had established a regular trade route in the eastern Mediterranean and Red seas. Trade with Nubia to the south enriched the treasury with goods produced in ancient Africa and the East. Copper, gold, bronze, silver, ivory, lapis lazuli, turquoise, and exotic spices were traded. Copper, bronze, ivory, and spices were produced in Egypt while gold, silver, lapis, and turquoise were traded for on the international market.

Art and Architecture. The intellectual creativity that had produced writing and calculation now developed architecture. A century after the first pharaoh was enthroned, Egyptian builders had discarded the timeworn use of sunbaked bricks for the sophisticated emplacement of

Thousands of Years Before the Common Era

Anyang, China; Olmec civilization develops in Mexico; Israelites leave Egypt ■ 1—Dorians invade Greece; Assyrian empire is founded;

stone. Again, the authorities were able to buy the manpower necessary to quarry and dress the huge stone blocks and transport them at will.

Within two centuries, the great pyramids at Giza were completed. Recent excavations at Giza have uncovered pictures, statues, and inscriptions that provide details of daily life. The workers were not slaves; they were hired. After sunset they had free time. In succeeding reigns, the stone builders erected some of the most impressive monuments, tombs, temples, and statuary the world has ever known. These remarkable structures can still be seen along 800 miles of the Nile from its delta to Abu Simbel.

Architecture and art went hand in hand. Since the late Paleolithic, the Nile artisans had created beauty and symmetry that enhanced even the most prosaic items. Flint knives, stone or pottery household vessels, pins and combs of bone and shell were decorated and colored to delight the eye. During the period of the three kingdoms, Egypt's aesthetic quality multiplied and a highly sophisticated art flourished.

For the next 3,000 years, Egyptian art knew greatness. Sculpture assumed massive proportions as artists tried to convey immense power through size. Painters added vivid pigments to the works of the sculptors and covered temple walls, columns, and obelisks with representations of official life; religious, battle, and pastoral scenes; and almost every aspect of both daily routine and imagery that fanciful imagination could convey.

Prosperity and Leisure. Under the pharaohs' ministrations, Egypt prospered and the people had a relatively good life. Occasionally the social order was broken by war, political unrest, famine, or plague, but in the normal course of events life flowed on serenely. As with all ancient civilizations, the lives of the laboring peasants were hard, with little free time for amenities. However, in return for their labor, the peasants knew security and had fewer anxieties than their Mesopotamian contemporaries, whose lands were periodically despoiled by conquerors. During most of the year, the peasants labored without ceasing from before dawn until dusk, then after a frugal meal they tried to sleep. When the Nile flooded, however, it was festival time, a religious occasion when all work paused long enough for everyone to celebrate with feasts, games, and ritual.

As Herodotus describes them:

They gather in the fruits of the earth with less labor than any other people . . . for they have not the toil of breaking up the furrow with the plough, nor of hoeing, nor of any other work which all other men must labor at to obtain a crop of corn. . . .[11]

The great pyramids at Giza.

© Corbis-Bettmann

Thousands of Years Before the Common Era

Phoenicians become trading power in Mediterranean; Saul is king of Israel

Whether of high or low economic class, families were large and children were wanted and well cared for. Children were the proud possessors of many modern toys, such as marbles, bouncing balls, tops, and tenpins. Adults enjoyed wrestling matches, some form of pugilism, and bullfights.[12]

Social Elites. The aristocracy controlled the land, lived in considerable luxury, and knew immense leisure, with all of the recreational activities that wealth, imagination, and retainers could buy. The supreme goal of Egyptian aristocrats was to enjoy the pharaoh's largesse. The upper class was part of a small, closed elite—a hereditary caste of priests, soldiers, bureaucrats, and, rarely, a gifted commoner who rose by dint of outstanding talent. The leisured class of Egypt lived in opulence and comfort that would be duplicated only by the aristocracy of other imperial realms. All of this wealth depended on agriculture, and the upper class was rewarded by the pharaoh with huge grants of land.

Servants were a necessity. Each lordly house kept a full retinue of personal maids, butlers, musicians, cooks, bakers, launderers, dancers, and more. Feasts were a frequent and often raucous diversion. Guests consumed quantities of rich foods, wines, and beer. The women were elaborately coiffed, even to the extent of wearing cones of perfumed burning incense. A great deal of time was expended in preparing for and going to dinner parties and the like. The banquets were not unlike modern nightclub entertainments, with each course accompanied by acrobats, wrestlers, exotic dancing, storytelling, and music.

Such recreational activities contrasted sharply with the unleisured lives of the masses. But public festivals and processions did provide a break from the toil that was the peasants' lot in life—as well as propitiating the gods.[13]

For more than two millennia, the Egyptians overcame the problems of war, drought, famine, and pestilence. The civilization they built withstood the rigors of time and place. But, as with all previous kingdoms, a combination of forces began to erode the power of the central government, and Egypt's decline from greatness was assured. Starting with the 20th Dynasty, a steady reduction of the pharaoh's prestige, a shrinking empire, and the influence of the Iron Age toppled Egypt from its preeminence.

The Egyptian outlook on life underwent a fundamental change during the latter part of the Old Kingdom (2300 B.C.). The fundamental change had to do with the way in which political power was wielded and by whom, but not in terms of the trappings of the culture. Instead of concentrating on the afterlife and believing in a deified Pharaoh, the aristocracy demythologized the throne while preserving the panoply of power. Now the focus was on the present; people demanded happiness during life. The royal officer Ptah-hotep could afford to write that happiness would be magnified to the extent that work was reduced and leisure increased. As he wrote in his lessons:

> . . . *Be merry all your life;*
> *Do no more than you are ordered to,*
> *Nor shorten the time accorded to leisure.*
> *It is hateful to the spirit to be*
> *robbed of the time for merriment.*[14]

The nation became prey to internecine warfare as palace intrigue gave way to internal discord and the land was divided. After 1100 B.C., Egypt's role as a world power was forever eclipsed. There would be several remissions as certain Egyptian aristocrats regained the throne and provided a strong power base, but these were relatively rare. More often than not, Egypt was invaded by covetous neighbors and other foreign conquerors who looked upon the rich agricultural valley as a prize. From the expulsion of the Hyksos dynasty during the later Middle Kingdom to the overthrow of the ruling family by the Libyans, then the Nubians, the Assyrians, the Persians, the Greeks under Alexander the Great, and finally the Romans, Egypt was a subject province.

The Nile Valley had given birth to the people who created the first great united kingdom, devised the political institutions to rule a far-flung geographic region, initiated the bureaucracy to administer hundreds of miles and thousands of people, and planned, organized, and executed engineering and architectural projects on a large scale. The Nile River kingdom provided the climate, food supply, stability, and wealth for at least some people to enjoy leisure and perfect the graphic and performing arts. The dynasties of Egypt are part and parcel of Western civilization because Egypt was a cultural crossroads between East and West as well as the home of people who created the enduring art, literature, and leisure of the good life.

Babylon

From the west came the Amorites, a Semitic people who settled in a rural village called Babylon, located on the Euphrates upstream from Ur. After three generations of intermittent warfare, they succeeded in bringing much of what was then western Asia under their political and military control, surpassing Ur as the central seat of government. Under their great king Hammurabi (c. 1800 B.C.), the first Babylonian empire was founded, with Babylon as its capital city.

During Hammurabi's dynasty, Babylonia flourished as the greatest commercial and political center of that time. The arts, particularly literature and graphics, were generally developed to the highest form known in those ancient times.[15] Members of the upper classes indulged in many recreational activities: hunting, fishing, riding, wrestling, swimming, and the exercise of a variety of weapons. Typical of the philosophy of Babylon is the saga of the hero Gilgamesh.

> *Gilgamesh, why dost thou run in all*
> *directions?*
> *The life that thou seekest thou wilt not find.*
> *When the gods created mankind,*
> *They determined death for mankind;*
> *Life they kept in their hands.*
> *Thou, O Gilgamesh, fill thy belly,*
> *Day and night be thou merry,*
> *Daily arrange a merry-making,*
> *Day and night be joyous and content!*[16]

The Gilgamesh epic illustrates a life of warlike activities interspersed with leisure experiences of hunting, gaming, singing, dancing, and music making. Dancing and music were originally linked to religious rites, but they were also part of everyday occupation. Vocal and instrumental music were inseparable from the ordinary workaday world. Music lightened the monotony of shepherding and gave farmers rhythmic accompaniment during the harvest. Its purely recreational use was left for later cultures.

The orientation of "live for today" and enjoy life is self-evident. This rationale predates the earliest hedonistic philosophers of ancient Greece. It reflects the pleasurable existence that the upper classes could afford as a result of the pyramidal society on which Babylonian culture rested. The Babylonian empire's rise, the enterprises of peace and war carried on throughout the 400-year dynastic period, the myths, fine arts, dress, habitation, religion, and literature—all are documented in many texts, as well as archaeological sources.[17]

Gradually, Babylon grew decadent. Its military capacity was greatly reduced as it became more highly civilized. Its art was prolific, as were trade and commerce. But the fruits of a leisured society came under the covetous eyes of warriors from the East, and by 1400 B.C., the empire that had been Babylon gave way to the Kassites, who ruled (and were absorbed into) the Babylonian culture as a whole until the 12th century B.C.

The second Babylonian Empire was liberated by Nabopolassar and reached its peak with his son, Nebuchadrezzar II, who became the greatest of empire builders. By this time, 600 years after Hammurabi, Babylon had been conquered by the Kassites, destroyed, and rebuilt.

The city of Babylon was the unchallenged capital of the Mideast, the most extensive and imposingly beautiful metropolis of the time.[18] Not only was the city laid out according to plan, but it was magnificently endowed with statuary, decorative tiles, massive portals, spacious boulevards, parks, and gardens. In fact, next to Nebuchadrezzar's main palace was one of the seven wonders of the ancient world: the Hanging Gardens, supported on a spiral of colonnades.[19] These gardens enabled the ladies of the harem to spend their leisure in the cool shade of tall trees and luxuriant plants of all kinds, 70 feet above the ground and away from prying eyes.

Babylon was basically a commercial empire, founded on trade and agriculture. Its essential labor was carried on by slaves, who performed menial tasks, physical labor, and most of the personal services in the state. Thus, the monarchy, feudal aristocracy, commercial plutocracy, and middle-class citizens were maintained, for better or worse, in conditions of relative luxury and leisure. As always in such cultures, the free peasants had nearly as hard an existence as slaves. Their free time was dictated by religious communities or aristocratic order.

Some 30 years after the death of Nebuchadrezzar II, the Babylonian empire broke up. The materialism and greed of the people softened them, and they fell easy prey to Cyrus the Persian.[20]

Assyria

To the north of Babylon, Assyrian power had consolidated. The Assyrians raised warfare to a fine art. Under Tiglath Pileser I, they conquered all of Mesopotamia and forced Babylon to submit to them in 1150 B.C. However, their conquest was not absolute; for 400 years a power struggle ensued between Assyrian military might and Babylonian force.

Economically, there was not much difference between Babylonia and Assyria. After all, the two states were merely the north and south branches of the same civilization. Like the Babylonians, the Assyrians wrote history, kept commercial records, and developed some literature.[21, 22] Yet they were a brutal people whose kings gloried in slaughter and torture.

The king's leisure was invested in reading, horseback riding, hunting, archery, and an appreciation of artwork. The nobility had similar tastes.[23] Assyrian youth of the upper classes were brought up to hunt from an early age. The typical recreational pursuits of the laboring class, when leisure was occasionally made available, were simple games, dancing accompanied by rhythm instruments and other music, hunting, fishing, and trapping.[24]

It was not until the middle of the sixth century B.C. that a third Tiglath Pileser arose to found the New Assyrian empire with the final conquest of Babylon. The Assyrian empire

Hanging Gardens of Babylon.

lasted only until a new crop of lean and hungry men came from the southeast to overthrow the 150-year-old Assyrian kingdom. The Semitic nomads came from Chaldea, and in alliance with the Medes and Persians from the north, they captured Nineveh in 606 B.C. The Chaldean kingdom, with Babylon as its capital, lasted until Cyrus the Persian attacked and defeated it in 539 B.C.

Thus, the story of civilization is repeated in successive centuries as conquest follows conquest in an almost rhythmic pattern, with intermittent warfare occurring as fresh invasions from border races inevitably bring about the collapse of the more settled former invaders. The Sumerians give way to the Akkadians, who interbreed with the Sumerians and lose their identity as a distinct people. The Sumerian-Akkadian empire languishes and is set upon by other peoples. The Babylonians defer to the Assyrians, who give way to the Chaldeans and Syrians; the northern Hittites swallow the Syrians and become Aryanized; the Medes and Persians then dominate until they are finally subjugated by the Greeks.

The Tigris and Euphrates civilizations existed for some 4,000 years. As Winckler states in his 1907 text, *The History of Babylonia and Assyria*, "Eridu, Lagash, Ur, Uruk, Larsa, have already an immemorial past when first they appear in history."[25] Those civilizations, created out of the need for social organization and the appreciation for and use of leisure, have left an indelible stamp upon human history. It may be that leisure, not necessity, is the mother of invention. Only when individuals have the time to survey their needs beyond mere survival, and appreciate the significance of creating something utilitarian out of natural materials or something aesthetic out of a utilitarian item, does the veneer of culture thicken to become civilization.

Israel

Although Israel was not as politically significant as the kingdoms of Chaldea, Babylon, Assyria, and Egypt, its place is recorded in history because Judea (Canaan) was the most direct route for both trade and warfare between Egypt to the south and the Hittites, Assyrians, Syrians, and Babylonians to the north. The land was almost constantly undergoing attack and conquest or, as a tributary state, paying indemnification to some foreign power. As small and militarily insignificant as this country was, it nevertheless had a long and troubled history. The writings of its people made significant ethical and religious contributions to Western civilization. They also served to document leisure concepts and recreational pursuits.

Prophets, Priests, and Kings. The patriarchs of the Old Testament came upon the historical scene sometime between 2000 and 1800 B.C. The Pentateuch (the first five books of the Bible) provides a basic description of human history and a record of daily life. It recounts the Flood, which appears widely in ancient Near Eastern histories. This may have been an account of some great submersion that occurred in the Mediterranean basin during the Neolithic era.

Genesis gives a history of the founding fathers, along with Abraham's migration from Ur of the Chaldeas. It describes a covenant made with the deity called Yahweh, later anglicized to Jehovah. The next six books of the Bible recount the migration of Jacob's tribe to Egypt, the story of Moses, the exodus of the Jews from Egypt and their wandering in the desert before reaching Canaan, the giving of the Mosaic laws, and the consolidation of Israelite fortunes in Canaan.

The Hebrews never really held Canaan. The Bible says the Philistines consistently held the fertile seacoast region of the south and the Canaanites and Phoenicians remained in possession of the northern border areas. The initial victories of Joshua were never repeated, and the Book of Judges becomes a recital of the Israelites' trouble, defeat, and failure. The people soon lost their faith, deserted to pagan gods, and intermarried with many races. Under the leadership of several prophets and heroes, they continued to wage intermittent warfare (never completely successfully, and usually without a united front) against a series of enemies. They were conquered by the Moabites, the Canaanites, the Midianites, and the Philistines.

Then the first king arose.[26] Saul was no more successful against countering invasions than the judges and priests before him had been. The Philistines overwhelmed him and his army at the battle of Mount Gilboa. His successors were David (c. 990 B.C.) and Solomon (c. 960 B.C.).

With King Solomon, the division of Jewish society into haves and have-nots began. He tried to speed the transition from an agricultural to an industrial state by imposing increasing toil and taxes on the people. One consequence was the creation of an underemployed urban population that became a source of political discontent and corruption—a model that would later appear in Rome.

The end of the reign of King Solomon was also the end of Hebrew plans for expansion and glory. The growing division between the well-off and the poor, together with an increasing enmity between the rural and urban populations, probably produced a climate ripe for separatism. A schism developed between the northern and southern sections of the country as two separate kingdoms, Israel and Judah, were established. The divided kingdoms quickly succumbed, first to Pharaoh Sheshnle of Egypt, eventually to the Assyrians, and finally to Nebuchadrezzar.[27] The rest of the history consists of regicide, fratricide, religious conflicts, political maneuvering, mistaken alliances, and intrigues that go on for three centuries.

Israel was finally swept into captivity in 721 B.C. by Shalmaneser of Assyria. Judah remained partially sovereign until 604 B.C., when Nebuchadnezzar II annexed it. Several decades later he transported the majority of the people to Babylon, where they remained for more than two generations. Upon their return in 539 B.C. under the protection of Cyrus the Persian, a great change was noted in their character.

"They went a confused and divided multitude, with no national self-consciousness; they came back with an intense and exclusive national spirit. They went with no common literature generally known to them . . . and they returned with most of their material for the Old Testament. It is manifest that . . . the Jewish mind made a great step forward during the Captivity," wrote H. G. Wells.[28]

Out of this travail an intellectual awakening began that created a moral force of intense power. Ethical concepts were established to guide the entire community. The Third Commandment made sacred a weekly day of rest. Perhaps this was a custom from the Babylonian exile, where certain days of abstinence and propitiation were observed.[29] The human capability for grace and perfectibility runs throughout this prophetic religion and is seen in the subsequent establishment of Christianity and Islam as direct outgrowths of Judaism.

Sabbath, Leisure, and Recreation. Beyond the creativity and monotheistic aspect of the Jewish religion is a dominant meaning for leisure and for the entire concept of the Sabbath, or day of rest. The statement "Have peace and know that I am God,"[30] exemplifies the idea that some time had to be set aside from daily life when people were free to worship their creator. They were supposed to work from sunup to sundown, but every seventh day they must give thanks to the God in which they had faith. The Sabbath was a day free from the obligations of toil and concerned with the revitalization of the individual through prayer, feasting, and appreciation of a God-given world. The original Sabbath could not be considered free time because some form of worship was mandatory, but it became the basis for free time in modern society.

Of course, there were other leisure occasions as well. Aside from the weekly holy day (holiday), there were great festivals. Canaanite agricultural rituals associated with planting and harvesting, lunar and solar cycles, became Mazzoth, which commemorated the barley harvest. Shabouth celebrated the wheat harvest (later this would be the Christianized Pentecost); Pesach, or Passover, celebrated lambing in the flocks; and Rosh Hashana introduced the new year. It was not until much time had passed that these occasions came to recognize significant historical events for the Jews.[31]

Despite the seemingly endless series of political defeats and apostasies, the Jews clung tenaciously to a core of beliefs that produced some of the greatest lyrical poetry and prose in history. The Proverbs, Psalms, Song of Songs, and the various books of the Old Testament show that leisure was an integral part of life. Even professional writers needed free time to create and synthesize this literary output.[32] Jewish theology took no account of a heaven or life after death. Whatever rewards accrued from leading a virtuous life had to be in the here and now, not the hereafter.[33] Everyone needs enjoyment and personal satisfaction because life is short and death is forever.

Man that is born of woman is of few days,
and full of trouble.
He cometh forth like a flower,
and is cut down; he fleeth also as a shadow,
and continueth not. . . .[34]

Human beings cannot live on asceticism. They must periodically renew themselves in pleasurable activities. "Then I commended mirth, because a man hath no better thing under the sun than to eat, and to drink, and to be merry."[35]

Other leisure pursuits noted in Hebrew life included the usual hunting and fishing activities as well as the use of more warlike and defensive instruments such as the sling, bow, javelin, and short sword. Many biblical passages refer to physical activities; an outstanding example is Jacob's wrestling with "the Angel of the Lord."[36] Religious rites are often celebrated with dancing, singing, and playing of musical instruments,[37] but through it all the underlying cultural expression of Jewish life revolves around the Sabbath and the leisure that it brings.

SELECTED REFERENCES

Bernstein, P., and R. W. Green. *History of Civilization to 1648*. vol. I. Totowa, N.J.: Helix Books, 1987.

Breasted, J. J. *A History of Egypt*. New York: Scribner, 1927.

Contreveau, G. *Everyday Life in Babylon and Assyria*. London: E. Arnold, 1954.

Hobson, C. *The World of the Pharaohs*. New York: Thames and Hudson, 1990.

Kramer, S.N. *History Begins at Sumer*. New York: Doubleday, 1959.

Lols, A. *The Prophets and the Rise of Judaism*. New York: Dutton, 1951.

Orlinsky, H. *Ancient Israel*. Ithaca, N.Y.: Cornell University Press, 1954.

Wilkinson, J. G. *The Manners and Customs of the Ancient Egyptians*. London: J. Murray, 1837.

Wooley, C. L. *The Sumerians*. New York: Norton, 1965.

REVIEW QUESTIONS

1. Explain the contradiction between Pharaonic leisure and the leisure enjoyed by the masses in Egypt.

2. How do we know the Egyptian aristocracy had a great deal of leisure?

3. How does the mythology of ancient Mesopotamia reveal a rich, leisurely style of living?

4. Is leisure inimical to invention?

5. How can we reconcile the Sabbath, which was originally mandated as a day of worship and religious study, with leisure?

GLOSSARY

Akkad: an ancient region that is now part of central Iraq. Akkad was the northern region of Babylonia. The city of Agade was founded circa 2300 B.C. and was incorporated into a large confederation of city-states.

Bronze Age: The first period in the history of ancient cultures of Europe, Asia, and the Middle East in which metals were used. This period followed the Paleolithic and Neolithic ages. The date of its beginning varies in different regions depending on the use of the metals. Copper was used first, followed by bronze (an alloy of copper and tin).

Hebrew: A term used to denote the Israelites mentioned in the biblical Book of Genesis. The word is said to describe those who were the ancestors of Eber, which would include the biblical figure Abraham. It is also traced to the Akkadian term *Hapiru*, which denotes an ethnic or cultural subculture. The Hebrews were a branch of this group.

Hyksos: A group of Semitics/Asiatics who inhabited northern Egypt during the 18th century B.C. Identified by the historian Josephus as the Hebrews of the Old Testament, although this view is not shared by most scholars.

Chapter 3

ANCIENT WESTERN CIVILIZATIONS AND LEISURE

Objectives:

After reading this chapter, the student will be able to do the following:

Define *arétè*.

■

Explain why the Greeks played games.

■

Understand why leisure existed in Greek culture.

■

Explain how the Greeks used leisure.

■

Describe Aristotle's concept of happiness.

■

Discuss the transformation of leisure availability from early to late Rome.

FRITHERIKOS

FRITHERIKOS WAS AN ATHENIAN AND A MEMBER OF an aristocratic family around 400 B.C. Despite his family's wealth and position, he was expected to contribute his efforts and work at the family business. His father was an importer of Cretan goods. Although there were no routine working hours, Fritherikos arose each morning with the sun. Typically, he did not have breakfast, nor did he shave. He simply clothed himself with his blanket and left for the Agora, the central market and meeting place situated under the looming presence of the Acropolis.

Today, Fritherikos expected to visit the stoa of Epicurus, who taught that everything should be done in moderation. Along with other young men, he attended the early lecture and then set out for Piraeus, the port of Athens, where his father expected him to assist in recording the lading bills for the last shipment of merchandise from Crete.

After finishing his assignment, Fritherikos walked back to Athens to meet a friend before noon. They were to discuss the Epicurean lecture at the gymnasium, listen to a declamation by the visiting orator, and then wrestle in the forecourt. Afterward, they would probably go swimming in the pool.

If there was time before sunset, Fritherikos anticipated a visit to the theater. He had heard about a new play by Aristophanes called *The Birds* and he wanted to see who the writer was excoriating with his biting satire. The theater production was enjoyable, but he overheard some older men say it was an act of hubris to puncture the dignity of those who led the polis. Fritherikos thought that this was exactly how politicians should be portrayed. After all, they were always officious and sometimes hypocritical.

The play ended late in the afternoon. It was time to go home, have ground meal and watered wine for dinner, and then go to bed. There was no point in staying up because it was simply too difficult to read by firelight. It had been a day full of information, some work, and fun. Although Fritherikos could expect to participate in a variety of entertainments on any given day, since his leisure was what he made of it, the play was the high point. He thought it was absolutely right and very funny. His teacher had also given him a great deal to think about, especially the concept of obtaining pleasure from one's life without neglecting morality, temperance, serenity, and cultural development.

Years Before the Common Era

The great games were invented by the classical Greeks as a celebration of human life dedicated to Zeus, the king of their many gods. "Strip or retire" was the admonition over the gate to the Olympic Games stadium in Olympus. The Greeks competed in the nude, and only men were allowed in. Spectators were unwelcome. One either participated (stripped) or had to leave (retired). This reflected the Greek philosophy of citizen participation, whether in athletic contests, military expeditions, or government.

The Greek contribution to civilization was both mental and spiritual. Deeply embedded in its ideals of heroism, satire, education, political awareness, and aesthetics were the need for and use of leisure. Most Greek men spent time in the gymnasium each afternoon as well as attending the tragedies, comedies, and satires of the greatest writers and thinkers. Leisure brought happiness.

Despite powerful goddesses and oracles, women were excluded from citizenship and, in some instances, could neither inherit nor own property. Except for those married to wealthy men, women lived lives of drudgery and seclusion. Entertainers and prostitutes were the only women who could routinely expect a public life. In classic Greece, girls were thought to be unworthy of education. A respectable woman's leisure was regulated by the strict social taboos that were placed on her. She might engage in art, crafts, writing, or other practical outlets, but usually in the privacy of her home.

Sitting in the Colosseum in Rome, the spectator could look down on 60,000 screaming fans as an entire naval battle was staged on the water-covered floor of the arena. When that spectacle was over, the area was cleared and wild animals were released to attack one another. This was the heyday of bread and circuses.

Rome had begun as a small hill town that grew and annexed land and peoples. At first a republic, then a military dictatorship, it finally

The Roman Colosseum.

Years Before the Common Era

⇨ Babylon are at war; cuneiform writing develops in Babylon; Attica (Greece) is unified by Athenian kings ■ **850**—Hunting from chariots; Phoenicians settle in Cyprus; Etruscans appear in northern Italy ■ **800**—Greeks colonize Spanish coast; Carthage is founded; astronomy in Babylon and China ■ **776**—First recorded Olympic Games; Greek poet Hesiod is born; Zhou dynasty reigns in China

evolved into an empire. All roads led to Rome because, along with everything else, the Romans built and maintained the best road system in the world. Imperial Rome was the creation of Octavian. Later Caesar Augustus initiated the characteristics associated with an empire—rule over diverse peoples and subordinate kingdoms; the pomp and panoply of monarchy; the genuflection and salutation toward the emperor; the court ceremonies and required protocol; and finally the standing army and far-flung bureaucrats who governed and taxed subjugated populations. From an early citizenry willing and able to fight for their homes to the increasing use of mercenaries to battle for them, Western Rome eventually succumbed to bureaucratic fumbling, failed leadership, and external pressure. Remnants of the Eastern empire lasted in some degree right up to the final convulsions of the Austro-Hungarian and Russian empires in 1918.

Although Rome bequeathed structural and practical capacities to the world, it still set aside time for games, races, gladiatorial contests, and other amusements. The leisure of Rome permeated the known world. Its decadence produced antagonism among the early Church fathers that reverberated for centuries. Leisure and culture are the story of ancient Western civilizations.

Parallel with the ancient Near Eastern civilizations, another culture arose on the island of Crete. Remains at its capital of Knossos indicate an advanced civilization, much of which is now submerged beneath the Mediterranean. This island civilization is at least as old as that of Sumer, but political unification did not occur until about 2500 B.C. For the next thousand years, the Cretans lived in peace, prosperity, and safety.[1] They developed commerce with every civilized nation in the known world.

Secure in their island citadel and immune from invasion for more than 3,000 years, the Cretans were free to perfect their leisure habits. Their artisans produced sophisticated textiles, sculpture, painting, and jewelry. They enjoyed amenities quite similar to those of our modern life. Excavations show that the people of Crete devoted much time to the leisure arts and participated in a variety of recreational activities, such as shows, festivals, bullfights, gymnastics exhibitions, dance, swimming, wrestling, and other sports.

Crete presents a vibrant, unrestrained, exuberant picture of the good life, illustrated by the luxurious conditions surrounding the aristocrats—at the expense of the enslaved masses.[2] The slaves were too busy trying to survive to have much leisure, but their masters enjoyed a great deal of it. Clearly, security encourages leisure. Wherever humans have been safe for any length of time, they have been able to develop their arts, standards of living, and other cultural benefits to an amazing degree. It is not surprising, therefore, that the Cretans achieved such a society in light of their immunity to invasion and comparative freedom from want.[3]

We know that Cretans played a type of chess at home, patronized pugilistic exhibitions, and attended the theater in towns. Music and dance combined to provide entertainment for those fortunate enough to have spare time. Of all recreational activities, hunting seems to have had the dominant role during the leisure of Crete's soldier class and aristocracy. Many drawings and paintings of hunting scenes, especially boar hunting, have been discovered.[4]

The art of Crete captured the life and times of those who were privileged and those who served them. Whether frescoed on palace walls or some merchant's house, stamped on cups, embossed on shields, fans, lamps, or seals, sculpted as little figures, or molded in bas-relief, these artworks reveal a civilization with order and wealth, free time, and an appreciation for such experiences and ornamentation.[5]

THE HELLENIC AGE

As a sea power, Crete probably established colonies on the nearest shores, one of which was the Peloponnesus. From 1600 B.C., some of these communities rivaled Knossos as centers of Cretan culture. After the sacking of Knossos in 1400 B.C, Mycenae became the chief city of this branch of old Minoan or Aegean culture, known as the Mycenaean civilization.[6] This culture, from which many art forms have been gathered, lasted until the 12th century B.C. A final, engulfing invasion from the north by the Dorians completely overwhelmed it in a dark age for three centuries.

It is clear that a continuous series of minor invasions from the north harried an indigenous

Years Before the Common Era

■ **753**—Rome is founded; music is part of daily life in Greece; choral music develops ■ **750**—Greeks colonize southern Italy and Sicily; Celts migrate to England ■ **700**—*Iliad* and *Odyssey* are ascribed to Homer; Olmecs construct first American pyramid; Nineveh is capital of Assyria ■ **680**—Athens replaces kings with archons (ministers) elected yearly; first coins are issued; the city-states of Greece are formed ⇨

people who inhabited Arcadia and Attica from 1800 B.C. to about 1400 B.C. The incoming Hellenic people gradually imposed their language on and were culturally absorbed by the non-Hellenes. It was not until the Dorian invasion that a cultural break came. The chaotic period of death and destruction, upheaval and internecine warfare, terminated (perhaps from sheer exhaustion) in the eighth century B.C., after which classical Greece began to experience a renaissance of culture.

The Greeks and Leisure

The Greek national character was molded by the history of its culture, beginning in the aristocratic arena of early Greece, where human perfection was a coveted ideal toward which the upper class was steadily trained and educated.

To discuss the influence of Greek thought on Western leisure theory and philosophy, we must first survey the structure of the Greek mind, which conceived and directed such intellectual pursuits as ethics, morality, and education. To do this, we must be aware of the effect the ideal of *arétè* had on all Greek achievements, including recreation. *Arétè* combines the idea of what is best in all things and is worthy of emulation and adoration—complete mastery. To the Greeks, a thing had *arétè* if performed not just efficiently but excellently in the manner for which it was created. This view applied to people as well. As Werner Jaeger puts it:

> We can find a more natural clue to the history of Greek culture in the history of the ideal of arétè, *which goes back to the earliest times. There is no complete equivalent for the word* arétè *in modern English—its oldest meaning is a combination of proud and courtly morality with warlike valour. But the idea of* arétè *is the quintessence of early Greek aristocratic education.*[7]

The ancient tradition of heroic power was not enough to satisfy the chroniclers of a younger era. Their concept of *arétè* combined noble actions and noble thoughts. Human perfection was the ideal that joined exalted deeds with nobility of mind. This concept of unity forced its way into the very foundation of the Greek code of life that has been handed down to us in the modern meaning of recreation.

Unity and wholeness seem to be the salient features of the Greek psyche. They are best described by Kitto, who states:

> *The sharp distinction which the Christian and the oriental world has normally drawn between the body and the soul, the physical and the spiritual, was foreign to the Greek— at least until the time of Socrates and Plato. To him there was simply the whole man. The Greek made physical training an important part of education . . . because it could never occur to him to train anything but the whole man.*[8]

We know from Homer, who wrote about the Achaean Greeks at least 300 years after that age, that there were major and minor monarchies. There is no certainty that Homer ever lived.[9] Moreover, his works may have been oral histories that were written down long after the original storyteller died. Many times the stories were attributed to famous figures, though sometimes they were only locally famous. Every city had a king; only when power was consolidated did a chief like Agamemnon arise.

Although slavery was already an institution in early Greece, it was no shame for aristocrats to handle a plow and farm their own land. Noblewomen performed a variety of craft activities, including sewing, weaving, and spinning.[10] Artisans and crafters were never slaves and were accorded the respect due their skill. Since each household was essentially self-sufficient in its production of needed goods and articles, as well as homegrown staples, crafts were specialty trades and were performed to order. Even though they might work long hours on a given project, the artisans worked in a leisurely manner without the compulsion of a competitive market economy.[11]

The Games. Even war did not diminish the Greek passion for games. Children and adults engaged in contests of skill. For example, Penelope's suitors played at draughts and threw the javelin and discus. When Odysseus landed at Phaeacia, his hosts played at quoits and danced for his entertainment.[12]

But more important were the athletic games that were held to celebrate religious rites, commemorate the lives of heroes, or entertain a guest—or just for the pleasure of the playing. When games were held, other affairs were halted so that participants could come together

Years Before the Common Era

⇨ ■ **660**—Byzantium is founded by Greeks ■ **650**—Acropolis in Athens is begun; literature is well developed in Greece, Egypt, Assyria, China, India; Assyrians destroy Babylon; ornamented weaving in Greece; new musical forms ■ **630**—Zoroaster founds Persian religion; tyrants rule Greece ■ **621**—Minister Dracon enacts first written laws for Athens ■ **609**—Assyrian empire ends; Greek philosophy is well established

and compete peacefully. The leisure that was then insured by oath was used to satisfy the competitive urge as well as produce a spectacle for entertainment (as it still does). The funeral games described by Homer were the forerunner to the great Olympics.[13]

The Panhellenic Games were organized to honor the gods and were an intrinsic part of the Greeks' pantheistic religion. Every town had its own place of worship or sacred grove. Eventually, local games graduated from their original commemorative purpose to a more encompassing scope and became the Pythean, Menean, and Isthmian Games. The greatest games were given in honor of the Olympian deities; they are still held every four years, after being revived in 1896 by Baron de Coubertain of France. Although 776 B.C is the date of the earliest Olympic victor on record, the Olympic Games probably began much earlier and may originally have been held every year. The games were gradually secularized until only the athletic events held significance.

Over a period of several centuries, the Achaean civilization slowly lost its vitality, and northern outsiders noticed its weakness. By immigration or invasion the northern hordes all but destroyed the Mycenaean civilization in the Dorian conquest. Hundreds of years after the Dorians invaded the Peloponnesus and disrupted social, political, and economic life, the synthesis of invaders and indigenous populations produced a people of vigorous abilities and intellectual acumen.

Cultural Diversity. After centuries of interbreeding, the Greeks retained some vestiges of the Mycenaean culture. Preserved were social institutions for government, religious rites, craft skills, technology, commercial forms and trade routes, elements of art and architecture, poetry, literature, and song. The impact of diverse cultures (Cretan, Mycenaean, Achaean, and Dorian) gave new impetus to a dying civilization.

In the Greece of 400 B.C, there were two reasons for the leisure that gave rise to great intellectual, artistic, creative, and philosophical achievements. One was the owning of domestic, factory, and mine-working slaves upon whose shoulders the leisure of the well-to-do rested. The other was the simplicity of life. The standard of living was far removed from what we consider the bare necessities of life today.

Then, too, the Greeks saved time by not having to travel to work and back home, and there were no conventional hours of work. Kitto has put it quite well:

> *Again, the daily round was ordered not by the clock but by the sun, since there was no effective artificial light. Activity began at dawn. We envy, perhaps, ordinary Athenians who seem to spend a couple of hours in the afternoon at the baths or a gymnasium (a spacious athletic and cultural centre provided by the public for itself). The Greek got up as soon as it was light, shook out the blanket in which he had slept, draped it elegantly around himself as a suit, had a beard and no breakfast, and was ready to face the world in five minutes. The afternoon, in fact, was not the middle of his day, but very near the end of it.[14]*

It is significant that leisure to the Greeks, especially the Athenians, was not conceived as many of us see it today. Leisure was put to practical use in learning (education) or in participation in government. Or it was directed to the contemplation of philosophy, civic service, rhetoric, or artistic creativity. Free time was used to benefit the society in which the Greek citizen (that is, the nonslave) lived.

Platonic Idealism

The first profound writings on play, recreational activities, and leisure were contributed by two of the greatest thinkers who ever influenced the cultural and educational pattern of Western civilization, Plato and his pupil Aristotle. Certain conflicts between their philosophical outlooks laid the foundation for many of the diverse concepts about the function of human beings, morality, government, the individual's place in the scheme of total knowledge, and education.[15] Both Plato and Aristotle recognized the need for play in their respective designs of school curriculum. While they never defined play in structural terms, they made it an intrinsic part of their plans for educating youth.

Platonic Curriculum. The preeminent work on education, Plato's *Republic,* fits play into the natural growth pattern of the child.[16] Plato understood the relation between education (*paideia*) and play (*paidia*). In play, children learn by serious imitation of older children and

Plato conversing with a student at the academy. Mural painting by Puvis de Chavannes.

adults. They copy the physical movements of daily living. But play also gives rise to activities of the mind—flights of fancy, imagination, make-believe. This type of play helps children learn and equips them for the formal curriculum.

To the end of his life, Plato was interested in the subject of play. Nowhere is his interest clearer than in *The Laws,* the work of his old age.[17] Plato's goal was to produce individuals who were fit for their particular station in life, who would be happy at what they were doing, and who would be able to live a full life with nothing lacking in personality, knowledge, or ability to achieve. The Platonic concept of education and play attempted to develop people who could get along with others, whose background and training were broad, and whose intellectual outlook was searching. Such individuals would be able to make a greater contribution to the maintenance and administration of their society.

In music and gymnastics, Plato saw the two balancing forces of mind and body that would train the person to build later intellectual and physical prowess.[18] Music in the Platonic era was not only rhythmic and harmonious; it also combined the poetic art and probably drama. Gymnastics, too, had a more profound meaning than physical exercise. It included rhythmics and dance, which are closely aligned to music. Together the two interdependent processes aimed for unity and for the cultivation and improvement of the whole person.

The use of music in gymnastics, which also included various of the aesthetic arts, made for what today would be called a well-rounded recreational program. We conceive a basic program for any recreational service agency to include music, dramatics, literature, rhythmics, the plastic arts, and dancing. Active sport and games and passive appreciative activities were included in the basic model of Greek education. Greek leisure was not thought of as time opposed to

Years Before the Common Era

551—Confucius is born; art forms develop; temple-building proceeds in Greece ■ 525—Aeschylus, Greek dramatist, is born; Themistocles, Athenian statesman, is born ■ 520—Pindar, Greek poet and composer, is born ■ 500—Pericles of Athens is born; first temple of Saturn in Rome is built; height of Etruscan political power in Italy; Phidius, Greek sculptor, is born ■ 496—Sophocles, dramatist,

work; it was just part of daily life. It blended seamlessly from the daily round of activity to early afternoon at the gymnasium. Not until Aristotle discriminated between schole (free time) and aschole (occupation) did the divergence of leisure and work become apparent.

Plato's belief in the immortality of the human soul and in the highest good—immutable perfection, or God—produced his earlier existence theory. He believed our existence on earth is just a shadow of our real existence in the world of the Supreme Being. Plato saw humans as creatures who turned away from the true reality of being and saw it only as someone facing away from a fire would see shadows on the cave wall, a dim reflection of the real world. To him the material world was, in fact, unreal. His real world was the world of pure idealism and ultimate good.[19] Plato believed that humans had prior lives in the spirit world (the real world) of the Deity, and their present existence is a hollow substitute for the time when the soul-spirit was united with God. He perceived our being on earth and our day-to-day experiences as a mere recollection of a time when the human soul was joined with the divine.

Play and Morality. Plato's idea of recall provides us with a philosophical concept that sets play as a standard of morality; from his point of view, there is a close relationship between the most important aims of human life and play. Plato associated play with the aesthetic truth of religion. He wrote:

> I say that about serious matters a man should be serious, and about a matter which is not serious, he should not be serious; and that God is the natural and worthy object of our most serious and blessed endeavors, for man, as I said before, is made to be the plaything of God, and this, truly considered, is the best of him; wherefore, also, every man and woman should walk seriously and pass life in the noblest of pastimes, and be of another mind from what they are at present. . . . And therefore, as we say, every one of us should live the life of peace as long and as well as he can. And what is the right way of living? Are we to live in sports always? If so, what kind of sports? We ought to live sacrificing, and singing, and dancing, and then a man will be able to propitiate the gods, and to defend himself against his enemies and conquer them in battle.[20]

For Plato, living the good life and dedicating it to God were best done through play. The thought of humans as God's playthings is an idea of humor and optimism. He advised us to live life as play, not to take ourselves too seriously, and above all to be free to change our minds from base materialism to a higher aesthetic plane, to live the good life, and to recognize God, who alone is worthy of serious contemplation.

It is in this work *The Laws* more than anywhere else that we can see the concept of *arétè* in the ideas of Plato. The ideal had undergone a metamorphosis. Plato considered *arétè* not an equalization of mind and body, a whole-person approach, but as a more one-sided affair. To him, the mind received the lion's share of attention and the body was tolerated because it contributed to a higher mental state by keeping the organism healthy. Plato's *arétè* was occupied with spirit as it pertained to increased knowledge and mental perfection. Body conditioning was included in his educational program to provide the purely physical chambers with a strong, healthy foundation fitted for the job of aiding intellectual and psychological growth.

Aristotelian Method

Plato and his star pupil had differing views on what constituted the material world. While Plato was an idealist, Aristotle was an empiricist. Nevertheless, their ideas on education were remarkably similar. Both saw the need for educating the whole person. Both knew that education was the key to developing the soundest society. Both required that play be part of their respective educational systems.

Aristotle included play in the curriculum because he believed it was necessary in the growth pattern of children. He probably saw that play was the way children could be educated to accept further teaching. Play allowed them to develop at their own rates, with personal and physical powers unfolding in their proper sequence. When the time came for more difficult instruction, each student's mind and body were so ordered that they could grasp the meaning of the instruction and hurdle the more troublesome phases of educative thought. But Aristotle went beyond merely fitting play into the educational scheme of things; he offered the world a design for living through his writings on ethics and morals.

Years Before the Common Era

Human Motivation. To Aristotle, the purpose for all human action was to obtain a measure of happiness (*eudaemonism*). Happiness was the universally sought end, being a natural inclination or deep-seated instinct. In the Aristotelian sense of the word, happiness was a product of the good life, a way of living within moral and ethical boundaries that equipped individuals to work and serve to the best of their abilities. Happiness was a product of action set in leisure because it included those values that were innate in schole (free time)—health, strength, virtuous conduct, self-reliance, and intellectual satisfaction. The interaction of these values created the whole person: cultured, educated, and loved. In other words, the product of these qualities was happiness. Even the modern world would have to admit that this epitomizes what we call the well-rounded person.

The word *eudaemonism* comes from the Greek prefix *eu-* for good and the root *daemon* for spirit. It describes what ethical conduct the individual should follow to achieve a good spirit. It should not be confused with the hedonistic philosophy that places all human motivation on the sensory level of mere pleasure seeking. The Aristotelian concept states that happiness is the outcome of a disciplined way of life. It can be achieved only through ethical practice. This is in contrast to the hedonistic doctrine that people should focus their living patterns so as to obtain pleasure and avoid unpleasantness.

In the history of human thought, eudaemonism has played a considerable role. Certainly, Aristotle developed his ethical doctrine to its most profound level in his Necomachean Ethics. Hedonism, which provided recreational activity with its usual content, was laid at Aristotle's door and was said to have issued from his writings, but this is simply not true. On close inspection, hedonism is revealed as an unethical type of behavior that has been promoted in modern times. It might be better said that Aristotle's philosophy has been corrupted to hedonism.

Basic hedonistic thought seems to stem from this bit of Aristotle's advice: "But to live well and do well, as we say, is nothing else than being happy. Being happy, then, and happiness consists in living well, and living well is living in accordance with virtues. This then is the end, and happiness is the best thing."[21]

The heritage of Aristotle's *Politics* is the Grecian golden age of philosophical thought. He said:

> *Nature, as has often been said, requires that we should be able, not only to work well, but to use leisure well; for as I must repeat once again, the first principle of all action is leisure.*
>
> *. . . But leisure of itself gives pleasure and happiness and enjoyment of life, which are experienced, not by the busy man, but by those who have leisure. For he who is occupied has in view some end which he has not attained; but happiness is an end, since all men deem it to be accompanied with pleasure and not with pain. This pleasure, however, is rewarded differently by different persons, and varies according to the habit of the individual.*[22]

The Aristotelian concept of happiness as the highest good is synonymous with leisure and presumably those activities performed during leisure. Naturally, leisure is meant to be taken in the Greek way.

Play and Catharsis. Central to Aristotle's concept of play was the cathartic process by which the individual was to act out in dynamic form tensions or aggressive acts. This sublimated release of directed energy in nonhostile behavior was to be achieved through play and in the play-forms of the dramatic arts. In his *Poetics,* Aristotle states:

> *Tragedy, then, is the imitation of an action that is serious and also as having magnitude complete in itself; in relationship with pleasurable accessories; each kind brought in separately in the parts of the work, in a dramatic, not in a relative, form; with incidents arousing pity and fear, wherewith to accomplish its catharsis of such emotions.*[23]

Thus it is that catharsis, or release from emotional involvement through acting out of focused behavior, serves as a fundamental support for play.

Schole. Because leisure was a basic ingredient in producing one of the world's greatest cultures, it was naturally used in educating the young. The word *schole,* from which we derive

Years Before the Common Era

⇨ ■ **431**—Peloponnesian War between Athens and Sparta begins ■ **430**—Temple-building in Greece reaches height after Parthenon consecrated ■ **429**—Pericles dies; Greek theater blooms ■ **427**—Plato is born ■ **411**—Coup d'etat in Athens, people's assembly takes power ■ **408**—Athenians capture Byzantium ■ **407**—Plato becomes pupil of Socrates ■ **405**—Peloponnesian War ends ■ **400**—The Ten

the word *school,* is Greek for leisure. Edith Hamilton observes, "Of course, reasoned the Greek, given leisure, a man will employ it in thinking and finding out about things. Leisure and the pursuit of knowledge, the connection was inevitable—to a Greek."[24]

The love of play and the desire to free people for the most important aspects of their lives, namely participation in government, the creation of art, and the never-ending search for knowledge, impelled the Greeks to use leisure as time for creative activity.

The Greek concept of education is joined with freedom, and their concept of freedom is tied up with leisure. On the combination of freedom and education, in conjunction with *arété* or excellence, a philosophy of leisure can be based. These separate facets of a single whole form what to the Greeks was completeness of mind and body to produce the complete person—at peace with self and the environment. All the person's faculties are in harmony, and there is no tension, strain, or discord. Such a person is truly re-created.

How different is our conception of leisure today. Many people consider it the antithesis of work, labor, or study; a time for loafing rather than living. The Greeks took their leisure seriously and spent it wisely in the pursuit of knowledge for living. But we take our leisure and use it to no purpose. We spend our time by letting it pass, "killing" it, with no thought of what we can make with it. The Greek concept of leisure was one of participation, stimulation, learning, and living. Our concept of leisure is a time for doing nothing, or at best watching someone else do what we don't have the skill or the energy to do.

The Decline of the Greeks. Economic rivalry was the essential factor in the conflict that ultimately led to dissolution of the Greek city-states. Only a short period of unity occurred while the war with Persia was concluded under the leadership of Athens. Unfortunately, after the common enemy was defeated, enmity and suspicion returned. Athens and Sparta fought each other in the Peloponnesian War. When it was over, so was the glory of ancient Greece. Impoverishment, destruction, and depopulation reached a depth from which the city-states never recovered. They were ripe for the armed takeover imposed by Rome.

THE ROMANS

Traditionally, Rome is supposed to have been founded by Aeneas of Troy sometime about 1200 B.C. Many myths describe in minute detail the construction and development of the city by Romulus. However, these stories do not stand the test of critical evaluation; they are merely part of the elaborate heritage of folklore to which the uneducated masses subscribed in the days of ancient Rome.

The Neolithic Italian culture existed before 3000 B.C. For 500 years thereafter, there was little change in that stagnant society. When foreign migrations started in 2500 B.C., progress in social culture was made. During the Chalcolithic age, metalworkers from beyond the Alps began to move into the region of the Po Valley. It was basically from these emigrants that Italy would gain its first knowledge of civilized life.

While the people of the Italian boot were adopting themselves to Chalcolithic culture (about 1700 B.C.), a new wave of invasions began in central Europe. The Achaeans moved into the Greek peninsula, and ripples of migrant pressure were felt throughout the northern Mediterranean region. One of these groups, the Terramara people, left a deep impression upon the peninsular Italians. Profound contact with them led to great advances in both material and cultural institutions.

Migration and Population Movement

Some six centuries after the Chalcolithic culture entered Italy, a new flood of migrations brought violent repercussions to the lands along the Mediterranean Sea. One result was the Dorian invasion of Greece. Another was the drive southward by the inhabitants of the Po Valley to new locations in the central region of the peninsula.

About 800 B.C., Italian culture underwent another remarkable change for the better when invaders from Asia Minor, the Etruscans, overran much of western Italy. They rapidly transformed the land they conquered. They taught the natives how to drain the swamps, log the forests, and grow grapes and olives. They worked the local iron, tin, and copper mines, and the practical trades of smithing, stone masonry, carpentry, and weaving soon ap-

Years Before the Common Era

Thousand under Xenophon retreat; Carthage occupies Malta; Indian civilization in Mexico ends ■ **399**—Socrates dies; trumpet-playing competitions are held in Greece ■ **384**—Demosthenes, statesman and orator, is born; Aristotle is born ■ **356**—Alexander the Great is born; Great Wall of China is constructed ■ **352**—Philip II of Macedonia becomes king ■ **350**—Etruscan power declines; India's ⇨

peared. Timber was transformed into ships, which were soon plying the trade routes among Italy, Sicily, Sardinia, and Corsica.

Once their position had been consolidated, the Etruscan aristocrats began to enlarge their sphere of influence. They went south and invaded Latium and Campania—thus probably founding Rome. The Greeks, too, had colonized parts of the Italian peninsula. Once the Etruscans headed south, it was only a matter of time before the two would clash. From the sixth century on, the two peoples were almost continuously occupied by war. It was not until 535 B.C. that Carthage and Etruria formed an alliance to expel the Greek colonists from Corsica.

By 500 B.C., however, the tide in Campania and Latium had turned against the Etruscans, and after repeated revolts by the native populations, the Etruscan empire toppled. The growing power of Rome was an important factor in this defeat. Between 500 B.C. and 265 B.C., Rome first became the dominant power and then engulfed and united all of Italy into one state.

Life and Culture in Early Rome

Life was simple and somewhat crude during the third century B.C. The culture was not very diverse. Class distinctions had weakened, and there was neither a very wealthy nor a very poor class. The economy was based on agriculture. People lived by traditions, and family unity was strong. These Romans cared little for aesthetics or for the niceties of civilization.

Under such conditions, work, not leisure, was the central theme. Everyone in the family worked hard and lived simply. Yet they still had some leisure and the diversions that free time usually spawns. Religious holidays were numerous. Citizens were obliged to attend public hearings and pass laws in Rome. Markets or fairs were held every ninth day in and about the capital as well as in the rural areas.

Slaves in early Rome were often captives of war used mainly as agricultural laborers. There were so few slaves during this period that they contributed little to the leisure of their owners. It was not until much later that large numbers of captives from Asia, Greece, and central Europe were cruelly exploited by their owners for purposes of luxury and vice. As might be expected, the early Romans, busy coping with a harsh environment (both human and natu-

ral), did little in terms of the fine arts and literature. However, in the eminently practical arts of architecture and road and aqueduct building, they were unsurpassed.

Education was largely home-based. This was especially true of the patrician class, even though they had the means to patronize organized seminars, lectures, and other instructional experts outside of the homes. The well-to-do typically sent their sons off on grand tours, usually ending in Athens.[25]

Roman children had many games, most of them well known in other lands throughout the ancient world.[26] There were various games with dice, dolls, bones, nuts, and the forerunner of checkers, chess, and backgammon.

As they grew older, the children's games gave way to more physically demanding activities. A constant concern for *mens sana in corpore sano* (a sound mind in a strong body) required participation in hunting, riding, running, jumping, swimming, wrestling, boxing, and throwing. Males could exercise for recreational and military purposes each day beside the Tiber at the Campus Martius, Rome's first gymnasium.

The public games, which flourished during the later Republic and throughout the imperium, were organized almost from the beginning of Rome. By the end of the Republic, 66 days out of the year were celebrated by public games in the circus or arena. The Ludi Magni and Ludi Romani were like the Greek Olympic Games except that they were celebrated annually.[27]

Physical activity in the early Republic was utilitarian training for war or labor. Romans disciplined natural play tendencies to military purposes. As their horizons broadened, through conquest and greater contact with older and more sophisticated societies, prejudices against leisure-inspired physical activity diminished. Whereas the contrast between Greek and Roman participation was as contestants and spectators, Greeks were inclined to participate in games while Romans were content to be observers.[28,29]

Life and Culture After the Roman Conquest

After about 265 B.C., Rome began to dominate the western Mediterranean world. During Rome's consolidation of the Italian peninsula, its wars seemed largely defensive. However, as

⇨ "Mahabharata" is written ■ **336**—Alexander becomes king when his father is assassinated, begins conquests; Zeno, founder of the Stoic school, is born; Aristotle lays the foundation of musical theory ■ **325**—Papyrus is used in Greece; Alexandria is center of Greek learning ■ **323**—Ptolemy Soter founds new Egyptian dynasty after Alexander's death; Euclid publishes his geometry ■ **320**—Hellenistic period of

A Roman aqueduct.

it continued to win, it had to protect new frontiers. This led to increased expansion. Inevitably, Rome's sphere of influence clashed with that of Carthage, which at that time controlled much of the western Mediterranean area. The conflicts resulted in the Punic Wars. Rome emerged victorious and by 200 B.C. was well on the way to imperial overlordship of the Mediterranean world.

With Carthage defeated, Rome was the strongest military power in the civilized world. Again, new frontiers led to new antagonisms and wars of both defense and aggression. The stage was set for Rome's assumption of power over the eastern Mediterranean as well. Until now Rome's foreign policies had been based on opportunism, and it had had little contact with the Greek states. Now it came into direct contact with them and was involved in an endless series of wars.

In 167 B.C. Rome emerged as the dominant power in the eastern Mediterranean as well as the western. From then until the decline of the Roman Republic in 79 B.C., Rome engaged in a series of major and minor wars that subjugated all of the former kingdoms and empires of the ancient Near East as well as Asia Minor, Greece, Spain, and the Danube region.

One of the unfortunate results of this imperial expansion was the decadence of Roman society. Increased wealth and might led to a marked inequality between the rich and the poor. So many slaves were available that the wages of citizen workers declined. The well-to-do no longer performed manual labor or lived the simple life of their ancestors. A new leisure class arose.

Public festivals and amusements became more numerous and varied for both rich and poor. From Campania came the gladiatorial combats, which were first held in Rome in 264 B.C. but took decades to gain popular support. Theatrical performances, horse racing, and acrobatics were some of the events held to entertain the people. By 50 B.C. the aristocracy, by virtue of its reliance upon slave-worked ag-

Years Before the Common Era

Greek arts ■ **312**—Appian Way is under construction ■ **301**—Palestine is under Egyptian rule ■ **300**—Rome continues to expand ■ **287**—Archimedes is born ■ **275**—End of Babylonian history; ball games, dice, and board games played in Greece and Rome ■ **264**—First Punic War between Carthage and Rome begins; first gladiatorial combat in Rome ■ **255**—Greek version of Old Testament is written ⇨

riculture and other commercial enterprises, lived a leisure existence on a scale hitherto unknown. As C. E. Van Sickle states:

Indeed, many of the richer members and the spendthrifts who strove to imitate them at times adopted gaudy splendor and coarse luxury which was the scandal of their own later times. Eating, drinking, flashy clothes, expensive furniture, handsome slaves, and gambling cost these worthies enormous sums, and they went to the most absurd and revolting lengths to procure the objects of their desire.[30]

Yet for all this misdirected activity, there is abundant proof of rich cultural development during this period. The Romans were very creative and found means of self-expression in both the fine arts and literature. History, poetry, oratory, and the didactic essay were integral parts of Roman literature. Architecture, sculpture, and painting flourished. Roman architecture formed a style of its own. An age of leisure produced Virgil, Horace, Livy, and fine arts whose merits cannot be denied.

The years of the Republic's decline and abandonment, caused by the corruption and degradation of senatorial power and some men's illegal taking of office during emergencies, cannot be laid on any single person. When the first tribune of the people was murdered, the basic sanctions against tribunician immunity from harm were lifted. One consequence was the rise of a variety of warlords who hastened the decline of the Republic. After the triumvirate and subsequent rise of Gaius Julius Caesar as a general and statesman, the fate of the Roman Republic was sealed. The triumvirate, as the term denotes, is the rule of three. It refers to the classic Roman office of three co-equal administrators or governors. In this instance, the office was filled by Ceasar, Pompey, and Crassus in the first triumvirate. Civil war between Caesar and Pompey, proscription of enemies, dictatorship, assassination, and the war of succession heralded the Augustan Principate.

Early Imperial Society

The aristocracy stood at the top of Roman society. It included the wealthy few who, through ownership of estates and shares in commercial ventures or through corrupt politics, had gathered the financial means to pursue a life of luxury. Estates were cultivated by tenants and slaves. With abundant leisure and opportunities for education, the aristocrats followed cultural pursuits that were denied to the masses.

The urban middle class, or curials, also enjoyed excellent educational opportunities. Through wise investments, a strong sense of civic duty, and other reasonable factors, they served Rome diligently until they were financially ruined by sustaining the cost of imperial government in the third century A.D. In the fourth and fifth centuries, the surviving curials were no more than slaves of the state.

The urban proletariat was a composite of hard-working, frugal freemen, hired laborers, and slaves. Because of slave competition, wages were very low and most workers lived lives of squalor and bare subsistence. In Rome, the emperors had to take over the task of feeding and amusing the urban population. The ruling class provided free food, entertainment, public baths, and other doles. These were the famous bread and circuses designed to distract the people from the unfairness of their lot.

Much more numerous than the city masses were the free peasants who cultivated the soil. Although slavery never played a major part in agriculture, some slaves worked with them. Tools and implements were primitive, and the free peasants worked hard for a small return and little leisure. Their lives were hard and bitter. They had to pay their rent and taxes and face forced labor drafts and other imperial levies. They had no part in the brilliant, if wasteful, urban life that produced the appearance of great prosperity for the empire in the second century A.D. Peasants had no educational prospects and very little culture. Their freedom, such as it was, became a farce by the end of the third century.

For 250 years after the death of Augustus in 14 A.D., the Greco-Roman culture of the Roman Empire was sustained by the intellectual and aesthetic traditions of its past. But the decay of classical culture had already begun. During the first century of this era much of value was produced. Then routine and stagnation set in, and for the next century taste and artistic form declined rapidly. Van Sickle states:

Literature succumbed to a taste for showy rhetoric and to blind worship of the past, and of the arts only architecture was producing anything which was destined to win the approval of later ages. Science and philosophy lingered a little longer, but before the accession of Diocletian they, too, had succumbed to the forces which were bringing the classical world to an end. The decline of economic prosperity, the breakdown of political absolutism, and a caste-ridden social order—all contributed to create an environment in which none of the distinctive products of earlier ages could flourish. Hence, they withered away.[31]

Late Imperial Society

The decadent fourth and fifth centuries witnessed the fall of the classical tradition in the Roman empire, as well as the destruction of orderly government, sophisticated urban life, the economy, art, literature, science, and philosophy. In the harassed and regulated cities of the fourth and fifth centuries, survival rather than leisure was the focus. Few people had the wealth to indulge in free time. Economic support was no longer sufficient for building programs. Artistic activity died out in communities continuously under attack by invading barbarians (not to mention their own soldiers and rapacious bureaucrats).

The society at this time was one of conformity, complicity, and stagnation. The urban middle class had been pinched out of existence because they could not compete in an economy founded on slavery. The landed aristocracy, the great senatorial landowners, lived in seclusion on their vast estates, enjoying their wealth, leisure, and whatever culture there was during the late empire.

The Roman Empire was doomed to destruction. Many factors influenced its inevitable decline, though no one knows exactly why Imperial Rome finally dissolved. The splendors of the classic era were routinized and strangled by an effete aristocracy and an ignorant peasantry. The indulgences of the senatorial aristocracy amid the ruin of the other classes were scandalous. In every period of the later Roman Empire, there are traces of degeneracy. For sheer waste and brutality, the gladiatorial contests and orgiastic or sybaritic entertainments cast a pall that would not be dispelled for centuries. Little wonder that members of the various Christian sects condemned leisure over the

next 1,400 years. A final commentary on the social conditions of Imperial Rome is offered by Johan Huizinga:

Rome grew to a World Empire and a World Emporium. To it there fell the legacy of the Old World that had gone before, the inheritance of Egypt and Hellenism and half the Orient. Its culture was fed on the overflow of a dozen other cultures. Government and law, road-building and the art of war reached a state of perfection such as the world had never seen. . . . The Roman Empire . . . was spongy and sterile in its social and economic structure.

Rome in its later days . . . was slowly degenerating and being suffocated under a system of State slavery, extortion, graft and nepotism, circuses and amphitheaters for bloody and barbarous games, a dissolute stage, baths for a cult of the body more enervating than invigorating—none of this makes for a solid and lasting civilization. Most of it served for show, amusement and futile glory.[32]

The grandeur that was Rome was copied to a large extent from the Hellenistic culture. The Romans adopted the leisure style of the Greeks but added certain refinements and debasements, among them the gladiatorial schools for slaughter and daredevil competitive events. Leisure excesses were so prevalent and leisure so demeaned that there was a negative reaction against all things recreational. The disapproval of most leisure activity or seemingly purposeless experiences has remained in one form or another in most Western cultures since the early Christian Church denounced frivolous conduct, particularly after Saint Augustine wrote against sensuousness in human affairs. We can even see this tendency in contemporary society. An example is the 1961 U.S. Supreme Court ruling that upheld the legality of blue laws, which prohibit certain activities (like the selling of liquor) on Sundays.

SELECTED REFERENCES

Archer, L. J., ed. *Slavery and Other Forms of Unfree Labor.* London: Routledge, 1988.

Baddeley, St. C., and L. D. Gordon. *Rome and Its Story.* New York: Gordon Press, 1977.

Downey, G. *Constantinople in the Age of Justinian*. New York: Dorset Press, 1990.

Finley, M. I. *Ancient History: Evidence and Models*. New York: Penguin Books, 1987.

Fornara, C. W. *The Nature of History in Ancient Greece and Rome*. Berkley: University of California Press, 1983.

Grant, M. *The Visible Past: Greek and Roman History from Archaeology*. New York: MacMillan, 1992.

Green, P. *Classical Beginnings: Interpreting Ancient History and Culture*. New York: Thames & Hudson, 1989.

Irwin, T. *Classical Thought*. Oxford: Oxford University Press, 1989.

Jaeger, W. *Paideia: The Ideals of Greek Culture*. Translated by G. Highet. 3 vols. New York: Oxford University Press, 1939-1944; Oxford: Oxford University Press, 1989.

Kinzl, K. H., ed. *Greece and the Eastern Mediterranean in Ancient History and Prehistory*. Hawthorne, NY: Walter De Gruyter, 1977.

Massey, M. *Women in Ancient Greece and Rome*. Cambridge: Cambridge University Press, 1988.

Onians, R. B., ed. *The Origins of European Thought*. Salem: Ayer, 1987.

Petronius. *The Satyrican*. Translated by P. G. Walsh. Oxford: Oxford University Press, 1996.

Sansone, D. *Greek Athletics and the Genesis of Sport*. Berkeley: University of California Press, 1988.

REVIEW QUESTIONS

1. Why was leisure so important to the Greeks?

2. Every citizen in the Greek city-state had leisure every day. How was such leisure possible? Are there any parallels between ancient Greek leisure and modern Western leisure?

3. Why does Aristotle say that people who are too busy cannot be happy?

4. Leisure assumed great significance for the Roman masses during the late empire period. Why was this so?

5. Was the condemnation of leisure by the early Christian patriarchy logically conceived?

GLOSSARY

Arcadia: Mountainous region of the Peloponnesian peninsula in ancient Greece.

Aristotle: Born 384 B.C., the son of the court physician to the king of Macedonia. Studied under Plato for 20 years. Opened the Lyceum, a center for learning, discourse, and research, particularly in the fields of biology and history. He was the tutor of Alexander the Great.

Attica: Ancient district of east central Greece with Athens as its main city.

Campus Martius: A floodplain area adjacent to the Tiber River in Rome. Originally used as a practice ground for military exercises, it was the site of the altar to Mars and the temple to Apolo in the fifth century B.C. The area was later drained and many structures were built there, including the Pantheon. The remaining buildings are all of Byzantine style.

Carthage: A city founded by the Phoeniceans in 814 B.C. The city was well protected by hills and the Gulf of Tunis. The city of Carthage engaged in wars with Rome called the Punic Wars between the third and second centuries B.C. and fell to the Romans in 146 B.C. Carthage flourished under Roman rule until it was destroyed by the Vandals.

Empiricism: The philosophy expressed by the doctrine that all knowledge of matters of fact is based on experience. The nature of the world cannot be understood through reason or reflection but only through experiential data. Empiricism has been combined with the philosophical viewpoints of the early Greek Sophists, Christian philosophers in the Middle Ages, and the logical positivists.

Years Before the Common Era

⇨ ■ **146**—Third Punic War ends ■ **133**—Asia Minor becomes a Roman province ■ **106**—Marcus Tullius Cicero is born ■ **100**—Gaius Julius Caesar is born; Chinese ships reach India; Great Stupa is erected in India ■ **90**—Civil war in Rome as Sulla takes control ■ **71**—Revolt of slaves under Spartacus is crushed ■ **63**—Pompey conquers Palestine; Gaius Octavius is born ■ **60**—First triumvirate is formed

Etruscan: A resident of Etruria in what is now Central Italy. Etruscan civilization reached its height in the sixth century B.C. The Etruscans greatly influenced the growth of the Roman civilization. Many artifacts of Etruscan civilization have been discovered in the region of Lazio, which now includes the present-day city of Rome.

Eudaemonism: A theory that makes the happiness of man and personal well being the chief good of humans. Because of the difficulty in defining the subjective state of happiness, ethicists today tend to avoid using the term.

Homer: Little is known of the life of Homer. He is thought to have been an Ionian Greek born in the ninth or eighth century B.C. The great works of ancient literature *The Iliad* and *The Odyssey* are attributed to his composition and/or inspiration. Both epics have had a great impact on Western literature and have been translated into modern languages many times.

Idealism: A philosophy that emphasizes the importance of the abstract relations found in the world over the reality of objects perceived by the senses. There are six different tenets of idealism that are shared by all schools of idealism.

Mycenae: An ancient Greek city dating from the late Bronze Age; the capital of King Agamemnon. Excavation of the site has produced numerous artifacts now in the National Museum in Athens. Mycenea was burned and destroyed by the Dorians around 1100 B.C.

Pantheism: A doctrine that states that all things in the universe make up God and at the same time there is no specific being called God, just the combination of forces, substances, and natural laws. This idea is reflected in many ancient religions and was developed into a distinct philosophy by Spinoza in the 17th century. The term can also mean the worship of many gods.

Peloponnesian War: The war fought between the two leading city-states of ancient Greece, Athens, and Sparta lasting from 431 to 404 B.C. By 411 B.C. Athens was experiencing political turmoil and was eventually defeated due to a Spartan blockade.

Plato: A student of Socrates. He developed a philosophy based on the existence of Ideas as the perfect representation of universal concepts or absolutes. Plato founded the Academy in Athens as the seat of learning and dialogue for the development of this theories. Included among his students was Aristotle. His principal teacher was Aspatia of Miletos, known as the first lady of Athens.

Punic Wars: A series of three wars over the period 264 B.C. to 146 B.C. between the city-state of Carthage and the Roman Empire. The third war resulted in the destruction of Carthage; only 50,000 of the original 500,000 residents survived until the surrender.

Years Before the Common Era

(Caesar, Pompey, Crassus) ■ **51**—Caesar conquers Gaul ■ **49**—Caesar crosses Rubicon ■ **47**—Great library of Alexandria is destroyed by fire ■ **44**—Caesar is murdered by conspirators ■ **40**—Herod is appointed king of Judaea ■ **30**—Octavian, renamed Augustus, becomes emperor ■ **9**—Roman army invades Germania ■ **6**—Judaea becomes a Roman province ■ **4**—Probable date of Christ's birth

LEISURE DURING THE MIDDLE AGES

Objectives:

After reading this chapter, the student will be able to do the following:

Understand why the Dark Ages were so named.

Discuss the impact of feudalism on leisure.

Explain why walled cities were built.

Differentiate between aristocratic and peasant leisure.

Explain why town life promoted leisure.

Describe the guilds' influence on leisure.

Differentiate between medieval and renaissance
people's attitudes toward leisure.

Discuss how the Reformation influenced leisure.

Explain John Calvin's view of leisure and recreational activity.

Agnes Dupuis

Agnes Dupuis of Senlac was married to a villein in the year of A.D. 1100. At 23, she had been married five years. She was a partner to her husband and shared in the daily drudgery six days a week. She might also work on Sunday by spinning or weaving to earn extra income in the hope of purchasing additional land or other necessities. She cooked, cleaned, made the family's clothing, and helped to produce the food. She soaked, beat, and combed out the flax; fed the poultry; sheared the sheep; milked the cows; made cheese and butter; and worked in the vegetable garden. Her outside chores included sowing, reaping, gleaning, binding, threshing, winnowing, and sometimes helping to repair the cottage in which they lived. She even drove the oxen while her husband handled the plow.

Today, however, Agnes looked forward to a day of rest after attending Mass and the Sunday service in the cathedral. Although she couldn't read, Agnes loved the stained-glass windows, with their depictions of the saints and biblical stories. When the sun streamed in, the cathedral was alive with glowing color. In the early afternoon, Agnes and her family walked from their holding to the village because a fair was in progress. It was one of the experiences that enlivened her existence. Agnes eagerly anticipated the mystery play she would see this day, for a band of players had set up their cart-stage at the fair site. Such productions were always enjoyable.

For the most part, Agnes's life consisted of the routine labor that was her lot. But on special occasions, such as Sundays or feast days or church-sanctioned holidays, she had free time to visit acquaintances, dance and sing at the local tavern, or participate in some rare revelry. Agnes might drink a prodigious quantity of beer as she watched her friends dance a reel or took part herself. The day ended with the long walk home. Leisure was fleeting and had to be made the most of while there was opportunity.

Years in the Common Era

476—Roman Empire ends in the West; cave temples at Yun-Kang, China ■ **481**—Clovis succeeds to kingdom of the Salian Franks, eventually founds the Merovingian dynasty ■ **483**—Justinian I (the Great) who will be Byzantine emperor, is born ■ **484**—First schism between Western and Eastern Churches ■ **493**—Clovis I converts to Christianity ■ **500**—New Testament is written in Greek and Latin;

The Age in the Middle occupied a millennium. The thousand years after the fall of the western Roman Empire (455 to 1455) saw the rise of a central Christian religion with the most spectacular edifices ever built, the cathedrals. During this period Islam was born out of Arabia and an Islamic empire enveloped North Africa, Spain, and the Middle East.

The rivalry of the Byzantine and Catholic churches created a schism that was never healed. Feudalism and town autonomy permitted the emergence of the European fledgling nation-states. Banking, accounting, and public finance were invented. Trade, travel, and industry augmented economic development. Islamic scholars collected and protected the classical works of knowledge and became a ready source for translation when reason replaced superstition.

Leisure was an integral part of life during the Middle Ages. The workers' toil was punctuated by the Sabbath, church festivals, holidays, and aristocratic largess. The leisure of the latter was always more abundant, but shared to some extent by tradition. By the end of this era, the nations that would comprise western Europe had been forged. Great centers of learning were founded. Sectarian and secular art flourished and ushered in a rebirth of classical ideals. If the Renaissance forcefully influenced cultural expansion, it also heightened people's leisure, and they used it to great effect.

Religious upheaval generated both the Reformation and the Counter-Reformation. The reformed church tried to tame the people's leisure and succeeded in producing a theocracy whose influence was projected to the New World. We are only now shrugging off that legacy.

The thousand years between the fall of the Roman Empire and the Renaissance are typically called medieval. During this period national cultures grew; Western civilization solidified to a point where its character would determine the shape of succeeding eras. There was only one church—the Church of Rome. The downfall of the Roman Empire in the West brought the scourge of barbarism to Europe. The Hunnish invasions caused the fierce tribes of the north to migrate. In the process the Franks, Visigoths, Ostrogoths, Jutes, Angles, Saxons, and others overran the boundaries of the Roman Empire and finally brought down its government.

With the destruction of Rome, the great illumination of classical civilization went out. The ensuing 500 years were, with good reason, called the Dark Ages. Although new knowledge indicates that a great deal of positive activity occurred during this period of alternating chaos and torpor, cities declined to towns and villages became mere crossroads. Farms were left to rot, roads decayed, isolated fortified places existed, and wild animals roamed where herds of domestic animals had pastured.[1]

THE DARK AGES

From 544 A.D. until the 11th century, Europe was in decline. The surge of Islam and the flowering of Byzantium did nothing to stop it. The Moslems gained control of the Mediterranean. Normans, Magyars, and Saracens invaded the towns and coasts. Migration, conquest, and plague devastated morals, government, and economies. The 500 years of this epoch were filled with fear, hunger, and disease. Survival constantly prodded people to seek out the protection of stronger neighbors. Looting and raiding were continual threats.

There were intervals of order. England, France, and Germany knew the ruling hands of Alfred, Charlemagne, and Otto. Education was revived by Alcuin and philosophy by John Erigena. Moslem science took hold. Leo IX and Gregory VII restored the Catholic Church. The Romanesque style of architecture came into existence. But not until the 12th century did Europe begin to emerge from the darkness.

An individual's real hope of protection lay in local chiefs strong enough to retaliate or stand off a raider. This fact was soon evident in the European countryside. The early medieval community was a clutch of huts set in close proximity to the manor house in which the local lord dwelt. But for survival, the free peasantry of Europe paid an enormous price—freedom. In exchange for being protected by the lord of the manor, many peasants gave up their freedom for serfdom, which bound them to the manor for life.

There were, of course, degrees of serfdom. At the bottom of the heap were the cotters, who were given three or four acres to farm but also did menial work at the manor. Villeins were given up to 40 acres of land to farm but had to labor a certain number of days each week on the lord's farm and supply him with produce from their own small holdings.

⇨ first plans are made for Vatican Palace in Rome; music is introduced in Christian church service ■ **511**—Merovingian kingdom is divided into four parts when Clovis dies ■ **517**—Emperor Wu-Ti introduces Buddhism to China ■ **519**—End of first schism reconciles Eastern and Western Churches; Chinese bronze sculpture (T'ang period) flourishes ■ **521**—Boethius introduces Greek musical letter notation to the West

Agriculture was the basis for the economy, and it proved to be a precarious enterprise, especially in the northern climates. Famine was endemic. The high aristocracy moved from place to place as provisions in one manor gave out. The king's court might be perpetually on the move throughout the realm. Unhappily, the burdens of this destitute society fell most heavily on the serfs. The load was severe and the requirements exacting. Every serf on the manor performed two kinds of labor: fieldwork and handwork. Ditch digging, manure carting, tree cutting, road repairing—all of the tasks normally associated with the term "handyman" were required. Serfs also had to plow, seed, and harvest the manorial acres. As if this weren't enough, they had to show gratitude for the lord's protection by supplying even more labor, called boon work, over and above all of their other chores.

WORK AND LEISURE IN MEDIEVAL EUROPE

In his *Colloquium,* Aelfric recites a dialogue between a serf and a visitor:

M. What do you say, ploughman, how do you do your work?

P. Oh, sir, I work very hard. I go out at dawn, driving the oxen to the field, and I yoke them to the plough; however hard the winter I dare not stay at home for fear of my master; but, having yoked the oxen and made the ploughshare and coulter fast to the plough, every day I have to plough a whole acre or more.

M. Have you any companion?

P. I have a boy who drives the oxen with the goad, and he is even now hoarse with cold and shouting.

M. What more do you do in the day?

P. A good deal more, to be sure. I have to fill the oxen's cribs with hay, and give them water, and carry the dung outside.

M. Oh, oh, it is hard work.

P. Yes, it is hard work, because I am not a free man.[2]

Hard toil and heavy penalties were the serf's expectations. Taxes came in many forms. The lord could impose a head tax, an income tax,

"Spring Planting Work" by Abel Grimer (Musée des Beaux-Arts, Antwerp).

Years in the Common Era

■ **527**—Justinian I becomes Byzantine emperor; Saxon kingdoms of Essex and Middlesex are founded; Church of the Nativity is reconstructed in Bethlehem ■ **529**—Justinian I closes the 1,000-year-old school of philosophy in Athens; St. Benedict founds monastery of Monte Cassino and the Benedictine Order; Justinian's Codex Vetus (civil law code) is issued ■ **531**—Persian culture and arts flower ■ **532**—Construction ⇨

and fees or charges for using his mill, oven, or wine press. It was not unusual for male serfs to have to pay for the right to marry and for female serfs to have to yield their virginity to the lord on their wedding night. Serfs did not escape even when they died, because the lord might confiscate the contents of their cottage.

It was possible to flee from serfdom. Serfs who could make their way to a town and remain there for a year and a day, paying the town's taxes, were freed from bondage. Occasionally they could purchase their freedom directly from the manor. If willing to work even harder than normal, on feast days as well as a few hours before dawn or after dusk, serfs might eventually amass enough money from the surplus produced to buy their own liberty.

Typically, however, holidays provided an all too infrequent break. That free time was needed to rest and recuperate from the unceasing toil that feudal society demanded. It was a time for raucous activities, for letting go, singing indecent love songs, dancing around a flowery maypole, and watching a traveling show with its mumming, masques, and dancing animals. These respites were brief, but the peasants deemed themselves lucky to stay alive and asked no more than the security they received from their masters. A medieval rhyme suggests that the human order was determined by God and one should not attempt to change the system. There were three castes—nobles, clergy, and aristocracy—and the function of the peasantry was to serve them.

Feudalism

The duty of peasants to support the ruling classes brought with it certain reciprocal responsibilities. The serf served the lord of the manor, the clergy ministered to the spiritual needs of both serf and aristocrat, and the noble had to govern and to provide security. Within the aristocracy itself, there existed a complex mutuality of privileges and responsibilities. The concept of noblesse oblige (the responsibilities conferred by noble birth) was the foundation on which medieval society rested.[3] The relationship between noble and serf was manorialism; that between noble and noble was feudalism.

The term *feudalism* stems from the Latin word *feudum,* or fief—a grant of land by a superior to a lesser lord, or vassal, in return for services performed and homage received. The rise of feudalism may be attributed to the kind of economy and insecurity that resulted from the barbarian invasions of the western Roman Empire. Constant harassment led to the demise of many clans, and geographic proximity assumed greater importance than blood relationships. Landowners became closely bound to neighbors whose lands adjoined theirs. By joining forces, they were often able to withstand threats of incursion or actual attack. Since the economy was essentially based on bartering, the exchange of services seems a logical extension.

The feudal relationship cemented a bond between two individuals, both responsible and accountable for their actions. Due to the religious unity of the times, vows assumed a sanctity and meaning that have seldom been seen. The feudatory act was sealed by a formal pledge of homage in which the vassal placed his hands between those of the overlord and was kissed in return. The superior not only gave the fief the assurance of his protection against all enemies, but also provided a court for the settlement of any disputes that might arise.

In the hierarchy of medieval nobility, vassals could have their own vassals and be subject to several overlords. Whoever was at the top of the pyramid—whether king, emperor, or pope—numbered hundreds or thousands of the aristocracy as inferior vassals. The services rendered by a vassal to a lord might be civil, monetary, and/or military. The vassal might be called upon to administer justice in the fief through various payments, to supply lodging if the overlord came through the fief, and to supply military service in times of need. This could mean castle guard duty and combat.

When summoned, vassals had to appear with whatever retinue they were called upon to provide. This might mean a mounted regiment made up of their own vassals, who provided their military services in much the same way. Feudal armies came to be based upon the mounted man, or knight. The term *chivalry* came from *chevalier,* French for knight.[4]

Warfare was common in medieval Europe. Invasions by Arab Moslems bent on converting all to Islam were a constant threat after A.D. 660. Sweeping out of Africa after the vision of Mohammed, the Moslems threatened western Europe many times. The structure of the feudal system slowly developed after the

Years in the Common Era

of St. Sophia Basilica begins in Constantinople ■ **533**—North Africa becomes a Byzantine province ■ **535**—Chinese roll paintings are created ■ **542**—Bubonic plague spreads from Egypt to Europe and kills half the population ■ **549**—Music, dancing, chess, and hunting flourish in the Sassonid dynasty of Persia ■ **550**—Kingdoms of Mercia, East Anglia, and Northumbria are founded in Britain; Toltec kingdom

great seven-day battle at Poitiers, in southern France, in October 732. The Christianized Franks defeated the Moslems, and warfare was now based on the cavalry rather than the infantry. Charles Martel, ruler of the Franks, decreed that to receive his protection, his vassals would have to provide their own horse, armor, and supplies. Poitiers proved to be the high-water mark of Moslem incursions in the West. While the armies of Islam would continue to harass the fringes of Europe (particularly Spain, southern Italy, and the Mediterranean islands), they would never again menace the European heartland.

The Carolingian Monarchy

Charlemagne was crowned king of the Franks at Aix-la-Chappelle in 768 and brought the reigning Martel family to the height of its power. The restoration of Roman imperialism was the focal point of Charlemagne's life, and he succeeded brilliantly. In St. Peter's Cathedral on Christmas Day 800, Pope Leo III crowned him emperor of the Roman Empire in the West. All of western Europe except England, Scandinavia, and the Islamic territories in Spain and Italy was under his control.

Charlemagne's acquisition of the crown launched a struggle for supremacy between church and state that would drag on for 600 years. His heirs lost the empire within 150 years after his death. But it was revived by the great German king Otto I as the Holy Roman Empire, this time minus France but including Germany and northern Italy. This imperial power would exist until the 13th century, and remnants would be observed by the Hapsburg emperors of Austria until 1918.

Charlemagne's empire was a monumental legacy to later generations, despite the political and religious disputes that he left unresolved. He became the patron of learning in Europe, and the schools he founded encouraged the spread of literacy and scholarship. Universities were established that supplied society with doctors, lawyers, bankers, administrators, and men of commerce. The Carolingian Renaissance anticipated the wave of aesthetic achievement immortalized in Romanesque and Gothic architecture, sculpture, and manuscript illumination.[5] Charlemagne is thought to have sponsored new methods of agriculture that increased food production. Charlemagne did much to promote rationality, education, and the restoration of classical learning to Europe, although this illumination was short lived.

After Charlemagne's death in 814, Europe had to defend itself against the savage raids of the Vikings and other Norsemen. Towns had to be newly fortified and thick surrounding walls constructed, and Europe gradually took on the form that is still associated with the word *medieval*.[6]

Many medieval towns grew up alongside a burg or fortress situated at a strategic high point, overlook, river, or seacoast. Here their merchant founders were conveniently based for trade and relatively secure from raiders. Some burgs were small castles, others were citadels. Outside the burg, the traders built a market and their homes, enclosed by a surrounding wall. The residents of these new burgs soon had a name to distinguish them from old burg dwellers such as knights, clerics, and serfs. They were called *burghers* by the Germans, *burgesses* in England, and *bourgeois* in French. Although these terms originally included all economic levels, they soon came to denote middle-class affluence. *Burg* passed into the vernacular, showing how successfully the way of life associated with medieval Europe was assimilated.[7]

Even as medieval towns were growing and a new middle class was beginning to appear, life was still brutish. Every castle, however small, had a dungeon. Punishments were extraordinarily cruel and debasing. Malefactors were burned, branded, mutilated, and eventually killed. Torture was typical. Justice was determined in primitive, superstitious ways. For example, if the accused floated when thrown into water, he or she was guilty. Hot irons and trial by combat were habitual. The one way an individual could refrain from being the victim of physical brutality was by joining the Church. As more and more people made this choice, they had a tremendous collective impact on medieval Europe. As the greatest spiritual power and now as a temporal kingdom, the Church had an enormous role to play.

DAYS OF TOIL AND HOLIDAYS

Only about 10 percent of all medieval people resided in towns; most of the rest were peasants dwelling on manorial farms. The aristocracy (landowners) amounted to less than two percent of the entire population and controlled

in Mexico maintains Teotihuacan civilization; Wales is converted to Christianity ■ **552**—Shotoko Taishi becomes emperor of Japan, beginning of Asuka era; European silk industry begins ■ **570**—Mohammed, founder of Islam, is born ■ **595**—First record of decimal reckoning in India ■ **598**—First English school is founded at Canterbury ■ **600**—Architecture and sculpture flourish in India; smallpox ⇨

all the rest.[8] The average peasants had a small patch of land and a cottage with thatched roof and dirt floor. For this largesse they were required to labor almost unceasingly. Their view of the world was contained by their village, the manor house, and its fields and woods.

If one piece of equipment symbolized the peasants' life, it was the plow. They lived by the seasons. Each autumn they sowed wheat and rye; each spring they planted other grains plus legumes; each summer both crops were harvested. Between these periods of backbreaking labor came many lesser chores and brief reprieves. The peasants' toil brought them mixed rewards but shortened their life spans considerably. Typically, a peasant was old and used up by age 30 and could be discarded like any chattel.

Spring on the manor began as soon as seasonal rains had softened the earth for plowing. The peasants sowed their own plots as well as their lord's with the crops memorialized in the old song "Oats, peas, beans, and barley grow." In fact, peas and beans were a staple of the medieval diet for both serf and noble, as shown in the rhyme "Pease porridge hot, pease porridge cold, pease porridge in the pot, nine days old." Each family had its own vegetable garden and its own livestock to pasture. In April, when the cows could be milked, the women were kept busy making butter and cheese and setting aside the eggs that were due the lord at Easter.

Spring planting was finished by Holy Week, and for a few weeks thereafter a welcome respite was allowed. The peasants thronged to church for the impressive ceremonies heralding Easter. Shortly afterward they celebrated another, more pagan, festival—May Day—with dancing, singing, and licentious behaviors. Despite such free exercise of their limited leisure, the peasants knew that May was also a month of continuing labor. Houses had to be repaired. Barns required patching. There were always fences, hedgerows, and drainage ditches to work on. Flocks needed protection from marauding wolves, and the peasants had to stalk these predators in the woods.

The summer months brought even harder work. Early in June vinedressers in France and Germany had to see to their vines. English and Flemish herders washed their sheep, and shearers, supervised by the lord's steward or bailiff, clipped the wool. The fields had to be weeded.

By Midsummer Day, June 24, the dawn-to-dusk work of the hay harvest began. Women and children labored alongside the men haying. Naturally, they brought in the lord's share before their own. Haying had to be finished by August 1 before the two major crops, wheat and rye, were ready for harvest. Reaping the grain usually took all of August as the peasants fought heat and exhaustion to finish. It was not until late September that they could stop laboring and give thanks for the long-anticipated harvest-home supper.[9]

Autumn was a time for food storage and husbanding supplies in preparation for winter. The peasants brought in vegetables from their own small gardens, picked fruit in the orchards, gathered firewood from the manor's woods, and collected acorns and other nuts to feed their pigs. Now it was time to thresh the harvested wheat—by hand. In October the grapes of France were picked and trampled and the juice was placed in fermenting casks. October was also a time for slaughtering the animals that would provide meat for the coming year. In November Flemish peasants scutched dried stalks of flax to separate the pith from the fiber they would use to make cloth. Feed for the animals was always in short supply, and this was a time for driving livestock to market.

December brought some respite to the men, but the women continued to work. The 12 days of Christmas brought the high point of the peasants' long holiday season of feasting, churchgoing, and celebrating folk festivities. The main meal on Christmas Day was traditionally served in the lord's manor, and all of the peasants were invited. Roast pig and blood pudding were a typical repast and often the men were permitted to sit and drink after dinner.

After the holidays, harsh weather generally put a stop to outdoor work, but the women still had to cook, weave cloth, and make clothing. Sometimes they were required to wait on the lord or his minions. Through January little could be done outdoors, but in February, the peasants began spreading the fields with manure and sharpening their plows for the labor of another year. Thus the seasons passed, the peasants' calendar remained full of toil, and life was short, hard, and unrewarding. Only the holidays provided the leisure for rest and recuperation before another round of intense manual labor began.

TOWN AIR IS FREE AND PROVIDES LEISURE

Medieval towns were little better than a hodge-podge of dwellings with stores or stalls for selling or trading goods and services, together with open sewers and animals rooting in the dark, narrow streets (alleyways). Sanitary facilities were almost unknown, and disease incubated by filth was rampant. Anyone who walked through town was assailed by the putrid odors of feces, garbage, and swilling pigs. Space was a luxury few could command, and crowding was endemic. Except for the thrilling sight of a Gothic belfry or church spire, townspeople could find little inspiring in the noisy, physically confining town.

There was, however, one absolute benefit to living in town. The air might be odoriferous, but it was free.[10] Unlike the serfs on the manor, the town dwellers could drink as they pleased, work or not, and speak their minds on any is-sue. Although the physical aspects of the town might be restrictive, people's emotions and intellect were given free rein. The hustle and bustle of urban life produced the social, political, and economic elements that would eventually change the Western world from medieval to modern.

Aside from the few cities that had survived the downfall of the Roman Empire, most towns of the Middle Ages were founded after the year 1000. Reconstituted trade encouraged their evolution. Essentially, international rather than local trade tended to support commerce. At the hub of East-West trade lay Constantinople.[11] For western Europeans, Constantinople beckoned to be taken. Christian military forces overcame Islamic strongholds on the northern borders of the western Mediterranean basin, and this encouraged the traders of Venice, Genoa, Marseilles, and Barcelona to build and equip ships for commercial enterprise with the East.

Carcasonne, a medieval city.

Years in the Common Era

national religion ■ **650**—Hindu empire reigns in Sumatra; weaving is developed in Byzantine empire ■ **664**—St. Peter's in York (boys' public school) is founded; plague hits England ■ **685**—Winchester Cathedral in England is founded ■ **687**—Pepin the Younger unites Frankish kingdom; Carolingians gain power ■ **700**—Greek becomes official language of Eastern Roman Empire (Byzantium); Easter eggs

The torpor of the early Middle Ages was now being shaken off. A new spirit of involvement arose. People started to travel again, some on pilgrimages, others back to rural areas that could be opened up for farming because of new agricultural procedures. With agricultural advances came greater prosperity and consequently population growth. People began to realize that life could have greater meaning than the day-to-day struggle for survival.[12]

Venice in History

The history of Venice encapsulates the story of Europe from the breakup of the western Roman Empire to its most splendid period. Forced to flee by the ravaging Lombards, the inhabitants of the mainland north of the Adriatic Sea found refuge with the fisherfolk who resided on the small islands formed by the Piave and Adige rivers. They founded the city of Venice. As with all pioneers, the need for survival took precedence. Merely finding potable water was a major undertaking. Because they had to use the only commodities at hand, fish and salt, to trade with the mainland, the Venetians became market oriented and lived off the gifts of the sea.

The separate islands consolidated to form a united government at the Rialto Bridge. Protected by the shallow waters of the lagoon and the marshes, the citizens turned their energy to trade, construction, and defense. Slowly their spreading network of markets and sailing skills brought them into contact with the Near East, Central Europe, and the West. Gradually commercial enterprise gravitated to Venetian ports. For a thousand years the Queen City of the Adriatic, Serenissima (the serene republic), retained its freedom and popular government under the successive rule of 117 doges. Not until Napoleon Bonaparte incorporated the republic into his empire in 1805 did Venice fall.[13]

With its formidable seafaring reputation and its protection from predatory invaders, Venice was able to expand its domain to mainland Italy and the Dalmatian Coast. It became rich and powerful and was given most favored status by Constantinople as an independent ally. These privileges permitted Venetian trade to reach the Black Sea and the Islamic trade. One of her sons, Marco Polo, penetrated the caravan route of the silk trade to the court of Kublai Khan, emperor of China.

Protected and secure, the Venetians found time to build magnificent palaces, churches, and their major cathedral, San Marco. Now the traditions of lifestyle accumulated. Each Ascension Day the reigning doge, from a highly decorated yacht, flung a consecrated golden ring into the sea and pledged marital devotion to the waters.[14] In time this became a regatta. To some extent, it is celebrated today with a procession down the Grand Canal and gondola races.

By the year 1000, Venice was a thriving cosmopolitan city known as "the golden" from the color of its stone buildings. The Venetians were already famous for their luxurious attire, literacy, civic loyalty, and pride. The world came to be awed by the wonders of Venice, and her people gloried in their commercial and architectural success. Class divisions along economic lines deepened. Factions arose and outsiders tried to intimidate Venice. Through it all, the great republican empire sailed on until its diplomacy and military might could no longer stop a conqueror. In its thousand-year history as an independent state, it became a treasure trove of art and artifacts, trade and artisans, aristocracy and commoners. Venice was envied and respected throughout Europe.[15]

There was leisure and enjoyment for all. Festivals, processions, celebrations both public and private, held everyone's attention. The city hosted all of the leading sovereigns and prelates of the day, and each was overwhelmed by the lavish hospitality.[16] Even as misfortune came to Venice in terms of losing battles, backing the wrong political or ecclesiastical faction, losing territory or commercial rights, Venetians knew how to enjoy themselves.

The carnival of 1510 was celebrated with so many festivities, fireworks, and masquerades that one might have imagined the city back in its golden age. At the wedding feast . . . 420 guests sat down to dinner, after which there followed an elaborate masque with singers and dancers, theatrical companies, clowns and acrobats, which continued until the sun was high in the sky.[17]

Fairs, Trade, and Leisure

As Venice grew wealthy, Europe as a whole began to respond to a resurgent economy. In this salubrious climate, the introduction of exotic goods from the East stimulated appetites for more. Although most of the wares were prohibitively expensive, there were many items to

Years in the Common Era

which lesser persons could aspire—among them sugar, spices, dyes, and fabrics. In the beginning, Europe had only one manufactured item for export: cloth. Eventually, grain, fish, flax, salt, and wines were added. Later, there were furs, timber, hemp, honey, and caviar. Out of the stimulating contacts and ideas developed in East-West trade came an expansion of local European trade and manufacture.

The results of such commerce could be observed at the traditional fairs, where the artistry and craftsmanship of native Europeans could compete with anything that originated in the East. As trading places, the fairs were unique.[18] The feudal lords who sponsored them and obtained revenue through taxes on them guaranteed safe conduct through their regions. Large fairs might draw traders from all over Europe and the Near East. International monetary units changed hands through obliging moneychangers; from this rude beginning, the banking system developed.

But for all of their advantages, the fairs could not really satisfy the need for trade. People had to travel to reach them, and travel was dangerous. Significantly, the fairs were seasonal. Increasingly, the merchant-traders required a stable place in which to buy and sell. Out of this need came the towns.

Situated at crossroads, on waterways, or in close proximity to fortified places, the towns grew. Inevitably towns attracted people other than traders; before long they were populated by artisans and crafters seeking outlets for their skills, serfs fleeing bondage, itinerant workers, footloose mercenary soldiers, the younger sons of nobles (who would not inherit anything), and others who provided them with amenities. The fabric of urban life was woven swiftly.

The new towns began to build defensive walls.[19] As populations grew and space became even more limited, towns were enlarged. Old walls were torn down and replaced by new, bigger ones. A town's progress toward maturity could be reckoned by the successive sites of the advancing walls. Between 1100 and 1250, the number of towns with charters that enumerated inhabitants' rights multiplied rapidly.

The Rise of the Commune

The growth of the towns stimulated a new concept of political control. Under the feudal system, the lands on which towns were built were owned by nobles or clergymen who exacted a number of obligations in return. As the towns prospered, fiscal exactions enriched the aristocracy. The urban populations quickly perceived the healthy position they were in and began to bargain their way out of political and social constraints. They felt no need to get the lord's permission to marry, to migrate, to own and dispose of property, to participate in military exercises, or to make other personal choices. They wanted their own courts and their own laws, the better to administer business affairs. By joining together to press their demands, town inhabitants frequently negotiated successfully for these rights. The town charter, which enumerated the citizens' duties, obligations, and privileges, became the basis for individual freedom and self-government.[20]

The Guilds

A double exercise in solidarity existed to help townspeople gain and retain their charters and freedom. One was the commune, in which all town dwellers joined to obtain political liberties. The other was the guild, which furthered both economic and social welfare. Originally, there were two kinds of guilds: those of merchants and those emphasizing specific crafts. The guilds became the cornerstone of social and recreational life, such as it was. There were guildhall banquets, saint's-day celebrations, pageants, and processions. Guild members were visited by their fellows when they were sick and were supported financially when out of work or too infirm to continue their trade. Guild funds might provide a dowry for a member's daughter, care for his soul through prayer when he died, pay his funeral expenses, and support his widow.[21]

Those not associated with guilds hired themselves out to perform whatever chores or assistance might be needed on any given day. Their leisure was a direct result of church celebrations and traditional holidays. They might also frequent taverns to drink, dance, and socialize after work. Sunday was also free time.

The power of the middle class, made up of townspeople, grew increasingly formidable. Dependent as they were on bourgeois wealth for their own revenue, the aristocracy, particularly kings, gave the rich merchants places in their councils. The merchants supported centralized authority and discouraged the feudal system, which responded by evolving into the nation-state. In whatever guise they assumed, whether as bankers, business tycoons, or masters of crafts, the bourgeoisie inexorably altered the social environment of Europe. Although the clergy remonstrated against its capitalistic competition and the nobles condescended to it as nouveau riche, the affluent middle class could not be kept out of the medieval spectrum.

Having acquired surplus capital by their determined labor, the bourgeoisie now aspired to heights that belied their low-born station. They built magnificent mansions, schools, and churches, clothed their families in furs and silks, became patrons of the arts, collected manuscripts, commissioned musicians and painters, and benefited posterity with the way they invested their wealth. They wanted to educate their sons in the new universities, to endow their communities with great cathedrals, fountains, public plazas, and sculpture. Medieval civilization flourished in consequence of the new towns' new middle class.

THE BURGHER'S LEISURE

During the course of their daily rounds, urban dwellers had enough leisure to dine on enormous meals (a custom still observed by many businesspeople who take clients to lunch or dinner on an expense account). Guild members could drop in at the guildhall, gossip about prices, drink wine or ale, and then return home for meals.

Since there were several guilds in every town and each had a time for festivals, parties, and public processions, there must have been much free time to forsake the business rituals and participate in or view these festivities. Naturally, the holidays were celebrated in the towns as were other public or private occasions when townspeople could enjoy social intercourse. Traditional May Day, saints' days, weddings, funerals, or commemorations were celebrated with song, dance, costumes, parades, drum and trumpet flourishes, and other decorative devices. Churchgoing was an obligation, but it was also a joyful occurrence filled with the symbolism, chanting, and choral music integral to the service.

Although the town dwellers preferred not to participate in military adventures, they did maintain a guard to watch from the city's walls and they learned archery for defensive purposes. Shooting at archery butts, bear baiting, dogfights and cockfights, some forms of dice, passion plays, and other entertainments were common. Some medieval towns had competitions among the various guilds that might include horse racing, flag throwing and catching, processionals, or other exhibits. Strolling singers, acrobats, jugglers, storytellers, musicians, and masquers also provided entertainment when they passed through the community.[22]

The trade fair, primarily designed to introduce commerce beyond the local area, was a time for lavish display booths. It enabled merchants to visit beyond the confines of their own towns and attracted all types of buyers and sellers in a mosaic of color and sound that could also serve as a recreational outlet. Dancing bears, wrestling contests, stage shows, mountebanks selling the latest snake oil, and an occasional hanging or other form of public punishment contributed to the leisure amusement of travelers. Although the first fairs preceded the towns, many of the finest and most enduring of them were held in the town whose name they bore. Today's Leipzig Trade Fair is a holdover from its medieval forerunner.

Town dwellers had free time because they were not subservient to a demanding lord and the vagaries of nature like the serfs. Since a guildsman was his own man, inhibited only by the regulations of the guild or community to which he belonged, he could do with his time as he saw fit. He engaged in the give-and-take of capitalistic enterprise as either a crafter, trader, or provider of amenities. When he decided to quit work for the day, he could do with his time as he wished. With leisure and accumulated wealth, the townspeople desired a better life.

The monuments in art, architecture, and learning they left us prove that the middle classes succeeded in upholding civilization. The greatest Gothic cathedrals were lovingly supported by money made in the towns in which they stand. The donor windows in Chartres Cathedral, for example, list the various guilds that supported its construction: window numbers 6 (Shoemakers), 7 (Shoemakers), 13 (Fishmongers), 16 (Vinegrowers and Bell-ringers), 24 (Shoemakers), 25 (Tanners), 30 (Masons), 34 (Bakers), 37 (Furriers and Drapers), 38

(Furriers), 39 (Weavers), 41 (Shoemakers), 42 (Masons, Stone-cutters, and Sculptors), 43 (Masons), 45 (Carpenters, Joiners, Cartwrights, and Coopers), 59 (Blacksmiths), 60 (Haberdashers and Apothecaries), 61 (Bankers), 62 (Drapers), 63 (Wine-merchants), 64 (Coopers, Carpenters, and Wheelwrights), 68 (Bakers and Pastry Cooks), 77 (Turners), 78 (Turners), 111 (Curriers), 117 (Bankers), 118 (Clothiers), 119 (Bakers), 120 (Bakers), 121 (Hosiers), 122 (Butchers), 123 (Bankers), 160 (Ploughmen), 164 (Bankers), 167 (Curriers), and 168 (Furriers).

The carved stone and wooden sculptures also depict the various divisions of labor dating from A.D. 1150. The royal door, for example, shows scholars of the medieval period as well as the workers who toiled year round. The north porch has another cycle of labor including mowers,

A window in Chartres Cathedral.

sowers, and farmers. The right bay shows a vine pruner, a flaxener, a harvester, a vintager, a sower, and a pig farmer. The arts, including agriculture, music, metallurgy, medicine, architecture, painting, philosophy, and magic, are also displayed. The left bay incorporates a woman working in wool. The roll call of these living monuments is a gorgeous reflection of the leisure life on which guildsmen and merchants lavishly spent their revenue. Chartres, Rheims, Amiens, Notre-Dame in Paris, Mont St. Michel, York, Canterbury, Strasbourg, Ulm, and Cologne are but a few of these great structures that still inspire all who visit them.

ARISTOCRATIC LIFE AND LEISURE

At the top of the social system was the nobility. Growing out of the wreckage of the Roman Empire, the barbarians developed ethnic ties and managed to form a new breed of people who would succeed the Romans. Ancient clan chiefs and their families formed the nucleus for the new aristocracy that came into being as Pax Romana withered. Into the vacuum created by the vanquished Rome, northern tribes hurried to establish their claims.

They too were pressed by migrating eastern hordes and needed surcease from continuous fighting. At strategic locations, clan chiefs and their families established fortified dwellings from which they could sally forth to infiltrate other areas, defend their own holdings, or enlarge their own domains. As they consolidated their possessions, always in land, feudalism became the dominant social system. There was no such thing as a central government, although a few powerful kings and emperors attempted to centralize their rule. Individual feudatories ruled over western Europe during the Middle Ages.

Originally, the aristocrats spent much of their time subjugating surrounding territories, engaging in military adventures, or just plundering the regions through which they marched. Once established as the ruling class, they quickly sought to gain advantage by imposing obligations on those who sought to live and work on their lands. The manorial system served to maintain the relationship between aristocrats. They and the clergy controlled all life in the early Middle Ages. Later, the devel-

Years in the Common Era

in Germany; astrolabe is perfected by Arabs ■ 874—Northmen settle Iceland ■ 879—Oldest mosque in Cairo is built ■ 895—Earliest Hebrew manuscript of Old Testament is found; Fujiwara dynasty rules Japan ■ 900—Alfonso III of Castille begins reconquest of Spain; Mayas migrate to Yucatan peninsula, Mexico; Constantinople is world cultural and commerical center; Vikings discover Greenland

opment of trading centers, towns, and the crusades to the East would forever change and finally bring down the feudal system.

By the 12th century, increasing security and trade had transformed the aristocracy from itinerant warriors into a stabilized rural nobility. As warfare became set piece, governed by tradition and season rather than by strategy, roving knights could settle down to their hereditary fief and turn their attention to their own pleasures. As long as his overlord did not require his military presence, a knight could enjoy much leisure, land tenure, and a number of life's amenities. Many aristocrats rebuilt early wooden forts into elaborate stone castles staffed by many servants. With a continuous stream of visitors, they banqueted, danced, and gambled. They imported chess from India and indulged in backgammon, dicing, and other board games popularized by returning Crusaders.[23]

The castles that served to guarantee protection to the surrounding area were constructed to withstand siege and house their noble proprietor, his family, and their retainers. The typical day was spent in the routine of seeing to the lands and livestock that were their economic base. The local council helped set policies regarding planting and politics. When guests were in attendance, the lady of the manor entertained them. Knights and squires practiced fencing and tilting. When lessons were over for the day, children were free to play—girls with dolls, boys with tops, balls, horseshoes, and bow and arrow. In fact, archery was a universal favorite in the 12th century.[24]

When the occasion demanded, tremendous amounts of food were prepared, served, and consumed. During these feasts, the diners would be entertained by jokes, songs, dancing, and games of various types. Gambling, chess, lawn bowling, and similar activities were all pastimes of the nobility.[25]

These zestful, willful men did not remain indoors when the weather was good. They rode to hounds, hunted stag and wild boar, engaged in falconry, archery, horse racing, and the knightly tournaments. They trained in gymnastics, ran races, and practiced with arms. As with older civilizations, sport replaced warfare as the activity of the nobles' leisure. For country aristocrats, a stream of visitors to the castles had to be fed and entertained. This could mean boating in a nearby river or lake, hunting parties, picnics, or, for the knights who no longer had to worry about war, romance.

The knights of the 12th century were absolute masters of their own castles and everything in them, including their wives. Male chauvinism was complete. But a new force entered the picture with the spread of courtly love, whose praises were sung by the traveling troubadours. This cult assumed tremendous recreational significance and was one of the uses to which the gentry's leisure was put.[26]

The Age of Chivalry

Courtly love encouraged the relationship of a knight to his chosen lady—which really meant any woman not his wife. There was an elaborate code of invitation, words, gestures, musical interludes, and, perhaps, assignations. According to formula, the romantic knight must be happy, ardent, discreet, and courteous. No matter how long it took the lady to consummate or reject his suit—weeks, months, even years—the knight had to continue his courtship. While much of knightly romance was spiritual and platonic, it did encouraged infidelities. The mythic romance between Queen Guinevere and Lancelot typifies the secret ritual of romance and dalliance that the new leisure encouraged.[27]

The Decline of the Middle Ages

By the end of the 14th century, nation-states were well on the way to replacing feudatories. The various monarchies gained more control over the central administration of government and law. France and England were the leading exponents as early as 1066 when William, Duke of Normandy, overcame Harold Godwinson at the battle of Hastings. This was the first stirring of centralized government. Over the next four centuries there arose the concept of trial by jury and equal justice under the law. Although the Magna Carta, signed in 1215, was a completely feudal doctrine, it nevertheless provided the basis for many of the rights that free people now assume naturally.[28]

In France during the same period, the kings tried to enlarge their tiny strip of land, the Ile de France. Paris was, of course, the international marketplace of Europe, and taxes poured into the treasuries of Philip I and his successors Louis VI and Louis VII. These were the kings who consolidated the monarchy. France developed its national existence at the beginning of the 13th century under Philip II (Augustus). By 1314, Philip IV had created an assembly composed of all the classes that would eventually be known as the Etats-Generaux (Estates General), named for the three estates of the kingdom: clergy, nobles, and commoners.[29] Schools were built and supported by a newly enriched middle class, as well as by prelates and the nobility.

Medieval people were fascinated with the effects of color and light. Venetian glassware is a product of that curiosity, as are the magnificent stained-glass windows that permit sunlight to illuminate the vast interiors of the Romanesque and Gothic cathedrals constructed at this time. Science and medicine were beginning to advance, and in the 13th century the scientific method was articulated by Roger Bacon.[30] As the practice of medicine spread, the containment of disease and public health were addressed. The first hospitals were developed.

But with all of these fine advances came regressions. Between 1350 and 1450 famine, war, plague, peasants' revolts, schism within the Church, and other crises disrupted European life. Many noble families were wiped out economically, and bubonic plague killed off nearly half the population of Europe. The social fabric was torn, and many of its threads would never be seen again.

Eventually the horrors of war and plague passed away and winds of change blew everywhere. Blocked from trading with Constantinople when the Turks overran that city in 1453, Europeans looked to the West for new territories and trading routes. With the discovery of the Cape Verde Islands in 1456, sailors began to think of the possibilities beyond the western horizon. A new age was beckoning.

The medieval mind and mores were fairly crude, but around 1350, etiquette became an important accomplishment. Men and women of the upper classes had to learn the manners of the court (courtesy) and know how to comport themselves, whether at home or in the hunt.

The Spectacle

Public assemblies held by the king, cavalry maneuvers, ecclesiastical pageantry or princely panoply, tournaments, and public trial by combat were the treats that entertained the masses. Staged spectacles were an important aspect of medieval life. Church processions, political parades, and guild commemorations filled the towns with colorful flags, floats, statues of saints, merchants, men on horseback, and band music. Traveling players gave short performances in the square; musicians sang and played instruments; jugglers, acrobats, fire-eaters, and strongmen all added to the festivities; a circus sometimes came to town.

The aristocracy, as always, hunted and jousted. Hunting, or as the French called it, *chasse,* was a passion. Falconry was a prime amusement, and nearly all great estates had aviaries containing a variety of birds.

Many sports and games had practical application. Almost all youths learned to swim and in the northern countries to ice-skate. Horse racing was popular, particularly in Italy. All classes participated in archery; the lower classes also fished. There were bowling, hockey, quoits, wrestling, boxing, tennis, and soccer. Tennis originated in France and received its name from the word *tennez* (play), by which the server announced that the ball was in play.

Social behavior was boisterous and sometimes indecent.[31] May Day was still an occasion for the English to raise Maypoles, light fires, and dance around them in a nod to pagan fertility rites. At Christmas a lord of misrule was appointed to organize recreational activities for the populace. Strolling players in masks and costumes performed on the streets, pulled stunts, or sang carols. There were festivals to mark the agricultural seasons, national and local victories, saints' days, guild celebrations, and any other conceivable event. In a Feast of Fools, the lower clergy parodied Church ritual by wearing silly garb, chanting risque hymns, using the altar as a gambling table, and performing other funny but irreverent acts. Eventually the indecency became so outrageous that the Church was forced to condemn it.

Centralized monarchy was slower to develop in other countries, but laws were written and representative government began to appear all over Europe. The pace of medieval life quickened with the advance of technology, trade, and the arts. The first of the great seats of learning was founded.[32]

The dawn of the 14th century was the climax and the decline of the Middle Ages. The results of medieval culture were everywhere apparent. Politics, economy, technology, medi-

Years in the Common Era

Western Europe ■ **1000**—Venice dominates Dalmatian coast and Adriatic Sea; Mayan civilization reaches peak; potatoes and corn are planted in Peru; Chinese invent gunpowder ■ **1040**—Duncan of Scotland is murdered by Macbeth, who becomes king ■ **1053**—Robert Guiscard founds Norman empire in southern Italy ■ **1066**—William of Normandy conquers England; Halley's Comet is observed ■ **1070**— ⇨

cine, education, and social services were expanding to meet the needs of all. Medieval people had established institutions to govern, to adjudicate, and to educate. They had political freedom and used it to enlarge their minds and make their place in society. They had the leisure to participate in both secular and religious activities that uplifted them, renewed their spirit, and provided the fun and entertainment that made life worth living.

The Middle Ages had reached their zenith, but new methods of warfare, continued religious problems, and economic reality required intellectual expansion and new solutions to problems. The medievals had done what they could; now it was another generation's turn.

THE INFLUENCE OF THE RENAISSANCE ON CULTURE AND LEISURE

The Middle Ages did not disappear suddenly; medieval life and civilization gradually waned for more than a century before the Renaissance burst out in full force in Italy. As in past upheavals, the new urban culture required methods and knowledge that feudalism and theological study could not provide.

The outburst of intellectual endeavor that attempted to model itself on the classical antiquities of ancient Rome was intensely humanistic. People were conscious of a changing world around them and reveled in the idea that they were part of this evolution. The old anchors of feudalism and dedication to other worldly efforts were slowly giving way to the emerging nation-states and the revival of interest in ancient Roman legal and literary studies. The center of this intellectual ferment boiled out of the Italian peninsula between 1350 and 1525. The coastal and interior Italian towns, situated as they were in the center of the Mediterranean trade routes, served as both ports of entry for seaborne goods and trade centers and transhipment markets on overland routes. The cities of Venice, Genoa, Rome, Florence, and Milan were admirably suited to carry on the trade with western Europe that a closed-off East made necessary.

The papacy left Rome for Avignon, France, in 1305 and did not return until 1375. This hiatus permitted the former papal territories to become secularized and governed by leading local families, who founded independent city-states. By 1315 these city-states had achieved a political position that allowed them to be independent. They no longer had to depend on the great monarchical powers to the north and west that had previously influenced them so heavily. At the same time, the larger Italian cities became immensely prosperous through successful trading. This economic development heralded a power structure that differed from other regions. Economic and political power resided in the cities instead of with the landed aristocracy.

The bubonic plague, which devastated much of Europe in the 14th century, could not dampen the enthusiasm and patronage for great art, architecture, and education. The Renaissance required a utilitarian kind of education that could not be found within theological study. The demands of business necessitated the study of law. Scholars began to search for the original Roman codes and indexes, which led them to the study of other classical works. From the diligent study of the classics for business purposes soon grew the desire to read for pleasure.

This ambition to imitate and learn from long-dead Romans led to the exploration of historical treatises. It was a short step to reading those who made the laws and placed their personal stamp upon their culture. The writings of Quintilian and Cicero, which emphasized the qualities of character and intellect that people needed to meet the challenges of the ancient world, fascinated readers in the 15th century.

One Ciceronian quality that probably endeared itself to the Renaissance world was that of the stoic-humanist, which combined the life of action and that of contemplation. For humanists, a person is the measure of all things.[33] The men of the Renaissance felt obligated to serve the community as well as to learn as much as they could about the rational world. Cicero offered a model that the students of ancient Roman thought could follow.

Of the four virtues (wisdom, justice, fortitude, and temperance), Cicero considered justice most important. It contains two elements, social cohesion and beneficence. The former involves consistency and truthfulness, while the latter is the most human of all concerns. Beneficence is the spirit of public giving, but performed in such ways that the recipient's character is not harmed. People who receive charity should not be made to feel that they

⇨ Amalfi merchants found Order of St. John in Jerusalem; York Cathedral is constructed ■ **1094**—The Cid conquers Moorish Valencia; gondolas are used in Venice ■ **1095**—Council of Clermont (France) is held; Pope Urban II proclaims First Crusade ■ **1097**—Crusaders defeat Turks and conquer Nicaea ■ **1099**—Crusaders take Jerusalem ■ **1100**—Decline of Islamic science begins ■ **1104**—Crusaders take Acre

are beggars. Nevertheless, beneficence also means that individuals must be able to sustain themselves before they offer aid to others. Therefore, charity begins at home.

One typically Roman trait that became the hallmark of the Renaissance man was universality. The complete man had mastery over many facets of life. Leonardo da Vinci may be the epitome of this ideal. He explored every subject under the sun and excelled in almost everything to which he put his hand. He had so many diverse interests that even though he was one of the greatest artists in an age of many great artists, he had little time to paint. What he did paint ranks among the world's most sublime art.

Da Vinci's curiosity and genius drove him to study and extend the range of knowledge about anatomy, botany, geology, mechanics, and astronomy. He was an engineer, inventor, hydrologist, cartographer, optician, and writer. He worked on every problem that caught his attention with the unlimited enthusiasm of a man who was in love with life and learning. In this way he was the embodiment of his age.[34]

Da Vinci was not the only person of his time with expertise in many fields. Certainly Michelangelo, Cellini, and Lorenzo de' Medici (Il Magnifico) would qualify for the role of Renaissance man.

The Spirit of Leisure

The Renaissance was an age of spectacles, filled with the mock combat of festival sports, the pomp and circumstance of processions, the uproar of great citywide celebrations. Almost any occasion—a saint's day, the arrival of visiting nobility, the anniversary of a great battle, even the political reverses of some feared or hated prince—was reason enough for crowds to fill the streets with revelry. When there were no opportunities, however meaningless, to celebrate, the joyousness of the age found outlet in hunts, ball games, horse races, boxing matches, snowball fights, racquet games, gambling, dancing, musical entertainments, banquets, and tableaux.

The People's Leisure Activity

Every city had its trumpeter heralds. With flourishes and martial blare, they would announce the town criers, accompany brides to church, enliven banquets, and precede nobles or town councilors through the streets. A Renaissance procession was a civic spectacle that is rarely duplicated in the modern era. It brought together in one magnificent display the luxuriously robed nobles, magistrates in full regalia, leading citizens, military companies, contingents of clergy, and hordes of musicians, acrobats, clowns, riders on horseback, and animal handlers. The entire community turned out for the event. Thousands marched, while from housetops, doorways, windows, and the streets, thousands more beheld the display.

Processions commemorated a variety of circumstances. Each city-state had a patron saint whose feast day was celebrated with a processional. Each ward, represented by companies in colorful costumes and following a float symbolizing its emblematic animal, would march around the central square amid the waving of banners and the brilliant sound of trumpets. After the procession there would be general feasting and, perhaps, games. "Procession of the Contrade," an oil painting done by Rustici Viricenzo in the second half of the 16th century (now in the Soprintendenza alle Gallerie, Florence) captures the atmosphere.

Venice again typifies this form of leisure behavior. During the years of famine in 1527 and 1528, the crops were ruined. This was followed by bubonic plague, a typhus epidemic, and hordes of refugees trying to evade the imperial army of Charles V as it hacked its way toward Rome. Still, J. J. Norwich writes, "Carnival was celebrated with undiminished gaiety, the balls and masques and marriage feasts were more sumptuous than ever they had been. . . . Scarcely a day went by without some magnificent procession, public or private, religious or secular. . . ."[35]

The energy and enthusiasm of the Renaissance found expression in a wide variety of sports and games. Schoolmasters considered physical activity an essential part of the curriculum.[36] Exercise was deemed a necessity for both young and old. The forerunners to tennis, baseball, and bowling were very popular. Physical activity was both utilitarian and enjoyable. It provided for the sound body in which a sound mind could exist, and it was fun.

Spectator sports played a significant role as well. The rough-and-tumble horse races, or Palio, with which Florentines honored their patron saint were run in the streets and squares of all Renaissance cities. The Palio is

"Procession of the Contrade" by Rustici Viricenzo.

still an annual tradition in Siena today.[37] Florence also espoused boxing and a variation on football. Each city had its traditional sports, and no festival was complete without the excitement of these events. Some places were famous for their bullfights, others for jousts. The gondola regattas of Venice were known throughout Italy. In Pisa, the most popular sport was a mock battle on a bridge, commemorating a historic defeat of the Saracens. So important were these activities to the citizens that even during periods when the city was threatened by invasion, gunpowder was actually taken from military supplies to provide fireworks for the festival.

Aristocratic Leisure and Recreation

Renaissance society was steeped in pageantry. When musicians played, they often wore masks and elaborate costumes. The tumbling of acrobats enlivened the most formal of courtly gatherings. Dinner parties' courses were announced by herald trumpets. When actors performed, the content of the play was of less concern than the scenery and costumes. Fantastic spectacles were usually staged between the acts. Leonardo da Vinci was employed by the Duke of Milan to produce elaborate displays to delight the Duke's guests. The greater the effect, the more pleasure was induced in the spectators. Impresarios tried to outdo each other in inventing special events. It was an age of supreme sophistication in the arts and superficial stimulation to titillate the senses.

The pageantry of a Renaissance country hunt was a match for the spectacles of the city.[38] A supreme gift from one aristocrat to another was a well-trained hunting falcon. The chase required stores of wines and food supplies, colorfully costumed hunters, teams of beaters, dog handlers, stewards, and other servants who were always close at hand to do the hard labor while the lords cantered easily and rode up for the kill. This amusement is vividly depicted in Paolo Ucello's painting of the hunt.

Physical activity was a mainstay for the aristocrat. No less a writer than Castiglione pointed out:

Years in the Common Era

⇨ King of England, begins Plantagenet dynasty ■ **1155**—Genghis Khan is born ■ **1163**—Construction of Notre Dame in Paris starts ■ **1170**—Thomas à Becket is murdered in Canterbury Cathedral ■ **1174**—Leaning Tower of Pisa is built; earliest horse races take place in England ■ **1189**—Richard the Lionhearted becomes king of England; Third Crusade begins ■ **1191**—Richard I conquers Cyprus and sells it

Also it is a noble exercise, and meete for one living in Court to play at Tenise, where the disposition of the body, the quickness and nimbleness of every member is much perceived, and almost whatsoever a man can see in all other exercises. And I reckon vaulting of no less praise, which for all it is painefull and hard, maketh a man more light and quicker than any of the rest.[39]

The Italian Renaissance also experienced its share of catastrophes. There were intermittent invasions as the monarchical states continued to cast covetous eyes upon Italy. Internecine warfare was endemic among the princely houses that ruled the various peninsular city-states. The Borgias, Sforzas, Estes, Gonzagas, and the Medicis were rising to power. Political intrigue, attempted Church domination, schism within the Church, and the selling of indulgences were rampant. The religious revivalism that reached epic proportions in the pronouncements of the Dominican friar Savonarola was not confined to Florence. Preachers had been speaking out for two centuries about licentious behavior, vanity, and other improprieties. In the end, however, his political supporters and disciples fell away, and Savonarola was burned at the stake.

While leisure was now available to the great mass of people, they still had to work hard before they could enjoy their free time. Except for public festivals and recreational activity during holidays or other memorial occasions, the proletariat struggled for the basic necessities. Life remained hard for the farmer, apprentice, or urban shopkeeper. By contrast, the wealthy hereditary nobility had the time and the talent to utilize leisure expertly. They became school builders and hospital founders. They supported the arts and commissioned composers to write music for them.

This is what Huizinga has to say about Renaissance Italy:

If ever an elite, fully conscious of its own merits, sought to segregate itself from the vulgar herd and live life as a game of artistic perfection, that elite was the circle of choice Renaissance spirits. We must emphasize yet again that play does not exclude seriousness. The spirit of the Renaissance was very far from being frivolous. The game of living in imitation of Antiquity was pursued in holy earnest. Devotion to the ideals of the past in

the matter of plastic creation and intellectual discovery was of a violence, depth, and purity surpassing anything we can imagine. We can scarcely conceive of minds more serious than Leonardo da Vinci and Michelangelo. And yet the whole mental attitude of the Renaissance was one of play. This striving, at once sophisticated and spontaneous, for beauty and nobility of form is an instance of culture at play. The splendors of the Renaissance are nothing but a gorgeous and solemn masquerade in the accoutrements of an idealized past.[40]

The high point of the Renaissance was reached in Florence, a city unmatched in all of Europe for its dynamism and intellectual achievements. In the arts, sciences, diplomacy, literature, banking, trade, and manufacturing Florence soared above all the others. In poetry, it had Dante and Poliziano; in prose, Boccaccio and Machiavelli; in painting, Giotto, Masaccio, Ucello, Verrocchio, Fra Angelico, Fra Filippo Lippi, Botticelli, Leonardo da Vinci; in sculpture, Donatello, della Robbia, Ghiberti, Michelangelo, Cellini; in architecture, Brunelleschi, Battista Alberti, and the Sangallo brothers. The Medici were associated with banking, and Florence produced its share of popes, cardinals, and saints.

Of course, other cities had their share of greatness too. The serene republic of Venice was considered one of the greatest cities of the world during the height of its power. Pisa, Genoa, Siena, and Milan were also cities to be reckoned with before and during the Renaissance.

Invasion Spreads the Renaissance. The invasion of Italy by Charles V propelled the doctrine of an independent peninsula and hastened the spread of the Renaissance beyond the Alps and into France, Germany, and Britain. The Church's hypocrisies and immoralities were protested by certain theologians, resulting in a schism that has not healed to this day. The Lutheran revolt in Germany picked up steam. England became Anglican in 1531, while Denmark, Sweden, part of Switzerland, and the northern half of Germany separated from the Church completely.

The aristocracy of the high Renaissance raised good conversation (*bel parlare*) to a flourishing art form. Italy led the Christian world in dancing, fencing, and most other recreational

Years in the Common Era

activities. The ballet was very popular, as was card playing. Pope Leo X was addicted to cards, and huge sums changed hands at the gambling tables. In Venice, gambling ruined so many noble families that the high council prohibited the sale of cards and dice.[41]

Upper-class Italian men were trained to ride, use a sword or lance, and tilt in tournaments. During some holidays, the town roped off space in a square where contests could be held. Bullfighting was introduced to Rome in 1332.[42] Hunting, falconry, horse racing, foot races, regattas, tennis, and boxing were activities of choice. Urban dwellers could stroll along the banks of rivers or ride out to the countryside; flowers were cultivated for homes and gardens. Water festivals were held in Venice, Florence, Mantua, and Milan. Spectacular fireworks displays marked state and religious holidays. Great processions filled the streets with floats, flags, bands, and dignitaries. Such cavalcades might be arranged in the manner of a Roman triumph for a victorious general, as when Leo X visited Florence.

During carnival everyone wore masks, sang, danced, played tricks, or made love in preparation for the denial of pleasure that the Lenten season demanded. Dramatics had its inception in the sectarian plays of 15th century Italy. These farces, or *commedia dell'arte,* became modern comedy.

Music was a major enjoyment among all classes at all times. Street singers could be heard in every city. Considerable knowledge of music was demanded of any courtier.[43] After 1400, universities offered courses and degrees in music; every cultured individual could read simple music at sight, play some instrument, and participate in impromptu musicales.[44] Cathedrals, churches, monasteries, and nunneries used music as an integral part of the liturgy. The Sistine Chapel choir became the supreme venue of music during the Renaissance. However, France was the leading exponent of music. French songs were sung throughout western Europe and transported to Italy, where they metamorphosed into the madrigal.

The flood of peace and prosperity continued until 1494, when Italy was overrun by Charles VIII of France. In swift succession the Italian cities were stormed, taken, and sacked. But these disasters did not destroy the Renaissance culture. For a century afterward, cities such as Genoa flourished. Smaller principalities remained independent, although overseas rule was common. Though they were defeated in battle, the Italians were not obliterated. Once the riots were over and peace settled in the peninsula, the shops reopened and life continued. The cultural rebirth that had long dominated Italy was now being exported to the northern and western European countries.

To suggest that these countries had been drifting and now suddenly began a cultured growth would be inaccurate. All the European countries had vital national cultures throughout the Middle Ages. The great German cathedrals, the poetry of Francois Villon in France, and the allegorical tales of Geoffrey Chaucer in England attest to that. However, in the 16th century a cultural explosion took place that was markedly different in tone from the culture of the Middle Ages.

Humanism and Enjoyment. Italian humanism was exported to the northern countries by travelers and the returning soldiers of the numerous wars fought for the tempestuous rulers of France, Spain, and Germany. The Renaissance came to Germany first, but it was short-lived. The invention of printing and the fact that men like Erasmus of Rotterdam could disseminate the philosophy of humanism throughout Europe, but especially to the German-speaking peoples, helped to spread it. The greatest name in German art, Albrecht Durer, eagerly took up the new naturalism and popularized the classical revival in his homeland. From 1494 until the first years of the 16th century, Germany was home to the Renaissance, but all too soon it was lost in the squabbles of the Reformation.

In France, the Renaissance had its greatest impact in the middle years of the 16th century. In art it is associated with the Italian painters who were employed by Francis I. No less a personage than Leonardo da Vinci was commissioned by the French king. In fact, da Vinci died near Amboise in the Chateau country of the Loire River. With the publication of *Pantagruel* by Francois Rabelais in 1532, French literature came to the fore.

In England, the dictatorial tendencies of Henry VIII prevented the humanist creed from developing. It was not until Elizabeth I that the English Renaissance came into full flower with the writings of William Shakespeare, Edmund Spenser, Christopher Marlowe, and Sir Thomas More.

Years in the Common Era

Spain reached toward the humanist impulse during the last part of the 16th and early 17th centuries. The creative talents of the playwrights Cervantes and de Vega and the painter El Greco were not immediately accepted. However, as Spain slowly educated itself to the new age, their works became beacons by which the Spanish Renaissance was measured.

As the concept of humanism spread throughout Europe, the influence of the Italian Renaissance was viewed seriously by other countries. They threw off their medieval role and accepted the fact that a new cultural epoch had arrived. Although Italy did not change the course of political and economic events, it did make the entire modern world aware of the intellectual ferment that naturalism inspired in politics, art, music, literature, and science. Moreover, Italy rescued a knowledge of how to enjoy life that had been in danger of being squashed by the insecurities and otherworldliness of medieval preoccupations. Because the Italian Renaissance gave unparalleled opportunities to ability and genius for more than 250 years, people all over Europe found its attitudes toward life and toward the arts a stimulus to their own aspirations. Thus, the Renaissance made way for still further adaptations as people explored new ways to look at life.

As the Renaissance came to an end in the 16th century, Italy was viewed as the mother of this exuberant distillation of arts, manners, government, science, and humanism. The Renaissance was an age of freedom, passion, commotion, and overindulgence. It was an age of aristocratic wealth, culture, and leisure raised upon the labor of the masses, who had little leisure and less money but shared the pride of civic accomplishment. It advanced classical learning and formulated art that was human and profane rather than religious. It saw the creation of the first modern literature. In graphic and plastic arts, it was sublime. It ended the thousand-year reign of Eastern thought in Europe. It taught the modern world the joy of living and brought forth questioning minds that would not accept the status quo.

THE REFORMATION, CALVINISM, AND LEISURE

In the 15th century, northern Europe was a troubled mass of ignorance, blind faith in the Catholic Church of Rome, and a belief in an afterlife that was more real than the harsh life that ceaseless toil imposed on the masses. Europe had fallen on hard times. England and France had been fighting for more than a hundred years. Regicide was not unknown. The peasants of Europe had revolted and been beaten down. The black plague had infested Europe. Trade declined; fields lay fallow; hunger, disease, and death lurked everywhere. The few advances made at the height of the Middle Ages fell into a state of decay. Fear was constant. Hellfire and damnation, rather than eternal bliss, were the incentives to righteous living.

But by 1350, the constant warfare was over. The Italian Renaissance had begun to turn people's minds from a deferred paradise to the pleasures of life on earth. Exploration of the uncharted seas had begun. The invention of the printing press brought a flood of information to countries whose literacy rate was growing. This was a time for new criticism, debate, and a desire for political independence.

The Monk, the Church, and Schism

Twenty-nine years after his birth, Martin Luther of Mansfield, Germany, took his doctorate degree at the University of Wittenberg. He was an Augustinian monk who would rock the Catholic Church to its foundations and create an entirely new Christian outlook. The year was 1517.[45] The Augustinian friar had long since traveled to Rome, had seen the Masses being read with such indecent haste that little comfort could have been taken from them, had witnessed the theological inconsistencies and dubious legalisms practiced by Pope Julius II in his desire to construct St. Peter's Cathedral.

All of this, plus his own intellectual questioning of basic Catholic doctrine, led Luther to the Wittenberg Cathedral. He nailed his list of concepts, in the form of 95 theses, to the door for public debate. The people typically dismissed academic discussion among theologians as obscure and abstract, but they were electrified by this statement. For the first time in centuries, someone had articulated what the masses had hardly dared to think.[46]

As Luther's ideas gained popular support, he wrote many treatises and pamphlets that spread his ideas even more rapidly. Now the Roman Curia began to take an interest, and

Luther was summoned to have one of his statements judged by Italians. The pope consented to Luther's being examined in Germany, so in 1518 he traveled to Augsburg to confront Cardinal Cajetan, General of the Dominican Order. The discussion produced only more argument and additional charges of heresy. Luther was now ready to denounce the pontificate as a manmade fabrication that perverted the Christian faith.

In a debate with the eminent theologian John Eck in 1519, Luther attacked not only the pontificate but the Church Council. He said it had been wrong to condemn Jan Hus to be burned at the stake 100 years earlier. By 1520 Luther had published several new tracts, which resulted in an irreconcilable break with Rome. Pope Leo X issued a bull condemning Luther's works, and his excommunication followed.

Emperor Charles V convened an assembly, the Diet of Worms, to hear charges of heresy. Despite the fact that the people were overwhelmingly in support of Luther, the young emperor decided to brand him an outlaw. Elector Frederick, concerned for Luther's safety, arranged for him to be taken to the Wartburg, a mountain fortress, where he remained in hiding for almost a year. Neither the Edict of Worms nor Luther's seclusion could stop the ferment that boiled over Germany. The Reformation had begun and would not be stopped.[47]

The Rise of Calvin

John Calvin was born in 1509 in Noyon, a cathedral city of Picardy in northern France, where his father was the diocesan notary. As a child, he was remarkable for his precision of mind and perfectionism. He imposed as harsh demands on others as on himself, but it is reported that his school friends liked him.

Calvin went to Paris because he expected to enter the priesthood, but his father decided he should study law at Orleans. Although he never practiced law, its study and his appreciation of it were to shape his life. At Orleans he studied with some humanists, but the contemporary humanist position, that worldly pleasure was ethical and desirable, appears to have had no impact on him at all. What really impressed him in his study of the classics was stoicism, the Greek philosophy that exalted discipline and preached impassivity in the face of both

pleasure and pain. This doctrine became Calvin's fundamental creed.

During this time, Calvin discovered the literature of reform and associated with reformers. Fearing arrest in consequence, he left France and moved to Basel, Switzerland. Here he began writing a text that would influence the Reformation significantly and lead to his installation in Geneva, *The Institutes of the Christian Religion*.[48]

This book was a defense of the reform movement and a textbook of instruction. It had more influence on the Reformation than any single work of Luther's and was the first complete, logical statement of reform beliefs. Its tone was far more funereal than the writings of Luther. Whereas Luther had envisioned God as merciful and fatherly, Calvin perceived God as a vengeful figure who zealously guarded His total sovereignty over everything. Drawing on the Old Testament, the writings of Sts. Paul and Augustine, the Scholastic theologians, and the reformers Zwingli and Luther, Calvin collected the views of those who had preceded him and synthesized them into a clear, systematic statement of reform beliefs.

The *Institutes* opens with an exposition of the Ten Commandments. It goes on to deal with creed, affirming belief in a trinitarian God, the divinity of Christ, and resurrection after death. Calvin wrote that salvation is only for the elect, or God's chosen. He also taught that original sin is passed on to all humanity and that no one can rise out of the state of disgrace without God's help. Finally, the *Institutes* deals with the relationship between church and state. Calvin stated that "man is the subject of two kinds of government," civil law and God's rule. "Civil government is designed . . . to establish general peace and tranquility. It is impossible to resist the magistrate without at the same time resisting God himself."[49]

After publication of the *Institutes,* Calvin set out for Strasbourg. He stopped en route at the city of Geneva, where he had intended to spend one night only, and stayed for the rest of his life. In Geneva, the proud Swiss, who had recently thrown off the yoke of Savoy, submitted to Calvin's theocratic rule and personal domination, so reminiscent of their former political fealty.

Calvin established an austere regime in Geneva at the behest of the Genevese themselves. Adhering to his concept of strict discipline and stoicism, he abolished gambling, drinking, singing, and dancing. Not quite ready for such an extreme program, the city council exiled Calvin. But it soon recalled him to improve the people's morals and uphold the reform movement.

When Calvin returned, he persuaded the city council to appoint a commission, with himself as head, to draw up a legislative code that would henceforth guide the community. The Ecclesiastical Ordinances became the constitution for the Reformed Church, which was to be supported by the state. According to the ordinances, the Bible was the law; the pastors were the interpreters of the law; and the civil government was required to enforce the law as the pastors interpreted it. The constitution also formed a consistory, or presbyter, which supervised worship, oversaw the moral conduct of every citizen of Geneva, and inspected every house each year.

Calvin's rule extended into all phases of society. He introduced sanitary regulations, financed new industry, founded what would become the University of Geneva, and preached endlessly. His was a rule based on discipline, and his doctrine of the elect flattered the Genevese into believing they were God's chosen people.

Calvin believed leisure was simply idleness, which he equated with mischief and the devil's work. His rules for the conduct of public inns prohibited dancing, dice, and card games, which were considered dissolute and immoral. However, Calvin himself was not an ascetic; he indulged in a variety of recreational activities.[50] He justified such recreational activity on the grounds that it permitted citizens to recuperate their powers so that they would be able to go back to work. This was wholly consistent with Calvin's doctrine of the elect. Any individual who was successful in his or her work received the benediction of God. To sustain the physical and mental ability to work, there had to be some time for rejuvenation. Recreational activity was necessary to promote the primary virtue, work. The fact that it could be enjoyable did not make it wrong; the only thing that was intolerable was idleness.

Because Calvin's creed was not colored by nationalism, as was Luther's, it was better able to surmount international borders. The Calvinist doctrine spread throughout Europe, and by 1559 it had reached as far as Scotland. There it was taken up by John Knox, who added a Scottish flavoring that was even more somber than the founder's.[51] Much of Knox's Calvinism found its way to the colonies of Massachusetts Bay and Connecticut when they were incorporated in the early 17th century.

LEISURE ACTIVITIES OF THE MASSES IN THE 16TH CENTURY

In the year 1500, four out of five Europeans were still tied to an agrarian economy. While many had risen from serfdom to become free or tenant farmers, paid handymen, or village crafters, most remained heavily burdened by taxes and services to their lords. Only in the village or town could people find some companionship and relief from imposed service or heavy toil. Isolated, self-sufficient, and close-knit, the peasant village was united by its communal pleasures as well as by shared hardship. The peasants' lot had been the same for centuries. Now, however, winds of change were sweeping through Europe, slowly but surely touching this most depressed underclass. Eventually there would be protests, petitions, and finally bloody revolt.

Among the artists who recorded the joys and sorrows of peasant life, none has ever matched Pieter Brueghel in depicting the vigor and tone of the times. His paintings are notable for their depictions of sports, games, social activities, ceremonies, and the drudgery in which the peasants passed their lives. A free afternoon might be whiled away at an outdoor tavern. Drinking, squabbling, courting, and listening to the bagpipe might constitute a social occasion.

A peasant wedding, as depicted in Brueghel's paintings "The Peasant's Wedding" (c. 1568) and "Wedding Dance" (c. 1566), was an opportunity to really let go. Prosperous peasants celebrated the event with a lavishness that would be remembered for some time. Manners were coarse, talk free, and drinking prodigious. Undernourished and overworked, peasants might consume a gallon of wine or beer each day; at weddings they drank even more. They danced reels as the bagpiper played.

Farm and church holidays were free days, respites from backbreaking toil. The clowning and foolery often alarmed the higher clergy, but the Church continued to create new holidays. By the start of the 16th century, 20 saints' days

Years in the Common Era

becomes center of the Renaissance and humanism ■ **1452**—Leonardo da Vinci is born ■ **1465**—First printed music is published; Hans Holbein the Elder, German painter, is born; Edward IV of England forbids bowling ■ **1475**—Michelangelo Buonarotti is born ■ **1477-1600**—Renaissance artists, architects, and sculptors flourish ■ **1479**—Spanish state under Ferdinand and Isabella begins; Brussels is center of ⇨

"Wedding Dance" by Pieter Brueghel.

were observed each year. This was a time for carnival festivities, and with an irreverence that worried Church fathers, the peasants flocked to a central field where costumes were judged, a variety of games were played, food and drink were plentiful, and music and dance abounded.

LEISURE ACTIVITIES OF THE ARISTOCRATS IN THE 16TH CENTURY

As always, the nobility enjoyed leisure far more than did the peasant and town-dwelling masses. Their wealth permitted them to live on a grand scale. The rare commoner could aspire to this estate, and self-made merchants sometimes acquired such riches that even crowned heads of state held them in awe. Jacob Fugger of Augsburg was typical of the powerful financiers. To the extent that the nobles of Europe could spend their time as they saw fit (particularly when not engaged in wars or up-

risings), they participated in recreational experiences that were gracious, invigorating, amusing, and educational.

The royal travels of Elizabeth I can be looked on as the height of leisure, but they were not considered extraordinary in an age where nine-tenths of the people labored to keep one-tenth in magnificent state. Two months out of every summer, Elizabeth led her court from London for leisurely rides through the country.[52] Provisioned by some 300 wagons and carts, the queen rode horseback or in an open litter. When her retinue stopped at a castle, there was a lavish display of presents, entertainment, music, dancing, pageants, and other amusements to capture the queen's attention.

When royalty was entertained by an outdoor show, townspeople crowded around to see the sights. Attractions usually included jugglers, tumblers, trained animal acts, and very rough sports such as log rolling or a forerunner of football. Bear baiting by fighting dogs, fireworks displays, and sumptuous banquets were all part of the program. Gentlemen would run at

Years in the Common Era

⇨ European tapestry industry ■ **1480**—Inquisition begins in Spain; explorers make many discoveries ■ **1483**—Richard III becomes King of England; Martin Luther is born ■ **1485**—Richard III is killed at Bosworth; Henry VII begins Tudor dynasty ■ **1492**—Spanish take Granada and destroy Moorish kingdom; Jews are expelled from Spain; Christopher Columbus sails to the New World ■ **1530**—Portuguese colonize

a quintain in a variation on the ancient game of jousting. There was always some danger of injury in these activities. For example, if the target was missed, it might swing around and knock the rider off his horse. Apparently the scent of danger and the possibility of maiming added to the thrill of the show.

England was brightened by music during the Elizabethan reign. Virtually every Briton, including the queen, could perform on a lute or virginal. Every country inn rang with the sound of madrigals. To the love of singing was joined a fondness for dancing. Common folk might dance a jig or reel, but the queen performed in stately pavanes and graceful lavoltas.

But nothing suited the queen more than a stag hunt. She was an expert horsewoman and deadly with a crossbow. In full cry, the quarry would be chased and finally dispatched.

Other countries' monarchs could be far more brutal. In Russia, at the court of Peter the Great, dwarfs were used to provide amusement. Many monarchs kept dwarfs as pets—or tormented them as the mood of the royal personage changed.[53]

By the end of the 16th century, Protestantism had established itself throughout Europe. England had thrown off Catholicism during the reign of Henry VIII and tolerated only a short period of reaffirmation under Queen Mary. The development of Puritanism, however, led to problems wherever this variant of Calvinism flourished. The Puritans were repressed by both Elizabeth and her successor, James I. It was during the latter's reign that the most radical Puritans, unwilling to compromise with the Church of England and frustrated in their desire to change the episcopal hierarchy and elaborate ceremony, fled to the New World.

The Calvinists believed that citizens demonstrated their fitness for salvation by obeying the law and being industrious, sober, and frugal. The Puritans started with Calvinist doctrine and grafted on their own brand of sobriety, individual responsibility, and unremitting work to form a creed that would take root in the northern colonies. Their unbending zeal required that they leave their homeland. Escaping from religious persecution, the Puritans (like reformers before them) persecuted others in their turn. Once they settled in the New World, they would force others to seek haven from their strict faith and domination. The American adventure was about to begin.

SELECTED REFERENCES

Cantor, N. F. *The Civilization of the Middle Ages.* New York: HarperCollins, 1993.

Geanakoplos, D. J. *Medieval Civilization.* Boston: Heath, 1978.

Gies, J., and F. Gies. *Life in a Medieval Castle.* New York: Harper & Row, 1974.

Gies, J., and F. Gies. *Women in the Middle Ages.* New York: Harper & Row, 1978.

Goffait, W. *Rome's Fall and After.* London: Hambeldon Press, 1989.

Grant, M. *The Fall of the Roman Empire.* London: Weidenfeld and Nicholson, 1990.

Grimm, H. J. *The Reformation Era: 1500-1650.* 2d ed. New York: Macmillan, 1974.

Hays, D. *Medieval Centuries.* New York: Harper & Row, 1977.

Holmes, G., ed. *The Oxford Illustrated History of Medieval Europe.* New York: Oxford University Press, 1988.

Howarth, D. *1066: The Year of the Conquest.* New York: Barnes and Noble, 1993.

Johnson, S. *Rome and Its Empire.* London: Routledge, 1989.

Jones, A.H.M. *The Later Roman Empire.* Oxford: Blackwell, 1993.

Jones, N. *The Birth of the Elizabethan Ages.* Oxford: Blackwell, 1993.

Lot, F. *The End of the Ancient World and the Beginning of the Middle Ages.* New York: Knopf, 1931.

Matthew, D. *The Medieval European Community.* New York: St. Martin's Press, 1977.

Miskimin, H. A., et al., eds. *The Medieval City.* New Haven, CT: Yale University Press, 1977.

Morris, J. *The World of Venice.* New York: Harcourt Brace Jovanovich, 1974.

Murray, P., and L. Murray. *The City of the Renaissance.* New York: Thames and Hudson, 1985.

Musset, L. *The Germanic Invasions: The Making of Europe A.D. 400-600.* Translated by E. and C. James. University Park, PA: Pennsylvania State University Press, 1975.

Payne, R. *The History of Islam.* New York: Dorset Press, 1990.

Randers-Pehrson, J. D. *Barbarians and Romans: The Birth Struggle to Europe AD 400-700.*

Stickelberger, E. *Calvin.* Translated by D. Gelser. Greenwood, SC: Attic Press, 1977.

Tuchman, B. W. *A Distant Mirror: The Calamitous 14th Century.* New York: Knopf, 1978.

Years in the Common Era

Brazil; spinning wheel is in general use ■ **1564**—William Shakespeare is born ■ **1538-1565**—Mercator uses the name America for the first time; voyages of discovery are made and European colonies are planted in New World; Elizabeth I reigns in England; tremendous advances take place in music, drama, and literature ■ **1574-1600**—First theater opens in London; great masters of literature, art, theater, medicine, ⇨

REVIEW QUESTIONS

1. Why did the amount of time for leisure nearly disappear in Europe immediately after the western Roman Empire was destroyed?

2. Explain the periodic causes of the decline of leisure throughout the Middle Ages.

3. Why did town residence promote more leisure than rural dwelling?

4. People of the Renaissance appear to have defied the survival theory of leisure. Is this a valid statement or not?

5. Why did people's attitude toward leisure change during the medieval period (as opposed to the Renaissance era)?

GLOSSARY

Aelfric: An Anglo-Saxon prose writer born around 955 A.D. His writings were considered the most important of his era and were used to spread the learning of the 10th century monastic revival.

Anglo-Saxon: Members of a Germanic people, Angles and Saxons, who ruled England from the fifth century to the Norman conquest in 1066.

Byzantine Church: A schismatic division of the Christian/Catholic faith developing by the sixth century, which was centered in the eastern portion of the Roman Empire and had a separate liturgy. It represents the beliefs of the Eastern Orthodox Christian Church. Thirteen canonical rites, or regional practices, are celebrated within the Byzantine Church.

Doge: A term used in Venetian Italian to denote a duke or leader. It was the highest office in the republic of Venice between the 8th and 18th centuries. The office was a lifetime appointment. The power of the doge was slowed by the development of constitutional bodies, which acted as governing agents.

Heresy: A theological doctrine that is rejected as erroneous by church authorities. Heretics were often excommunicated or expelled from the Church to protect its doctrines and beliefs.

Humanism: Inspired by a resurgence of interest in the classic Latin writings and the humanities, this philosophy emphasized humans' free will, their relationship to God, and their superiority over nature. Humanism made man the measure of all things. Its current use refers to a value system that upholds the importance of humans without acknowledging a God.

Magna Carta: The charter of English liberties issued by King John in 1215. The United States Constitution has ideas and actual phrases taken from this document.

Palio: A festival of medieval origins, held each year in Italian cities, usually involving bareback horse racing. The most famous of these is still held twice a year in the main square of Siena.

Pax Romana: The Roman Peace, symbolic of the relative peace that existed in the world due to the pervasive influence of the Roman Empire from the years 27 B.C. to A.D. 180. The Romans governed the many provinces of empire but allowed a great degree of home rule.

Years in the Common Era

⇨ astronomy, mathematics, navigation flourish; there is constant warfare between European nations and Turks, Pacific islands, India, and North America are colonized; Sir Walter Raleigh discovers and names Virginia; first French botanical gardens are established; skittle alleys become popular in Germany

Puritanism: A religious reform movement of the 16th and 17th centuries that sought to remove the last remnants of Roman Catholicism from the Church of England. The Puritans' struggle to have their way of life become the standard for all of England resulted in civil war and their eventual migration to the New World.

Rialto: A bridge over the Grand Canal in Venice that represented the engineering expertise developed during the Renaissance. The bridge was completed toward the end of the 16th century.

Savonarola: A Christian preacher and reformer born in Ferrara, Italy, in 1452, Girolamo Savonarola set up a democratic republic in the city of Florence after the fall of the Medici family in 1494. His efforts to fight corruption within the government and the Catholic Church led to his unfair trial, torture, and execution.

Villein: Any member of a class of serfs or peasants who had become free in their legal relations to all others except their lord, to whom they remained entirely subject.

Chapter 5

THE AMERICAN EXPERIMENT

Objectives:

After reading this chapter, the student will be able to do the following:

Discuss leisure in colonial America.

■

Explain how the Enlightenment affected leisure.

■

Describe how the onset of the Industrial Revolution influenced people's leisure.

■

Discuss the spread of egalitarianism and its affect on people's leisure.

■

Tell how the American Civil War influenced the transfer
of traditional recreational activities among regions.

■

Explain why people need leisure.

■

Discuss the influence of urbanization on the growth of the recreational service movement.

■

Discuss the sectarian attitude change toward leisure.

■

Describe the transformation of the recreational service movement.

Wat Smith

Wat Smith awoke as usual at 4:30 this morning, but he couldn't help feeling a little excited. Today was his 16th birthday, and he enjoyed the thought that with each passing year, the end of his apprenticeship was getting closer. Wat's father had apprenticed him to the village blacksmith when Wat was 10; now there were just four more years left until his apprenticeship would be over. Wat liked his work, and this morning he laid the fire and cleaned the smithy happily before sitting down to his breakfast of hot porridge and buttermilk.

Wat hoped that if he worked unusually hard today, his master would excuse him before sundown, his usual quitting time. Wat dreamed of what he'd do with the extra free time he might get. Of course, he'd have to practice his catechism and arithmetic, but he'd do those lessons quickly today. Then he might have time for some of the things he loved best.

Wat had heard of a new stage play that sounded interesting, but the city fathers warned against attending because of the danger of contracting a contagious disease. Although Wat was a sturdy lad and he so enjoyed the music and storytelling at these events, he did fear an early death. His friend Jed Smith had died last year of typhus and his master had lost a daughter to the plague this spring.

Instead of going to the play, Wat thought, he might practice his longbow. At the last feast day, he'd just missed winning the marksmanship prize. With a little more practice, he was sure he could win the next contest. Or, if Alp Plough and Hugh Branfeld were able to finish plowing early, he might invite them to a game at the bowling alley.

Wat's thoughts of what he'd do with his leisure occupied his mind until the midday meal. As he'd hoped, his master said he could be excused after he'd finished one more chore. Suddenly Wat knew what he'd do. A pain in his shoulder had been troubling him for weeks. He'd go to a spa and see if he could get some relief. In addition to the healing waters, Wat loved the entertainments he'd see there. He would avoid the dice and card games because his father had taught him to be thrifty with the little money he had. But the bear baiting, bull baiting, and cockfighting always made an exciting diversion.

The spa's waters did the trick, and afterward Wat felt invigorated enough to join a soccer game. He drank heavily throughout the game and, as usual, got into a fight after the match.

It had been a good day, Wat thought, as he walked back to his attic bed at his master's cottage. He savored it all the more because such free time was so seldom available. He tried to keep the thoughts at bay, but he couldn't help looking forward to the next time he'd be able to enjoy such leisure again.

Years in the Common Era

1607—Jamestown, Virginia, is founded ■ **1608**—Samuel de Champlain founds Quebec ■ **1609**—Henry Hudson explores Delaware Bay

Exploration for trade and profit as well as for dominion sent sailors around Africa, into the Atlantic, and finally to circumnavigation of the globe. Between 1420 and 1620, any country that bordered a sea could be reached. The great navigator Columbus opened up the Americas.

Europeans looking for adventure, wealth, or freedom from persecution reached the North American shore with their rituals, tradition, beliefs, and biases. Two very different colonies were founded in Virginia and New England. One had an aristocratic outlook; it desired leisure even as survival took all its time and energy. The other, based on Calvinist theology, denied the need for leisure and human enjoyment. One disappeared and the other changed radically. The original Virginia settlement was obliterated and the New England colonies eventually threw off the yoke of Puritanism.

Colonial growth led to an independence movement and revolution. The nationality of the epoch called for a free and equal people to pursue happiness. The opening of this country, its travails and civil war, culminated in a nation spreading from Atlantic to Pacific. Its pioneers, living in isolation or seeking paradise in the West, turned their hardscrabble lives to self-sufficiency, developed leisure traditions, and learned to use work forms in creating recreational experiences.

Industry, which had furnished the means to conduct the Civil War, now began mass production and called for better, more practical education. Science was ascendent. The technologies invented created more leisure for all—and the acceptance of leisure as a legitimate part of life. The colonial period saw a secularization of thought.

The struggle between the humanistic philosophy of the Renaissance and the darkly stoic attitude of Calvinism brought about many problems and societal divisions involving the work ethic, religious convictions, and the continuing demand on each person's time to engage in activities essential to subsistence. The spread of protestantism assured a place for Calvin's teachings. His ideas traveled well and were accepted by English-speaking peoples as well as those who spoke French, German, and Dutch. It was only a matter of time before religious persecution and mercantile operations would carry these convictions to the New World.

LEISURE IN COLONIAL AMERICA

Two essentially different settlements, guided by opposite views of life and religion, were established on the American continent during the early years of the 17th century. The original settlement at Jamestown in Virginia was made up of aristocracy, gentleman traders, and adventurers who saw their new colony as an opportunity to claim uncharted lands and untold wealth. They came to the south with a good English background of sports and games, love of theater, good books, music, and physical exercise. They saw no reason to give up these pastimes simply because they had a colony to build.

Yet as soon as they realized the magnitude of their undertaking and the peril in which they lived, they found that they had no free time for recreational activity. They faced starvation, malaria, Indian attack, and anxiety. Just staying alive was a full-time job. It came as no surprise when the governors of Virginia passed strict ordinances against the frivolous waste of time in recreational activities. The authorities wanted the settlers to use their energies to put the colony on its feet, economically and physically. As soon as the threat of disaster passed and conditions of daily life eased, restrictions against leisure pursuits were lifted. The colonists were free to enjoy their increasing opportunities.

Life was similar for the founders of the Plymouth Bay colony. They too faced hardships and an uncertain future. The basic differences between the two regions were the religious view and the philosophy that provided a frame of reference. The era of settlement in America provided a seed of religious dogmatism as well as a hodgepodge of political and social colorings.

The colonists of the 17th century, especially in New England, were under the theological domination of Calvinist thought. Under the leadership of the clergy in association with the governing authorities, the Puritan ethic spelled out taboos and restricted social gatherings. The Calvinist teachings of predestination, frugality, and intolerance for idleness profoundly influenced modern social life. In New England (although not elsewhere), almost all forms of recreational experience were prohibited by law,

Puritans spent most of their time in work or worship.

partly because of their leisure base and decidedly because they were enjoyable.

During the years immediately after Europeans settled on the American continent, their attitude toward leisure and recreational activity was particularly unfavorable, especially in the New England communities. In this time of terrible hardship, survival was uppermost in everyone's mind. So productivity became the measure of the good life. The early Puritans, bringing with them as they did the orthodox preachings of the Reformation, limited atonement, and irresistibility of grace, sought to stamp out the human desires for pleasure and amusement by restricting what individuals could do in the daily process of living.

In New England, where the stern rule of Calvinism condemned idleness and amusement for their own sake, the tradition that life should be wholly devoted to work ("that no idle drone be permitted to live amongst us") held its ground. The magistrates attempted to suppress almost every form of recreation long after the practical justification for such unrelenting attitude had disappeared. The intolerance of Puritanism was superimposed on economic necessity to confine life in New England within the narrowest possible grooves.[1]

The unproductivity of the land and the stunning experience of frontier living combined with the stark pessimism of Puritan life to form a philosophy that valued frugality, hard work, self-discipline, and strict observance of civil and religious codes. This approach to life considered play to be the "devil's work," and any time not given to productive labor or worship (which was obligatory) was wasteful and therefore condemned. In a society where survival pressed the inhabitants daily, the people readily accepted legislation suppressing activities of a recreational nature. The magistrate was the law, the law was the literal interpretation of the Bible, the Bible was handed down from God, and God was to be obeyed.

Years in the Common Era

■ **1626**—Dutch colony of New Amsterdam is founded at mouth of Hudson River   ■ **1650**—First coffeehouse opens in Oxford, England;

Time passed, and the struggle for existence ceased to pervade all the waking hours of life. The problem of getting through each day eased. Land was fenced off for common pasturage, protection, and tillage. People now had time to talk of social issues with their neighbors. Meeting grounds, later to become parks, were established as the stress of emergency living relaxed.

When the agricultural economy was established, trade and commerce—first between colonies and then with foreign contacts—allowed a leisure class to develop. People still performed their daily work, but those with more financial security, land holdings, mineral rights, or other valuable assets, found others to carry on the more onerous, detailed, and time-consuming tasks. This provided blocks of unoccupied time for these privileged few. This wealthy minority constituted the ablest, most learned, most astute, and sometimes most ruthless and unprincipled colonists. Their background and education made them long for the modes of living they had left behind. Soon bowling on the green, cricket, horse racing, fox hunting, card playing, dancing, musical concerts, theatrical entertainments, and the common sports became popular again.

As the vigorous and aggressive leadership receded from Calvinist idealism, people tended to replace it with concepts more pleasing to their newfound security. By 1700, the Dutch settlers of the eastern seaboard pursued many pleasures within the environs of public houses. In addition to drinking, games similar to modern golf, handball, skating, tennis, and sleighing in season, and the more indiscreet activities such as gambling and prostitution, were carried on. These leisure activities spread throughout the colonies, despite denunciations from the pulpit, and by the time of the American Revolution (1775-1783), masques or theater parties, balls, entertainments, extravagant dances, drinking, gambling, animal baiting, and other pleasurable activities were flourishing, despite being censured by both the Congregational and the Calvinist churches.

THE ENLIGHTENMENT

The mature Renaissance gave way to an even more rationally oriented philosophy. Scientific evidence and the Enlightenment were the underlying bases for the emergence of a human-ist, romantic, secular philosophy that counteracted stoicism, asceticism, and religiosity. The orthodoxy of theological concepts based on religious sanctions gave way to an insistence on human reason rather than divine law, natural rights instead of supernaturalism, the scientific method rather than received truths, social contracts and personal liberty rather than authoritarian mandate, and a humanitarian and democratic belief rather than aristocratic preferment. This change, or enlightenment, from the German word *Aufklärung,* gave the age its name.

The Enlightenment was an 18th-century philosophical movement that freed people's minds from dependence on the supernatural and otherworldly rewards. The afterlife would no longer shape the here and now. Fear and ignorance were to be expunged as society sought self-perfection. This was a time for learning based on scientific inquiry. The humanist-oriented concept that man, not God, is the measure of all things played a great part in the recovery of leisure as an important aspect of human life.

From this liberation of thought developed more reasonableness toward activities performed during leisure. The great educators had always been interested in play. In the Enlightenment era, educators began to stress children's needs for recreational experience. Locke, Comenius, Montaigne, and Froebel revitalized the use of recreational activity in the formal school setting. They and their contemporaries influenced later recreational and leisure activity development through their writings and practices.

In the more than 150 years of the colonial period in America, an increasing shift away from religious and otherworldly foundations and toward those based on secular and human studies could be discerned. Utilitarianism gained in scope and significance as the practicalities of life were contemplated. Although the classics were still part of aristocratic tradition, there was also notable growth of the physical sciences, social sciences, and the vernacular literatures.

INVENTION AND HUMANISM

The most spectacular accomplishments were in the applied sciences that produced technological progress. The mechanical and material

Years in the Common Era

Harvard College is granted charter; modern Japanese Noh drama begins; overture develops as a musical form ■ **1706**—Benjamin Franklin is

sciences came into their own. The science of navigation required more accurate measuring devices, so compasses, telescopes, barometers, and the like were pressed into service. The study of heat, light, electricity, and mechanics led to the development of machines and procedures that revolutionized mining, farming, animal husbandry, manufacturing, communication, and transportation. The industrial and agricultural inventions of the 18th century, in concert with political and social philosophy, paved the way for a liberalism in which ordinary people sought a larger say in their own affairs. The privilege of aristocracy began to fade, and popular government emerged.

By the time Americans were ready to declare their independence, a new industrial technological era was being ushered. James Watt offered the world his steam engine in 1782. Jethro Tull's seed-planting drill had been invented in 1701, iron smelting with coke in 1709, the steam pump in 1712, threshing machine in 1732, flying shuttle in 1733, Sheffield silver plate in 1742, beet sugar extraction in 1747, spinning jenny in 1768, and winnowing machine in 1777. Mill-rolled iron was made in 1784, the cotton gin in 1793, and the improved lathe in 1800. The sum of all this technology was that the individual was free to pursue whatever goals hard work, frugality, honesty, and perseverance would bring.

What was happening in England was reflected in the colonies. The beginnings of social reform were evident, much of it originating from an awakening of social conscience and the desire to improve the lot of the poor and disadvantaged. The world was changing. The 18th century was being radicalized by the views of David Hume, Adam Smith, and Jeremy Bentham. Bentham's creed was "the greatest good for the greatest number." His influence brought about a number of reforms in English government. He is credited in large part with alleviating the unjust criminal laws, curing defects in the jury system, eliminating imprisonment for debt, removing usury laws, repealing religious tests for public office, and passing public health laws. His enlightened vision extended to almost every aspect of life.

The egalitarianism of humanist impulses and the theory of the natural rights of man rejected the Puritans' concept of the steward-ship of the elect and embraced the idea that man is worthy of respect and equal in the sight of God. Secular leaders campaigned for more humane treatment of prisoners, welfare agencies, and support for the underprivileged. Humanitarian services developed from Rousseau's contention that human nature is inherently good.

American liberals, steeped in the tradition of German Romanticism, accepted the doctrine of the perfectibility of human nature. This meant poverty and lack of opportunity were the result of environmental deprivation, not personal inadequacy. Social reforms were urged to help people achieve better conditions. The cause of the common folk was advocated by Jefferson, Paine, and Franklin. These thinkers helped to change the method of improvement from personal charity to organized effort, even the radical solution of government programs to promote the general welfare. This shift to natural rights as the basis of government was forever established in America in 1789, when our Constitution was adopted with the preamble "We the people of the United States."

LEISURE AND RECREATIONAL ACTIVITY AFTER THE REVOLUTION

The adoption of the Constitution was followed by decades of rapid expansion. Settlers began to migrate westward, where they carved new lives out of the harsh wilderness. Remote from the usual security of the towns and cities of the coast, the agrarian family had to be self-sufficient. Almost everything needed to maintain life—food, clothing, shelter, and the utensils and tools to operate the farm—was made at home. Each member of the family shared in the struggle for existence. The family was the basic unit of social life.

Attitudes toward leisure underwent another change after the War of Independence. Recreational activity had assumed a place in the eastern seaboard cities and towns, but the backcountry farmers and frontier families remained relatively untouched by the quest for diversion. Their free time had to be useful, not merely enjoyable. The pioneers on their way west converted their essential laboring activities into recreational experiences. Straight-fur-

Years in the Common Era

born; first evening paper is published in London   ■   1720—First collective settlement is founded in Vermont   ■   1775-83—American

row plowing competitions, horse or oxen weight pulls, and cooking contests became typical leisure activities. Group efforts such as barn raising, sheep shearing, corn husking, crafts, church suppers, quilting bees, turkey shoots, community fairs, and town meetings drew the interest of the rural people, who saw the benefits of voluntary cooperation in getting a particular job done. Individuals participated in communal activities of their own volition in this society of free and equal families.

The migration of people seeking a new and better life on the western side of the Appalachian Plateau helped to spread the doctrine of egalitarianism, the natural rights of man, and humanitarian faith. Politically, economically, and socially, frontier agricultural life exerted a profound influence on the mosaic of American democracy. It not only introduced the principles of freedom, equality, and individualism to the frontier but had considerable effect on the older, more populated sections of the country. The small frontier farmers had a huge impact on the struggles over suffrage. In the eastern states, ownership of property was still the screen used to determine who could vote. The growing pressure of western migrants for one man, one vote did much to open up voting to all citizens. The frontier states were also the first to allow women to vote.

The westward movement was strengthened by the attraction of empty lands (empty at least from a white point of view, since the current residents held no deeds to their property) for immigrants and the growing populations of the east. People could start over. If they had the cash, the courage, and the skill, they could homestead. This migration brought with it isolation, but it also brought freedom from the conventional restraints of east-coast life. Recreational activities were centered in the home, and the family was the whole social world except when roads or rivers were passable enough to permit all the families of one district to meet for common feasting, dancing, marketing, or other such enterprise. Life was severe and short

People migrated west to seek a better life.

© Corbis-Bettmann

Years in the Common Era

for the unwary settler, and the pleasurable pursuits of social intercourse and other leisure activities were few and far between.

In effect, then, the leisure activities of the rural and frontier regions mixed recreational activity with work. The natural elements as well as survival techniques were used. In the well-developed, settled areas of the East, and later on in the West as civilization inexorably pushed back the frontier, a leisure class grew. Its typical recreational activities were games of chance, extravaganzas, the more aesthetic entertainments, and other forms of individual and social activity. There was never a year after 1630 that didn't hear a discussion of continental expansion. These ideas were quickly put into practice.

First, trappers filtered into the region between the Appalachians and the Mississippi River. Frontier settlements were established as pioneer families trekked westward in search of free land. The federal government sent exploratory expeditions to map the vast continent and set boundaries. As the Midwest began to fill up, other emigrants continued to search for a promised land until they reached the Pacific Ocean.

The expansionists could trace their lineage to Governor John Winthrop of Massachusetts, Thomas Paine in 1776, James Madison in 1787, and Thomas Jefferson, who in 1803 authorized the Louisiana Purchase. This westward flow became a veritable flood with the discovery of gold in California in 1849. Railroad construction, land settlement, development of manufacturing, the need for markets, and the financial gain of all these activities combined to increase the pressure for expansion right up to the Civil War.

Industrialization and Social Issues

The causes of the Southern rebellion and the attempt to secede from the United States are not in question here. More pertinent are the exchange of recreational ideas, the invention of certain games, and the use of recreational activities to fill the soldiers' leisure and raise morale. War has always been a contest between hurry up and wait. One of its insidious elements is the boredom that envelops combatants when they are not actually fighting or maneuvering.

The Civil War was no exception. Except when men fell down from exhaustion or hunger and slept whenever and wherever they could, the stand-downs, reorganizations, and camp life in general were, for the most part, completely boring. During lulls in fighting or marching, soldiers were thrown back on their own resources to fill their free time. Unsatisfied leisure produced poor morale and disciplinary problems. The better commanding officers filled free time in a number of ways and saw an improvement in discipline and morale.

Since recruits came from all regions of the country, urban and rural, were from different ethnic groups, and had varying recreational skills and experiences, the war brought disparate individuals into close contact. These differences served to leaven the boredom. Soldiers learned new and different forms of sports and games, music, dance, theatricals, and the great attraction for men at war—religion.[2] Several times revivalist fever swept the opposing armies, and men who had never shown any religious inclination stepped forward to pray and be baptized. This was not surprising behavior for men on the firing line of battle. Religious services were important social events and morale builders during the war.

In fact, buildings that were constructed primarily as churches doubled as theaters and venues for many recreational activities that occurred. When the soldiers had free time, they visited their friends in other units of the camp, established instrumental and singing groups, staged plays, and indulged in other activities.[3] During a lull in the campaign in the winter of 1864, hundreds of soldiers in several brigades waged a snowball fight that lasted several hours.[4] It was not considered odd that the commanding general participated in this mock combat to break the monotony of camp life.

Parochial views were altered and leisure skills broadened by the war. Traditional regional recreational activities were displayed and learned as the men intermingled in the training camps and during the various campaigning intervals. A great deal of knowledge about many activities was traded back and forth within and between armies. Those who came from rural areas learned about urban ways and those from the cities learned to better appreciate rural pastimes. Northern soldiers were just starting to play a form of baseball. It was an adaptation of Duck-on-a-Rock, and General Abner Doubleday would forever be associated with its origin.[5] The Civil War also assisted the spread of organized recreational activity (by courtesy of the different military units).

Horse racing became a fad during the war, and huge crowds attended racetracks in Boston, Washington, and Chicago.

The years between the Civil War and 1900 saw advancing forms of a mechanistic technology, the explosive effect of Darwin's theory of biological evolution, and a humanitarian appeal. All exerted pressure for a new approach to the latest discoveries of the day. The advances in the physical and biological sciences produced such profound changes in people's worldview, their relationship to the environment, and the possibilities for education that not only was reappraisal necessary to reconcile these diverse concepts, but a radical change was required if any practical use were to be made of this new knowledge.

Education began to take rapid professional strides as labor, a newly awakened force in the economy of the United States, insistently demanded a place. There was a call for more education better suited to those who worked at the manual trades and for their children upon whose shoulders their hopes for better lives rode. As education progressed, it carried with it (albeit more slowly) the as yet unestablished field of recreational service. Industrialization and mass production called for new educational techniques. The demand to produce more and cheaper goods stressed advances in communications, transportation, metallurgy, scientific analysis, and chemical research.

Advanced techniques in science and industry after 1865 turned the attention of educators and economists toward utilitarianism and materialistic philosophies of life. Businessmen wanted education to orient their workers to a useful, practical knowledge. They were eager to underwrite institutions of learning that would produce employees who could fit into their particular form of economic enterprise.

Coupled with this outcry for a utilitarian education was the swift growth of the natural sciences. Science became the byword for industrial growth and development. This rapid acceleration in an area of learning that had formerly reposed behind ivy-covered walls opened new vistas to the intellectually minded. Encouraged by the demand for better ways of doing things through industrial crafts, which needed the sciences for operational inventions, the natural and physical sciences gained ascendancy over the humanities in institutions of higher learning, and a new round of philosophical thinking was inaugurated.

MOVING TOWARD PART II

The book to this point has traced the evolution of leisure from prehistory through the early American period. You've learned about the major events that have affected the development of leisure. Now it's time to move from a study of events to a study of concepts and from a global view to a mostly American view of leisure. The rest of this chapter begins that move from events to concepts, but it continues to place the concepts in the context of historical development of leisure in America. With this transition, you'll be prepared for the issues to come in part II.

The New Leisure and Recreational Service

The increasingly important role played by recreational activity is due to a variety of causes, beginning with those that gave rise to the Industrial Revolution of 1792. The age of discovery brought the age of invention; the age of invention brought the age of power; the age of power brought the age of leisure. As in the past, new technical processes improved productivity to the point that the hours of work were reduced without reduced wages. In the past 60 years, the hours of factory labor have been reduced in some industries from 60 per week to 35. State and federal legislation has imposed restrictions upon the number of hours children can work. White-collar and professional workers enjoyed similar reductions in hours. One result in the apparent reduction of leisure, because of "moonlighting" or other self-imposed decisions to work more hours, is accompanying stress—both physical and mental. The value of participating in recreational activity can be observed in the reduction of stress and the greater likelihood of a more healthful mental outlook. Recreational activity, particularly of a vigorous physical type, does much to develop cardiopulmonary efficiency, strength, flexibility, and fitness as well as a perception of psychological soundness.

A shift in public health agencies' interest from curing gross environmental ailments to extending life and physical well-being means the average person may contemplate from 12 to 20 years of life expectancy after retirement—which should have considerable effect upon the activities of leisure. Medicine has done much to reduce poor health among the aging. As science pushes back the frontiers of the unknown, it will surely find remedies for the diseases that now account for most morbidity at advanced ages. This will lead to an increase in the leisure of older adults and proportionate growth of their interest in community recreational service programs.

The American people have been extremely ingenious in devising ways to employ their leisure. The amusements, entertainments, and diversions designed to provide vicarious experiences, not to mention activities for direct participation, are inexhaustible. They partake of nearly all our innate capacities for feeling and action and are multiplied by the development that these capacities undergo in the experience of living. Their complexity is increased by inventive genius; they are not limited by utilitarianism but conditioned only by their ability to give human satisfaction and enjoyment.

Innumerable hobbies and group activities in literature, science, crafts, games, sports, music, art, and clubs abound. By 1995, there were 150 million aquatic enthusiasts, 40 million bowlers, 16 million tennis players, 30 million joggers, 21 million golfers, 41 million softball players, 53 million anglers, 54 million bicyclists, 39 million walkers, 14 million boaters, and unnumbered archers, riders, hunters, collectors, birdwatchers, and faddists of one kind or another. Add to these the spectators at concerts, opera, theater, cinema, professional sports centers, television, racing fans, and nearly everyone participates in some form of recreational activity.

Creativity and Leisure

As the number of hours spent working decreased, people came to depend more on lei-

A few of the 21 million Americans who golf during their leisure.

sure activities for full expression of their abilities. In the preindustrial era, workers found outlets for a wide range of their faculties in their vocation. Work was not highly competitive; it was performed leisurely. It required various skills. It gave the opportunity for creative experience and invention and for individuals to place the stamp of their own genius on the character of the product. It also provided the opportunity for social intercourse in the productive processes. Work was life in the full.

Today work in the trades and professions alike does not tap workers' full potential. Their success is almost directly proportional to the degree of their specialization. In the factory, workers often use the accessory and not the large skeletal muscles. This does violence to their physiological and emotional balance, so they must find relief in large-muscle activity during leisure. In their recreational pursuits, they have a chance to live creatively and give expression to the wide assortment of human capabilities with which they are endowed but which atrophy through disuse if not released and cultivated in leisure.

> *Because the satisfaction of basic human needs was inherent in the work of our predecessors, they did not need as much time for recreational activity as we do today. Few of us, at the present, can see the completed result of our labors, and even if we do we cannot readily identify ourselves with a particular product since we may have performed only one of the thousands of operations required for its completion.*[6]

Individuality and self-expression are needed in an environment that restricts conduct and demands conformity. Creative leisure allows individuals to realize their skills and talents and to engage in experiences that are uniquely personal. Freedom is the essence of recreational pursuit; people select their leisure activities and participate to the limit of their being, shaking off the confines of routinized daily living and slipping into the realm of self-determination.

In no other activity are individuals free to be so uninhibited. However, recreational activity is not escape from life. What people choose to do in their leisure has an impact on their character. Because people do what they want to do when they want to do it during leisure,

they are likely to seek creative activity to satisfy their basic needs for achievement.

The Economics of Leisure

Fortunately, the processes that changed the nature of work and reduced its hours created a greater national wealth. This made possible many improvements and commodities that were needed if leisure was to bring compensatory satisfactions and values. Labor-saving devices, competitive decreases in the cost of entertainment, better and faster transportation and communication—all served to provide leisure and its opportunities. Much of this wealth has been reinvested and consumed in the processes of further production; much has been wasted in wars and other enterprises that produced few social values; and much has been expended on social betterment, education, and recreational experience.

Realization of the potential values of our leisure has been enhanced by increased national wealth. True, some of the recreational activities that people enjoy the most can be done at no cost, such as walking, swimming in a pond, or reading a book from a library. Other activities, such as skiing, going to the theater, or making crafts, can be expensive. People who can't afford the equipment or fees aren't allowed to enjoy these activities. The benefits of leisure before World War II had never been as universal as they are today, due in part to the unequal distribution of wealth.

Yet almost every American family has always spent some money for recreational services, materials, or activities.[7] Even when people could not afford certain recreational commodities, they could patronize public and other community facilities open to all. These include not only those available through agencies specifically established for recreational services, such as parks, playgrounds, and beaches, but those that are offered by public schools, youth service agencies, churches, libraries, and other community enterprises. These facilities are still not uniformly distributed, nor are they by any means adequate for existing needs, but they are increasing in number as demand increases.

Urban and Suburban Development Fosters Recreational Service

Urbanization has provided fertile soil for the growth of leisure activities. The phenomenal increase of public recreational service agencies in cities as compared to rural communities may be explained by the traditional rural distrust of government enterprise of any kind. Many urban dwellers, on the other hand, have been willing to cede to government the responsibility for establishing agencies to serve people's needs. With rapid development of urban centers came a corresponding growth of municipal recreational service departments.

Approximately one million farm families in the United States moved into cities between 1940 and 1945. The obvious attraction was wartime industry, which required a labor force and paid premium wages. For the next 40 years, there was a continual migration of rural populations to metropolitan areas, although the trend has begun to reverse in the last decade. Some central cities have attracted poor rural populations because of welfare benefits. Courts have consistently upheld the rights of indigent persons to receive welfare assistance without having to establish previous residency in the community. Thus, many cities have received poor migrants while simultaneously losing their more affluent citizens to the surrounding suburbs.

Today, more than 200 million people, or 80 percent of the nation's total population, reside in metropolitan areas. The metropolitan and nonmetropolitan areas are currently growing at the same rate. A metropolitan area is a community with upwards of 50,000 people. In addition to a central city, it includes all adjacent and contiguous civil subdivisions and incorporated places with a population density of at least 150 people per square mile. A rural community has fewer than 2,500 residents and is usually situated beyond the urban fringe.

Since 1970 there has been a decrease of about 2 percent in the population of central cities (chiefly those of more than a million people), while the suburban population continues to increase. The net loss of cities to suburbs is a factor in service provisions and economics.

The great significance of internally migrating populations for leisure and the subsequent growth of public recreational agencies is that the sharp line between rural and urban living no longer exists. There is more similarity between urban and rural life than ever before. The rise of the suburbs led to a movement away from the central city, but to areas close enough to use commercial and recreational facilities.

Suburban living and rural dwelling have become equal in terms of information due to television and greater mobility.

Rural and suburban areas have become quite interested in public recreational service. An increasing number of communities with populations of 800 to 2,000 people want to provide their children and themselves with the recreational facilities and activities they need. This is evident throughout many rural regions of the United States.

The development of full-time public recreational service departments is somewhat slow in the most rural areas. This is because small populations do not yield enough taxed revenue for professional leadership and facilities and because farmers get more creative satisfaction from their work than most people. However, rural communities are beginning to consolidate services. Two or more small towns within a given geographic area vote to share personnel and facilities. The benefits of publicly organized recreational services are spreading to the most exurban of communities.

The Acceptance of Leisure and Recreational Activity

The growth of the field of recreational service has also been accelerated by the breakdown of traditional cultural prejudices and religious taboos. A recognition of the importance of leisure and recreational activities in terms of human and social value has gained general acceptance. As work has receded from its preeminent place in Western culture, religious leaders have reconsidered the place of leisure in human life. The churches have been forced to incorporate leisure into their philosophy and theology.[8] The Puritan tradition, which viewed work as the antithesis of leisure, has been largely dispelled. Churches often support leisure and recreational activities, adopting techniques developed by practitioners in the field of recreational service.

In our pluralistic culture, it would be difficult for any one clerical system to suppress much recreational experience performed in the new leisure. Even the most fundamentalist sects are developing recreational aspects for use in their own churches. Although laws still prohibit certain recreational activities on Sundays, and a minor academic prejudice against the applied arts exists, the tendency to consider leisure insignificant has broken down rapidly. Religious groups' attitudes toward recreational activity and leisure pursuits have assisted the great development of recreational service by public agencies and the new awareness of leisure by private groups and individuals.

The last quarter of the 20th century in America has been an age of massive human leisure. In no epoch of the past has there ever been a hope (if not full realization) of time free from unremitting toil for nearly everyone. Except for the early hominid period, all cultures have had some leisure, but only a privileged few could afford it. In societies with slaves, leisure was a commodity to be purchased. The rise of leisure can be traced to the recapture of time formerly spent obtaining food, clothing, and shelter. The development of civilization, with organization, division of labor, mechanization, mass production, and automation brought leisure within the grasp of all. Only when time was gained through labor-saving devices (e.g., the wheel, better agricultural implements, irrigation methods, sailing vessels, steam, internal combustion engines, and atomic power) did leisure become a universal possession.

Leisure has been an element of life throughout the thousands of centuries since the first true human being had the time to think. Significant advances in culture have been due largely to the creative use of whatever leisure was available. Free time, used to increase one's knowledge or abilities or to provide benefits to a community and by extension to society as a whole, affords a matchless step forward in the progress of civilization. The American tradition for recreational activity began to develop during the 18th century. The inventions of that century laid the foundations for the industrialized nation of the 19th century and ensured the growth of mass leisure.

The innovative outlets Americans have found for their free time have been documented in all of their varied forms for at least a hundred years. Increased leisure demanded constructive experiences. Individual striving was followed by collective concern for the masses of people who poured into the country in successive waves. Several social movements had profound impacts on the provision of public recreational service. Farsighted men and women from disparate trades, vocations, and economic strata began to examine private organizational administration of recreational service and found

it inadequate to serve the needs of such a diverse population.

First, private philanthropic agencies and altruistic people came forward to offer recreational assistance to induce new converts or to implement their specific doctrines. Then public-spirited individuals banded together to urge government action. This brought about a movement that is even now coming to full maturity. Americans learned to use their leisure for personal satisfaction and in most cases coincidentally benefited their communities. During this period of growth and learning, the recreational service movement was established.

Transformation of the Movement

By 1900, only a few cities had made provision for public playgrounds. Today nearly all cities have recreational areas available, some with highly organized programs supervised by professional practitioners. Writing in 1922, Clarence E. Rainwater traced nine transitions in the play movement:

1) From provision for little children to that for all ages of people; 2) from facilities operated during the summer only, to those maintained throughout the year; 3) from outdoor equipment and activities only, to both outdoor and indoor facilities and events; 4) from congested urban districts to both urban and rural communities; 5) from philanthropic to community support and control; 6) from "free" play and miscellaneous events to "directed" play with organized activities and correlated activities including manual, physical, aesthetic, social, and civic projects; 8) from the provision of facilities to the definition of standards for the use of leisure; 9) from "individual" interests to "group" and community activities.[9]

Twenty years later, George Hjelte formulated five more transitions:

1) From a "play" movement to a "recreational" movement; 2) from a local municipal only, to a state and national movement; 3) from programs detached from public education, to programs integrated with the educational curriculum and system; 4) from organization limited to urban communities to that inclusive of suburban and rural areas as well; 5) from an organization largely under quasi-public control with subsidies from public funds to full acceptance of recreational service as a public function.[10]

To these transitions we can now add the following: (1) from programs operated by laypeople to those operated by professionally prepared and, in most instances, highly qualified practitioners; (2) from an amenity service to one considered essential to the health, welfare, and cultural development of all; (3) from a voluntary service to a professionalized occupational field of applied social science; (4) from a relatively universal dependence on the merit system of civil service classification for the employment of personnel in the field to a mistrust of such procedures, at least in many urban centers; (5) from a reliance on a career ladder process whereby recreationists could aspire to administrative positions to the use of seasonal, provisional, and specialist personnel limited to specific, timed assignments without hierarchical possibilities, particularly where economic pressure forces the restructuring of agencies; (6) from a nonpolitical position to a highly sophisticated use of political procedures to gain departmental advantages; (7) from an effort to serve most of the constituency to the initiation of a few well-publicized projects designed to satisfy high-profile special interest groups; (8) from a position of serving only those who have the physical and mental capacity to seek service to an attempt to identify and serve disabled populations, either through mainstreaming or through specialized grouping and programming.

Recreational activity is now universally recognized as one of the basic needs of human life. When a need is deemed significant to society, then government, as well as private and philanthropic enterprise, enters to help administer it for the mutual benefit and welfare of all concerned. Recreational activity is such an important aspect of life that modern society would suffer an inestimable loss without it.

In this chapter we have seen how recreational service has evolved from a private and personally directed leisure experience to a highly complex, governmentally administered organization. Public, private, and voluntary institutions work side by side to provide essential opportunities for recreational activity.

SELECTED REFERENCES

Berkhofer, R. F., ed. *American Revolution: The Critical Times*. Waltham, Mass.: Little, Brown, 1971.

Bremer, F. J. *Puritan Experiment: New England Society from Bradford to Edwards*. New York: St. Martin's Press, 1976.

Byington, E. H. *Puritan as a Colonist and Reformer*. New York: AMS Press, 1976.

Carlson, R. E., et al. *Recreation and Leisure: The Changing Scene*. 3d ed. Belmont, Cal.: Wadsworth, 1978.

Dorson, R. M., ed. *American Rebels: Personal Narratives of the American Revolution*. Westminster, Md.: Pantheon Books, 1976.

Dulles, F. R. *A History of Recreation*. 2d ed. New York: Appleton-Century-Crofts, 1965.

Gay, P. *Enlightenment—An Interpretation—The Science of Freedom*. vol. 2. New York: Norton, 1977.

May, H. F. *Enlightenment in America*. New York: Oxford University Press, 1976.

Neumeyer, M. H., and E. S. Neumeyer. *Leisure and Recreation: A Study of Leisure and Recreation in Their Sociological Aspects*. New York: Wiley, 1958.

Scheiber, H. N. *American Economic History*. New York: Harper & Row, 1976.

Shahan, R. W., and K. R. Merrill. *American Philosophy*. Norman, Ok: Univeristy of Oklahoma Press, 1977.

Shivers, J. S. *Introduction to Recreational Service*. Springfield, Ill.: Charles C. Thomas, 1993.

Warner, S. B., Jr. *American Experiment: Perspectives on Two Hundred Years*. Boston, Mass.: Houghton Mifflin, 1976.

REVIEW QUESTIONS

1. How did the Pilgrims view leisure? Why?
2. Why was the Puritanical appreciation of leisure abandoned?
3. How did westward migration affect leisure?
4. Is leisure good?
5. Has industrialization produced more or less leisure for the average American? Why?

GLOSSARY

Asceticism: From the Greek word *askeo,* "to exercise or train," it is the practice of denial of physical or psychological desires in order to attain a spiritual ideal or goal.

Enlightenment: A period of intellectual development experienced during the 17th and 18th centuries in western Europe. The power and use of reason was felt to be the most effective way to understand the world. Reason was ultimately used in the examination of religion, which held the primacy of faith over reason. This argument of faith versus reason is constantly debated by philosophers, theologians, and Red Sox fans.

Stoicism: A philosophy of the Greco-Roman period that the world is fundamentally rational and governed by fate. Each person's role is to remain calm and reasonable in order to be one with the universe and attain a higher moral existence. Meanwhile, people should play an active role in public affairs.

PART II

Leisure in
Social Context

All leisure developed in a social environment. From its origins, leisure could first be discerned when survival necessitated cooperation from at least one other. Out of this early scenario grew all of the forces that shape people and guide their respective behaviors. No human being could thrive without the contribution of a supportive society. The central core of our identities is intimately related to social participation. Where such an association is absent or failed, the consequence will be a misanthrope.

People who, as a result of an inadequate social environment, do not develop are usually lacking in objective or motivation. They have no interest in achievement. They have no defining goals and are merely carried along by the tide of occurrences. They typically resort to puerile behavioral patterns in response to the claims made on them.

In the last decade of the 20th century, we are witness to a growing underclass of discontented people whom society has failed. Without a nurturing family situation, without clear guidance defining right and wrong behavior, without socially acceptable values, with role models who may be immoral at best and criminal at worst, these people tear at the fabric of the social order. Ignorance, poverty, crime, and early demise seem to be their lot. Not all the members of the underclass experience these negative prospects, and some who are not so categorized certainly do. But there are many thousands of people who have not known the influence of a supportive society.

There has always been an underclass in every culture. The causes may differ, but class or caste distinction and separation from the privileged few has been a recognized human condition. As we have observed, leisure has always been available. To some much was given; to others, little or nothing. As culture enlarged and became civilization, the ability to obtain leisure increased because the social system encouraged it through traditions, taboos, and law. Recreational experience was provided as holidays, celebrations of various sorts, or simply entertainments designed to divert the populace's attention from unsatisfying social conditions. Eventually, such entertainments could no longer counter the effect of social imbalances. Rebellions, revolution, and civil war were inevitable.

As technology advanced, factories replaced home production. Industrialization of society created mass leisure and, along with a system of transportation and communication, contributed to intense urbanization.

When at last people's basic survival needs were met, it became clear that we also have social, emotional, and intellectual needs. Some of these needs are satisfied by recreational activity. The recreational service movement grew out of social situations arising from population migrations, urbanization, industrialization, mass education, mobility, mechanization, and leisure. This outpouring of effort is in part a response to the changing role of the family and other social institutions. The recreational pattern formerly focused on the home has been replaced by the school, sectarian agencies, local recreational centers, and the community at large.

Today, people often choose to have more leisure rather than to work more hours and earn more money. With the economic means to do more leisure activities, wider horizons as a result of mass communications, and education to identify a variety of leisure pursuits, they spend less time enjoying their leisure at home. This displacement of family recreational involvement has produced an upsurge in individual interest in voluntary service and community affairs. Although recent trends seem to suggest that more people are spending their leisure at home, or "cocooning," there is less here than meets the eye. A greater proportion of young- and middle-aged persons still look to out-of-home activities for their chief recreational interest. More older adults are also seeking enjoyable experiences away from home either through travel or other cultural and developmental activities.

Meanwhile, people demand consumer products and commodities they perceive as enhancing the quality of life. The work ethic remains, but it is slowly being overtaken by a leisure ethic. There is a universal sentiment in favor of leisure, and we should not lose sight of the fact that it is not inherently good or bad. Used well, it enriches; used badly, it is time ill spent.

We now live in an age where the smokestack industries based on coal, iron, and steel have given way to mass communication, computer information networks, and service performance. The basis for the new economy and social institutions of the 21st century will be light, air, chemicals, and sand. Light will power fiber optics; air will be separated from gases to produce semi-conductor washes; chemicals will be used for plastics and catlytic processes; and sand will be used for silicon, lasers, and crystals. Together with increasing farm product exports, both the social and economic base of our society's order will offer untold free time to those who have the intelligence and education to permit them to take full advantage of the opportunities.

Chapter 6

UNDERSTANDING LEISURE AND THE RECREATIONAL EXPERIENCE

Objectives

After reading this chapter, the student will be able to do the following:

Understand the free-time definition of leisure.

■

Describe the various ways leisure accumulates.

■

Explain the Aristotelian concept of leisure.

■

Discuss leisure as a state of being.

■

Describe the nature and functions of leisure.

■

Explain the nature of recreational experience.

■

Discuss the values of recreational activity.

The concept of leisure as time free of obligations is the most effective and meaningful definition yet proposed. Instead of encrusting leisure with restrictive consequences and hedging it with certain values, activities, or partial time references, the free-time definition is theoretically sound and unambiguous.

Certainly, one hesitates to label anything completely free, because almost every theory about human behavior is shaped or constrained by factors and forces within the culture. Thus, some scholars perceive free time as being restricted by forces that impede or actually prevent human leisure due to limitations of choice, economic means, knowledge, skill, or motivation. But this does not really concern leisure as free time. It is simply a device to give the definer a sense of appropriate fit. In fact, some analysts believe that there is no free time because some humans daydream. The act of contemplation on a routine basis is viewed as a constraint on free time. If everything is by prior disposition subject to some restraint, how can there be free time?

This basic concept has been twisted to fit every theorist's idea of what is attractive and plausible. Free time allows for comparisons within and between cultures and for the removal of artificial boundaries.

What is leisure? This deceptively simple question has a variety of conflicting answers because scholars of different orientations have attached all manner of philosophical, sociological, anthropological, and psychological qualifications to the word. Cutting through these layers to reveal the nature of leisure and its impact on behavior, economics, and politics is the function of this chapter. An understanding of recreational activity is also a concern.

THE FREE-TIME DEFINITION OF LEISURE

Leisure is simply free time, that is, the time that an individual has to dispose of in whatever way he or she sees fit.[1] Unlike idiosyncratic views, which tend to obscure leisure, the free-time definition has been included in every reputable unabridged dictionary. Most define leisure as freedom from the demands of work or duty; free or unoccupied time; free or unrestricted time, and so on. The *Oxford English Dictionary* says leisure is "free time; time at one's disposal. Opportunity afforded by free time."[2]

In other words, this is an objective, value-neutral definition; personal attitudes about leisure do not obscure its meaning. A value-loaded definition (like those in many textbooks) would create an egocentric orientation. The individual who encrusts leisure with certain values promotes a particular concept that has nothing to do with free time but rather with how such time is used or perceived. The free-time concept hasn't disappeared; it has merely been overlaid with ideological baggage in terms of personal constraints, usage, capacity to perform, and other artificial encumbrances. All this because the free-time definition is too simple or not positive enough for some to appreciate.

How is this discretionary time generated? Where does it come from out of the normal 24-hour day and how is it made available to the individual? Free time can be produced or accumulated in several ways: (1) through economic ownership; (2) through technological advance; (3) by procrastination or failure to fulfill obligations; (4) by restriction of activity or enforced idleness; (5) through retirement; and (6) by completion of required activity. Let us examine each of these possibilities to determine whether the free-time definition covers all categories of leisure production.

Leisure Through Economic Ownership

The easiest way to obtain leisure is to have the economic means not to have to work for a living. If you do not have to work during any given period, that time is free to do with as you wish. Economic ownership, whether derived from inheritance, accumulated wealth from earnings, gambling success, or patronage, enables the owner to indulge in discretionary activity because that individual is no longer obliged to work within certain time frames. Thus, leisure becomes available to those whose economic resources can ensure their freedom from an obligatory, time-consuming occupation.

Leisure Through Technological Advance

A great deal of the time-consuming drudgery that attended the labor of our forebears and that of people throughout much of the world today has largely disappeared in the United States. Unfortunately, there are people in this country who cannot afford the labor-saving devices that enable them to accumulate free time. Still, millions of people do reap the rewards of additional free time because they no longer have to perform repetitive or time-consuming tasks. What was formerly done by hand is in many instances accomplished by mechanical means, freeing the user of technology for other activities. The user of frozen foods, for example, accumulates free time by not having to prepare the food.

Some forecasts predict that we are rapidly heading for a future in which a wide variety of mechanical devices will virtually eliminate the need for any physical or time-consuming labor. This will generate abundant free time—at least for those who can afford the technology. Labor-saving devices are now available in automated factories, homes, schools, and commercial enterprises and may become the basis for massive future leisure in this society.

However, persuasive contradictory evidence is now available. Technology, it is said, has resulted in not more leisure but less. In fact, with few exceptions, technology has cost rather than saved time.[3,4] According to some analysts, many people use the time they save with technology to work at a second job (perhaps to pay for their time-saving gadgets).

Leisure Through Procrastination

If you put off doing something that is required, the time you save by not meeting the obligation becomes available for discretionary use. Of course, sooner or later retribution catches up, and you are forced to fulfill your obligations. Whatever the task or obligation might be—whether it is writing a book report for school, running an errand, visiting a relative, or making an important decision—the time that was obtained by postponement will eventually have to be taken to discharge the obligation, displacing the leisure that was accumulated. Truancy from school, lateness in performance, or failure to carry out assignments because one has used

the time for other purposes is eventually made up by cultural penalties that reduce leisure. Checks and balances may be in effect here.

Leisure Through Restriction or Enforced Idleness

Prisoners, patients in treatment centers, and individuals confined in institutions have a great deal of leisure through circumstances beyond their control. A patient may have to undergo various treatments each day, but the time between therapy or between meals or other imposed routines is idle time from which there is no escape. The periods of enforced idleness are leisure—not the kind that is earned, as in the case of a worker's paid vacation, but free time that is imposed. To the extent that the illness or affliction permits, the patient may do whatever he or she wishes within the constraints of the institutional setting.

With prisoners, however, enforced idleness is somewhat different. Prisoners have transgressed society's laws and are confined for

The Princes of Wales

While enforced leisure does not cause behavior (that being the province of personal character traits, values, and upbringing), it does allow certain proclivities to manifest themselves. The enforced leisure of reigning royals provides excellent examples of how free time can be used positively or negatively.

The heir to the throne of Great Britain is the Prince of Wales. The future Edward VII, son of Queen Victoria, was not allowed productive participation in any aspect of the kingdom. Instead he led a life of dissolute leisure. Despite his flair for setting fashion trends and fads, he was a notorious womanizer, involved in numerous scandals, and behaved badly until his mother's death.

The future Edward VIII, Victoria's great-grandson, was an international favorite who did not care about propriety and was disinclined to conduct himself responsibly. His enforced leisure took him all over the British Empire, into and out of sexual adventures that ended in his romance with an American divorcee. He came to the throne on his father's death, abdicated after 10 months to marry his American lover, and spent the rest of his life in self-imposed exile where, among other things, he was a Nazi sympathizer.

The current Prince of Wales, Charles Windsor, although a naval officer, still must contend with enforced leisure. He is not permitted to participate in government. However, he has turned his lively intelligence toward architectural criticism and environmental conservation and has established an institute of architecture, which has had a positive impact on contemporary building in England. Charles also plays the cello, plays polo, and is an excellent painter. He was commissioned by the British Postal Authority to paint English castles for use on stamps.

punishment. Whatever free time they have comes from being unable to do anything independently of the penal authorities and the incarceration environment. Ironically, prisoners earn their leisure much as any worker does, by performing various jobs. The time available after working hours may be considered free time—but only if it is not otherwise restricted by the institution's rules and regulations. Thus it is unquestionably *enforced free time*. Prison restricts the possible choices of the inmate, but it does generate leisure.

One other restrictive source of leisure should be mentioned, although it is far less common. It occurs among reigning aristocracy. Tradition prevents monarchs from indulging in most gainful occupations while they reign or rule. This produces a tremendous amount of leisure for them. Aristocratic leisure has a long history. Since reigning aristocrats could not participate in commercial enterprise, and the preoccupations of government, warfare, or other traditional tasks did not consume all of their time, they compensated for the buildup of leisure by indulging in sport, patronizing the arts, or erecting monuments and public buildings.

The enforced idleness of the aristocracy, fenced in by taboo, ritual, or custom, gave them much leisure to use or misuse as they saw fit. Even today we hear about the antics of the idle rich and wealthy nobility cavorting with the jet set or seeking entertainment in ways quite beyond the reach of ordinary people. The historical restrictions on what aristocrats can do frees them from the more mundane occupations that use up the time of those who must work.

Leisure Through Retirement

The Calvinist tradition that a work-centered life is the only way to salvation has been a fixed idea among Western societies for 400 years. This idea has held sway because it supports the economic system of production and distribution under which the individual produces goods or delivers services and is paid money in exchange. This permits the individual to survive.

What happens when an individual is no longer employed or employable? In enlightened societies, measures are taken to ensure the survival of those who are no longer able to work or whose services are no longer wanted. Pension plans and retirement plans of all sorts have been set up in the public and private sectors to enable retired persons to live out their lives in relative comfort and security. Unfortunately, this is not always the case. Too often the individual has barely enough to survive on, much less to enjoy life. Yet some retired people are quite well off thanks to pensions, Social Security, savings, investments, or other accumulated wealth.

Retirement generates leisure. When an individual no longer must consume time by being employed, that time—which some look upon as a reward for working—can be used or not as the person desires. When work ceases, the individual loses not only monetary rewards but also the many satisfactions that come with one's position and active involvement as a productive member of society. Something else must replace the occupational pursuit that was formerly the focus of existence. The time accumulated during whatever remains of a person's life is retirement-generated leisure.

Leisure Through Completed Activity

Certain individuals in our society have minimal obligations to fulfill before they are free to use their time in a discretionary manner. Among these are young children, whose only time restriction is that they must perform given tasks or engage in normal existence activities such as eating. Youthful assignments may be to attend school, run errands for parents, or carry out specific chores around the home. Otherwise, the young person has leisure and may be free to do whatever he or she wishes until a required activity impinges on that free time.

Free time may occur regularly or intermittently, depending upon the age and competence of the individual to be entrusted with responsibilities. Very young children probably require close supervision of leisure activity to prevent mishaps. Their leisure is punctuated by meals, naps, or the availability of a parent to supervise activity. As children mature, additional requirements are imposed, cutting the leisure allotment. From the time the child completes the required activities satisfactorily until another set of obligations is imposed, there is a certain amount of free time available. This routine succession of required performances, whether of a survival or a cultural nature, continues throughout one's lifetime until either the accumulation of wealth or the mandatory re-

Retirement generates leisure.

tirement from employment frees up more leisure.

Other Leisure Concepts

Having examined the ways in which leisure is produced, it might be interesting to look at a few other concepts. A number of theorists do not accept the equating of leisure and free time. Rather, they define leisure in value-laden ways. Let us review some of these ideas.

Leisure as Pleasure. The Aristotelian concept of leisure did not negate the free-time concept; it merely attached the pleasure principle to it. According to Aristotle, leisure is the natural objective of all thinking people because it is associated with the most pleasurable of all activities—contemplation. Leisure provides the time to think. For a philosopher of Aristotle's nature, thinking and leisure would be intertwined. Since nothing could be of greater value to a thinker than thinking, the conclusions that Aristotle drew would follow logically.

To a certain extent, the theory of leisure as pleasure is still held today. However, leisure cannot be defined as pleasure. The contemplative act, which Aristotle believed could occur only during leisure, is a specific kind of activity that some say can actually occur at any time. Moreover, thinking is an activity, not a time period. A particular activity should not be equated with what is clearly a period of time.

Leisure as Activity. A number of theorists define leisure in terms of what people do in their free time. Kelly, among others, states, "Leisure is defined . . . as activity chosen in relative freedom for its qualities of satisfaction."[5] Unfortunately, when leisure is defined in this way, it cannot be separated from any of the myriad activities in which humans engage. The whole purpose of definition is to set limits by determining the boundaries or precise outlines of a word. It explains meaning by stating the nature or distinguishing characteristics of a thing. When leisure is defined as activity, it can mean almost anything. This definition merely causes confusion because, for example, one person's leisure may be another person's work. Attaching utilization to leisure opens the term to many meanings that depend on individual perceptions.

Defining leisure as free time does not deny that it is used, but the use is immaterial to the definition. Unobligated time does not have to be used in any particular way. It can be allowed to pass without purpose or to some purpose. Yet value-laden definitions abound in the literature. There are those who perceive leisure as a consummatory state. Thus, Csikszentmihalyi, in *Beyond Boredom and Anxiety,* chooses the word *flow* to refer to leisure that completely absorbs the individual.[6] Again, it is not leisure that absorbs, but the activity in which the individual chooses to participate. Leisure is a neutral term, neither positive nor negative. It is the setting or opportunity for whatever experiences the individual desires. How a person uses free time imposes a positive or negative judgment but does not explain what leisure is.

Leisure as Work. Leisure defined in a work context was enunciated by John Calvin (1509-1564), a leader in the Reformation movement.[7] Calvin maintained that the purpose of leisure was to recuperate in order to work better. Consequently, in Calvin's view most leisure was mere idleness, not to be tolerated by the authorities. Work alone was seen as the way to salvation. Anything that enhanced the ability to work was accepted; all else was condemned. The time-honored formula was that the individual had to be doing something; simply loitering about or doing nothing was sinful.

Leisure as a State of Being. Leisure defined as a state of consciousness has been articulated by a number of writers. Two of the foremost are Sebastian de Grazia and John Neulinger. They believe that leisure is a state of existence clearly differentiated from time and that it can occur regardless of what the individual is engaged in, including work. For these theorists, leisure is the epitome of self-actualization, the ability to achieve one's potential. Of course, according to their reasoning, the individual would have to be unencumbered by anything as ordinary as having to work for a living. In fact, de Grazia suggests that real leisure can occur only when the individual is freed from the need to worry about survival. Thus, leisure is set on a lofty pedestal and stands quite outside the realm of ordinary human existence.

Neulinger conceptualized leisure as perception. If the individual perceives something as leisure, it is. How this could be reconciled with pathological perceptions or even with perceptual errors is not explained.

You have some free time for leisure so you join a drama group. You get cast in a play with scheduled rehearsals. Is the time you spend in rehearsal part of your leisure?

THE NATURE AND FUNCTIONS OF LEISURE

Now that leisure has been defined as free time, it is possible to ascertain how it can be used. Although occupations take up an important place in civilization, for each person life holds something more than the work required for survival. That something added to complete the whole of life may be identified as leisure. Of course, everyone has other commitments besides work. Some are self-imposed obligations; others are culturally imposed. For the most part, these experiences are a direct outcome of

work (conferences, institutes, retreats, union meetings, etc.) or are performed during leisure (attending religious functions, visiting relatives, transporting children to various activities, etc.). The primary means for determining if an activity is leisure based is whether or not one can enter or leave the activity at personal discretion.

Leisure is not a withdrawal from life. What we do during leisure helps to shape the person we are. There are countless ways of using time away from obligatory activities, and we have to choose. Every decision about leisure activity is significant because it affects the course of our development. A great deal of most people's time is now spent in leisure. Furthermore, unlike employment, leisure is almost always looked upon with favor. It is not viewed as something unpleasant, punitive, or threatening, but rather as a reward and a benefit. What we do with our leisure, since the activities are freely chosen, is an accurate reflection of interest, personality, and character.

Leisure may be perceived in several different ways, among them relaxation, enjoyment (active or passive), release, and recuperation. Let us examine these perceptions and their influence on personal development. They may also be seen as elements in an inclusive perspective on leisure, each having its own important role to play.

Relaxation

One form of leisure is the pause from activity, the temporary cessation from exertion. An extreme manifestation is complete rest through sleep. When sleep is a physiological necessity, it is not leisure. Nevertheless, rest and relaxation are integral to some aspects of leisure. Sometime during each day, most people simply stop physical or mental expenditure of energy and try to relax. This may be why the coffee break has become an institution in this country. It gives people a chance to sit, talk, think, and compose themselves for the next round of activity.

Every individual takes a break in his or her own way. Some people do it by reading a book, newspaper, or magazine. Some relax by watching shows, games, or performances. Others indulge in hobbies or in various contemplative pastimes. In many different ways, people take time out from the daily grind to reaffirm themselves. This renunciation of high energy output in daily business or conduct in favor of change to a relaxed state is a highly effective way to regain the purpose one tends to lose during the routine of everyday life. It helps people achieve an attitude of complete openness and observant receptivity to what seems consonant with their personal capacity.

Enjoyment Through Activity

Leisure is almost always used enjoyably—if the individual has the knowledge and skill necessary for such participation. Leisure experiences are a deliberate attempt to produce pleasure. There are too many recreational forms to list here. Pleasurable experiences can be generated by an assortment of activities ranging from the study of astronomy to zoology; from engagement in one or more of the performing arts to mountain climbing or caving; from touring, reading, writing, or game playing to hobbies of all sorts. Indeed, distinctive traits of leisure pursuits are their tremendous variety and the intensity of interest and energy they elicit.

The appeal of leisure activity for enjoyment stems from the fact that human beings are living, active organisms who derive satisfaction from using their innate abilities. Pleasure is a subjective emotion produced from performance of the human organism in harmony with its appropriate powers. It is the emotional dividend restored from the expenditure of personal talents. There is little real pleasure in mere idleness and in unused qualities. Leisure may permit the employment of personal abilities in activities that evoke pleasure, but it is not synonymous with recreational experience. The former is simply residual time and the latter is activity that uses that time.

Not all forms of leisure activity are desirable to all people. The choice must be an individual one, because each individual has a value system against which to judge the kinds of activities available. One criterion in selecting leisure activities for pleasure is the positive or negative outcomes that will flow from such participation. A negative activity is one that detracts from the well-being of the individual participant and of others. Activities that are illegal, immoral, or harmful are negative. Although some people may derive pleasure from indulging in antisocial activities, such preferences surely indicate a set of values and sense of personal worth that are highly suspect.

Any number of other standards may be used in evaluating pleasurable activities to make enlightened decisions about participation. The important thing to bear in mind is that personal preferences are acquired, not inherited. Leisure participation for pleasure must be based on value systems that distinguish the more worthy from the less worthy free-time possibilities.

Passive Enjoyment

Instead of regarding leisure as an opportunity for enjoyment through active participation, we may view it as a source of passive pleasure. We may choose to watch others participate and seek diversion through entertainment. That spectator forms of entertainment have become big business is borne out by the multimillion-dollar salaries commanded by professional athletes, popular singers, actors, musicians, and other entertainers. Michael Jordan, for example, earns millions of dollars from endorsement alone. The mass media are largely responsible for the astronomical success of this business. On any given evening in the United States, more than 100 million people watch television in prime time, and TV's pervasive influence is a worldwide phenomenon.

The attraction of entertainment comes from the stimulation we get out of vicarious participation. Watching a performance, the spectator identifies with the performers and has the impression of actually experiencing the activity. While the spectator's involvement may appear to be passive, it is actually a suggested, internalized experience. The biggest drawback to this type of experience is that it becomes a substitute for action.

A benefit of vicarious experience is that it may serve to enhance the observer's knowledge. Another plus is that it affords a greater degree of appreciation than could be achieved by personal activity. Few people can match professional performance in terms of execution, yet it is probably beneficial to share vicariously in what these highly skilled people do. A great performance can also elicit a heightened intensity of feeling and provide the catharsis of emotional release. Furthermore, professional performances set a high standard for the activity, which can motivate spectators to become participants.

Release

Many people think of leisure as a way to escape from the dissatisfactions or boredom in their lives. Perhaps their work has become routine and unstimulating, or maybe they cannot find pleasure in typical pursuits and seek new forms of release. For such people, leisure experience must be as different as possible from their everyday lives. This may account for the rise in unconventional behavior as well as in activities that may be thought of as extreme at best and grotesque and life-threatening at worst.

The upsurge in high-risk leisure activities may reflect increasing attempts to escape from much in life that is humdrum and monotonous. Hang gliding, mountain climbing, caving, parachute jumping, shark hunting, auto racing, motorcycle and motor-sled racing may be symptoms of this desire for some form of escape. Other forms of release-seeking activity include drug and alcohol abuse, pornography, and other vices. The attraction and proliferation of various cults and "religious" sects are also manifestations of this desire.

The desire to escape from reality is often an expression of feelings of inadequacy. The well-adjusted person has learned how to cope and does not regard the normal activities of work, school, or social obligation as intolerable or dull. Individuals who look for "kicks" in risky or antisocial pursuits in order to escape from reality need to be exposed to positive, socially redeeming activities long before instant gratification becomes the sole purpose of their lives.

Leisure can give every individual the opportunity to practice appropriate skills and indulge in wholesome interests. Ideally, such experiences might guarantee a positive attitude toward all aspects of life so that no one falls prey to escapism, withdrawal, and self-destructiveness. However, this utopia does not exist. Achieving it would require a complete reorientation of personal attitude, government intervention, and other collective action.

Recuperation

According to its usual meaning, leisure is a time for self-renewal, refreshment, and recuperation. From such leisure the individual should emerge free of encumbrances, looking forward to new experiences and anticipating optimistic outcomes. People who have participated in rejuvenating activities experience a new lease on life. Instead of giving in to the doubts and frustrations that are part of the daily routine, they now hope for achievement and the possibility of satisfying endeavors. The best uses of leisure produce a sense of heightened energy, new outlook, and promise.

Some people choose high-risk leisure activities.

© Terry Wild Studio

Do you think that high-risk activities are appropriate ways of using leisure? For what reasons (other than the desire to escape) might people participate in high-risk activities? Would a person who is fully satisfied with his or her job and life ever choose this type of leisure activity?

WORK AND LEISURE

Leisure is sometimes defined as the antithesis, or direct opposite, of work. This understanding requires thoughtful analysis and explanation. There are significant relationships between leisure and work that underscore the significance of each. We will examine four paramount modes of looking at these relationships.

Work as Leisure

According to the view promulgated by John Neulinger, leisure can occur during work if the individual's attitude makes leisure out of work.[8] Naturally, no one would claim that all work is leisure, but some thinkers believe that the elements of refreshment, satisfaction, enjoyment, and ego involvement found in some work do not differ from those elements found in leisure; therefore, the two must be the same.

Some occupations are indeed so interesting and satisfying that the worker feels genuinely restored after carrying them out. Some types of work actually provide more enjoyment and fulfillment than certain leisure pursuits do. Indeed there are people who find their work a more effective means of escape from life's stresses than leisure. According to some social psychologists, many enterprises that are supposed to be work are, in effect, games. Simulated games are used to explore serious problems in industry, business, government, and other arenas. The deadliest business of all—war—is often referred to as a game.[9]

Work that rejuvenates is, without question, inestimably more valuable than assignments executed out of a sense of disagreeable necessity. It is also probably performed more effectively. Occupations that incorporate incentive and reward continuously encourage energetic efforts. However, it is futile to discuss the interchangeability of work and leisure. They are separate domains. Despite the fact that both can have identical features, they cannot be viewed as indistinguishable. Work is not leisure. Its obligatory nature negates the essence of leisure—relative freedom to come and go as one chooses.

Leisure as Work

The sameness of leisure and work may also be observed from the opposite view. Just as work may have many characteristics of leisure, so leisure can also take on the appearance of work. Many people bring the same approach to their free time as they do to their occupations. They cannot differentiate between free time and obligated time. They use leisure as something to be gotten over. Many participate for reasons other than enjoyment. For example, people work out at health clubs to maintain fitness, or they go bowling with the club because of group pressure.

Although it is quite normal for a person to approach work and leisure in much the same way—after all, it is the same personality—if the typical attitude toward work is applied to leisure, it negates many of the restorative and enjoyment aspects. One's attitude toward leisure has a great effect on the benefits it confers. If one cannot approach leisure with spontaneity and unrestrained anticipation of enjoyment, then a great deal of the value that leisure should have will be lost.

Work for Leisure

The third orientation sees work and leisure as completely separate. The purpose of work is to provide the financial resources for using leisure. Many workers, particularly those engaged in routine assignments (such as factory hands or laborers), think of their job as an unavoidable task, performed only to earn the money to be spent during leisure. When an individual does not find satisfaction in work, leisure may represent the ultimate in relief, comfort, pleasure, and hope of achievement. The duller the job, the greater the expectations.

It is unfortunate that work should be onerous and leisure looked on as the realization of aspirations. Not infrequently people will toil and stint all year in order to splurge on their annual vacation or go on a single glorious spending spree. People whose leisure base is so narrowly concentrated often face frustration when their expectations are not fulfilled. Leisure that must make up for the staleness of work is also likely to become an escape rather than a rejuvenating experience.

The same is true of many pensioners. Workers who are covered under retirement systems or who have saved enough throughout their work lives to underwrite their old age may look forward yearningly to the freedom of discretionary time, which will vindicate all their efforts. But all too often, they find that retirement does not live up to their expectations.

Leisure for Work

Another view distinguishes between leisure and work but considers the former a means for abetting the latter. The purpose of leisure is to permit recuperation so that they may perform the job more efficiently. They use leisure simply as refreshment so that their capacity to work is unimpaired. This approach is typical of workaholics, people whose commitment to and interest in their work is so intense that they would be at it constantly if human physiology did not demand a break. This attitude is just as narrow and short-sighted as that of the worker who hates his or her job and pins all hopes and dreams on leisure pursuit.

To evaluate leisure purely on the basis of its support of the job is really to make it part of work and to steal from it the freedom and spontaneity that are its hallmark. Although in some sense the best work has leisure qualities, work and leisure are not identical. It is a deprivation of life to require that leisure be justified as an instrument of work. Recognizing the separate domains of each and taking opportunities to actualize human potential can lead to achievement of the good life.

How would you categorize your perception of the relationship between work and leisure: work as leisure? leisure as work? work for leisure? leisure for work?

THE NATURE OF THE RECREATIONAL EXPERIENCE

Recreational experiences are those activities that are *voluntarily entered into for pleasure during leisure without being negative.* This emphasis on wholesomeness, on activity that is not detrimental to the individual or to society, is fundamental to the definition. The entire concept of recreation is based on the restoration of the individual to a state of well-being; there is no room in it for destructiveness, immorality, illegality, or personal deterioration. This section examines the basic characteristics of the recreational experience.

Choice

Almost all recreational activities are entered into freely. This means that the individual must be as autonomous as possible in selecting them. For the most part this is so, but there are exceptions that prove the rule. Sometimes social,

economic, or other pressures influence involvement in what should be a recreational activity. When the individual is compelled to participate, the activity in question is not recreational but an extension of obligation. The decisions as to what, where, when, and degree of participation should be up to the participant. Except in those rare instances where the individual is completely dependent on another, there is no necessity to seek permission, no obligation to belong to a particular group, and no concern about one's right to make a decision.

Certain qualifications, however, are built into the decision-making process. Among these are ability to perform; knowledge of one's options; the time available for participation; possible impediments such as lack of financial resources; supplies, materials, and equipment needed; conflicting demands for the use of the same space; and other variables that may affect one's choice. All of these factors can influence participation, but the underlying element remains the individual's own desire to engage or not as he or she sees fit. This is what is meant by the *voluntary* aspect of recreational activity. If the activity is forced or imposed, by any means whatsoever, it becomes something other than recreational.

Again, there are extenuating circumstances. When an individual is under some obligation but then comes to enjoy the activity intensely and gain benefit from it, it is not initially a recreational activity but it becomes one as the participant's attitude changes. An activity that starts out as distasteful or compulsive may with experience become so satisfying that it will be pursued voluntarily. Once the individual achieves enjoyment, obligation is no longer a factor. But people who are required to participate in an activity forgo one of the inherent values of a recreational experience—the spontaneity and change provided by freedom from the constraints of everyday affairs. In recreational activity, participants have the chance to learn, develop skills, enhance their sense of personal worth, and realize their potential.

Pleasure

People do not participate in recreational activity unless they expect to get enjoyment or satisfaction from the experience. In a word, fun is the primary motive. While it is true that individuals who are new to an activity may experience some initial frustration because of deficient knowledge, skill, or coordination, the intrinsic motivation of fun serves as a continuing stimulus. Novices usually accept the fact that they cannot expect a skilled performance in the beginning. But the anticipation of learning and achieving helps to sustain interest. Even the learning and skill development stages can be fun. The attempt itself is rewarding.

Fun is the motive for all recreational activities. However, not all recreational activities are fun for all people. Individuals have their acquired tastes, biases, likes, and dislikes, and what is recreational for one person may be boring drudgery to another. No one can account for individual taste. Thus, no matter how many falls a novice skier or ice skater may take, the fun of learning plus the prospect of even greater pleasure with greater proficiency keep the individual trying. The same may be said for any of the countless recreational forms. Attitude and anticipation are the twin energizers that encourage participation.

Performed During Leisure

All recreational activities are performed during leisure. Regardless of motives or emotional response, unless an activity is engaged in during free time it is not recreational. The root of recreational experience lies in the freedom of choice to do what one wishes, within certain limitations, to the extent that ability and interest permit. It is fundamentally a manifestation of individual freedom.

Although many activities may have qualities similar or even identical to recreational experience, they should not be confused with this wholesome leisure pursuit. In fact, many of the values generated in recreational activity may also be produced at work, in school, in church, or in numerous other settings where achievement, satisfaction, and enjoyment are integral to the activity. The clearest mark of separation between these experiences and recreational activity is the absolute need for the experience to be performed in leisure.

A Positive Act

Recreational activity, by definition, cannot be anything but worthwhile and socially acceptable. Nothing can take the place of acts that enhance the individual in some positive way. This may be in terms of skills learned, abilities sharpened, happiness enjoyed, self-realization, companionship found, or other helpful and socially beneficial experiences.

© Richard B. Levine

People pursue recreational experience even when the activity engenders initial frustration.

The word *recreation* comes from *re-create,* to create again, renew, refresh, or rebuild. It cannot denote activities of a destructive, pathologically debilitating, or purposely deteriorating nature. Renewal is a valuable standard for determining the worth of various activities. If participation in a given activity produces impaired judgment or results in a deliberate weakening or diminution in mind or body, that activity cannot be called recreational. Of course, many recreational activities have risks, but the object is not to injure oneself. Accidents happen and may cause injuries, but the primary purpose is never injurious.

Stealing a car for an "innocent joyride"; setting a forest fire on a dare; vandalizing a school or cemetery for a lark (or to practice the "art" of graffiti); tormenting and torturing animals for kicks; mugging and beating the elderly "to let off steam"; abusing drugs and other substances—these and other vicious, destructive, antisocial acts can never be condoned as recreational. It would be a perversion of the definition to include such negative behavioral manifestations. That is why referring to "the recreational use of drugs" is oxymoronic. It would be much more accurate to say "the leisure use of drugs."

How do leisure and recreational experience overlap as concepts? Can you have recreational activity without leisure? Leisure without recreational activity?

RECREATIONAL ACTIVITY AND SELF-FULFILLMENT

So far, these discussions have focused on the relationship between leisure and recreational activity and between work and leisure. To better understand these relationships, we need to see what roles leisure and recreational activity play in human development.

The recreational experience satisfies a basic human need. Every member of society is obliged to engage in some gainful employment and to discharge responsibilities toward family, community, and nation. These responsibilities continue more or less throughout life and influence the kind of life we lead and the kind of people we are. Recreational participation offers opportunities to offset these obligations

through activities that contribute to the creation of a well-rounded, balanced personality. So while the demands of occupation and social setting tend to restrict the kind of life one leads, through recreational activity the individual can develop complementary modes of behavior that help to develop a complete person.

The concept of completeness suggests that recreational activity normally succeeds when there is marked distinction between the activities of employment and those of leisure, when the two are different enough that the combination creates a balance. There is little research in this area, but it appears likely that the most beneficial kind of recreational activity for any person is based on individual interests, skills, and job duties.

There is a certain amount of logic in performing different kinds of activity during leisure from those performed on the job. Renewal and completeness are more likely if the change in activities is dramatic. For example, the sedentary person should engage in regular physical activities. The solitary person should engage in socially involving activities. The person who works indoors should take to the outdoors for renewal. This does not mean that a writer can't take up stamp collecting or a construction worker shouldn't join a hiking club. It simply suggests that individuals should seek out activities that will complement and round out their lives.

Human life, in common with all living organisms, is characterized by a regular, cyclic recurrence of elements, or the stroke-glide principle. Energy output and rest follow one another in successive swings, with a general tendency toward equilibrium, a swing from one extreme to the other, a completion of orbit. Recreational activity set in leisure offers opportunities for the free exploration and uninhibited participation in pursuits that can produce the whole person.

Individualism

Similarly, recreational activity contributes powerfully to the production of human uniqueness. Each person enters into recreational participation voluntarily. No one is forced to engage in one activity rather than another. We may be made to conform to custom in most societal situations, but within reason we reveal ourselves in the recreational forms that we choose. Unless those choices are freely made and express our real desires, a danger exists that mass activity forms may dominate.

Society actually does attempt to regulate the kinds, times, places, and circumstances in which recreational activity can be pursued. There is a place for organized recreational service, but it should not preclude the discovery by each person of those attractive, personally chosen interests through which individuality can best be explored.

Sense and Outlook

A profound and recurring human need is to seek the meaning of life. An awareness of vocation in employment is one way to derive a sense of life. Yet this consciousness is almost impossibly separated from intermittent withdrawal from labor as a necessary step in recovery and renewal. During leisure and with participation in recreational activities, there is time to think about the pattern of one's life and to evaluate one's objectives. Through such periods of withdrawal from the dictates and stresses of everyday transactions, one can stand off and gain some perspective on life and relationships.

Recreational activity makes possible a disentanglement from the preoccupations of daily existence. To gain an overall view of how the parts relate to the whole, we must be able to step back and take a broad, objective look at the total picture. Keeping one's nose to the grindstone can dull an individual. Those who run the risk of becoming warped by sticking to the narrow concerns of work can benefit the most by routine withdrawal from stultifying conditions into complementary forms of recreational activity. Learning to free oneself from the cares and responsibilities with which most people are generally preoccupied through participation in recreational pursuits is indispensable in gaining meaning and proportion in life.

Fun

A sense of fun is one indication of a carefree spirit. Fun is a difficult word to define, but it probably has two basic ingredients: First, the ability to recognize that which is inconsistent with the ordinary state of affairs, and second, the ability to delight in the unexpected or incongruous. Incongruity and spontaneity are parts of a sense of playfulness. This ability to feel pleasure in the fanciful is important because it exists in the human consciousness. Mentally and physically healthy people don't take everything seriously. The underlying motivation for all recreational experience is fun.

The Whole Person

Much of what we have said about the contribution of recreational activity to human satisfaction and fulfillment may be epitomized in the concept of the whole person. To be whole is to have the capacity for infinitely enhancing one's sphere of perception through intelligence and imagination. The liberated, reasoning human being does not simply receive an environment and conform to it; rather, he or she dreams about what might be and attempts to make the dream come true. This can happen in all phases of cultural activity, including work. However, it is particularly in recreation that the naturalness and limitlessness of the human factor may be evident.

The pressures of life often bind us to our jobs and to the responsibilities of family and citizenship. Recreational activity enables the individual, through imagination and disengagement, to surmount those obligations and renew his or her own uniqueness. Further, it provides a perspective not only on what one is but on the person one has the potential to become.

Imagine you're a 30-year-old executive in line for a nice promotion. It's Friday evening, you've put in a hard week, and you're looking forward to sleeping in tomorrow before going boating with your wife. Your boss stops by your office on his way out the door and tells you he's included you in a golf foursome tomorrow with himself, another supervisor, and the company's vice president. "Tee time's at 7:30 A.M. See you there," he says. Does that golf game fit our definition of recreational activity? Does the answer depend on whether you like golf? Would the answer be different if your boss had arranged an afternoon boating excursion instead of an early-morning golf game?

THE NEW BEHAVIORAL CONCEPT

Humans have always had to work in order to survive. Today, relatively few people have the economic freedom to enjoy total leisure, but in the future, leisure may be an accepted focus of existence. The means of production and its consequent output will not require human participation. The human factor in industrial and agricultural production may well become obsolete. Leisure may become the dominant concern of people's lives. Technology can produce a social and cultural situation that finally frees them from the time-consuming and in many instances wasteful decisions that can impinge on their quality of life. A gradual readjustment to this reality will be necessary.

Therefore, a clarification of leisure in culture and its meaning in terms of attitude and emotion is appropriate here. Just because the past 30 years have seen a gradual diminishment of leisure as hours of work have increased does not mean that the future is already decided. As Schor suggests, changes in government intervention, union involvement, professional associations, and other collectives' concerns, as well as changes in people's attitudes, are needed to realize the promise of free time that lies before us.[10]

Essential to the development of the new leisure ethic is the transformation of society by automation, cybernation, and miniaturization, so that all repetitive forms of human labor and much of what is now considered to be within the realm of human decision making will be performed by self-maintaining mechanical devices. They will gradually replace the human labor force until very few people are employed. A new social existence will see leisure, not vocation, as the focus of human affairs.

Even if we did not face this technological prospect, we would still need a social philosophy built around the concept that leisure is an undoubted good and a necessity in human life. Equating leisure with immorality produces the kind of guilt feelings that have haunted millions of people and stopped them from realizing quality living. The biblical injunction that "man does not live by bread alone" may be the conceptual basis for a new leisure ethic. Leisure as a social good brings its own reward and needs no other justification in human society. It will become the focus of existence rather than a peripheral and guilt-laden response to work. Of course, this will require total reeducation of the present population.

Where the economic market is not the controlling factor, people will have to make lives that depend on individual, inner-directed activities instead of external influences. There will have to be a radical redesign of teaching methodology and education. It is likely that in a nonmarket world the home will be the school, and a computer hooked up to a central storage bank may be the major teaching system. Learning and the interests, skills, and knowledge that will accrue from leisure activity may well become lifelong concerns. If the enjoyment of leisure is taught in the schools from the earliest possible time, and if leisure is looked upon as the objective of the good life, surely a new leisure ethic will come to fruition.

SELECTED REFERENCES

Dare, B. G., and W. Coe Welton. *Concepts of Leisure in Western Thought*. Dubuque, Ia.: Kendall/Hunt, 1987.

Graefe, A., and S. Parker, eds. *Recreation and Leisure: An Introductory Handbook*. State College, Pa.: Venture, 1987.

Ibrahim, H. *Leisure and Society*. Dubuque, Ia.: Brown, nc., 1991.

Ibrahim, H., and J. S. Shivers, eds. *Leisure: Emergence and Expansion*. Los Alamitos, Cal.: Hwong, 1979.

Kelly, J. R. *Leisure*. 2d ed. Englewood Cliffs, N.J.: Prentice Hall, 1990.

Kelly, J. R., and G. Godbey. *Sociology of Leisure*. State College, Pa.: Venture, 1992.

Quarrick, G. *Our Sweetest Hours*. Jefferson, N.D.: McFarland, 1989.

Chapter 7

COMMUNITY COORDINATION FOR LEISURE SERVICE

Objectives

After reading this chapter, the student will be able to do the following:

Discuss the need for government intervention
in the provision of leisure services.

■

Explain the association between human nature and social organization.

■

Describe social education.

■

Indicate the functions of governent.

■

Understand the need for community coordinating efforts.

■

Differentiate among means of coordination for recreational service.

Government is necessary to preserve the common good and protect constitutional guarantees against encroachment. There is much that government, at all levels, can and does do to carry out that mandate. However, there is little that government can do to eliminate disparities in economic level, education, or intellect. It has, of course, attempted to redistribute wealth through taxation, but this has come to be viewed as an extreme measure.

Government cannot mandate the leisure aspect of life, except in terms of creating national holidays. But there is at least one way government intervention fulfills people's needs and spends tax money equitably. The coordination of people, material, and financial resources into a smoothly ordered recreational service can do much to enhance the leisure of all.

Coordination is the ability to combine personal and material resources in such a way as to create an environment that will optimally serve the people's leisure. This means allocating money, personnel, and goods or services to produce greater opportunities for the recreational use of leisure, without undue duplication of effort or waste.

Diversity of interests, needs, philosophy, and programs within any community require determination of a common course so total recreational service can be offered. The process of community cooperation in the interests of all can be achieved only with coordination among all agencies concerned with the provision of recreational services. Human beings are social and political animals. They rely on interdependence to survive and create government to ensure social stability and security.

The solitary hunters of prehistory met death far more often than did those who banded together in family, clan, or tribal units. Mutual protection offered survival. As human society achieved a high degree of complexity, reliance on others increased proportionately. The basic factor that produces this interdependence in modern society is the complicated specialization of labor. This intricate division necessitates an involved and ramified social organization to coordinate the many functions on which society depends. An overview of the agents and agencies that meet our survival, educational, recreational, and occupational needs illustrates our mutual dependence and the organization required to assist the individual.

Indeed, it is the very complexity of modern existence that demands this type of government involvement. To cope effectively with its health, educational, recreational, economic, social, and ideological problems, society needs an understanding of human development, social interaction, and the function of government in these services.

COMMUNITY COORDINATION AND ORGANIZATION

Individual development is influenced not only by face-to-face contacts in family encounters and direct personal friendships, but also by membership and participation in classes, aggregates, and other groups. These inclusive social clusters, unlike the more personal relationships, are public concerns.

The community is judged on its production of citizens who are able to function competently and effectively in a competitive society. The caliber of citizen effectiveness depends almost entirely on the services, tangible and intangible, the community establishes for its self-preservation.

In this era of mass leisure, sufficient opportunity for recreational experiences to enhance individuals' lives is basic to the fabric of social relationships in a worthwhile community. Legislative considerations to the contrary, choices about how to render these developmental opportunities must be made locally.

COORDINATING COUNCILS

Recreational service is assumed to be a local responsibility and partially a function of government. In nearly every community of any size, there are organizations outside the public sector that also provide many opportunities for the attainment of recreational skills and the practice of leisure arts and interests. Their provisions are augmented and made more comprehensive in depth and scope when the community accepts its responsibility to establish a public recreational service department supported by taxes. Like other government functions, a tax-supported recreational program has qualities that can strengthen and enlarge upon the offerings of other agencies. However, all agencies, both public and private, play an important role in satisfactorily meeting the expressed needs and interests of the public.

One way to coordinate all sectors of the community is with some type of central council representing all the agencies with any interest in the provision of recreational services. Because the council is open to all, it offers a forum for interested professionals and laypeople alike to participate in community planning for recreational services. It allows open discussion and debate on how best to meet community needs. It can also serve as a clearinghouse for the exchange of ideas and the dissemination of information about current problems, crises, and conditions that demand immediate attention.

The purposes of the coordinating council are to promote community betterment through recreational services and to provide an exchange of ideas, experiences, problems, possible solutions, and cooperation through representatives of those agencies that make up the council. The coordinating council for recreational service may be defined as a primary policymaking body designed to promote civic betterment through planned community examination and positive action.

A coordinating council is brought into being by local ordinance. It is established as a

A council must strive for broad representation and inclusiveness.

legal arm of government, by voluntary association of social agencies interested in cooperative effort, as a result of citizen demand, or any combination of these factors. The council will probably encourage close cooperation and coordination of activities by member groups and will make plans for meeting and improving recreational services to meet community needs.

Recreational service coordinating councils have developed from the work of an individual or a small group who realized the need to establish a public recreational service system or improve an existing department. In some instances, the council arose because public officials wanted to institute a department. Some councils grew out of the voluntary cooperative endeavors of public and private agency officials. Others were established as one branch of a parent body whose interests cover all phases of community life and function.

Representation

Broad representation and inclusiveness must be the basic tenet of a council. A list of civic, service, social, commercial, religious, business, professional, fraternal, educational, and labor groups within the community should be made, and each of these organizations should be invited to supply a representative to the coordinating council. It may be that a hierarchy of councils within a large community—from the neighborhood, district, and regional councils to the local jurisdictional council covering the entire community—will send representatives. The total community should be represented. There is a place for every voice, and every interested party should be permitted to participate in the equitable solution of recreational problems confronting the community.

The public recreational service department acts with the authority of government, supported by tax moneys. It has the power to acquire the proper physical plant and properties and to develop these areas for optimum use by the public. It has the financial means to offer a stable organization, and since it was brought into being by local ordinance and state enabling legislation, its permanence is relatively assured. Its control ultimately rests with the people of the community, not with any group of individuals. It answers to all the people because it was established by their will.

Government is the instrument by which people obtain certain results that they require but cannot attain by themselves. An agency of government, in this case the recreational service department, acts for the people in supporting their needs and meeting the conditions that arise in the community. The objective of community recreational service cannot be completely realized unless the coordinating body truly represents all sectors of the community. It cannot be left to voluntary participation and accidental cooperation. The initiative must come from an agency that is chiefly concerned with organizing the entire community for recreational services.

To achieve optimal community recreational service, the public recreational system must coordinate its efforts with those of all other agencies that propose to offer recreational activities. Certain innovations may be more fruitfully developed under the auspices of private agencies. A sectarian, commercial, or voluntary agency may be better equipped than the public recreational service department to operate a particular activity.

Instead of attempting to offer the same activity and running the risk of an inferior performance as well as duplicating what is already being done more effectively, the public department will best serve community needs by encouraging, cooperating with, and stimulating special interest organizations to even greater efforts. It is unwise and unnecessary to compete with another community agency in that agency's special field. There are so many other recreational activities to be offered that any duplication can engender only bitter feelings, unwelcome comparisons, wasted time, drained financial resources, misused personnel efforts, and needlessly restricted programming. Of course, if the public agency can do a better job in providing certain services, it should compete.

To assist in the development of cooperation and coordinated action by community agencies, the council should disseminate policies throughout the community to alert all other recreational agencies and educate their operating officers to the idea of a centralized coordinating body. The council is established to gain cooperation from all community agencies. It encourages an environment of mutual trust and provides a common meeting ground where reciprocal commitments among agencies offering recreational opportunities can be fostered. The council must stimulate agency representatives to look beyond parochial limitations and adopt an attitude of community concern.

One function of the council is the continual examination and evaluation of recreational opportunities, problems, and ways to eliminate or improve inadequate or underdeveloped recreational services. Communitywide projects require the resources of all agencies. Of major concern today are the location and utilization of specialized physical resources such as recreational centers, golf courses, aquatic facilities, camps, and other extensive developments. These are especially important to private agencies catering almost exclusively to youth (as differentiated from public or private groups that may serve older adults and agencies that act as catalysts for the stimulation of recreational programs instead of actually operating programs).

Council Organization

To put together a council, the public recreational service department should start by inviting all community agencies with direct or implied interest in the provision of recreational services to send a representative to a meeting sponsored by the department. The public department should organize and steer the council because it is the primary agency concerned with total recreational efforts in the community. It should do some groundwork first by conducting an educational campaign explaining the need for a council.

The council must be wanted by the community and its agencies. This means that all prospective participants should feel that a council is necessary to accomplish total community recreational service. Since the chief purpose of the council will be to speed action and eliminate gaps in recreational service, its organization should be uncomplicated. Its functions and responsibilities must be precise, easily identified, and comprehensible to all. They should be developed in precouncil conferences with future participants. The lack of a clear definition of functions and responsibilities leads to misunderstandings and poor relationships among members of the council.

If the council is large, it may need a small steering committee to streamline the transaction of business. Every council needs several permanent committees, which will perform much of the groundwork. They are responsible for long-term functions, which often involve some of the most important problems confronting the community. Among the standing committees of the council are public relations, physical plant and resources, financial, programming, human resources, and legal. It is customary for the chair of the council to appoint committee members.

Good councils do not operate in a vacuum. Instead, they seek to enlist technical and professional people from many fields of endeavor to serve as resources. Intelligent, competent professional assistance is essential to smooth and efficient performance. Council members must be willing to commit adequate time to council work. The amount of time needed will be in direct proportion to the extent of activities carried on and the individual and agency commitments made to the council. Attendance at council meetings is a prime requisite of membership. At least one council meeting each month is prescribed for effective coordination of community activities.

The council will assign setting of the meeting agenda to a particular executive officer. If the council has a steering committee, responsibility will rest with it. However, exigencies and conditions will have a great deal to do with what the council discusses and resolves. Standing committees of a council play a large role in selecting and evaluating items that require the council's attention. The calendar of business for the year and the agenda for each council session require careful study and planning. The agenda for each regular council session should be planned at least one week ahead and distributed to all representative agencies for comments, suggestions, and additions. Such advance notice will ensure that members give thought to agenda items and allow them to discuss intelligently the various actions to be taken.

If the council is established by municipal executive order, the city may provide offices, supplies, and secretarial assistance. If the council is initiated by the public recreational service department, the department must furnish the needed space, facilities, and staff personnel. Because the council is advisory and acts as a clearinghouse and coordinating body, it needs no budget per se. Agency representatives are expected to be on salary and council participation becomes a regular part of their assigned functions. The constitution and bylaws spell out the specific functions for which the council was established. When the council is activated by executive order, the order is codified and becomes the basis for all council action. When the recreational service system implements the council, specific duties and functions are developed by the membership sitting in session.

Can a community run a successful recreational program without government involvement? Can you suggest an optimal combination of public and private agencies to provide leisure services? What are the pros and cons of a public agency providing subsidized programs already offered by private agencies? Is it justifiable for public recreational service agencies to offer programs in areas that are usually the domain of private agencies?

NEIGHBORHOOD ADVISORY COUNCILS

The recreational councils established in each neighborhood are usually organized by the public recreational service department. In some cases, interested neighborhood residents have generated enough enthusiasm to form their own councils to support the public program. In brief, the functions of the neighborhood recreational council are as follows:

1. Representing neighborhood interests within the greater scope of city- and communitywide planning for recreational services.
2. Coordinating existing activities and determining the need for additional facilities and services.

Community Action Makes a Difference

While the government has a responsibility to provide for the common good, it cannot necessarily tailor activities to meet the particular needs of each segment of the population. Often it takes community-minded individuals to identify what is needed at the local level and to organize and mobilize the municipal and civic organizations that can supplement general governmental services.

Poquonnock Bridge holds a unique place in the makeup of the town of Groton, Connecticut, and in the history of shipbuilding in the United States. What for centuries had been an expanse of farmland reaching along the shores of Long Island Sound was transformed into housing units during the massive shipbuilding efforts of World War II. Groton was home both to the U.S. submarine base and Electric Boat, a company that remains the foremost submarine production facility in the world. The temporary housing constructed during the war was planned somewhat haphazardly, without real concern for long-term habitation. The original intention was to tear down the housing at the end of the war. At the war's end, however, when production of submarines had slowed, many inhabitants remained in these modest homes.

Some of the homes were purchased and refurbished by residents, some were bought by real-estate managers, and others were neglected and abandoned. As years passed, the neighborhood experienced severe blight due to the homes' substandard construction, lack of attention by landlords, and transient population. In contrast to the problem housing, some of the neighborhood comprised a core of homeowners who remained, improved their properties, and encouraged their children to stay in the area (many of whom now rent or own their own homes).

Poquonnock Bridge is unique within the town: This neighborhood primarily contains single-family homes, yet it is economically and racially diverse in relationship to the rest of Groton, a Yankee town dating from the 1600s. Because of the racial diversity and the population density, Poquonnock Bridge qualified for block grants intended to improve conditions in the neighborhood. Federal and state moneys were used to refurbish homes but the area continued to suffer from many social maladies. It was evident that material improvements were not enough to change the neighborhood.

The Poquonnock Bridge Neighborhood Association was formed with the mission of creating a safe, drug-free environment in the neighborhood. The association's members sought to improve the appearance of the area, encouraging all neighbors to take an active role in the maintenance of their properties. They encouraged cooperative efforts among neighbors and with municipal and civic groups to accomplish the improvement. In the few years since its inception, the association has experienced many successful endeavors. A well-written, professional-looking newsletter informs all residents of upcoming community events, such as cleanup days, crime-watch programs, fund-raisers, and an annual block party.

The success of this organization is due in part to the close relationship the group has with the local police department, social service agencies, town planning and zoning officials, and the parks and recreational department. Programs have been developed by all these agencies to meet the specific needs of the resident populations. Police have added bicycle patrols to the area. The youth and family agency runs a neighborhood center providing parents and youth with opportunities to develop the skills necessary to positive living. Zoning officials have helped by removing junk cars and enforcing the laws pertinent to the safety and well-being of the residents. Furthermore, recreational programs in the neighborhood now serve those residents who cannot transport themselves or their children to other sites.

The association's newsletter and regularly scheduled monthly meetings have raised the awareness of both residents and local officials to the problems—and the potential—of the Poquonnock Bridge neighborhood.

How would you, as parks and recreation director, justify providing special recreational programs for a specific neighborhood?

As program director, what types of programs could you develop to bring residents from different neighborhoods together?

What, if any, are the negative aspects of neighborhood based municipal services?

3. Establishing and consolidating social relationships within the local neighborhood. Putting people into contact with one another where such contact did not previously exist.

4. Making an inventory of neighborhood resources in terms of physical properties owned by city, school, quasi-public, and private agencies. Compiling a list of the various recreational facilities that might contribute to the total neighborhood program.

5. Providing information about the public recreational agency to everyone in the neighborhood to gain popular financial support for making better recreational services available to the neighborhood. Educating the public to the need for professional personnel and high standards of competency.

6. Assisting the public department in planning recreational activities as well as requesting certain facilities or equipment for specific placement within the neighborhood.

7. Supporting referendum campaigns designed to raise capital for buildings, land acquisition, and special equipment for the particular neighborhood.

8. Securing volunteers to supplement professionals.

9. Advising the public department on the neighborhood customs, opinions, and demographics.

10. Sponsoring special ethnic events, which can be included in citywide recreational planning.

11. Sending a representative to sit on a district coordinating council in order to affect community or municipal decisions affecting the neighborhood or influence community attitudes toward neighborhood needs.

12. Supplementing public funds with private donations for activities, equipment, or facilities to be used in the neighborhood.

Neighborhood advisory councils are one way to plan for and facilitate social growth and development. A neighborhood advisory council will involve people in efforts that enhance their own enjoyment and let them feel like part of a significant undertaking. It offers residents a chance to help shape the course of recreational activities within their neighborhood. It enlists the interest and support of citizens at the grassroots level and educates them about the value of public recreational service. The ultimate goals of neighborhood planning and cooperation are (1) to serve as the medium by which local residents can articulate their recreational needs, interests, and problems and (2) to provide the focal point from which coordination will emerge among any and all agencies having responsibility for recreational service.

Neighborhood recreational councils, especially in large metropolitan areas, are the recipients of much attention from community coordinators. Such groups are particularly fit to perform the typical activities of study, planning, enlistment of assistance, support, and awareness. Neighborhood councils are concerned with attempting to satisfy the needs of local residents. In the largest urban centers, they are essential to facilitate total community planning of recreational services. Neighborhood councils can never replace centralized coordinating bodies, but they most assuredly render such bodies more effective.

Neighborhood councils offer citizens the opportunity to shape recreational programs in their neighborhoods.

Does any organization at your institution, such as a College Activity Board, serve in the same capacity as a neighborhood advisory council? Does the group carry out the 12 functions discussed on pages 111-113? If you were part of the group, what issue would you want at the top of the agenda? How do you see the group offering students "a chance to participate in shaping the course of recreational activity" within the campus setting? Consider becoming involved in this group.

COORDINATION THROUGH OTHER EFFORTS

The range of agencies in the modern community having communitywide interest is so varied that they often duplicate work and waste time and money. Because all these organizations are autonomous and tend to act independently of one another, there is a great deal of overlapping, parallelism, and omissions in community recreational service.

But agencies that have similar interests and concerns do not have to be in conflict with one another. Infringements on agency prerogatives and interference in functions can be largely avoided by coordinated planning. Coordinated effort can be realized if agencies can agree on community objectives. Procedures found effective in coordinating agency activities include the following:

- a policy of coordination,
- informal meetings,
- conferences, institutes, and workshops
- contracts,
- an employed coordinator,

- a shared executive, and
- interlocking board memberships.

Policy of Coordination

A basic policy can be established emphatically stating that the agency has a fundamental responsibility for coordinated action with other socially oriented organizations within the community. But policy cannot merely be announced by an executive and left for subordinates to enact. The policy of coordination must be made the responsibility of every worker. Each employee of the agency requires preservice orientation concerning pertinent philosophy and guides to implement it. If new workers are directed to coordinate with members of other community agencies in order to achieve specific communitywide goals, coordination will probably become part their job.

Executive decision does not ensure that policies will be carried out. The executive's decision to coordinate efforts with other agencies is only a starting point. From the time the decision is made, the concept of cooperative action must permeate the entire organization. Every employee must be imbued with the idea that cooperation and mutual planning are vital to agency success. Unless front-line employees regard coordination as essential to carrying out their functions, policy statements by the executive mean little.

Informal Meetings

Widespread publicity concerning recreational planning in the community is helpful in arranging meetings. Notices should be sent to every interested agency and private citizen requesting their attendance at a specified time, place, and date. The location of the meeting should be as central as possible. A luncheon meeting is the simplest device for providing and exchanging information about recreational services within the community. At the meeting, coordinated plans can be drawn up and disseminated. Offering a program dedicated to cooperative action in an informal and highly social setting enhances the possibility of success.

Meetings are arranged through the staffs of all agencies that wish to be represented as well as those agencies confronted by problems of mutual concern. It is wise to hold them on a routine schedule, much like the luncheon meetings of social, civic, or fraternal associations. Instead of having a guest speaker or lecturer as the featured program, during the coordinating meeting the members discuss recreational plans, schedules of activities, mutual problems, conflicts that arise, and any other situations that appear to be hindering coordinated effort.

The meeting form of coordinated activity does not in itself secure coordination. As usual whenever close relationships are needed for the production of any service, personality factors play a significant part. Without interpersonal goodwill, most coordinating efforts will not be successful. Mutual feelings of cooperation and good official relations tend to grow out of informal social occasions, personal friendship, and continual joint planning. Any cooperative enterprise that brings together the representatives of agencies on various levels to study responsibilities of mutual concern can be useful, if it strengthens the bonds of goodwill between the representatives and provides for an exchange of information about what each person is doing and can do in achieving the common good.

Conferences, Institutes, and Workshops

A more formal procedure for coordinated action is the periodically scheduled conference, institute, or workshop. The duration of any formal sessions will depend on the size of the community involved and the number of agencies concerned with recreational problems.

The easiest method of the three is the frequent exchange of information through conferences for representatives of concerned agencies. The conferences may last one to three days, although a shorter time period may be of even more value if the conferences are arranged at closer intervals. They may even become a routine device, with agencies hosting a meeting once a month.

Institutes and workshops, by their very nature, are scheduled less frequently than conferences, although they too may become regular, routinely attended functions. Institutes are intensive sessions in which a great many problems and possible solutions are discussed and analyzed over a stipulated period of time, anywhere from three days to two weeks. Because of the length of the institute and the concepts to be scrutinized, complicated and detailed preparation is necessary to ensure its success. Usually specialists are brought in, either from the community or from outside sources. Special lectures, publications, program resources, and pertinent data that have been painstakingly collected are offered for the participants' enlightenment. These sessions are intended to produce new involvement and a rededication to the precepts of coordinated effort. The success or failure of an institute is reflected not only in attendance but in the outcomes and problem resolution.

Workshops are intensive practical sessions lasting not more than three days. A series of planned demonstrations and talks by specialists and outstanding practitioners can show dramatically how tasks can be accomplished. In planning the workshop, the managers should select the areas and instructional methods that will contribute most to the de-velopment of communitywide coordination. The topics offered and the techniques used to handle them should be designed to stimulate the largest number of participants to want to do the best possible job. Since there will probably be laypeople in the audience, subjects and techniques suited to their levels of experience and skill should be included. An effort should be made to motivate them to get involved.

Contracts

Two or more agencies may seek to solve common problems by mutual agreement or contractual obligation. A contract results in a more restrictive type of enterprise; only those activities stipulated will be acted upon. The danger is that unmotivated individuals may seek ways to restrict joint projects by adhering to the letter of the contract. However, the contractual form of coordinated undertaking may be a good

Workshops are intensive and practical.

way to start a working relationship with another agency. Such a contract can lead to closer agreements and ultimately produce a permissive climate where harmonious working relationships can flourish. Wherever possible and by whatever ethical methods are feasible, the method of coordination is justified by the end product.

Employed Coordinator

Two or more agencies may jointly employ an individual to work at the supervisory level and perform only those duties that concern coordination. The coordinator is free of all managerial functions and is directly responsible to the executives of the agencies in question. He or she has access to all personnel records, employees, reports, facilities, equipment, program plans, and other operational factors. The coordinator is, in effect, an assistant executive for each agency, and authority is granted depending on the situation. It is the coordinator's duty to keep several units in constant connection and concurrence with each other.

Specifically, the coordinator's immediate functions would comprise the following:

1. Interpretation of the role of each agency in the overall plan of community recreational service

2. Interpretation of the philosophical orientation of each agency to all other agencies in terms of community recreational service

3. Investigation of community recreational needs and problems that could be solved by coordinated action by several agencies

4. Recommendation of cooperative endeavors by which each agency would complement another agency's efforts

5. Arrangement of conferences, meetings, institutes, and workshops to resolve mutual problems, conflicts, and unfamiliarity

6. Development of joint policies, rules, regulations, and procedures that would result in the presentation of a coordinated and comprehensive program of recreational services for the community

The idea of employing a coordinator who would be free of executive functions suggests that coordination deals with every facet of agency operation, not just policymaking. This form generally commends itself to large urban centers where complex, constant relations with a variety of agencies require a person of high intelligence, tact, and ingenuity.

Shared Executive

Two or more agencies may employ an administrator who serves, say, as a director or an assistant executive of some phase of a school system, as the superintendent of recreational services in a municipal recreational department, and as director of the park department. The executive receives one-third salary from each agency and reports to the superintendent of schools and to the mayor or other managing authority in the municipal system.

This plan may work well in small communities or in sparsely populated rural regions that cannot afford to employ a highly paid executive. When several agencies combine to hire one executive, each agency provides only a fraction of the overall salary.

There are serious drawbacks to having an executive employed by two or more autonomous agencies. The complex and sensitive relationships of the position are almost overwhelming in magnitude, and it is unlikely that one person will be able to assume responsibility for two or more full-time jobs and give only half or one-third time to each. Few people have the expertise to administer two or three separate agencies, each calling for a specialist in the position.

The administrator may become so entangled in the intricacies of managing and directing more than one public system that he or she cannot fulfill obligations to any. Not having the time to become familiar with all facets of each agency, the administrator may not be prepared to handle the intimate details of operating procedures to effect coordination. The employee may fall back on stating policy lines, which does not ensure actual cooperative and coordinated practice.

Nevertheless, in communities where two different systems (for example, school and recreational services) share an administrator, the employee can integrate the curriculum with the teaching of leisure arts and skills and the municipal department's offerings with educational subject matter. Each aspect reinforces the other. This form of coordination may give small communities the same positive results as a large metropolitan center can reap by employing a nonexecutive coordinator. The doubled (or tripled) responsibility makes the job much more difficult to perform effectively, but the right coordinator *might* be able to do it.

Interlocking Board Memberships

Where policy or advisory boards or councils are established for a variety of agencies with the recreational service function, joint or interlocking memberships are an excellent means of overhead coordination. In this plan, one or more individuals, adroitly selected for broad points of view and genuine interest, are asked to serve on several separate though related boards—for example, the recreational service board, the park board, the school board, and the library board.

If the person has both the time and the inclination, he or she will be in the best situation to observe and comment on the needs of the various agencies in question, to supply information about each agency, and to sympathize with the problems and needs of each. A board member with voting rights is in a strategic position to call attention to duplication of services, glaring examples of uncoordination, and poor or faulty relationships between personnel, as well as to focus public scrutiny and professional study on such conditions in an attempt to correct them.

Exchange of Board Members

Like the interlocking membership plan of coordination, the exchange plan is an attempt to solve agency difficulties by inviting members of one board to be voting members of other boards whose agencies are directly concerned with the provision of recreational service in the community. Except where board members are publicly elected to serve, any board may request (by invitation and appointment) that an individual already serving as a member of one agency's board participate on another agency's board. When membership is by public election, the invitee may still serve in an *ex officio* capacity. A member of the school board may be asked to serve on the recreational service advisory board; a member of the recreational service board may be requested to serve on the school board.

In each case, these board members bring to the respective boards an understanding of the

What coordinating activities would be most effective for a small town? For a large city? If a group of agencies is interested in coordinating its efforts to provide community recreational service, what questions should it ask to help determine how best to work together for the good of the community? Do the questions differ with the size of the community? Is it possible for public and private agencies to work together in a cooperative organization?

functions of the system with which they are familiar. In turn, they learn about the departments with which they have less experience. When these people broaden their knowledge, they will more clearly recognize problem areas that confront the agencies and seek to establish a harmonious atmosphere.

COORDINATION AND COOPERATION

Coordination can exist only where the parties want to cooperate. Efforts to organize the community and its various agencies of recreational service must culminate in the building and maintenance of goodwill with all the operating agencies and associations. It is easy to criticize, analyze, and recommend solutions. But each autonomous agency must act in a manner consistent with its frame of reference and is ultimately responsible for its own actions. Working solutions may be derived through mediation, consolidation, and education, but in the final analysis, the agency's decision to coordinate systematically with other community-based groups is its own and must be respected.

SELECTED REFERENCES

Benest, F., et al. *Organizing Leisure and Human Services.* Dubuque, Ia.: Kendall/Hunt, 1984.

Brager, G. A., et al. *Community Organizing.* 2d ed. New York: Columbia University Press, 1987.

Crimando, W., and T. F. Riggar. *Utilizing Community Resources: An Overview of Human Resources.* Orlando, Fla.: P. M. Deutsch Press, 1992.

Graham, P. J., and L. R. Klar, Jr. *Planning and Delivering Leisure Services.* Dubuque, Ia.: Brown, 1979.

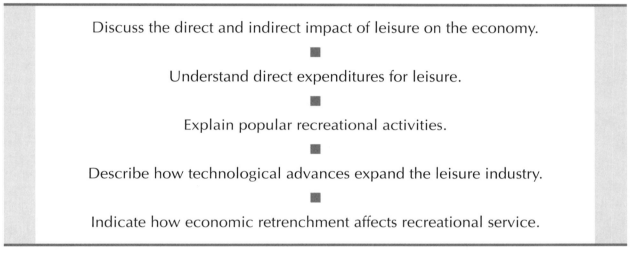

Chapter 8

THE ECONOMICS OF LEISURE

Objectives

After reading this chapter, the student will be able to do the following:

Discuss the direct and indirect impact of leisure on the economy.

■

Understand direct expenditures for leisure.

■

Explain popular recreational activities.

■

Describe how technological advances expand the leisure industry.

■

Indicate how economic retrenchment affects recreational service.

What is the good life? It may mean anything that is personally satisfying or brings happiness to the individual. Although it is said that the best things in life are free, more and more individuals realize that it takes money, and lots of it, to buy the products and services that enrich a person's life.

Essentially, the leisure industry reaches into every aspect of living. Leisure considerations may influence how we travel and where, the clothes we put on, the hairstyles we wear, the chairs we sit in, the cars we drive, and a host of other factors ranging from the mundane to the exotic. Spending on leisure seems to be growing exponentially. Even in times of economic recession or depression, leisure expenditure by individuals increases. Economically, leisure has assumed a significance that should give us pause. Billions for self-serving experi-

ences, but not one cent in taxes to enhance anyone else's life.

America's mass preoccupation with leisure activity is reflected in the vast amounts of leisure-related goods and services that are produced and sold each year. We spent an estimated $350 billion directly on leisure in 1995; if indirect, or spillover, amounts were included, total recreational expenditures might almost equal the gross domestic product. This may sound like a wild exaggeration—but not if we think in terms of all moneys being spent, in a sense, for enjoyment, to achieve the good life.

Before we examine the direct expenditures made in pursuit of leisure and recreational activities, let us first consider some of the indirect ways leisure permeates the economy and affects supply and demand.

119

INDIRECT EXPENDITURES ON LEISURE

Many products that have nothing to do with recreational activities per se are nevertheless related because they contribute to the good life. Vacuum cleaners, refrigerators, washing machines, fuel to operate vehicles and to heat and light homes, frozen foods, washable and no-iron fabrics, cosmetics and drugs, easy chairs, automatic garage-door openers—all these products (and many, many more) contribute in some way to eliminating time-consuming chores or making life more comfortable and satisfying. In fact, under the "pursuit of happiness" clause of the Declaration of Independence, we might include just about everything as being related to leisure or recreational activity.

The focus on recreational living may be seen everywhere. More recreational facilities and spaces are being constructed throughout the nation. There are hundreds of commercial amusement parks and theme parks like Disneyland and Busch Gardens, and many more are being built. So successful has the Disney Corporation been that it now franchises the Disneyland concept. A Disneyland opened in Tokyo in 1983 and another in Paris in 1991. Thousands of smaller-scale amusement places have been constructed along main highways or near metropolitan areas since 1945. Attendance is in the millions, and people spend huge sums at these places.

Industrial Development and Leisure Expenditure

Some developments have been concerned with historic, scientific, aesthetic, or other stimulating aspects of local, national, or international flavor. The construction of art and science museums, zoological gardens, wildlife and game parks, historic restoration—such as the renovation of Boston's Faneuil Hall and the adjacent harbor area and the reconstruction of Baltimore's harbor district—are examples of this kind of development. There has also been a tremendous upsurge in the construction of civic centers, auditoriums, stadiums, performing arts complexes and the like. Hundreds of millions of dollars are spent annually, by both builders and those who seek diversion by attending performances or exhibitions at these places.

Despite recessions, inflation, and other economic problems, Americans continue to spend vast amounts of money on leisure activities. Governmental austerity programs and high unemployment have not deterred us.

Among the industries indirectly associated with leisure are the automobile, construction, petroleum, metal, glass, rubber, forest products, electronic, publishing, alcohol, tobacco, and chemical manufacturers. They are actually affected by leisure spending in both direct and indirect ways. For example, most people buy cars primarily for transportation and secondarily for leisure use. But even when gasoline prices are very high, people still use their cars for recreational purposes. If only 25 percent of auto use were for recreational purposes, it would add a significant sum to the amount of money expended during leisure. However, other expenditures must also be included in such a calculation, because automobile production uses metals, chemicals, lubricants, plastics, glass, rubber, electrical systems, cloth, and

Disney Corporation builds many amusement parks, and millions attend.

© W. Lynn Seldon

other items. All of these other industries have a ripple effect on the amount spent on recreational investment.

All of these industries are involved in the production of goods that are used directly for recreational activities—fishing gear, hunting equipment, playground apparatus, radio and TV receivers, tape cassettes and records, craft supplies, and so on. With some industries, however, the involvement is secondary. For example, the highway construction business, with its spinoff industries (asphalt, concrete, steel, chemicals), has attained economic power because of transportation demands—including recreational travel.

Virtually every industry and service organization that contributes to the gross domestic product also contributes, in some way, to leisure expenditures. Chemicals, for example, find their way into paint, cars, clothing, recreational equipment, highways, fuels, illumination. So although the chemical industry is not normally thought of as being affiliated with leisure, nevertheless it supplies products that are directly or indirectly used for leisure and recreational activities.

Finally, there are negative nonrecreational activities that account for economic trade in the hundreds of billions of dollars. Illicit, antisocial activities like drug selling, prostitution, pornography, illegal gambling, and joyriding (stealing vehicles for unauthorized riding) have become a significant economic factor.

Predicast Forecasts, a source of statistical information concerning manufactured products for each industry in the United States, reports the number of units of every item produced and sold and issues predictions of industrial expansion or contraction. For some industries, forecasts are made to the year 2005. According to Predicast's latest report, personal recreational expenditures by American consumers in 1995 reached $350 billion, while government expenditures for recreational purposes were calculated at $70 billion. By 2005, based on an estimated annual increase of 4.1 percent, personal expenditures for all forms of recreational activities are expected to reach $500 billion.

These are incredible sums of money to spend directly on recreational goods and services, but they are quite reliable estimates, as past records show. Furthermore, we can expect the growth in population to increase the demand for products old and new, and even with minimal inflation there is bound to be an increasing cost for the delivery of recreational goods and services.

Economic Circulation or Percolation

Industries involved in the production of products for recreational use have a multiple impact on the entire economy. The ripple effect is sometimes very widely felt. To illustrate, we can track the purchase of a motorized sled in a given community. In the first (primary) cycle, the money the customer pays the retailer permits repayment on a bank loan that went to finance the original purchase from a wholesaler or from the manufacturer. This money is then used to refinance the entire operation. In the secondary cycle, the salesperson in the retail store earns a salary or commission on the sale, which in turn permits him or her to pay the rent or reduce the mortgage and pay for food, clothing, and fuel; this generates additional momentum as bills are paid, balances are accounted for, and the local economy is stimulated.

The manufactured goods used for various recreational activities have an impact far beyond their costs for many facets of the economy. More money was spent for recreational activities in 1995 than for national defense. Recreational outlay also exceeds the total outlay for new home construction and is far more than the combined incomes of all American farmers. Recreational spending is increased by longer vacation periods, longer weekends, shorter workweeks (about 2,000 companies have adopted a four-day week), and earlier retirement programs—although this last may not remain a factor if attempts to raise the retirement age are successful.

Perhaps the most important element in increased leisure spending is the swift rise in personal income. Even though inflation has increased too, the amount of discretionary income has still grown. This means that more

Can you think of an industry that lacks some sort of economic link with leisure or recreational activity? Is the widespread influence of leisure activities on the economy a modern development or an impact leisure has had on society throughout history?

people are spending more money for recreational experiences, and this pushes leisure-related industries and services into one of the areas of most rapid economic expansion.

DIRECT EXPENDITURES ON LEISURE

Americans spend more than $350 billion for recreational equipment, admissions to sporting events, cultural programs, and other commercial leisure activities. Total purchases of recreational equipment have increased more than 50 percent in the past five years. Outdoor recreational activity is one reason for the great boom in leisure spending. More and more people want to return to nature, and they are doing it by purchasing more camping equipment, recreational vehicles, boats, and aquatic sports equipment.

A number of leading indicators suggest that spending for recreational activities and leisure experiences will continue to climb in the foreseeable future. It must be remembered that such reporting is partial; that is, not every recreational activity or expenditure for leisure is measured and noted. Gaps in information for a variety of common recreational expenditures can only be guessed at. If the illegal and questionable forms of leisure activity were included in the total, the 1995 gross expenditure would be hundreds of billions of dollars higher.

One example is tobacco and tobacco products. Aside from the federal subsidy tobacco farmers are granted each year, some $20 billion was spent in 1995 for tobacco use. Whether or not smoking or chewing tobacco is a recreational activity, it is a leisure experience that is indulged in by many, especially because of the addictive nature of nicotine. Thus, the nation's tobacco consumption habits must also figure in the total leisure expenditures.

Any attempt to appraise the total participation in recreational and leisure activities in the United States is subject to widespread error. Since it is impossible to survey everybody, the best estimate is only a sample, which is bound to include some inaccurate interpretations. However, a variety of studies have provided interesting information about the leisure habits and behavior of Americans. The ubiquitous shopping malls are primary and secondary leisure and recreational facilities.

People use them for relaxed and protected walking, to browse around the various shops, or for recreational opportunities that are located to appeal to both spur-of-the-moment patrons and deliberate selectors. Movies, bowling alleys, billiard parlors, and other primary recreational facilities are there because both city and suburban dwellers are coming to the malls in greater numbers. Although higher gasoline prices may cut some attendance, these malls offer recreational opportunities to large numbers of people.

Home recreational and leisure involvement may be estimated by the amount of goods and services purchased. For this there are accurate reporting methods. Such studies must include the sales of both casual apparel and clothing specifically designed for recreational use, such as gym shoes, jogging outfits, swimsuits, tennis shorts, and ski jackets. There is of course no way to determine when ordinary clothes are put to recreational use. The new suit or dress for the office may also serve as the outfit of choice for dining out or attending a concert performance.

The costs of home barbecues, tennis courts, swimming pools, gardens, and the like can only be estimated in terms of popular appeal. Furthermore, it's a matter of opinion whether such tasks as mowing the lawn, pruning shrubbery, and chopping firewood are recreational activities. And there too, costs must be guessed at. Many women frequent beauty salons for elegant coiffures, but some go for the social experience.

If you were assigned to collect data on direct expenditures for leisure or recreational activity on your campus, how would you categorize that spending? Would you include cigarette purchases? Does the purchase of a hobby item always constitute a leisure expenditure? Would you count the expense of growing or canning fruits and vegetables for home consumption in your leisure expense study? Would you count the purchase of pornography? Leisurely window shoppers may not purchase anything immediately, but eventually they may spend money on items suggested by their perusals: Does this delayed buying constitute a form of leisure spending? How would you categorize a computer purchased for business but used occasionally for playing computer games?

POPULAR RECREATIONAL ACTIVITIES

A number of studies have developed lists to identify the most popular recreational forms. These lists probably suffer from sampling errors and inaccurate reporting, but certain common denominators do emerge that enable us to make a few generalizations about the kinds of leisure pursuits and recreational opportunities Americans prefer.

Americans like activities that are easily accessible, relatively inexpensive, easy to perform, and predominantly self-directed. Home-based activities tend to be among the most popular. Watching TV, listening to music, reading, cooking, puttering around, and home hobbies are high on the list. More elaborate activity forms that require a greater financial outlay may still be home-based. Electronic games, table games (cards, checkers, chess), table tennis, darts, workshops, do-it-yourself auto repair, and the like are gaining in popularity.

Away from home, people still gravitate toward activities that are relatively inexpensive, are easy to perform, and require little or no organization. Swimming, walking, birding, bicycling, and similar activities are among the many recreational experiences that are simple and free.

To examine leisure and recreational activities more specifically, we will use the following classifications: (1) athletics and participation sports; (2) spectator sports; (3) motor-oriented activities; (4) travel and tourism; (5) high-risk activities; (6) nature-oriented activities; (7) the arts; (8) crafts; (9) cultural activities; (10) publications; (11) technological activities; and (12) miscellaneous hobbies.

Athletics and Participation Sports

In numbers of participants, athletics and sports far surpass all other forms of recreational activities, with swimming, running, and walking at the top of the list. Involvement in physical activity usually begins in childhood and continues for many people throughout life, although participation may begin to fall off after they leave school if the activity is not readily accessible.

The 19 most popular physical recreational activities are shown in table 8.1.[1] The increasing popularity of certain athletic activities is whetted by television, especially during the Olympic Games and world competitions. Enthusiasm is also generated by the publicity individual stars receive when they go professional.

Participation in all forms of athletic activities is a major contributor to the American economy. Spurred on by athletic equipment manufacturers, promotion and advertising agencies, the mass media, and local newspaper ads paid for by retail outlets, the expenditure for all kinds of equipment used in athletics represents an outlay of billions of dollars. One piece of equipment, in-line skates, is a case in point. Used originally by off-season hockey players, they have gained many adherents despite their expense. When these equipment costs are added to the costs for the provision of athletic fields, custodians, coaches, trainers, and referees, the amounts are staggering.

Spectator Sports

Watching others compete in individual, dual, and team sports and games seems to be one of the most compelling leisure pursuits in the United States. Paid admissions to professional athletic events reached more than $4.1 billion in 1992. Even during the 1995 baseball strike, attendance totaled 50.4 million. Perhaps that explains the multimillion-dollar contracts awarded to star players in baseball, football, basketball, hockey, and tennis. Professional golfers, boxers, ice skaters, skiers, race-car drivers, and jockeys also command impressive payoffs as long as they win (although heavyweight fighter Mike Tyson earned more than $10 million in his title-losing bout).

All of the professional sports leagues have expanded the number of teams playing. If the owners feel that their teams are not being supported by the community, they are quick to switch to other cities, which sweeten any deal by offering to build stadiums at public expense. Presumably the taxes expected from such real estate development and box-office trade are seen as an economic asset by the jurisdiction involved.

No small contribution to the economic growth of professional spectator sports has come from the mass media, particularly television. The major networks have millions of dollars tied up in sports broadcasting. This is evident when the amount of time given to such events is calculated

Table 8.1 Most Popular Physical Recreational Activities in the United States, 1995	
ACTIVITY	PARTICIPANTS
1. Exercise and walking	95 million
2. Swimming	75 million
3. Fishing (freshwater)	65 million
4. Bicycling	55 million
5. Camping	54 million
6. Hiking	50 million
7. Basketball	50 million
8. Bowling	45 million
9. Exercise with equipment	40 million
10. Golf	40 million
11. Aerobics	39 million
12. Sledding	35 million
13. Hunting	35 million
14. Softball	34 million
15. Ice skating	30 million
16. Canoeing and kayaking	28 million
17. Horseback riding	26 million
18. Sailing	19 million
19. Skiing	12 million

in terms of coverage and money spent for exclusive rights. Every TV station covers some aspects of sports every single day and evening. During spectacular events such as the Olympic Games or world championships, stations broadcast many hours of coverage each day that the event continues. Newspapers and magazines devoted to professional and amateur athletics also contribute to this avalanche of words and pictures. All kinds of physical games have become economically important because the mass media, with television leading the way, keep insinuating athletics into the American consciousness.

Live attendance at even the biggest sporting events, such as the Indianapolis 500 or the college bowl games, cannot compare with the vast audiences that watch these events on TV. Eighty million viewers watched a recent professional football game, while world championship events draw hundreds of millions of viewers.

Motor-Oriented Activities

The American love affair with the automobile began with the first production car and persists today. While it is difficult to separate the recreational use of driving from transportation uses, it is clear that Americans think of cars primarily as recreational vehicles. And an entirely new industry has developed to keep pace with the leisure use of motorcycles, motor bicycles, mopeds, and motor scooters. Dune buggies, campers, motor homes, all-terrain vehicles, airplanes, motorboats, snowmobiles, and motor surfers are some of the motor-driven vehicles used for recreational purposes. The RV market is in excess of $5 billion.

There was a drop in the manufacture and sale of motor homes, travel trailers, and truck campers during the first oil crisis in 1973 and to some extent in 1990, with some small setback for the market as a consequence of increas-

Millions of fans make spectator sports popular recreational activities.

ing fuel prices. But these vehicles continue to be sold in increasing numbers.

General aviation is a rapidly expanding industry. More than a million people are flying in rented, leased, or personally owned airplanes. This activity was quite inexpensive until the fuel problem raised the price of flying along with everything else. But this has not deterred those who look to flying as a major recreational interest. Flying clubs organized and sponsored by public recreational service departments spread the costs of lessons and use of aircraft among many people. Some flying schools offer the first lesson free on the assumption that after only one try the customer will be hooked on flying. The general aviation industry has great potential, particularly as more people fly commercially.

Travel and Tourism

One of the major recreational pursuits of Americans is traveling and tourism. Expenditures for activities directly related to tourism, including overnight accommodations, eating, transportation, souvenirs, luggage, clothing, and similar items, probably accounted for more than $100 billion in 1995. Whether in the form of weekend, vacation, holiday, short excursion, or overnight trips, the travel industry reaches into almost every segment of the American economy. The car-rental business generates $14 billion annually.[2] Travel and tourist agencies and the major carriers—airlines, steamships, trains, and buses—are highly competitive and attempt to attract customers with public relations campaigns, more services, package deals, fringe benefits, or simple snob appeal.

Lodging. The hotel/motel business goes hand in hand with tourism and travel. Motels are no longer just places for motorists traveling to some distant point to stay for the night. Today they are comprehensive resorts that have become the destination of preference. They have become purveyors of sports, spectator events, variety shows, square-dancing exhibitions, stamp-collecting bourses, art exhibits, conventions, and the like. It is not unusual for people to leave home and travel to another state to spend a weekend at a motel or hotel.

Dining Places. Associated with travel and tourism is the growth in restaurants and fast-food businesses, which have literally transformed the countryside. Neon lights glittering with the names of different food places are the first sight that greets drivers in many towns. Restaurants in airports, museums, art galleries, and railroad and bus stations draw travelers as never before. In fact, eating out is one leisure activity that has created a growth industry. Food chains, famous restaurants in distant cities, and local restaurants are all beneficiaries of the American taste for good meals.

Tourist Destinations. Much, if not all, of recreational travel is tourism. Americans (and their foreign counterparts) are spending enormous amounts of money to tour at home and abroad. By 1995, American tourism of all kinds reached $100 billion annually. This is direct recreational spending for foreign and domestic travel, including transportation, food, lodging, entertainment, visiting local attractions, guide services, and purchases of local products.

Tourism appears to withstand the rigors of inflation, recession, and unemployment better than other leisure activities. More people are visiting more places than ever before. Britons, for example, continue to visit the United States, particularly Florida, because their money can buy more here. Inflation is so high in Great Britain that English visitors often come to the United States to shop, saving enough to pay for the trip.

Citizens of all the industrialized nations have the wherewithal to travel abroad. Around the world Germans and Japanese have replaced the ubiquitous Americans as the chief tourists, although Americans are once again traveling overseas in record numbers. If Americans cannot afford the time or money to travel abroad this year, they save for next year. If they still can't make it then, they travel domestically. Attendance at the national parks, forests, and other great natural attractions is growing. Cumulatively, Americans drive more than 300 billion miles to and from vacation areas. The trend toward travel both at home and abroad maintains its pace unabated. Special charter flights, airline tours, travel clubs, and package tours make the itch to go almost irresistible. Total travel expenditures exceeded $3 trillion in 1995.

High-Risk Activities

Not as popular, but still important in terms of economics and the number of participants involved, are the high-risk physical activities such as hang gliding, parachute jumping, rock climbing, caving, scuba diving, and skateboarding. To this may be added snowmobiling, which attracts some 14 million people annually, and sledding, with 37 million adherents. The high-risk activities, inherently dangerous because any miscalculation can lead to death or terrible injury, are among the more costly activities. All require special equipment, instruction, and

monetary outlays that far exceed those required for lower-risk activities.

Nature-Oriented Activities

Outdoor activities that are growing in popularity include camping, picnicking, hunting and fishing, hiking and backpacking, swimming, boating, and nature observation.

Camping. The camping industry comprises day camps and overnight, or residential, camps. Approximately 12,000 camps operate in the United States, with at least 10 million attendees. These camps have fixed installations, cabins, structures, trails, swimming facilities, and a host of other recreational areas that cater to the needs of campers. More than 54 million Americans camped out in various ways in 1995. To accommodate the large number of campers, government and private investments in the acquisition of land and the development of camping places have climbed rapidly.

Day camps are typically operated by government authorities, although some commercial operators have been very successful. Most are organized and administered by public recreational service departments or sectarian or youth-serving agencies. Some of these camps have elaborate facilities, but many have simply sanitary conveniences, some shelter, and game fields.

Residential camps are not just for children anymore. Many adults spend their vacations there. Sometimes camping for adults is connected with some educational or business enterprise that joins the learning experience with camping activities. Specialized camps for disabled people and those that concentrate on a particular skill also attract many. The investment by operators and the expenditures by participants are considerable.

Picnicking. This very traditional American recreational activity attracted more than 140 million people in all its aspects during the 1990s. Some picnics are adjuncts to other recreational experiences, such as attendance at a sporting event or a visit to a zoo, park, or fair. How much is spent for picnicking can only be guessed at. It varies with the number of people involved, the food and drink, and whether picnic supplies are bought on the road or brought from home. Picnics may also involve takeout from fast-food outlets.

Hunting and Fishing. Over 100 million people above the age of nine go fishing and/or hunting each year. Expenditures for equipment, supplies, and clothing probably exceed $6 billion, while licences, fees, taxes, and the like probably generate another billion dollars to federal, state, and local agencies. Additional costs for transportation, food and lodging, and sundries make the economic impact even more striking.

Hiking and Backpacking. Nearly 50 million people choose hiking as their preferred recreational activity. Unlike walking, hiking involves intense physical activity, a predetermined goal or destination, and usually some related experiences along the way such as sightseeing, camping, and picnicking. Hiking also offers opportunities for nature observation, ecological investigation, rock climbing, nature specimen collecting, hunting, fishing, and swimming.

Backpackers carry food, shelter, clothing, and other necessities in a compact pack so that they can remain outdoors at least overnight and sometimes for weeks. They usually like to travel through wilderness areas or places that are inaccessible by vehicle. The outlay for lightweight backpacks and the supplies therein vary, but so many people participate in the activity that it must play a significant economic role.

Swimming. Swimming continues to be a popular outdoor recreational interest. More than 75 million people in the United States engage in swimming and at least 70 million more enjoy wading and sunbathing. People travel to lakes, camp alongside rivers, and go to resorts overlooking ocean or gulf in order to swim. The construction and maintenance of outdoor home swimming pools and those installed and developed by public agencies contribute a great deal to the expenditures on this activity. The money spent on swimming paraphernalia (including swimsuits, goggles, earplugs, scuba gear, lifesaving devices, surfboards, diving boards, aquatic slides, wave-making machines, and other equipment) totals approximately $5 billion.

Boating. The boating industry includes power, sail, and personal forms of waterborne locomotion. More than 103 million people participate in some form of boating in the United States. Sailing has approximately 20 million enthusiasts; canoeing, rowing, and kayaking are enjoyed by 30 million people; power boating accounts for the rest. Boating offers opportunities for other water-oriented activities, such as fishing, swimming, scuba diving, and water-skiing.

About $10 billion is expended for all boating needs. This includes the purchase of the craft, maintenance, fuel (if necessary), supplies, materials and equipment, mooring fees, and any other accessories that boat owners feel they must have to enjoy boating. It does not include additional expenditures by public and private organizations to develop marinas, launching sites, and boat storage facilities, or the life protection offered by the U.S. Coast Guard.

Animal Keeping. That people love animals and keep them as pets is well known. The economically significant aspect comes in terms of industries that have developed as a result of pets. Training, pet foods, adornments, medicines, cemeteries, toys, cages, carrying cases, and innumerable other supplies or assistance cost hundreds of millions of dollars each year. Add to that the maintenance of animals for fun and profit—such as racing, showing, and breeding—and all the accoutrements, and the figure reaches billions.

Nature Observation. Birdwatching captures the interest of approximately 15 million people in this country. Millions of schoolchildren are introduced to nature study through walks in fields, marshes, bogs, and swamps, where they can collect frogs' eggs, birds' nests, pieces of wood, mineral specimens, flowers, berries that they can make into candles, leaves to identify, and so on. This early exposure often provides the individual with a lifelong hobby.

More than 100 million people visit zoos, parks, botanical gardens, arboreta, and the like to enjoy animal and plant life both in cultivated surroundings and in the wild. This figure is even more astounding if we add the six million people who go to natural settings to photograph them. While it is not very expensive to walk a trail or watch a bird, some enthusiasts equip themselves with special clothing, field glasses, telescopes, cameras, walking shoes, and many other costly accessories. Some nature lovers combine tourism with observation and photography—traveling to all parts of the world, from the Galapagos Islands to the Great Barrier Reef of Australia.

The Arts

Our estimate of participation in art activities—painting, sculpture, drawing, collage, or other aesthetic forms—is derived from commercial sales of the supplies, materials, and equipment used by artists and novices. This does not include those art activities that cost little or nothing because the artist uses scrap or found materials. Millions of people participate in some form of art activity.

Schoolchildren are exposed to art experiences when they scribble with crayons, draw, or learn art appreciation. Some individuals become lifelong enthusiasts; others drift into and out of art activities depending on the time available and other attractions competing for their attention. The costs of art participation vary in terms of kind of instruction needed, equipment needed, and art supplies, tools, and materials.

Crafts

Crafts cover a very broad area and account for a considerable portion of the leisure economy. By crafts we usually mean aesthetic objects that can serve a practical purpose. Survival crafts include campfire building, outdoor cooking, shelter building, food gathering or catching, and utensil making from natural materials. Decorative crafts include stitchery, weaving, and crafts using wood, metal, leather, glass, stone, bone, vegetables, and other materials. Crafts are commonly practiced in home workshops, school shops, camps, and other recreational facilities provided by the public, private, and quasi-public sectors.

The costs of craft activities include not only the materials, some of which are quite expensive, but also instruction, equipment, supplies, and sometimes fees charged for the work space. Some crafts are free in the sense that the basic materials can be picked up on beaches, roads, or dumps or salvaged from junk. But some expenditure is usually required, even for paper crafts. To be sure, the 35 million people who engage in arts and crafts activities each year make this a significant economic factor by sheer numbers.

Cultural Activities

There are 1,500 symphony orchestras, 40 million amateur musicians, 20,000 drama companies, 850 commercial dance companies, and thousands of noncommercial dance companies in the United States. Many performing arts activities are organized and sponsored by public recreational service departments. Dance performances now attract more than 20 million people annually, and dance is looked on as the art form with the greatest growth potential.

Opera companies, community theater groups, commercial theaters, musical productions, poetry readings, and many other facets attest to the cultural importance of the performing arts. To this may be added the $4 billion investment received directly for the performing arts and the echoing distribution of hundreds of millions, which eventually filters down through the economy.

Additional millions attend art and craft exhibitions, shows, gallery displays, and the like. Attendance at museums and art galleries in 1995 exceeded 350 million, with a total expenditure of $550 million. To this must be added the monetary contributions of government to these institutions and the manufacturing, wholesaling, and retail costs and sales this recreational activity generates.

Publications

All forms of publications—books, newspapers, magazines, literary supplements, digests, and the like—contribute to one of the most fascinating forms of recreational experience. Reading provides news and information. But more than that, it is entertaining and stimulating and permits the reader to enjoy vicarious experiences. Reading can also motivate an individual to try some of the ideas expressed. Book clubs, book discussion groups, and literature classes help make the publishing business lucrative. There are more books being published than ever before, about 50,000 titles a year. About $20 billion was spent on all kinds of books in 1995.

There are magazines devoted to virtually every form of leisure experience, both amateur and professional. Trade journals, general magazines, professional periodicals, and research journals provide required information, offer assistance, entertain—and direct readers to the ads that make magazines a commercial success. Although some long-established magazines have gone out of business recently, new

Cultural activities are popular recreational pursuits.

© Jack Vartoogian

ventures continually enter the field. With 10,000 magazines published and a circulation of 260 million, business is booming.

Newspapers have suffered the greatest decline among readers, no doubt because so many people get their news from television. However, almost 10,000 newspapers are daily or weekly publications with a readership in excess of 150 million people. Newspaper publishers employ almost 500,000 persons and sell $15 billion a year in advertising and newspapers, making this the "dominant advertising medium, receiving more ad dollars than radio and television combined."

Technological Activities

American ingenuity has not been limited to converting almost every participatory activity into a competitive game. Technology is used to change the environment so that people are guaranteed the climate, temperature, or location they want. Advances in the electronics industry have enabled travelers to take news and entertainment along with them, whether they dive, fly, ride motorbikes, or sailboats. Television and radio are the most popular technological instruments available for recreational purposes. Electronic games, which can be connected to TV receivers, activated by battery, or plugged into outlets and worked separately, are also popular. Computer simulation and game playing have been around almost as long as computers. Nintendo is only the latest of the electronic fads that entice young people to spend money.

One of the latest technological advances in the television industry is videodiscs, machines that reproduce recorded programs or movies for viewing on any TV set. It is estimated that the market for these devices, the next step up from VCRs, will eventually reach $1 billion annually.

But technology is not confined to electronic gadgetry. The winter sports industry, for example, has been revitalized by sophisticated snowmaking machines, which enable resort operators to turn barren slopes into snowfields. Lifts, tows, and gondolas also help make the participant's ride to the top of the hill possible.

The use of laminated woods, plastics, and other chemical products makes a variety of recreational activities possible and affordable. Lightweight surfboards, composite-wheel skates and skateboards, sports cars, snowmobiles, boats, and bicycles, among other products, have used the benefits of technology to enter the mass market, where millions of people purchase and enjoy them.

Developing the means to impound water, reconstruct cities or towns, irrigate the desert, or clear waterways of ice for pleasure boating are some of the ways technology has expanded people's recreational opportunities. By changing the way we think about recreational activities in terms of when, where, how, and at what price, technological progress provides conditions in which we can use our leisure as we please.

Miscellaneous Hobbies

Indoor and outdoor gardening and personal hobbies of various types can be performed in purely self-directed ways or as part of an organized effort. All told, these activities add up to an annual outlay in the billions of dollars. Adult education, elderhostels, seminars, skill lessons in groups operated by recreational service departments or other agencies, libraries, museums, art gallery or architectural exhibitions, gourmet cooking classes, wine-tasting tours— these and many others may all be part of formal and informal learning experiences.

Hypothetically if spectator sports like football, basketball, and baseball no longer received coverage by the various media, what would be the economic impact? Carry the consequences as far as you can: What would happen to professional athletes' salaries? What would the effect be on stadiums or arenas? What would happen to product advertising without athlete endorse-

ments? To sales of team apparel? Would the sale of equipment to other participants be affected (i.e., would more or fewer people buy basketball backboards to play their own games if fewer people were watching the games)?

RECREATIONAL SERVICE

Another way to illustrate the profound impact of leisure and recreational pursuits on the economy is by focusing on the commercial enterprises that manufacture and market finished goods, environments, or services for recreational use.

Recreationally Oriented Businesses

Recreationally oriented businesses have enormous profit-making potential and opportunities for employment and investment.

Sporting Goods Manufacturers. Sporting goods makers manufacture such items as baseballs, basketballs, bowling balls, footballs, golf balls, handballs, soccer balls, and volleyballs; camping equipment such as tents, backpacks, sleeping bags, air mattresses, cooking stoves and utensils, kerosene or Coleman lamps, and mosquito netting; golf clubs, bags, shoes, and other accessories; hunting and fishing gear and supplies; aquatic gear for swimming, boating, scuba diving, and underwater photography; bicycles; racquets of all kinds; protective clothing; skis, ice skates, toboggans, sleds, snowmobiles, and other winter sport paraphernalia; archery tackle; bats, bases, gloves, masks; parachutes, surfboards, and roller skates. This itemization does not begin to cover the range of sporting goods and related products.

Cultural Products Manufacturers. This category includes publishing houses, newspapers, and manufacturers of musical instruments, art supplies, dance shoes and accessories, photographic equipment and supplies, craft tools and materials, records, tapes, recording machines, radios, TV sets, filmmaking equipment, toys, and games of all kinds.

Travel Service Businesses. These businesses include individuals and companies engaged in any aspect of offering assistance to those who are traveling for recreational or other purposes.

Travel agencies, gas stations, airlines, bus lines, railroads, steamships, hotels, motels, restaurants, and roadside attractions are among the businesses that are part of this lucrative commerce.

Vehicle Manufacturers. Enterprises whose products are used in any way for recreational purposes, either in whole or part, are included here: cars, motorcycles, motorbikes, motorboats, airplanes, all-terrain vehicles, campers, vans, and the like. Also included in this category are the adjunctive businesses of auto insurance, auto accessory and replacement parts, wreckers, towers, metal and other salvage operators, and the auto adornment businesses, such as painters and custom builders.

Entertainment and Spectator Services. This group includes organizations and institutions in the spectator entertainment business, providing regional, national, and international competitions in, for example, jai alai, soccer, football, baseball, ice hockey, track and field, golf, tennis, gymnastics, boxing, and swimming. There are also horse and dogtrack racing and speedways for automobiles, motorcycles, stock cars, dragsters, and boats.

Among the possibilities for mass and individual entertainment are movies, stage plays, operas, ballet, modern dance, rock concerts, classical music concerts, art galleries, natural history and science museums, aquariums, zoological and botanical gardens, supper clubs, theater in the round, antique shows, stamp exchanges, fairs, parades, and festivals.

Indoor Recreational Businesses. All commercial offerings for which there is a membership fee or an entrance charge fall into this category. Examples are private athletic clubs, health spas, dance halls, billiard parlors, bowling centers, and organizations such as Jewish community centers, YMCAs, American Legion posts, VFW posts, and social, civic, business, and service organizations. Among the newest popular business ventures are arcades featuring electronic games.

Outdoor Recreational Businesses. Among the enterprises that provide outdoor recreational settings are residential and day camps, seasonal and year-round resorts, aquatic facilities, dude ranches, sightseeing tours, tower visits, historic sites, cultural shrines, adventure trips on waterways, and horseback trail riding.

Recreational Instruction Services. These businesses provide instruction, guidance, counseling, or assistance to help people learn a skill, gain a particular knowledge or appreciation, enhance personal satisfaction, or become better selectors of leisure alternatives. Such services encompass instruction in the performing arts, the fine arts, crafts, and photography. Also included are any ancillary services that enhance recreational enjoyment or comfort—for example, parking facilities at recreational areas; marinas and shipyards for recreational boats of all kinds; lockers for clothing and valuables; and concessionaires selling food, drink, suntan lotion, and other supplies or renting beach chairs and umbrellas.

Miscellaneous Recreational Businesses. These are commercial offerings that do not fit into other categories, such as time-sharing ownership of dwellings, facilities, or equipment at resort areas; alcohol sales at liquor stores and bars; off-track betting; and gambling casinos. In the next decade, it is estimated, shopping malls will become centers for a variety of leisure activities. They are already expanding their attractions with child- and adolescent-focused amusements, movie theaters, and gambling. Gambling centers like Las Vegas are introducing family activities in hopes of luring more players.[3] Of course, any activities that are immoral or illegal are not considered recreational, but they are leisure experiences.

Employment Opportunities

Hundreds of thousands of jobs are available in the commercial aspect of recreational service, both direct and indirect. These jobs require all kinds of skills and vary greatly in education and experience necessary. A small private campground, for example, is often a family-owned business in which one person performs a number of tasks. On the other hand, large hotels, resorts, clubs, and amusement parks employ a great many workers with specialized functions.

When all the assorted recreationally oriented businesses and the number of employees needed to operate them are taken together, we can begin to see the awesome commercial potential of the leisure industry.

Resorts draw recreators to the outdoors.

Marketing and Promotion

The leisure market is promoted by highly sophisticated forms of marketing approaches, advertising, and publicity. The net effects of these endeavors are to

- influence the buying behavior of potential clients,
- permit a high degree of personal, technical, and geographic specialization,
- offer consumers a wide range of choices among many different products that are reasonably adapted for their individual requirements, and
- give customers lower costs.

As the population continues to grow, commercial enterprises associated with recreational activities will expand and return a

Take a quick inventory of your dwelling. What items did you purchase for a recreational pursuit? What sacrifices did you make to purchase those items? What items were impulse purchases? How much use do those items get? What does all this say about the economic priority you give recreational activity? Are you satisfied with your answers?

profit. Although at least half of small businesses fail, enough will succeed, and many more entrepreneurs will enter the lists to infuse the leisure trade with new ideas, new products, and new ways to attract clients.

ECONOMIC IMPACTS ON RECREATIONAL ACTIVITY AND SERVICE

The attraction of climate, site, and facilities may induce hordes of tourists and seasonal visitors to descend upon some community or region. An influx of visitors can stimulate growth and prosperity in the local economy, and when this happens it is a big success story.

But sometimes this does not occur. The Winter Olympics held at Lake Placid, New York, in 1981 is an example of how poor planning resulted in monetary losses as well as a number of bitter experiences for the public and the officials. Badly organized transportation did much to cancel tourists' goodwill toward the community. Millions of dollars were lost. Even the facilities constructed for the Games will not be fully utilized because the community cannot afford the cost of maintenance. The money was lost because the facilities, which would have generated fees for use, remained closed. Such facilities, when not maintained, tend to deteriorate, also costing scarce dollars.

Many cities and towns use an annual fair, derby, or similar celebration as an occasion for cleaning up and refurbishing the community and building good public relations. Unfortunately, after the ball is over and the tourists leave, there may be a sizable deficit left, with no way to recover the costs of new construction. Poor planning is responsible for many communities overextending themselves and finding that they have a white elephant on their hands. They can neither keep up the new facility nor capitalize on the expected revenue. Instead of producing money, the facility turns into a loss.[4]

Federal Retrenchment

The budget-cutting of the Reagan administration undermined many of the social programs that the federal government had supported for the previous 30 years. The federal government has been cutting back on many programs and services concerning recreational activity, particularly the national parks and forests. Its noninvolvement in the provision of recreational activities for its national constituency will affect all other government expenditures as well. From a $10 billion annual expenditure, there has been a precipitous drop as agency budget-cutters begin to trim so-called frills.

That this has already happened at the state level is evidenced by the passage of Proposition 13 in California in 1979, Proposition 2 1/2 in Massachusetts in November 1980, and a similar proposition in Oregon in 1991. In all of these instances, the voters decided to limit the amount of taxes the state can levy and collect on property. In Massachusetts the referendum limited property taxes to 2 1/2 percent of market value. This meant that all local jurisdictions had to slash property taxes. The overall effect has been to reduce many public functions, including recreational services. Both California and Oregon have closed public parks, beaches, libraries, and other recreational facilities. Programs have been eliminated and employees have been laid off. When ill-advised tax limits become law, the result is either high user fees and charges or other taxes.

Effects on the Recreational Service Profession

Accompanying the national leisure boom was an expansion in the field of recreational service during the 1960s. A national study reported that in 1968 there were approximately 1.4 million full- and part-time workers in the field and predicted a serious shortage of professionally educated recreationists in the near future. Many colleges and universities attempted to meet the growing need for recreationists, only to find the progression of the field halted by the recession of the mid-1970s. Almost immediately financial retrenchment was translated into lost jobs and unfilled or frozen vacancies. The hard-fought gains in recreationist positions were wiped out overnight.

There were a number of reasons for these cutbacks. Chief among them was the economic decline that began in 1973. Inflation, two major recessions, the stock market collapse in 1987, and the threat of war in the Mideast contributed to this condition. This situation has produced a rise in unemployment and serious social problems, with high costs to all levels of government. Social problems include the spiraling costs of welfare and urban renewal and the increased costs of education, housing, law enforcement, fire protection, and health care. In addition, money spent on reducing pollution, ending civil service strikes, and operating municipal governments has meant a lack of funds available for recreational services. This is a real setback for recreationists and for the many people who rely on their services.

Possible Solutions

Setting priorities is the first step in solving the problem of recreational retrenchment. Revenue sharing, which formerly returned about $11 billion annually to the states, has been considerably reduced. The Republican-dominated Congress is determined to restrict financial support to programs that essentially serve the poor and lower middle class. So is all now lost?

Although public service employees have been around for 70 years, some political figures claim privatization is the best way to ensure municipal viability. Urban centers are being pounded by fiscal crisis brought on by a departing middle class, a deteriorating infrastructure, costly (read union) personnel, a core of nontaxpaying poor, and an environment that is increasingly a threat to human health and life.

Privatization may not be the solution, but shifting the burden to private companies who bid competitively to provide public services can help municipalities lift themselves from insolvency. Where unions have not been a major factor, in the South and West, more and more cities have contracted out public services.

Whether or not privatization can save money for local governments remains to be seen. Certainly, savings of better than 40 percent have been recorded.[5] However, the greatest savings occur from eliminating intensive services personnel. Unfortunately, the savings to one department may result in a loss to another. The branches of government concerned with welfare and health have to spend more because of higher unemployment among displaced city workers. Private companies tend to pay minimum wages and offer minimal health benefits.

Surely there are drawbacks to privatization, not the least of which is the potential for graft and corruption.[6] New York City's experience with contracting for the collection of parking fees led to exposure of criminal wrongdoing by highly placed political figures, as well as payoffs and other forms of bribery. This is precisely why public service was installed—to combat rampant corruption. In the final analysis, the savings of privatization may be negligible in terms of the total city budget, but the psychological impact on taxpayers and others may be

Retrenchments in the federal budget have adversely affected agencies involved with environmental protection and social programs. What is the outlook now for support of public leisure services? Should municipalities contract out to private sectors their formerly public leisure services? Should certain aspects remain in the public domain?

Public Land, Private Interest

Town officials in Groton, Connecticut, saw their hopes for the development of a minor-league baseball team disappear due to restrictions placed on land purchased by the town. Residents had approved an $8 million bond issue to purchase selected parcels within the town for conservation and recreational purposes. A 246-acre parcel appraised at $4 million was offered to the town for $3 million; the balance would be as a gift. Attached to the sale were a covenant establishing a board of overseers and restrictions on commercial use of the property. The town was experiencing growth at the time, and this was seen as protection of a valuable resource.

Two years later the town was approached by the New York Yankees, who were looking for a site for a minor-league stadium. Approximately $7 million was available in state economic development funds, and the project had the support of a regional coalition of community leaders. Meetings were held to explain the project, and negotiations began with the franchise owners.

Several local residents and open-space supporters protested the construction of a stadium that would house a professional baseball team. The argument centered on the definition of commercial use. The town would remain the owner of the facility and would lease the park on a seasonal basis. The facility would provide a venue for many other activities, such as community concerts and youth baseball tournaments, and had the potential to be a source of revenue for the town. The opponents argued that leasing the property constituted a commercial use and was prohibited by the covenant.

After much debate and legal opinion, the project was abandoned and the stadium was built in a neighboring town (which has withstood several lawsuits connected with the project). The stadium is a source of pride and economic enhancement for the city of Norwich. Groton continues to own the 246-acre parcel, with its board and covenant.

If you were a member of the board of overseers, how would you have voted on the issue? What criteria would you emphasize in making your decision?

beneficial. Safeguards must be intrinsic to any systematic attempt to privatize public service to prevent a spoils approach to the bidding and operating functions of contracting out.

ECONOMIC PRIORITIES

We have seen that Americans spend great amounts of money on leisure activities and recreational participation. Why, then, are we unwilling to support public and voluntary agency facilities and programs? Some of the money being spent on private recreational involvement could be diverted to meet the needs of the public, but this is not likely to occur. When new tax bills are introduced, they are met with a resounding no. Taxpayers are unwilling to pay any more for services but are quite willing to spend more than $200 billion on personal leisure. Again the word *priorities* must be considered. What is more important? What will a reduction of recreational facilities and employees mean to the American way of life in years to come?

SELECTED REFERENCES

Gratton, C., and P. Taylor. *Economics of Leisure Services Management.* London: Longman, 1991.

Owen, J. D. *The Price of Leisure.* Montreal: McGill-Queens University Press, 1970.

Rojek, C. *Capitalism and Leisure Theory.* London: Tavistock, 1985.

Chapter 9

LEISURE THREATS TO THE ENVIRONMENT

Objectives

After reading this chapter, the student will be able to do the following:

Discuss environmental issues with regard to recreational use.

■

Describe the ways leisure use causes environmental
pollution or spoliation.

■

Differentiate between land preservation and conservation
for recreational use.

■

Explain the public domain.

■

Tell how war influences natural resource conservation.

■

Discuss the recreationist's concern with environmental degradation.

■

Suggest possible solutions to the environmental threat of leisure.

Environmental degradation is not something that occurred recently. People have been polluting the world ever since they could cut trees, make fire, and get rid of waste products. But industrial development without controls increased the ability to produce waste, and this process has been hastened vastly during the last 100 years. Now, acids, metal tailings, and chemicals of all kinds seep into the water supply, while gases and other toxins pervade the atmosphere. Despite efforts to protect the environment, the struggle is slowly being lost.

Leisure threatens the environment no less than industry or domestic waste disposal. Activities directly stemming from leisure use include building vacation retreats in a wilderness, cutting ski trails through forests, racing off-road vehicles over fragile desert pictographs, motor boating and dumping petroleum products, and indiscriminate littering after a picnic or hike, among many other behaviors. All of the numerous recreational activities that eat up space and damage natural flora and fauna must be rechanneled or curtailed before there is nothing left.

All recreational activity requires some space. Whether artificially created or natural, environment surrounds us. However, when we discuss concepts of space, we are referring to the natural environment. Even artificial environments, such as buildings and other facilities, need original areas for their construction. Unless there is a concerted effort to save open space and natural places, land is simply taken for other purposes—industrial, commercial, residential, government, transportation, and other uses that promote society.

It is part of the professional obligation of recreationists and the agencies they serve to protect, preserve, and maintain the natural resources of the public domain against all forms and methods of waste, pollution, destruction, and encroachment in order to provide recreational experiences in outdoor places for present and future populations' use, enjoyment, and value.

FINITE RESOURCES

The limited resource that is earth supports a relatively resilient but easily damaged ecosystem, which is being dangerously tested as a consequence of modern humanity's manipulations. As the world's population approaches the 5 billion mark, people's infringement on the intricate and interdependent structure necessary for survival becomes more pervasive and thus more serious. Our habitations have proliferated from the few settlements along seacoasts and inland waterways to a vast network of megalopolitan extensions that stretch in unbroken array for hundreds and in some cases a thousand miles. Urban sprawl, if permitted to continue unabated, will use up all land space in a given region as communities stretch out along transportation corridors.

Perhaps such growth is inevitable in a finite world with a disinclination to control population. The rapid development of urbanized communities brings with it a need for amenities. Among the most popular amenities is recreational activity. A considerable part of industrialized society's time is spent in recreational activity during its leisure, which has been obtained as a result of labor-saving devices and a mandated or negotiated allowance of free time.

Conservation

Open space, the places in and on which recreational activity can occur, is essential to recreational service. Designated areas should be set aside so that people can participate in outdoor recreational experiences, both active and contemplative (for example, the appreciation of scenery). No matter how the potential recreator (user) sees fit to engage in the outdoors, land, water, and air are fundamental.

Yet, on every side, land is being gobbled up, taken away, broken, cut, excavated, constructed on, developed, leveled, tunneled into, or hidden under layers of concrete and asphalt. Trees and grass are fast disappearing from the scene of human habitation. The fish and wildlife that once abounded in many regions are being killed off by the number one predator—humans and their civilization.

Restrictions are being imposed on systems of recreational service because they cannot accommodate the growing population, the megalopolitan spread of strip cities, the widespread pollution of water, and the encroachment by private, commercial interests as well as by government agencies that take park and varied recreational resources and spaces and use them for other purposes.[1] The depletion of forests as a result of fire and soil erosion, their use as waste dumps, the wholesale destruction of landscapes by wanton strip-mining, each leaves a needless blight upon the face of the land. All these factors, some related, some correlated, by the sheer immensity of useless exploitation or foolish spoilage of property and natural areas reduce the space available for the public to use recreationally.

Maintenance and Exploitation

A great conflict exists between those who see in land a great storehouse of natural history and scientific, aesthetic, and cultural values that must be preserved and those who are mainly interested in profiting from the economic utilization of these same resources.[2] A similar dichotomy exists between those who wish to preserve open spaces for recreational purposes in their wilderness state and other, equally dedicated, individuals who seek to open up these wild regions by constructing access roads, utilities, and other amenities.

© Terry Wild Studio

Land is thoughtlessly being used for development.

The idea of multipurpose uses of land has divided those who want to preserve the land from those who want to conserve the depletable resources.[3] We must decide whether wilderness regions shall be preserved without undue civilizing influences, for the exclusive use of those hardy spirits who have the necessary interest, dedication, and rugged individualism to pack in to the back country, or whether road systems shall be expanded so that thousands, instead of tens, can reap the benefits of the natural environment.

Purists believe that wherever people go, they destroy the balance of nature in some way and bring with them a civilizing pattern that ruins its essential harmony. They say that with great mobility, leisure, and financial means, many more people have the inclination to visit the great natural wonders and get back to the soil—but only if there are roads, accommodations, and other conveniences.

Those for whom the outdoors is an entertainment objective tend to view the natural environment as a self-sustaining system that can renew itself regardless of human impact. The many, who want their way made easy, vociferously defend their need to use publicly owned places as an entitlement for paying taxes. They expect the government to give them access because it is their right to enjoy the outdoors. The wilderness is there for those who want to see and use it.

But if agencies begin to develop access roads and scar the vistas with resorts, and in the process cut the timber and eliminate the wildlife, the wilderness disappears. As Aldo Leopold writes: "All conservation of wilderness is self-defeating, for to cherish we must see and fondle, and when enough have seen and fondled, there is no wilderness. . . ."

Still, when all is said and done, space is the prime necessity. Space must be acquired for a variety of structures in which recreational activities occur; space is necessary for sports and games, for every aspect of the comprehensive program. No recreational program is complete unless it provides both indoor and outdoor experiences throughout the year in order to meet people's diverse needs. Available, accessible, and economically acquirable land is the key to these problems.

Yet public agencies are losing land on every side. Encroachment by other public agencies, by purchase (which takes the land off the market), by the development of private investors, and by other legitimate and even illegitimate means has created a crisis in land needed for a growing and mobile population.

This nation was endowed by nature with an abundance of riches and varied resources. It has minerals to mine, land to cultivate, scenery to enjoy, waters to control, develop, and fish, and timber resources to manage and use. Its flora and fauna have provided food, clothing, and recreational activity for millions of people. But what was once considered limitless and inexhaustible turns out to be a steadily diminishing resource. Nevertheless, planning and management have helped to perpetuate and conserve natural resources for, among other things, recreational purposes.

Land is increasingly in short supply, particularly in terms of natural environments and the proximity of people to them. Great reserves of land and water have been set aside permanently so that current and future generations will be able to appreciate and enjoy outdoor recreational activities. However, most of these conserved areas are far removed from population centers.[4] Many people cannot reach them. Of course, if they could, these natural areas would soon disappear under the impact of use. People are loving the wilderness to death.

Environmental Conflicts and Threats

The controversy is waged between two extremes: environmentalists who believe that all natural resources of whatever type must be preserved from waste and pollution versus commercialists (developers) who think that all natural resources can be exploited for profit forever. Between these extremes are the moderates, who believe that the environment contains some elements that must be forever preserved, some elements that can be conserved, and some that can be exploited for profit, as long as safeguards are provided.

The concept of multipurpose land use has become a barrier to communication between those who want to maintain the pristine outdoor environments untouched by human hands and those who feel that depletable resources require careful nurturing and constant monitoring. A confrontation is building around the question of whether the wilderness, our national heritage, will be protected against encroachments or whether access to the natural areas will be opened to the tens of thousands who can enjoy them instead of just to the hearty few who can get there through their own efforts, without needing public highways and amenities.

For example, the incongruous spectacle of backpackers fighting disabled people over accessibility to a remote area in New Hampshire is just one facet of the many-sided conflict of interests.[5] More extreme and potentially dangerous is the group known misleadingly as Earth First. Among its highly controversial dictums is equal rights for all species, including the smallpox virus.[6]

Loss of Potential Recreational Space

Of supreme importance for recreational activity is the need for space. Space must be acquired for a variety of structures and specialized play areas. Space is required for sports and games, camping, walking, and every aspect of an outdoor program. In fact, no comprehensive program can exist unless adequate and well-distributed recreational sites are available and accessible.

Yet encroachment on present and potential recreational places by public and commercial interests continues apace. After all, there is only just so much land available in the urban region. Some of this use is absolutely necessary if people are to have residential areas, government services, and the business and economic base essential to a viable community. But much land is also gobbled up by speculators and developers whose deals take them to relatively unused lands beyond the city fringe. Here they buy cheaply and sell to developers whose construction spreads the urban tide along the easy transportation routes. This takes land out of use for anything other than suburbs. This is invariably done with no thought to the amenities that all residential developments should contain. The speculators are concerned only with intensive land use and maximum profits.

It bears repeating that unless there is a logically developed land-use pattern in which all of the interests and concerns of the people are considered, land will soon be so scarce that most people will not be able to afford homes or to live within reasonable distance of a recreational space.

Poor planning and mismanagement of environmental resources are errors of human judgment. Such failures can be remedied by appreciation and compatible use of the natural bounty. Environmental degradation, on the other hand, may permanently destroy any use potential. With foresight, professional planners can eliminate or significantly reduce negative factors so that the environment can renew itself and continue to generate outdoor recreational opportunities of incalculable value.

There is no simple solution. The desert land in eastern California, for example, has a fragile ecology, and parts of it are protected. However, some people like to drive dune buggies, motorcycles, or four-wheel drive vehicles over the sand at high speed. This churns up the earth, pollutes the air, and disturbs wildlife. Moreover, these same enthusiasts destroy the great sand drawings left by earlier indigenous populations. They justify their actions by saying that this kind of activity is therapeutic for them; it is their way to escape from the pressures of city living. There are many similar situations occurring all over the country.

Should natural areas be closed off to thousands who seek enjoyment in this way? One answer might be to open for vehicular use selected areas that are closer to cities and are clear of wildlife habitats. Another possibility might be to prohibit all vehicles of any kind in areas where the ecological system can be easily disturbed and rely on some sort of mass transit, electric bussing program to take visitors to these outdoor areas and deposit them at some central location. Then they could walk, hike, camp, or pursue other recreational activities that have less impact on the environment than vehicular traffic.

Where do you fall in the continuum of views about land development versus land conservation? How might advocates of both positions use the utilitarian concept of "the greatest good for the greatest number"? How can we decide what interests to protect? Is there a limit to how far we'll go to maintain lifestyles of consumption? Are we willing to destroy natural resources in favor of manmade ones? Where's the line?

ENVIRONMENTAL DAMAGE AND POLLUTION

Pollution is the presence of excessive amounts of harmful substances that endanger health, degrade the environment, and restrict its use.

Americans are polluting their environment outrageously. This country is marked by consumer waste and industrial indifference. Poisonous materials are dumped by uncaring individuals, companies, and sometimes criminal conspiracies.

The Love Canal episode in New York State is a prime example of what happens when industrial companies' dumping of waste materials is not controlled. Now many toxic, radioactive, and hazardous dump sites are being found and exposed by an aroused citizenry whose health, homes, and children have been adversely affected by polluters. The government has finally stepped in to monitor and control the methods companies use to dispose of contaminated and poisonous water.

The American people throw away 1 million old cars, 48 billion cans, 26 million bottles, 4 million tons of plastic, and 58 million tons of paper in a typical year. And this is only a small part of the pollution picture. In addition, land space is rapidly vanishing, lakes and rivers are filled with wastes, beaches and coastlines are contaminated with garbage, sewage, and oil.

Fish and wildlife have not escaped the harmful impact of pollution; some species are becoming extinct. The single worst air pollutant is automobile exhaust fumes. A hundred million vehicles continue to pour exhaust gases into the air. Factories also contribute to the mounting unsatisfactory condition of the air we breathe. Photochemical smog in the skies of our major cities reveals the immensity of this problem. Radioactive fallout is present in the atmosphere. Insecticides, aerosol sprays, and some fertilizers are causing damage.[7]

Even nature conspires against us. The Mount Saint Helens volcano, which erupted in 1980 and continues to erupt at odd intervals, spread a cubic mile of ash, pumice, and harmful dust to the north and east of the volcano's site. A great deal of the displaced material destroyed lakes and trees, and winds carried ash across the United States. The oceans, too, are subjected to environmental degradation. A great natural resource and coastal land protector is constantly threatened by air pollution and global warming. The coral reefs of the world are starting to die.[8]

The Threat of Air Pollution

Between 60 and 80 percent of all air pollution is caused by emissions produced by internal

Pollution threatens our natural resources.

So widespread is air pollution that samples of Arctic ice have been found to contain concentrations of toxic chemicals that could only have been carried through the air. There does not seem to be one place of refuge where a person can get away from the pervasive air pollution—unless one remains indoors, and the air is sometimes polluted there too.

The government estimates that dirty air costs each person in the United States $80 per year in terms of damage to human health, residential property, materials, and vegetation. The total amount is $16.1 billion each year.

When health, sunlight, and climate suffer, so does the opportunity to participate in recreational activities. Pollution also affects the activities in which a person engages, how safe they are, and how much they can be enjoyed. All of these deteriorating factors concern recreationists because they interfere with people's enjoyment of their leisure. In some cities, for example, smog alerts curtail the usual recreational activity of those who are susceptible to pulmonary ills and prevent or greatly restrict outdoor leisure.

The Threat of Noise Pollution

Americans probably live in the noisiest country on earth. Excessive noise can harm not only hearing but the nervous system as well. It can undermine health and emotional stability and affect the entire environment. Noise contributes to the destruction of fish and wildlife habitats. It creates an atmosphere that is detrimental to high-quality living. In modern America, motor vehicles, jet planes, pneumatic drills, loud TVs and stereos, honking horns, factory and industrial noise, and the uproar that accompanies human congestion anywhere all contribute to the aural pollution of the environment.

Urban noise is doubling every 10 years. An estimated 13 million Americans live near an airport and suffer from the roar of jet engines, and 17 million work in dangerously noisy occupations. About 170 million Americans in urban and suburban areas are exposed to enough noise each day to degrade their quality of life.

The problem of noise is just as bad indoors. At rock concerts and nightclubs, the decibel level has been measured at 130, as high as the roar of a jet-fighter engine. Steady attendance at dance clubs will probably result in eventual

combustion engines of automobiles. To this may now be added all the other mass-produced motorized recreational vehicles, which have a debilitating effect upon the environment. Even the high price of gas has not reduced the use of these vehicles. Although the motorized camper was hard hit by the jump in gasoline prices, the switch to diesel engines brought a resurgence in its use.

Other culprits are the coal-burning industries and factories that emit chemical and other exotic compounds. Sulfur dioxide particles damage human lungs, especially when they combine with other atmospheric gases to produce acid rain. The distortion of the food chain is related to the highways' destructive dispersion of carbon monoxide and hydrocarbons. These products slow reactions and damage the heart; nitrogen oxides from high-temperature combustion engines and furnaces increase susceptibility to influenza. Photochemical oxidants from motors irritate eyes and increase asthma attacks. The result is deteriorated human health.

hearing loss. Another example of the toll that noise pollution takes is the number of working hours lost because employees stay home, take sick leave, or even quit their jobs to escape from noisy conditions.

Recreationists must be concerned with noise pollution, since one of the objectives of recreational activity is improved health. Rules proscribing loud radios and other noisy intrusions should be enforced at all recreational places. Regulating the use of radios, musical instruments, and other amplified sound systems in recreational areas can do much to alleviate the impact of noise on hearing and health. Finally, recreational settings should be so planned and developed that there is space available for people who want peace and quiet.

More important, recreationists should campaign for a quieter environment by mounting a public relations program to alert people to this persistent nuisance and health hazard. The problem is especially bad on buses, subways, and other enclosed areas from which there is no immediate escape.

The Threat of Water Pollution

Primarily chemical industries, but also effluent produced by human waste, oil spillage, contamination of aquifers by toxic wastes, and pollution of waterways by automotive emissions are just some of the ways in which humanity misuses one of its life-sustaining forces—water.

There is only so much water to be recycled through the hydrologic process. If vast amounts of impurities keep pouring into the waters of the world, we may yet see people vanish through thirst. Even if this catastrophic scenario is not reached, the damage to waterways impairs not only the thirst-quenching attributes of water, but also the propensity to use such a resource for primary and secondary recreational purposes.

The observation of water, in all of its forms, offers a spectacle of color, aesthetics, excitement, and physics. Participation in waterborne activities enhances the enjoyment and fitness capacity of the users. Unless some means are found to lessen the impact of pollutants on the earth's waters, people will be the losers.

Wildlife or Wild Life?

It is a scene reenacted throughout campgrounds and wilderness areas across the country. A family with small children plans a week-long vacation camping in a developed park campground that supplies a cleared site for tents and campers. They envision a time away from the daily distractions and hectic pace of everyday life. It is a chance to relax and to introduce the children to the wonders of nature.

Settling in at the campsite next door are six recent college graduates ready to celebrate their accomplishments and their newfound freedom. Their vision of camping is to hike, drink beer, swim, drink beer, play loud music, drink beer, and sleep when it is absolutely necessary due to exhaustion. They are unaware of the effect of their style of wilderness adventure on other campers.

You have been hired as a summer security officer at the park and are working the late shift, from 11 P.M. to 6 A.M. The father of the family comes to your station around midnight to tell you that the adjacent campers are consistently using profanities and playing loud music and appear to be drunk most of the time.

While he understands their need to have fun, his family has been deprived of their sleep for several nights, making the entire camping experience less than fun.

1. What will you say to the father?

2. What will you say to the college campers?

3. How will you enforce your decision?

Concern for and interest in the preservation of the national natural heritage, as well as the frightening prospects of water pollution, reached feverish intensity during the late 1960s and prompted the establishment of the federal Environmental Protection Agency (EPA) in 1970. This organization took on the monumental task of monitoring the effects that industrialization and domesticity have on the environment and any ecological imbalance which results from inordinate pollution, whether to the air, the water, or the soils. During the first few years of the EPA's efforts, the public was vitally interested in a cleaner environment. After five years of legislative enactments which had wide implication for commercial enterprise, employment, energy production, and community impact, there was a slackening of public excitement.

The EPA is still active in forcing industry to clean up toxic wastes. In 1990, for example, the EPA induced the AVX Corporation to pay $66 million in one of the largest settlements under the federal Superfund program.[9] Equally significant is the new attitude of federal prosecutors toward corporations who knowingly commit environmental crimes.[10]

The Threats of Damage to Land

The factors that contribute most heavily to land damage and misuse are urbanization, overcrowding, industrial pollution, highway construction, and commercial development to satisfy recreational demands.

Urbanization Problems. In the past, cities arose at the confluence of rivers or near natural harbors, where water was available for transportation. If the site was favorable for strategic, commercial, or industrial purposes, people flocked there. The city usually developed in a recognized pattern. First the inner core was established. Then succeeding generations, together with their economic, residential, and amenity needs, spread outward in concentric rings around the central city.

For the past 40 years, this pattern has not been followed. Urbanization has spread along new travel routes and has leapfrogged distances through developments that attracted a highly mobile population. Once workers could commute many miles to the urban center, the growth of suburbs and exurbs merely stretched the city's growth pattern in a linear manner

rather than in concentric circles. Now we live in an age of strip and edge cities, which grow in one direction only. The word for this growth is *megalopolis*. The process of urbanization has spread its tentacles beyond the city's limits to engulf entire regions. Today, it is difficult to recognize where one city ends and another begins.

Thus, the suburb, which once could be easily identified as a separate entity, has now become an integral part of the larger urban center. It is the source of labor for the central city. Suburbanites commute daily back and forth between city and residence. Even suburbs are beginning to develop an industrial base. As people move out of the central city and take up residence in the surrounding hinterland, lines of communication and transportation follow. Inevitably, these spaces are filled in and city growth continues.

The surge of the megalopolis has had several effects. There is the need to add highways between and through satellite communities as traffic loads increase and existing highways become obsolete. There is a loss of fish and wildlife, as the spread of cities continues to destroy their habitats. Industrial and human waste being poured into rivers and streams have damaged fish life and the recreational use of fresh water. Woodlands and forests are being depleted by manmade fires as well as by poor management. Open spaces for recreational purposes still exist, but they are at increasing distances from where people work and reside.

The rapid development of the suburbs was a compromise between accessibility to recreational areas and to employment areas. However, the growth of suburbia eats up more and more open space, as developers buy up former farmlands or woods and vacant fields and build citified suburbs. When people move to these outlying areas, they demand faster means of transportation. And the vicious cycle of additional highway development, with its encroachment on open space, begins anew.

As urban complexes grow, they create escalation effects on areas just outside of the city. People move out of the core and into these outer regions, which puts pressure on all of the natural resources in these regions. The consequences of the megalopolis are a deterioration of open space, a failure of natural resource conservation, and all the attendant ills of encroachment.

Urban encroachment on the land is part of the machinations of investors who speculate in land. As cities grow, they follow major traffic routes. People seeking housing outside the city's core also follow the traffic route. The ensuing housing development appears from the air like spokes radiating from a hub, but without any rim. Consolidation of the spaces along the spokes follows; these areas push out as additional migrations take place. Investors, noting population trends, quickly buy whatever land is available between the densely populated zones of the city and the rural areas.

Without intelligent planning and zoning, the outer areas are allowed to deteriorate while the land speculators reap a profit from their investment. The value of their interim property increases far beyond what it costs in taxes and capital gains. As Von Eckardt states:

Such unused land may profit the speculator but it is most expensive to the community— and not only in aesthetic terms. Such land can no longer be considered for the orderly planning of floodwater impoundments, roads, sewers, schools, and other vital facilities. New housing that is actually built is pushed farther and farther away from the city. This means longer and more expensive sewers, more utilities and roads, and greater transportation problems.[11]

One result, of course, is urban blight.

Overcrowding. Americans are crowding into cities, causing excessive congestion, noise, air pollution, deteriorating government services, high crime rates, and other problems. The U.S. Census shows that half of all Americans live within 50 miles of the west or east coast. Furthermore, although there are only 58 inhabitants per square mile, seven out of ten of them are living on just 2 percent of the land.

The growth of population, whether by increasing birthrates, immigration, or longer life spans, puts more pressure on the available space to support people. It isn't only that people want to live near a coastline, because there are also millions of people who live within the interior states of this country. It is the fact that despite the use of cities as the repositories of 70 percent of the population, people and their agents (usually government) are also ruining the rest of the land through faulty planning, ill-conceived regulations regarding the exploitation of natural resources, higher incidences of vandalism, and poor management of resources, which permits destruction of flora and fauna.

The environmental consequences of urbanization have been a growing threat since World War II. The most apparent problem has been the diversion of agricultural land to urban use. More than a million acres of farm land have

© Terry Wild Studio

Suburbs, a boom to land developers, encroach on woodlands.

been taken over for city use in each of the past 40 years. This loss is all the more serious when added to the million farm acres lost each year from soil erosion, flooding, and turning of farm land into forests.

The problem of water supply for the millions of residents who converge upon the city has become urgent recently. Although the water cycle remains constant, as does the total quantity of water available, its quality has deteriorated with urbanization, transportation, and industrialization. There is increasing competition for water use. We still pollute water, despite continued warnings and documented evidence of resulting health hazards to the population.

The 1990 census figures indicate that the nation appears to be developing more and more regional competition. Population growth for the heartland and the Northeast has stabilized. The Southwest has become the most populous region, displacing, after many decades, the Midwest and the East. Americans have been migrating to the South and West for the past 40 years. Three sunbelt states, Arizona, Texas, and California, have 10 million more people than they did in 1978. However, not all of this movement is due to departures from the snowbelt. A great many immigrants have played a role in this shift.

The feeling of being squeezed uncomfortably has always been the key factor in the movement out of the old central cities and to the South and West. Americans are not merely seeking work opportunities; more and more, they are looking for places with fewer people. Regionally, the Rocky Mountain states recorded the greatest growth rate during the past decade. Their current population is only 11,350,000, which means that 5 percent of the total population spreads out over the vast land area of these states.

Population of the giant urban centers dropped 4 percent to 39 million, but the next 50 largest cities gained 5 percent (up by 10 million), while the next 50 largest cities gained 11 percent (up more than 6 million). The continued escape from congestion cuts across the migration pattern from snowbelt to sunbelt. The dramatic unfolding of the American search for spacious living is best illustrated by California, which added 5.6 million to its 1980s population. Simultaneously, large numbers of people emigrated from California to the less densely populated areas of Oregon, Idaho, and Alaska. These people were willing to give up the sunny climate of California to escape air pollution, crime, congestion, and other troubles that accompany urbanization.

Still the cities remain popular. Americans are flocking to them in ever-increasing numbers as the urbanization process continues. One out of every four Americans lives in a city of over

Preservationists versus Preservationists

In 1961, Governor Herbert H. Lehman donated a children's zoo to the City of New York. It was a fanciful marvel whose structures featured a candy cane cottage, the three little pigs' houses, Noah's ark, Jonah's whale, and overhead lights designed as flowers.

Over the years, the city permitted the zoo structures to become dilapidated. When the New York Art Commission approved plans for a new children's zoo, preservationists joined battle—on opposite sides. The donor's granddaughter is suing the city to stop the destruction of the fairy-tale zoo. She is supported by architects who defend the gift and want to maintain the original structures. Just as adamant are opponents who argue that the Lehman donation was an inappropriate intrusion on the carefully planned landscape of Central Park.

The new children's zoo design fits better with the naturalistic intentions of Olmsted and Vaux, the park's designers. Furthermore, the Art Commission says the new design is playful and charming and lets small children interact with animals. The Landmarks Commission has yet to make a decision.

If you could vote on either the Landmarks Commission or the Art Commission concerning this question, how would you vote? What is the basis for your decision?

100,000, although smaller cities are beginning to attract more of the urban population. The 1990 census shows that Americans are on the move. The direction is away from old, congested urban centers in search of locations that offer a better quality of life.

One obvious result of urbanization has been the decline of open space in and around urban centers. What little open space is still available has become less accessible. Continual construction infringes upon all space, not merely what is necessary for the several uses of congested populations. Open space is required for maintaining flood plains, conserving water, conducting specific kinds of agriculture, absorbing noise, relieving crowding, and enjoying recreational activities.

Too many people in a restricted area lead to damage, litter, and unsightliness. The negative aspects of urbanization include congestion, high crime rates, air pollution, and the loss of tax-supported and essential city services and other amenities. There are some positive elements of urbanization. They include varied and readily available community resources, cultural developments, and opportunities for recreational experiences.

Industrial Pollution. Although some companies are genuinely concerned about the ecology and anxious to minimize the environmental effects of their industrial plants, there is no way to avoid environmental damage entirely. Industrial emissions and wastes contaminate the atmosphere. They pollute the air we breathe and the water we drink. They can be extremely hazardous if improperly disposed of and have already caused serious damage to waterways, land, wildlife, and people.

The menace of improper or illegal dumping of highly toxic materials cannot be overstressed.[12] Stricter enforcement and penalties for illegal dumping may have a salutary effect. The acid leaching from mines, the more than occasional misapplication of harmful chemicals that are emitted into the atmosphere, the infiltration of salt water into overpumped wells, and industrial effluents that pour into the air and waterways are a few examples of how industrialization hurts the environment.[13]

Every industry requires a furnace to generate artificial heat, light, and power. The outcome is an atmosphere that is becoming increasingly overburdened with noxious pollutants. Since the Industrial Revolution, the exploitation of all natural resources, including the taking of land for the construction of industrial plants, has gone on apace. Forests have been cut down, the land spoiled, and topsoil permitted to blow away. Minerals have been strip-mined in the states that permit it, leaving deep holes in the earth. The very shape of the land is being changed irrevocably as terrain features are blown up, excavated, tunneled through, pulverized, and otherwise modified for exploitative purposes. This is the legacy of unrestricted industrialization.

True, there can be no progress without industrialization, but it must be tempered with wise choices and controls that do not permit the aesthetic destruction of the landscape, the pollution of air and water, and the exhaustion of the environment. The law must be applied to all aspects of industrial expansion, or else the American people will live to regret unregenerate companies' obliteration of the ecological balance.[14]

We must remember that all organisms need to live in harmony with their environment. No species can remain in an environment unless it is a positively contributing member of an ecological group. Each member must interact with and compensate for the actions of all. We must learn that we humans are inescapably joined together with all living organisms. This understanding may enable us to survive the impact of industrialization. Recognizing this mutual interdependence, we should insist that the powers that be promote an environment in which we can lead healthy lives.

The Threat of Recreational Vehicles to the Environment

Americans now face another peril whose proportions cannot be overemphasized. The ownership of recreational vehicles increased dramatically during the 1960s. Minibikes, minicycles, motorcycles, snowmobiles, dune buggies, and other variants continued to show a rise despite an economic recession in the early 1970s. Now 10 million units are in use and about 85,000 more are sold annually. There are now 1.5 million snowmobiles being used in North America, almost a million of them in the United States alone. Off-road or all-terrain vehicles (ATVs) are projected to gain a 70,000-unit market by 1998. Powerboats are simply one more facet.

What impact will this proliferation of recreational vehicles have on the environment? All of these vehicles can harm the environment. All make such horrendous noise that it affects wild fowl and game. Wildlife does not become accustomed to the intrusion of its habitat by people on vehicles. ATVs used at the wrong time of the year can destroy upland birds' nests. Vegetation is damaged and heavily used motorcycle trails become gullies after rains. Scenic and historic areas are threatened with destruction as motorcycles and ATVs erase prehistoric etchings on the desert floor. Motorized vehicles must be controlled so that their use does not destroy the things people seek when they use the forest, reservations, national parks, or deserts.

Of course, any use of the environment for most active recreational purposes will have a deteriorating effect. However, motorized recreational vehicles use up space at a magnified rate, far more so than nonmotorized activities. As space grows increasingly precious and scarce, we must be concerned about those forms of recreational experience which take up or consume space so rapidly and in such a detrimental manner.

There are reasons why mechanized recreational activities may be considered necessary. However, their detrimental effect on the environment means that serious efforts must be taken to control this industry. Surely good planning, new technologies, strict user control, noise abatement programs, or other remediation can alleviate this menace to the world's health and hearing, not to mention its biota. One thing is certain: The current state of mechanized recreational activities is part of the escape psy-

Given a continually increasing population, how can we expect to control all forms of pollution and all the factors that contribute to land damage and misuse in our country? Should society protect its natural resources for recreational use by imposing a moratorium on industrialization? Should the government limit use of recreational vehicles that destroy natural habitats? To what extent should laws be enacted and enforced to govern use of recreational equipment? How much government intervention and expenditure of tax dollars would you allow toward this end?

chology that needs increasing stimulation and thrives on an inherent destructiveness, either of self or of the environment.

RECREATIONAL IMPACT ON THE ENVIRONMENT

Among the variety of activities that have direct impact on the environment are homes, land clearing, hunting, waterborne activities, and commercially operated facilities.

Vacation Homes

Vacation or second homes are usually built in scenic locations with lakes, panoramic views, mountains, or heavily wooded lands. The impact of such construction depends on the number of habitations developed within a given area—that is, on the carrying capacity of the land to sustain construction and use. With the building of houses come the inevitable questions of septic waste and its disposal, road construction, air pollution from the burning of fuel, thermal pollution of watercourses, and so forth.

If an area is attractive enough to induce developers and would-be vacation home owners to build permanent installations, the outcome is inevitably bad for the environment. The more scenic the area, the more people will pour into the region, and the added polluting load will hasten the breakdown of the environment. Vail, Colorado, is an excellent illustration of what happens to a scenic region that becomes popular and is overdeveloped by people who want to enjoy the great outdoors. Sooner or later the outdoors disappears under the surge of dwelling places, trade centers, nightclubs, and bowling alleys.

Land Clearing

When the land is stripped of trees and picked clean to provide recreational places, negative effects are almost sure to follow. Cutting down trees, eliminating ground cover, upsetting the ecological balance—these are some of the results when developers come to natural areas to convert them to recreational facilities. Ski and toboggan slopes and golf courses come quickly to mind. The cumulative and intensive use of these areas can destroy the natural environment. When these facilities are built indiscriminately, roads, amenities, sewage dis-

© TWS/Mark Anderman

Vacation homes have a direct impact on the environment.

posal, and other elements of urbanization are put into place. It is one thing to use and cultivate a natural slope with bare sections; it is quite another to destroy an entire forest so that people can slide down a snow-covered hill. Trees are the natural barriers to soil erosion. They help prevent mudslides and flooding. They provide oxygen and serve as noise abatement agents. Their destruction by scarification destroys our environment.

Hunting

The killing of wildlife for trophies or to sell their feathers, fur, horn, tusks, or other parts has pushed many wild species to the brink of extinction. Indiscriminate hunting hurts the flora and fauna of a habitat because it disturbs the balance between predators and their prey. When humans hunt, they upset this delicate balance. The wanton killing of predators permits the unrestricted growth of their prey, which then are forced into severe competition with each other for food. The result is slow starvation for many animals.

In the late 1970s, the Alaska Fish and Game Commission attempted to eradicate the entire wolf population in a region to induce growth of the caribou population. The plan was that large caribou herds would result, and the commission would charge fees to people who wanted to hunt them. But without natural predators, the caribou herds grew so large that they ate all their ground cover and ran out of food. The hunters had a good time, but the scheme served no useful purpose.

How can the natural environment be protected so that people can enjoy it without obliterating it? Does your municipal, state, or national government consider answering that question a priority? Should it be?

ENVIRONMENTAL GOALS

We must finally come to grips with the forces that threaten the use of resources for leisure purposes. People need to change their commuting habits; the environment must be helped to cleanse itself; and people must be educated about how a quieter, safer, more healthful environment, both urban and natural, can improve their lives.

SELECTED REFERENCES

Bryan, H. *Conflict in the Great Outdoors*. Auburn, Ala.: Bureau of Public Administration, University of Alabama, 1979.

Gaines, S., et al. *Taxation for Environmental Protection: A Multinational Study*. Westport, Conn.: Quorum Books, 1991.

Orloff, N. *The Environmental Impact Statement Process: A Guide to Citizen Action*. Arlington, Va.: Information Resources Press, 1978.

Patmore, J. A. *Recreation and Resources: Leisure Patterns and Leisure Places*. Oxford: Blackwell, 1983.

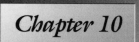

Chapter 10

SOCIAL PRESSURES AND LEISURE

Objectives

After reading this chapter, the student will be able to do the following:

Explain how social disintegration applies to recreational activity.

■

Discuss the social basis of urban life.

■

Describe the social institutions that promote change.

■

Explain how school influences leisure and recreational activity.

■

Understand how cultural institutions influence recreational service.

Human beings are profoundly social. Life and being are formed in the give and take of society. Personality does not develop in isolation, but largely through interrelationships with others. This growth happens in the course of many and varied types of association: first the family, then peer groups, citizenship participation, the workplace, and leisure activities. All of these relationships have significance for the developing individual.

The establishment of an appropriate environment helps the individual's inherent talents and interests to develop to maximum capacity. The emerging personality is encouraged to explore a value system that can be used as a guide to a better life.

Several social institutions are constantly at work to preserve and transmit cultural values, but there are insidious influences that steadily undermine that responsibility. The social significance of poverty, family disintegration, crime, immorality, personal irresponsibility, ignorance, and a lack of a work ethic carry over to leisure. Instead of recreational activity during leisure, we are currently witnessing negative leisure in an underclass that represents a point of view inimical to a workable social order. What can be done?

We are all intensely social. From birth until death, most of us are surrounded by people. We cannot escape them even if we want to, unless we go to extraordinary lengths to be alone. Even then, social influences pervade our every waking moment. Socialization is a fundamental need. The culture of which we are a part transmits the heritage of the past, along with new elements, through a variety of institutions—the home, school, government, religious authorities, and peer groups. These institutions and individuals confirm our worth, remind us of the debt we owe to the past, and offer expectations for the future.

Everything that is human is fashioned in the context and interrelationships of society. Traits and characteristics do not develop in a vacuum but through interdependencies in the community. This development takes place during the normal course of growing up and assimilating the values and ideas of the people with whom we live, work, play, worship, or learn.

HUMAN RELATIONS AND SOCIAL DEVELOPMENT

The relationships we develop over time occur within formal and informal groupings. We internalize the values and opinions of our family, peers, acquaintances, political cohorts, social groups, co-workers, and certainly our recreational partners. Social development occurs simply because we are in contact with other people. Sometimes the institutions of society, school, courts, or police intervene directly to

produce a form of behavior that is acceptable and desirable. Much of personal growth, however, is left to the coincidental associations of daily life.

The interaction between the individual and society produces either an assimilated, well-adjusted person or a dissatisfied, discontented, dissenting, rebellious individual. For the most part, social institutions mold "raw" individuals by a conditioning process that rewards conformity and penalizes real individuality. This attitude carries over into recreational pursuits. The traditional cultural activities are conservative in nature; they demand rigid adherence to form, ritual, and rules of performance. This is primarily observed in dual and team games, where no one wants to be called a spoilsport.

Other activities that also transmit the cultural heritage include art, music, dance, and drama. These activities contain customary methods of reproduction and/or performance. Attempts at innovation or radical departures from the accepted norm are often met with derision or ostracism. The brouhaha over the

---

Art: An Expression of Culture

From the cave drawings of southern France to the treasures of the greatest galleries in the world, society has benefited from and been inspired by the images created by artists. Primitive art was often a graphic representation of the activities of daily life. Religious beliefs and superstition were the object of much art as humans tried to explain the supernatural. Some of the greatest works of all time represent the human conception of the divine.

Equally prevalent was art depicting fertility, sexual prowess, and sexual activities. These facets of life have also engaged artists in capturing the mystery of human existence. Some of this art was produced strictly to cause sexual excitement and became a less accepted form of expression known as pornography. This type of work has been tolerated throughout civilization.

In recent years the National Endowment for the Arts has been under fire for allocating funds for artists whose work many people find to be pornographic or in very poor taste. Mapplethorpe produced horrific photos and other shocking images while he was funded by the NEA.

The issue calls into question the boundaries of art and good taste and the role of the government in sponsoring art. In a time when the federal government is downsizing, the NEA's budget has been cut drastically, due in part to misguided efforts like those mentioned above.

What role should government play in supporting the arts?

What are acceptable boundaries for government-supported artistic expression?

What role should censorship play when tax dollars are used to fund creative projects?

© Terry Wild Studio

Dance transmits cultural heritage.

photographs of Robert Mapplethorpe in 1990 is a case in point.[1] The work of this recipient of a grant from the National Endowments for the Arts award shocked some people. Protests against his photos resulted in the forced resignation of the chair of the NEA.[2]

Society's contract with the individual presumably offers a chance for personality development. It also requires respect for social values and behavior that contributes to the ongoing process of civilization. That this occurs in many different ways is a tribute to the variety of social influences and the interactions that are the warp and woof of the community fabric. There is hardly any aspect of human life that is not guided by, developed for, organized with, or controlled by people. The social forces affecting human behavior are produced by direct involvement with social institutions as well as by spontaneous associations.

In this chapter, the recreational needs of different segments of our society will become apparent through discussions concerning human ecology and the social basis of urban life. A variety of problems that currently beset our cities, as well as cultural changes that emphasize the family, youth, elders, women, and social planning in contemporary society, will be set against the background of city life and its organization.

When a municipality cuts property taxes, it must also cut spending. In the list of spending priorities where would you place cuts in spending for recreational services? How important do you think recreational service is to alleviating the social problems discussed in this chapter? Are public funds the only source of financing recreational service? Are they the most effective way?

THE INFLUENCE OF SOCIAL INSTITUTIONS

A social institution is an intentionally organized and formalized arrangement designed to achieve a particular objective. It is recognized by tradition and law as a separate social organization, with certain privileges and mandates. It takes its role from the entire social scene and is defined by its interrelationships with other institutions. Social institutions grow out of highly specific needs, which are culturally manifested as a society attains maturity and separates the diverse functions, obligations, and rights that compose social existence and order.

There are many social entities but only a few social institutions. Among the latter are the family, school, the law, government, religion, professions, and trades. These forms of association endure despite the fact that the individuals who give life to them come and go. Other social formats are temporary and informal, such as groups of friends or special interest organizations.

The social scene is in a constant state of flux. People live differently today from only five years ago. We are much more aware now of the problems in our cities, the problems of disadvantaged people, the incidence of crime, the energy crisis, and many other cultural changes that affect all of us. All of these problems that affect our society affect recreational services and settings.

Municipal Government: Current Problems

Urban government functions have multiplied tremendously during the last 25 years. These problems are highly technical and require the services of qualified, competent specialists. Specifically, city governments have expanded their functions in the fields of recreational service, health care, education, protection of life and property, public works, transportation, and social welfare. Until President Reagan announced his intention to cut the federal budget and with it hundreds of millions of dollars that would have gone to the cities to support a variety of urban services, municipal governments cooperated with state and federal authorities in activities that had once been relegated to the private sector.

Playgrounds, adult education programs, daycare centers, art schools, community centers, libraries, hospitals, garbage collection, aid to dependent children, and city marinas are only some of the vast array of specialized services city governments have attempted to provide. In light of severe recession, the enormous deficit with which the federal government has saddled itself, and the state of near bankruptcy facing a number of city governments, many of these functions will probably be sharply curtailed, if not eliminated.

Finally, there has been widespread dissent among taxpayers, who have demanded surcease from the constant tax burdens of state and local government. Some states (notably California, Massachusetts, and Oregon) have passed referendums that severely restrict property taxes and cut back on the services municipal governments can provide.

Problems of the Urban Metropolis

The growth of megalopolises, or urban clusters, has created problems of government that go largely unrecognized by smaller cities and towns. The satellite communities just beyond the urban fringe, whether incorporated or not, are integral to the metropolis in every way except political, and they want to maintain their political sovereignty. Although they may attempt to work with the major city on some common problems, many more problems arise. One consequence of this desire for autonomy includes the overlapping and duplication of functions, as well as economic waste and social disorder.

Many of the problems that confront central cities and their satellites infiltrate political boundaries and cannot be met by smaller communities that operate within the narrow confines of their municipal limits, no matter how efficient they are. For example, a transportation system cannot be coordinated when the small communities in the metropolitan region ignore the needs of neighboring municipalities and the region as a whole. One community may dump sewage or garbage whose end products find their way into aquifers, rivers, and other waterways and become a health problem for other communities. Crime does not confine itself to one jurisdiction. Poor people may move into any community that provides higher welfare payments. The maze of interlocking and conflicting problems of a political, economic, and jurisdictional kind have tremendous impact on people's lives.

The Social Basis of Urban Living

Cities by their nature offer a vast complex of influences that condition personality development, attitudes, and values. On one side are the mechanistic elements of urban culture; on the other are the myriad forms of social organization that are a constant source of psychological stimulation. The end result of interaction between the individual and the niche he or she inhabits is behavioral patterns that reflect the environment of the city dweller.

One characteristic of urbanites seems to be an apparent lack of concern for either social amenities or emotional ties with neighbors.

The city actually encourages impersonal relationships. In fact, one of the reasons people give for living in the city is that it permits many more choices and freedom. Moreover, there is a sense of superficiality in social relationships. The congestion of the city makes it impossible to get to know more than a fraction of all the people one meets. Thus the urban dweller is at once a member of a highly sophisticated cultural center and stereotyped in terms of the role he or she appears to play. Seeing people as roles rather than as individuals raises barriers to interpersonal relations. These barriers reinforce the impersonality of social relations.

Superficiality of Human Contact

The high density of people in a given area, coupled with their mobility and their numerous activities in business and the trades, produces contacts that are secondary. These contacts, although direct, are momentary and loosely defined. Many of the social contacts urbanites make are fleeting glimpses of one another in mass transit systems, as part of an audience, in the crowds of shoppers, in hordes of street vendors, and other equally anonymous faces that whirl past during the day. Most contacts of the city person range in intensity from a subliminal awareness of others to a casual, nodding acquaintance (for example, meeting neighbors in the elevator of their apartment building). The media also make indirect contacts possible, multiplying the number of secondary contacts without really extending primary relations.

As contacts have become increasingly sterile in the competitive, congested urban setting, formal social controls have been needed to undergird the primary controls that function so well where relationships are intimate. In the largest urban centers, such influences are so limited in scope that the normalization of human relations on a broader scale must be, almost by default, relegated to institutional control. This is the main reason that law and other rules of behavior take on significance in managing the conduct of urbanites. It is also why such functionaries as police officers, firefighters, judges, and probation officers play influential roles in urban life.

This is not to say that primary relations are unimportant, nor that they have been eliminated in the city. Some primary contacts reveal a surprising degree of vitality, especially the small informal recreational groups that have been established to satisfy their members' emotional and psychological needs. The multifarious recreational activities taking form as card clubs, informal dancing clubs, sewing clubs, book groups, and similar social groups in which adults participate are manifestations of the social forces at work in the city. So are informal recreational groups for youth, such as secret societies and clubs. They have supplanted many of the functions once performed by family, neighborhood, and church. They are primary in that the connections in them are informal and strictly personal.

Social and Moral Codes

In an urban setting, with its hodgepodge of cultures, ethnicities, races, religions, and other social distinctions, there is a great deal of tolerance and freedom. An individual may belong to several groups, each with a well-defined ethical code and recognized pattern of conduct. Because of their specialized nature, very few urban groups are able to fulfill all of the psychological and physical requirements of the individual. So the person joins as many groups as necessary to satisfy emotional and psychological needs.

The ability to lose oneself in the crowd often makes it possible for people to choose between one group and another without losing status or reputation. The city houses pluralistic social and ethical values that may exist nowhere else. One outcome of association with groups that have quite different behavioral and ethical codes is a multifaceted personality. The urban lifestyle is consistent with the paradox of carrying on a satisfying, though inconsistent, existence through relationships with groups that have divergent and often contradictory standards.

Social Disaffection and Urban Movements

Modern city life has been more adept at creating human desires than enabling their fulfillment. While urban life is highly competitive, that does not mean there is equality of opportunity to compete or that those who do compete all fare equally well. In urban America, powerful social pressures are concentrated on the individual to achieve specific objectives, particularly concerning social or economic status. Disaffection and dissension among the least successful are probably unavoidable. These thwartings may lead to emotional problems.

If shared with other people, they become focal points for social unrest and sometimes develop into a form of collective behavior. Thus, frustrations with the way things are can have a healthy outlet in the formation of social action groups that aim to change the current economic system; sectarian movements offering panaceas to those who are seeking themselves or merely a better life; movements for social betterment, to clean the air, water, and make the streets safe; and movements to reform, engineer, or modify aspects of the social order. The movements themselves represent the start of new social organizations, which may have influence far beyond their original boundaries. The recreational service movement was one such city-bred social reformation, and it has had profound effects on the social consciousness of America.

How might rich and poor communities differ in the recreational opportunities their social institutions afford? Should all people have the same opportunity for recreational experience? Would the social problems that exist in many poor neighborhoods be affected by well-funded recreational programs?

SOCIAL INSTITUTIONS AND RECREATIONAL EXPERIENCE

In order to be effective, social reconstruction must be based on genuine needs of the multitudes. These needs must be recognized as important in the life of every person, not merely fads that appeal to a small but vociferous special interest group. The chief function of social organization is to lend permanence, stability, and continuity to group life. It is these very qualities that make institutions, customs, and codes so difficult to change.

Inquiry into social organization also reveals the problems of social disorganization. Crime, poverty, class discontent, amoral behavior, and the inequities of life are evidences of failed so-

cial relationships and institutions. The relevance of these social factors to recreational services is readily apparent if one appreciates the connection between how and where people live and what they do to overcome perceived inequities that frustrate them. Of course, recreational participation is also part of the positive arrangements people find to suit themselves. Recreational activity can be the enlightened road to personal esteem, community recognition, and emotional and physical satisfaction.

The School and Recreational Service

Educational institutions are indispensable socializing agencies. Through the process of formal and informal instruction, the culture of society is passed along from generation to generation. In the classroom, the younger members of society are made aware of their social heritage. In a society that employs the schools as an acculturating institution as well as the major source of preparation for citizenship and the responsibilities of adult life, this force has an enormous influence throughout the childhood years and sometimes in adulthood as well. In many instances, urban schools have become substitutes for families due to the high breakup rate of students' families.[3]

To the positive aspects of school may also be added counterproductive outcomes. Schools not only reflect the problems and concerns of society but may exacerbate them. A case in point is a recent report issued by New York State's Social Studies Syllabus Review Committee. The committee's final statement mirrored academic multiculturalism and political correctness. It demonstrated the rush to separate ethnic and racial communities by challenging the melting-pot concept.[4,5]

Schools in all areas—city, country, or suburban—provide local, district, and regional recreational services to local children and youth. Of course, the kinds of recreational services provided vary from system to system. In some communities, the school system is the recreational service department as well as the chief formal educational institution. In others, only schools serving a neighborhood may be the physical facilities where some recreational activities are offered.

For children in school, a number of learning situations are coincidental with recreational experience. Among these are physical education activities, shop class, music activities, home economics courses, and art activities. In fact, the entire curriculum of the school has significance for recreational activity, because any study may become a recreational activity at the individual's leisure. The study of language for conversational purposes, science and math clubs, and many other classroom experiences may lead to recreational enjoyment.

Students may also participate in extended curricular activities organized and administered by the school. Examples are intramural activities of a sport and/or game, debating teams, choral groups, band performance, club activities, and the use of athletic facilities after school hours. Schools may also organize interscholastic athletic programs that are enjoyable for both performers and spectators.

Adult education has become popular over the years. Born of the exigencies of urban life, it has been a mainstay in providing formal and informal learning experiences for adults. The constantly shifting patterns of urban life may demand greater awareness of cultural surroundings, thereby producing the need for a continuing education. But adult education has proliferated far beyond the confines of the city. It is found wherever interested adults gather. Its offshoots assume great personal investment and offer opportunities for self-expression, fulfillment, and enjoyment in activities as diverse as public speaking, civic service, do-it-yourself home repair, lifesaving skills, and community theater. Education obtained during an adult's leisure is a primary recreational experience even if it occurs in a formal classroom setting.

The school, as one of society's great socializing agencies, offers innumerable opportunities for all age groups to participate in recreational learning experiences. It also comes complete with a physical plant. The extent of opportunity depends on how school officials perceive their responsibility. School system recreational services may consist of a comprehensive, full-time recreational program, activities offered only to school-age youth, activities only of an athletic type, or merely the use of the school plant by other community-based agencies. In whatever way the school system expresses interest in the worthy use of leisure, it can be a major source of recreational opportunity to the community it serves.

Mass Media and Recreational Opportunity

Perhaps no other social agency more accurately reflects the intellectual standards and interest of the people than the mass media. Here is a social institution that transmits information to and about people, places, and things, generates intense interest in a variety of subjects and topics, and entertains as well. Surely everyone

Schools provide recreational service.

now realizes the great impact of television, both as a news-gathering agency and as a medium for entertainment, on viewers. Of course, all of the media transmit significant information too, some of which is useful for the public to formulate opinions about effective social policies.

The complexities of modern society demand a free press that can supply (in its enlightened moments) needed information about the current events of the day as well as problems and situations we can know only vicariously. Moreover, the mass media shape taste and fashion, support worthy causes, expose political and other forms of corruption, dispense the news, and provide entertainment without peer. There is no faster or more economical method for the delivery of news, ideas, or pleasure.

The influence of the mass media cannot be denied. There is something for just about everyone: advice to the lovelorn and to parents bringing up a family, medical solutions to health problems, financial management, guides to dining out and tourism, places to go and things to do. The media provide commentary and criticism that stimulate, motivate, and guide behavior.

As opinion seekers and molders, the media operate throughout all levels of society. Information about special interest groups, political figures, world monetary trade, the local job market, or human interest stories tend to influence people's attitudes for or against an idea, a group, or some planned action. Just as they gather and dispense news, the media also play an extremely important role in developing an event into something controversial or bringing the obscure to public notice.

But their recreational effects are of greatest importance, because this is how most people perceive the media. They look on it as the pleasurable part of the day or evening when by reading, listening, or viewing, they can be entertained, informed, motivated, or lulled to sleep. The media also promote recreational experiences, among them sporting events, movies, concerts, museums, and art galleries. Public recreational service agencies use the media to inform the public about the where, when, and what of recreational opportunities. In short, the mass media not only function as recreational experiences themselves but also help shape the public's knowledge about and interest in other recreational activities.

Sectarian Agencies and Recreational Service

Religious institutions of all sects, denominations, and creeds have as their chief responsibility the propagation of their faith and moral instruction. Churches have always played an important part in fashioning attitudes toward people of other beliefs.

Just as churches influence the lives of their members, so too does the urban environment influence the viability and vitality of churches. Social stratification in any community, especially the city, is mirrored in the structure and functions of the churches—that is, in the types of individuals they attract, forms of worship, social and religious values, and relations with other organizations in the community. The rise of extradenominational churches is an indication of how sectarian agencies keep pace with modern life. Many of the established churches have failed to meet the needs of the culturally deprived and economically poor, at least in the United States. The rise of cults and involvement in mystical rites illustrate how far people may go in attempting to get religion to satisfy their emotional needs.

Religious institutions not only influence the faithful but also perform numerous activities that transcend purely religious principles. They have become a force in leisure-centered and social welfare activities. Sectarian agencies have come to realize that leisure is an important consideration in people's lives. If they hope to influence moral conduct, they must provide some appeal beyond creed. This is why so many of them offer comprehensive recreational programs and facilities to their congregations. It is not unusual for such social activities as suppers, picnics, game nights, dances, travel programs, exhibitions, displays, lectures, discussion groups, and athletic activities to be a part of the clergy's function. Everything from Bible classes to dramatic societies, music classes, domestic science, arts and crafts, summer camps, and playgrounds are more and more being sponsored, organized, and administered by churches.

Churches have also begun organizing and administering nursing homes, hospitals, classroom activities, day nurseries, employment bureaus, and other secular activates. All of these functions and responsibilities are considered integral to the role of the church in modern society. If churches remain the chief exponent of moral teaching and preservation of the faith, they are also an expanding force for the social betterment of citizens throughout the community via activities that bring satisfaction, self-expression, and enjoyment to their daily lives. Church no long means exclusively prayer of the faithful and attendance on the Sabbath; it includes a broadened approach to the demands of constituents, whose corporeal and leisure needs, not just spiritual needs, are seen to be important.

Cultural Institutions and Recreational Service

Libraries, art galleries, museums of various kinds, public auditoriums, musical ensembles, theater, and the like are excellent measures of the intellectual and social life of the community. Generally, only large urban centers have the resources to support notable cultural institutions, but libraries can be found in almost every community. Commercial and community theater; repertory groups; street performers; private and public art galleries; science, history, and natural museums; planetariums; and other cultural repositories exist wherever people have decided that they want to enjoy these kinds of endeavors. On the whole, cultural institutions are widespread throughout society, and millions of people are exposed to them when free attractions are offered in public parks, gardens, or municipal auditoriums. Naturally, millions more take advantage of commercial opportunities.

Libraries and other cultural institutions serve an extremely important function in the provision of recreational experiences. They often supply a professionalism that is worth emulating. Of even greater importance are their spinoffs—duplications of aspects of the great cultural institutions by amateurs, interested people, and groups who see in these experiences a lifetime of enrichment, satisfaction, and enjoyment through exposure to the great ideas of our civilization.

To what extent does the family shape a person's concepts of leisure and recreational experience? What effect does social disorganization have on leisure and recreational opportunities? Consider

this scenario: A neighborhood park in a large city is a haven for drug dealers and thieves. People are too afraid to come to the park, so it's no longer used for its intended purpose. Occasional attempts to police the park succeed in removing criminals for a while, but as soon as the police leave, the dealers and thieves return. The equipment at the park has been vandalized or stolen. No other park is near enough for people to walk to. Should the city pay to repair and maintain this park?

SOCIAL DISORGANIZATION AND ITS EFFECTS

Just as there is social organization to establish how society can benefit its constituency, there are also contrary forces at work that tear at the fabric of society. Any disturbance of the social and economic balance of the community is a form of social disorganization. The differences among individual interests and their expression, for instance, have the seeds of social disintegration about them.

This is not to say that diverse interests and differences of attitude or opinion are not welcome in a democratic society. Far from it. The very diversity of people and their interests is essential to the pluralistic and free institutions on which America has always depended for strength, progress, and resourcefulness. However, individual differences can be formidable barriers. Open conflict can arise out of prejudicial thinking, long-festering suspicions, racial hatred, religious bigotry, ethnic bias, economic inequity, and other equally reprehensible expressions of the dark side of human nature.

All communities exist in a condition of fragile equilibrium, with too little cooperation among various groups because of existing animosities, frequently due to cross-cultural misunderstandings. This state usually continues until something occurs that transforms long-held prejudices into open antagonism. This has been painfully evident for groups arriving in this country. The new immigrants are often exploited by the older, more established groups—who were once immigrants themselves.

Today's society has witnessed numerous instances of the breakdown of the law, reflecting a rejection of moral codes and ethical conduct.

Corruption of public officials, both elected and appointed, occurs at every level, from local to federal.[6] Congressmen and senators have been convicted of bribery, taking kickbacks, and selling their offices; mayors, governors, state legislators, and appointed officials who wield the power of the bureaucracy are implicated in criminal activities ranging from extortion, bribery, and fixing to racial, religious, and ethnic discrimination.[7]

Moreover, there is widespread corruption among the trades and professions; physicians and lawyers are indicted for lying, stealing, embezzling client trusts, and malpractice due to incompetence.[8] The disintegration of society finds its major outlet at the local level, where public and private individuals flout the law or are on the take.[9]

When the economy is listless or inflation is rampant, and people have little faith in their government's ability to do anything about it, conditions are ripe for disaffection, disunity, and social upheaval. When industries lay off workers and unemployment skyrockets, when businesses go bankrupt and cities cannot meet their obligations, the disintegration becomes a fact. People begin to leave the stricken region. Workers seek employment elsewhere; middle-class flight takes away the taxes that really support the community; business and industries leave, hastening the demise of the institutional structure.

The Family and Recreational Activity

The family is a microcosm of society. Modern life and its complexities have been given as reasons for the breakup of families. Statistics show that half of all marriages end in divorce. Battered wives, husbands, and children are no longer rare, if they ever were. Abused family members are seen constantly by medical facilities, domestic relations courts, and crisis centers. This is an indication that society is losing its cohesiveness and threatens to fly apart. As the family loses its instructive and customary power of transmitting traditions and cultural heritage, there is a simultaneous weakening of ethical conduct and the simple civilities that smooth the normal course of human relations.

The cultural changes in the American family have been enormous in recent years. Generally, children engage in few activities with their families. As they grow older, they want to be with their friends instead. One problem is that leisure activities often differ among family members. Each member may go his or her separate way. Between school, work, and different leisure activities, families rarely participate together in anything. Unless they have made a great effort to maintain the commonalities that each family should have—taking the time to instruct the children in recreational activities and keeping the family unit together during the formative years of childhood—there will be little that family members can do to promote cohesiveness and closeness. Physical separateness of family members leads to emotional separation.

There are many recreational activities the entire family can enjoy. They include bicycle trips, camping trips, picnics, swimming, tennis, hiking, fishing, and activities in and around the home such as cooking, table tennis (if there is enough space), hobbies, reading, and listening to music together. If family members find themselves going different ways all the time, they should set aside one night a week or an afternoon on a weekend to do something together. Of course, indifference and longstanding noncommunication cannot be undone quickly. Personalities, interests, and skills are shaped over a relatively long period of time. The enjoyment of family companionship must be developed from the earliest time. Unless insight and understanding are built in from childhood, there is little likelihood that they will develop later.

Attitudes toward recreational activity are generated from early childhood. How an individual views a specific activity will reflect, to a great extent, how he or she was introduced to the activity. Early mastery of skills, exposure to new experiences, and satisfactions of achievement during leisure all tend to enhance the individual's appreciation of recreational activities. The opposite is also true. The home environment is a huge influence on the individual's values, opinions, self-confidence, and attitudes toward leisure and recreational participation.

The influence of families on their children's expectations, aspirations, and cultural development can be positive or negative. Where home life patterns and family support have made a positive contribution, children are likely to grow up able to express themselves, adapt

Camping is a recreational activity the family can enjoy.

© Terry Wild Studio

to different situations, and persevere in the face of setbacks. A lifelong pattern of appreciation, participation, and enjoyment can result. In contrast, unsupportive families may raise children who dislike recreational experiences and miss out on their physical, emotional, and spiritual benefits. The family's responsibility for encouraging life-enhancing activities calls for intelligence, consideration, and a great deal of affection. With these to bolster them, this social force can be one of the most positive influences in all children's leisure life.

Poverty and Recreational Activity

The term *disadvantaged* is used to describe a person or groups of people who are culturally, economically, physically, or socially deprived. Most disadvantaged people live in inner cities, but they can be found in every part of the country. For example, Native Americans are one of the most disadvantaged groups, even though a majority of them live in rural areas.

Poor health, often due to inadequate nutrition, is often a problem for disadvantaged people. Many are unemployed or underemployed. The working poor live at a level barely above subsistence. Many of them are illiterate, and many are illegal aliens who have found a haven in the United States.

Ghetto schools are almost uniformly deplorable. Instruction is substandard. The buildings have broken windows and holes in the walls and have long since been defaced by graffiti. Even where there is an attempt to construct attractive and comfortable places, the vandals are soon at work. Recreational areas and facilities are nearly nonexistent in such neighborhoods. Most school buildings were constructed without any thought to outside space for recreational purposes. They were merely structures set in limited urban spaces. Drug use, alcoholism, petty crime, and violent crime are fostered by this deprivation. These problems threaten to overwhelm the law enforcement agencies, justice system, and other social organizations designed to contain this social malevolence.[10]

The leisure of the disadvantaged is much different from that of the upper or middle classes. Since many disadvantaged people are unemployed or school dropouts, they have more leisure than the higher income groups. The working poor and those who are exploited for their labor have even less leisure than their wealthier urban neighbors. In either case, disadvantaged people have neither the money nor the knowledge to appreciate and participate in the recreational activities offered by the government. But where facilities and programming are available, some poor people may be induced to try them.

However, the disadvantaged live in areas that offer little in the way of recreational facilities or organized programs. Many disadvantaged people do not participate in commercial types of recreational services. They usually do not own a car and rarely take vacations or attend spectator events, social functions, or cultural activities. This is due at least as much to the lack of money as to the lack of a constructive concept of personal leisure. Cultural deprivation may also produce attitudes of apathy and disaffection toward organized constructive recreational activities that are made available through public or voluntary organizations.

Peer pressure may cause inner-city youth especially to reject outright the values that are accepted by the majority of society. This attitude precludes their participation in many recreational activities. That disadvantaged people may in fact despise the programs society deems valuable can be attributed to a lack of exposure at early ages, insufficient support from their families, and nonacceptance by their peer groups or older members of the community who feel that such activities do not provide the kind of status or action that they crave.[11]

Crime, Delinquency, Civil Disorder, and Recreational Activity

The incidence and form of criminal behavior are closely related to social and economic conditions as well as public attitudes toward law enforcement. Organized crime is directly related to urbanization. Lawbreakers, especially those who have long records of antisocial activity, show the mentality of habitual offenders. Such individuals typically think of themselves as criminals, use a well-practiced method of operation, speak a criminal argot, see crime as a vocation, think of themselves as opponents of the criminal justice system, and invariably associate with other types of criminals (racketeers, prostitutes, pimps, drug pushers, and so on). Some felons begin relatively early, joining delinquent gangs and engaging in vandalism, petty theft, extortion, and street fighting; then they graduate to more serious illegal activities.

Social disorganization, which is both a product and a cause of crime, increases dramatically in the urban environment because of such factors as a high mobility, anonymous relationships, impersonalized social controls imposed by law and police agencies, and the opportunities for delinquents to become acquainted with each other. The associations they form reinforce

morally reprehensible conduct and a general disregard for socially acceptable behavior.

Antisocial activities of any kind place severe restrictions on recreational services and on the opportunities for recreational participation. Attacks in parks and other recreational facilities immediately force people to reassess their perceptions of personal security and tend to inhibit the use of such facilities for recreational purposes. As Robert J. McGuire, former police commissioner, stated:

> *Crime has enormous impact on the quality of life in the city. It dictates where you walk and what time you walk. Whether you go out at night or stay home. . . .*[12]

Little has changed in the past decade, except to get worse as city services decline. It is unfortunate that some people live in constant fear for their safety, even in the privacy of their own homes. In recent years there has been an increasing incidence of assaults on older people, but other age groups are not immune. A disdain for traditional authority seems to be sweeping the country. Students attack teachers in schools, gangs attack police officers, children attack children.

All of these threats, perceived or actual, influence participation in recreational activities and attendance at recreational places. Many parks, whether local, country, state, or national, are no longer recreational havens.[13] In fact, many neighborhood and city parks and playgrounds have been abandoned by the community due to nonmaintenance or takeover by undesirable elements. The presence of drug addicts, alcoholics, or homeless people is construed as a menace to others.[14]

Public recreational facilities are not being used by the patrons who frequented them less than a decade ago because they are apprehensive about going to places where antisocial behavior is rampant. Moreover, this unruly and outrageous behavior eliminates many of the kinds of experiences people are seeking when they attend recreational facilities. The quality of the recreational experience is demeaned when hostile elements threaten the patrons.

Whether performed by individuals or by anonymous groups, violent acts toward people and property decrease everyone's ability to participate in and enjoy recreational activities.

When antisocial individuals trash public facilities, wantonly kill or cripple animals in zoos, break windows, deface walls, set fire to structures, damage equipment, and, worst of all, molest people, recreational opportunities are reduced.

If people are afraid to go out at night, if they fear for their safety when they attend recreational events, the antisocial element wins. Destruction of public property reduces the ability of the system to provide opportunities; few cities can afford to keep replacing damaged equipment. Placing curfews on parks, playgrounds, and other recreational areas continues to reduce leisure opportunities. A vicious cycle of antisocial activities breeds such insecurity and actual damage that recreational places, programs, and enjoyable experiences are denied to the very people who need them the most.

A large city has a $1 million recreational budget and allocates $10,000 per year for facility repair. An uptown, public golf course has high maintenance fees and also takes in a lot of revenue, bringing in a profit for the city. The course needs repairs costing $10,000 on its irrigation system. Three other privately owned golf courses in the city allow the public to play. A downtown swimming pool in the city loses money: Attendance is high, but pool entry fees are low because the residents can't afford to pay much. Insurance fees and lifeguard salaries also contribute to the pool's operating in the red. The pool's filter system needs repairs estimated to cost $10,000. What issues should the city council consider as they decide how to spend the money?

ATTEMPTS TO SOLVE SOCIAL PROBLEMS

Is the social order in such disarray that nothing can be done to alleviate the dislocation and disintegration we observe on every side? The intricacies of social factors spread far beyond social interaction. Other variables in the pattern of the social fabric in every community include political realities, economic capacity, personal attitudes, custom, educational levels, health status, personal involvement in community development, and the ability of social institutions to transform behavior.

Public Planning and Urban Renewal

Despite the drastic federal cutbacks and less allocation of financial assistance to cities, there is little likelihood that the major cities of the United States will be left to bankruptcy and quick (or even slow) disintegration.[15] There may well be a need for state government to interpose to protect the state's people, whether they reside in rural areas or urban centers, from the disaster of budget retrenchment and the reaction of taxpayer revolts. Not only the states but other government agencies, as well as private and quasi-public institutions, must rally to provide the programs and the physical properties that offer amenities and an enhanced quality of life.

The purpose of any urban renewal project is to develop adequate housing for its inhabitants, neighborhood schools, and sufficient recreational areas (including parks, playgrounds, swimming facilities, and community centers) to meet residents' needs. A comprehensive redevelopment program can be successful only when it meets all the basic needs of the people. This requires good schools, employment opportunities, affordable and good housing, pertinent social services, and positive leisure outlets. If every sector of the community could work in cooperation to provide these necessities, a great force for social integration and renewal would be created.

Among the recreational services that can be expected to reinforce traditional values and social acceptance are those that improve the quality of the various neighborhoods, develop innovative recreational programs, and foster institutional improvements. The latter may be anticipated as public forums, discussions, advisory committees, and wider opportunities are made available to all citizens.

Community Involvement and Recreational Service

Community involvement is essential to the success of any recreational program anywhere. Recreational service planning should be oriented to the needs of small population groups and neighborhoods. Community participation must be sought before any decisions regarding park placement or other aspects of recreational planning are made. Citizen input is also essential in implementing programs. One major objective of recreational services should be to solve pressing urban problems.

Citizens must become aware of community problems and should be recruited to work with public administrators to create social reforms in their neighborhoods. Even some gangs are nonviolent and want neighborhood improvements, such as eviction of drug pushers, neighborhood cleanup, food distribution, and protection of mass transit riders against muggers.

The administrative decentralization of recreational services has implications for both community residents and administrators. Residents can

1. influence employment patterns and obtain training for careers in recreational service,
2. gain bargaining power,
3. gain more frequent and satisfying recreational experiences thanks to their involvement in the planning and implementation of programs, and
4. establish behavioral models to inspire community members and draw them into new areas of employment and social action.

Administrators can

1. create a new job market and work force of and for the community,
2. devise valid methods for appraising recreational programs, and
3. assess the leisure patterns of community members.

Recreationists in administrative positions must first meet with community leaders to determine what the responsibilities of the community will be in any recreational program. As the project progresses, the recreationist should solicit community members' feedback about the program. Major changes should be mutually agreed on. Once the program is on its feet, a great deal of responsibility should be put into the hands of community members. Community involvement provides jobs and maintains interest in the established program.

Social Sector, Interest, and Effort

The federal, state, and local governments, as well as voluntary and quasi-public agencies, all have much to contribute to every segment of the population. In the past, most federal and state provisions for recreational services have been for people who could get to regional recreational areas on their own and were knowledgeable about camping, swimming, and other outdoor activities. They were also able to pay for services and equipment necessary to benefit from these recreational facilities. Most federally owned land is remote from the great metropolitan regions, particularly those cities along the eastern seaboard. When a state park is near a large city, it is often difficult to get there by public transportation. Many inner-city residents lack knowledge of the city's transportation system, and many are not native speakers of English, which makes it hard for them to seek out relatively distant sources of recreational opportunities.

The local government has a great responsibility to provide suitable recreational services to all members of the population. Unfortunately, studies show that middle- and upper-income groups are usually favored in recreational programs. Even when programs are open to the entire community, they are often based on middle-class values and interests and are too expensive for most low-income families. For example, community swimming and tennis complexes are appearing in many of our smaller cities and townships. They are open to all, but disadvantaged families cannot afford the $100 to $300 annual membership fee. Even if they could, they would probably not be able to get to the facility.

Voluntary and quasi-public agencies must also share responsibility for community recreational services. YMCAs and YWCAs, Boys' and Girls' Clubs, and settlement houses do good jobs—where they exist. However, when neighborhoods begin to deteriorate and the middle class leaves, voluntary agencies often leave with it. This is an unfortunate reality of disadvantaged areas. But local government cannot flee when times are bad. It must attempt to reverse the trend and must direct time, money, and energy to programs that are designed to assist citizens, not simply maintain the status quo.

Local government must decide where to put its limited resources so that those in the greatest need will receive the kind of help they require. One innovative idea—urban homesteading—has come into its own recently (1990). Residents of deteriorating ar-

© Frances M. Roberts

Government has a responsibility to provide recreational service to every segment of the population.

eas have been able to buy dilapidated structures and restore them with low-interest loans. Some of these neighborhoods have become showplaces, attracting both middle- and upper-income people back into the heart of the city. These are the kinds of programs that local governments should push.

Compensatory recreational services, for example, is simply a plan to put the greatest effort into recreational programming for the disadvantaged segment of the population. It attempts to compensate some for their social and economic hardships.

Disadvantaged youth usually have a poor self-image. Their environment makes it almost impossible to achieve their goals. The disadvantaged grow up to expect frustration and defeat, and they are rarely disappointed. A meaningful recreational program can help these young people to think more of themselves and their futures—indeed, to realize that they can have futures. It is important that any recreational program provide suitable adult role models for young people. Ways of providing meaningful recreational experiences to poor children include planning self-help projects and hiring community members. Assignment of workers to target populations or outreach programs is part of this picture.

It is also important to recruit more minority and disadvantaged people for careers in the field of recreational service. Recreationists defi-

nitely have a responsibility for improving urban conditions. Educational experiences in the universities must be updated to include urban studies and exploration of recreational programs needed and desired by communities. Improvement of youth-oriented and counseling programs is needed to prevent future civil disorders.

People's attitudes about themselves and others play a major role in how they perceive themselves and how they confront life on a daily basis. While attitudes are learned early, they can be modified through contacts with social institutions. This is true with regard to sexism, racism, nationalism, ageism, and other biased ways of looking at and judging others.

No group of citizens should be denied recreational opportunity simply because they are no longer young, are disadvantaged, speak languages other than English, or have a different ethnic, religious, or racial orientation from those who can trace their ancestry in the United States back four or five generations.

For example, older people make up an increasing proportion of the total population of the country. The graying of America is not merely a slogan but a fact. Elders have the same needs for recreational services, with all that such a concept entails, as any other segment of the population. So do people with mental or physical disabilities. All levels of government, as well as private and voluntary agencies, should contribute to their mainstreaming.

As much as possible, recreational services and facilities should be open, available, and accessible to all. They are needed to help hold the fabric of social life together and encourage people to be more resilient, capable of resisting the erosion of self-confidence, self-sufficiency, and self-esteem that tries the life of every individual at some time. There are many social institutions that can help defend the individual and improve his or her situation in life. Recreational service is one of them—if it is given the essential resources to do the job.

Would you advocate student-loan waivers for new graduates who commit to performing five years of inner-city recreational service after graduation?

SELECTED REFERENCES

Andrew, E. *Closing the Iron Cage: The Scientific Management of Work and Leisure.* Montreal: Black Rose Books, 1981.

Clark, J., and C. Critcher. *The Devil Makes Work: Leisure in Capitalist Great Britain.* Urbana, Ill.: University of Illinois Press, 1985.

Iso-Ahola, S. E. *The Social Psychology of Leisure and Recreation.* Dubuque, Ia.: Brown, 1980.

Olszewski, A., and K. Roberts, eds. *Leisure and Life-Style: A Comparative Analysis of Free Time.* London: Sage, 1989.

Paul, E. F., et al., eds. *The Good Life and Human Good.* New York: Cambridge University Press, 1992.

Stebbins, R. A. *Amateurs, Professionals and Serious Leisure.* Montreal: McGill University Press, 1992.

Wilson, W. J. *The Truly Disadvantaged: The Inner City, the Underclass, and Public Policy.* Chicago: University of Chicago Press, 1987.

Chapter 11

LEISURE AND THE MARKET

Objectives
After reading this chapter, the student will be able to do the following:

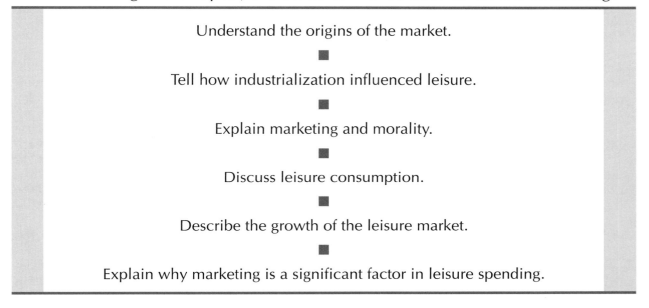

Understand the origins of the market.

■

Tell how industrialization influenced leisure.

■

Explain marketing and morality.

■

Discuss leisure consumption.

■

Describe the growth of the leisure market.

■

Explain why marketing is a significant factor in leisure spending.

Marketing has been around for as long as there have been goods to trade or an economy to make commerce worthwhile. Naturally, early marketing came in the form of direct barter or whatever caught the eye of the potential buyer. Transactions were simple and immediate.

The history of marketing is an outgrowth of early markets or centers of trade. As commerce flourished and goods from faraway places filled the market stalls, potential buyers had to be wooed. Competition, risk, taxes, and a desire for profit tended to set the price, but competition invariably caused price decline. It was necessary to attract buyers to purchase wares whose price was not the essential element. What attracted them was marketing.

The relationship between leisure and marketing is seen early on; as free time became available, it coincided with fairs, festivals, and other entertainment activities of the market. In time, wealthy customers were attracted to a wide variety of cultural opportunities and influenced others to emulate them. Fads and fashions developed from the caprice of the leisured population. This led to the marketing of those interests to the masses.

Contemporary competition for dollars spent during leisure uses market segmentation to attract customers to a particular product or service. In the same mode, but without a profit orientation, recreationists use marketing practices to draw consumers in the public sector.

If one considers the basic dichotomy between activities that are either essential to survival versus those that are a matter of individual preference, the implications of leisure in the marketplace are enormous.

Studies show that at least 75 percent of an average individual's time is taken up with activities considered essential to human existence. Experts may differ on exactly which activities constitute essential needs and which are seen as discretionary or elective—eating and clothing for survival in contrast to dining and dressing for pleasure. But most agree that essential behaviors involve physiological, emotional, and social well-being.

A 1972 statement from the editorial advisory board of *Leisure Today* is sexist and redundant, but it provides a good definition for the consideration of leisure as an integral part of a market economy:

> *that period of time at the complete disposal of the individual, after he has completed his work and fulfilled his other obligations. Leisure hours are periods of freedom, when man is able to enhance his value as a human being and as a productive member of his society.*[1]

Americans dispose of approximately 6 hours a day, 54 hours a week, or 2,808 hours a year that can be described as leisure. This does not include holidays or paid vacations. Since the earliest civilization, humans have sought out

The mall: A modern marketplace.

meaningful (and not-so-meaningful) pursuits during their leisure.

HISTORICAL FOUNDATIONS

To understand the relationship between leisure and the marketplace, one must understand history as it relates to both topics. Leisure preceded the marketplace. The evolution of civilization depended on the ability to gain security. Early humans were consumed with finding food, shelter, and protection from the natural threats posed by their environment. As they developed tools, brought the power of fire under control, and planted food crops, human beings began to create tools and items of special use and value. The invention and use of tools was so important that the ages of human development are historically divided by the mastery of various minerals and metals in the construction of tools: the Stone, Copper, Bronze, and Iron Ages.

Beginning in the Stone Age, agrarian societies fostered the development of pottery and various containers for holding grains and oils, as well as the invention of writing. Concurrently, the ability to manipulate metals encouraged the creation of hard currency, which eventually facilitated trade in goods and services.

Only after these events occurred could the concept of the market be realized. Leisure, resulting in part from the achievement of security, a recognized social order, the domestication of animals, and the refinement of agricultural practices, enabled the gradual emergence of stable communities at central locations. This eventually resulted in the appearance of economies in the ancient world. These economies centered on the existence of a marketplace.

Ancient Law and the Market

The ancient Near East offers many texts describing the market activities of the inhabitants. Writings of Sumerians, Egyptians, Syrians, Hittites, Assyrians, and Babylonians offer insights into the early market activities of these civilizations.

The Code of Hammurabi, written in approximately 1782 B.C., included laws to direct the lives and activities of people living under the Amorite Dynasty. These laws covered many areas of behavior, ranging from morality to legal liability, adoption, marriage and dowries, and mercantile activities. Trading occurred between two groups, the merchants and the traders. The traders brought their goods to the merchants, who would pay them in currency or barter for other items. Grain, sheep, cattle, wines, slaves, and currency were bought and sold in the marketplace. James Pritchard reports:

> If a man lend grain, wool, oil, or any goods at all to a trader to retail, the trader shall write down the value and pay it back to the merchant, with the trader obtaining a sealed receipt for the money which he pays to the merchant.[2]

The code also specified punishments and judgments:

> If a woman wine seller, instead of receiving grain for the price of a drink, has received money by the large weight and so has made the value of the drink less than the value of the grain, they shall prove it against that wine seller and throw her into the water.[3]

Apparently swimming was not considered an enjoyable pastime in ancient Babylonia.

The Market and Culture

Much market activity was associated with the rituals of the major religions of the ancient world. Animal sacrifice and offerings to the deity held great importance. Temple tariffs played a major role in the economy, with exacting payments required for the procurement of objects to be offered. In the city of Carthage, the following guidelines were found on fragments of stone blocks dating from the latter part of the third century B.C.

> Any citizen and any scion and any participant in a banquet for the god and anybody who shall offer a sacrifice . . . , those men shall make payment per sacrifice in a written document. . . . Any priest who shall accept a payment contrary to what is specified in this tablet shall be fined.[4]

The tariff further describes how animal sacrifices would be carved and divided between the priest-merchant and the worshipper. Undoubtedly, the trade of butcher had its start in the temples of the Near East.

The well-developed economic system of ancient Greece, whose influence reached through-out the Mediterranean, was centered on the city marketplace, or *agora*. The marketplace of Hellenistic times witnessed the trade of materials such as corn, olive oil, dried fish, wine, metals, timber, slaves, and manufactured goods. In each city, the agora became the gathering place or administrative center. Buildings included a council house, archives, and the *stoae* (shops and offices). The emporia or trading posts of the empire were spread throughout the Mediterranean basin.

The growth of the Greek empire resulted in the dissemination of its culture and the creation of a wealthy class of citizens as the profit from the various outlying markets was realized. This growth eventually contributed to the downfall of Greece as the market needs of remote areas were gradually met by local efforts and their dependence on the powerful city-states waned. By the first century B.C., the economic and cultural supremacy of Greece was in decline. The economic benefits realized through the systematic exploitation of its conquered neighbors failed to expand. It became difficult to obtain food supplies from foreign lands, maintain production at home, and continue economic and cultural influence over the foreign populations.

The non-Greek cities of Alexandria, Syracuse, Rhodes, and eventually Rome began to exert their own influence on the market economy of the ancient world. While these distant, ancient civilizations offer some insight into the concept of a market and the growth of trade, their remoteness from our modern reality makes it difficult to grasp these realities. If one has the good fortune to visit the site of an ancient civilization, the archaeological remnants often bring the past into much clearer view.

Consider the early activities that took place on a marshy lowland between the Palatine and Capitoline in central Latium. Residents of the area brought their livestock to this watering hole. Gradually they began to trade. The importance of this swamp grew as it became identified with the exchange of goods. Anthony Pereirra explains:

> It was in a true sense a market place, and temporary stalls soon changed into permanent shops; but with the passage of time the Forum proper gradually lost its original character, the traders were banished from the exclusive area and by doing so the first steps

were taken to make the Forum respectable and solemn.[5]

The area became the center of commerce, law, and religion for the mighty empire of Rome.

Classical Latin used the word *forum* to denote a market site set aside for the sale of goods. The Roman Forum was described in ancient writings as the "quo conferrent controversias et quae venderentur vellent quo ferrent, forum appelarunt"[6] or "the place to which they took their disputes and to which they brought the goods they wished to sell."

Juvenal gave advice on how to sell in the market:

Pares quod vendere possis pluris dimidio, nec te fastida mercis ullius subeant ablegandae Tiberum ultra neu credas ponendum aliquid discriminus inter ungenta et corium: lucri bonus est odor re qualibet.[7]

This translates to: You should produce some goods which you can sell at more than 50 percent profit, and do not be overcome with disgust at the type of merchandise which has to be relegated to the other side of the Tiber, or think that you should make any distinction between perfumes and hides: profit smells sweet no matter from what good it is derived.

Early on, the forum of Rome also became the site of special events, including livestock fairs and gladiator contests. The term used for the annual fair held in a town or a city was *mercatus.* Joan Frayn writes:

The important feature of the mercatus was not the unaccustomed gathering of the participants, for they probably all came from populated areas in or around urban centers. It was the amount and variety of the merchandise available.[8]

The forum evolved further into different market settings, including the macellum, the basilica, and the emporium, the latter being a market situated by the sea or the Tiber River. As the market aspect of the forum was banished, other market areas were developed in adjacent neighborhoods. Of particular note is the market of Trajan, which incorporated two types of market distinct from the macellum: a public retail bazaar and a porticoed exchange building.[9]

The business of the market took on a more permanent nature at this and other sites. "Tonsor, copo, cocus, lanius sua limina servant. Nunc, Roma est nuper magna taberna fuit."[10] ("The barber, the innkeeper, the cook, the butcher keep within their thresholds. What was largely one great retail store is now the city of Rome.")

Commerce grew from the central marketplace to the outlying neighborhoods and villages. Country dwellers had the opportunity to bring their goods to the city market every nine days (nundinae) and often returned home with goods not available in their remote environs. Historically, a radius of about 35 kilometers (21 miles) from the central market of a city was the practical limit of travel for country people wishing to market their goods in the city. As suburban areas grew in population, new markets were developed in those areas.

Rome benefited greatly from the manufactured goods of the region: the pottery from Arretium, the spears, picks, scythes, and chisels of Puteoli, the pots and pans of Capua. These goods were also traded to the remote areas of the empire. The Roman influence extended throughout Italy and beyond to Carthage, Macedonia, Syria, Greece, Egypt, southern Gaul, and Spain.[11]

With the growth of commerce between population centers and more remote areas came a natural transfer of information and culture between previously unrelated peoples. The trade routes of the ancient world were also its communication lines. As Rome obtained materials like grain, copper, tin, lead, wool, and hides from Gaul and Spain, these areas adjusted to and eventually absorbed many of the social and cultural practices of their occupiers. This may seem oppressive by modern standards, but it was a natural occurrence during this epoch. The spread of Christianity, for example, was greatly aided by the presence of Roman legions in the Middle East that were in contact with the government in Rome.

The major trade routes along the Via Aurelia, Flaminia, Appia, and other roads created a network for the distribution of goods and the acculturation of the local people. The success of the market economy of the Roman Empire allowed its beneficiaries to devote time and resources to advancing the leisure pursuits of education, architecture, sculpture, and the arts.

The ability of these early civilizations to maintain a healthy market economy and hence a thriving culture was paramount to their success and often contributed to their decline. This apparent contradiction occurred because when Rome developed markets at the periphery of her domains, they developed an autonomous economy no longer dependent on the central market of Rome.

The Market in Agrarian Society

The traditional mercatus of ancient Rome continued in the many European fairs that marked all significant holidays of the year.[12] The centuries passed and the disappearance of the Roman Empire gradually led to the establishment of the nation-states of Europe even while the ancient kingdoms of the Middle East and Asia were combining or breaking up to form new entities. By the 15th century, new explorations turned commercial eyes north and west. The shift of international commerce from the Mediterranean to the Atlantic and North Sea ports during the 16th century made the fairs and festivals even more critical elements of the domestic economy.

In the agrarian society, labor had not benefited greatly from technological advances for centuries. Life was hard, and work was long and seasonally dictated. During the planting and harvesting seasons, work was never-ending. During the rest of the year, many holy days (holidays), provided a respite from labor. In France in the 1700s, there were over 100 holidays a year, plus days when farmers couldn't work due to the weather. Fairs were both an economic and a cultural highlight of European life.

In the 18th century, at the English Stourbridge Fair, there were stalls not only for the sale of practical goods but: Coffee Houses, Taverns, Eating Houses, Music Shops, Building for the Exhibition of Drolls, Puppet Shews, Ledgerdemain, Mountbacks, Wild Beasts, Monsters, Giants, Rope Dancers, etc. . . .[13]

Clearly, festivals were a central part of the leisure market of the growing economy of western Europe.

Daily life prior to the Industrial Revolution centered on home-based activity. Families engaged in farming or some craft or skill in or around the home. While leisure was discernible at this stage, there was no well-defined division between the obligatory demands of life and those pursued for pleasure or enrichment.

The Market and Industrialization

The change from an agrarian economy to a manufacturing one was as significant as the introduction of agriculture had been centuries earlier. Just as the end of nomadic wanderings led to the establishment of villages, cities, and stable economies, so too did the industrialization of the workforce forever change the underlying tenets of society.

With the introduction of factory-based manufacturing, workers (most often males) found themselves separated from home and family for many hours every day. Separation occurred with respect to gender, age, and suitability for the workforce. The family began to experience both work and leisure in segmented and separate ways. Leisure activities became specific to the place of the individual in society economically, socially, and institutionally. As the amount of leisure fluctuated with the demands of society, entrepreneurs, entertainers, businessmen, and malefactors attempted to capitalize on people's desires to fulfill themselves during leisure.

The relationship among industrialization, the home, and sex roles during the rapid industrial growth of the 18th and 19th centuries produced significant changes in people's lives. The Industrial Revolution lengthened the work year beyond the seasonal agrarian demands, also opening smaller segments for leisure. It replaced past recreational outlets with a more rational approach to fitness, education, and cultural enrichment. Instead of having to rely upon the capriciousness of the weather or changing climatic conditions which led to odd dollops of free time, industrialization gave rise to more certain schedules and expected segments of leisure. Thus, it made the home a focal point for leisure activities as work was performed in a separate and somewhat isolated setting.[14]

The Market and Morality. The demands of industrial societies took their toll on workers and families. Leisure activities, in consequence, often led to excesses and antisocial behavior. Heavy drinking and violence marked the evening and weekend leisure pursuits of many factory workers. Others were too tired and alienated to be interested in personal enhancement.

The evolving leisure market of the early industrial era became a battleground for moral leaders. Government intervention and interdiction, as well as a new leisure reform movement, sought to address the negative developments in leisure activities. The growing need to fill the evenings and weekends of workers and their families with activities fostering healthy interaction and personal growth—as well as many vices—had created what would become the largest, most pervasive market for industrial and postindustrial consumers. Whether that development was positive or negative still remains to be seen.

The market demand was met by commercial enterprise, publicly supported programs, nonprofit organizations, and industrially based recreational activities. The economic realities of society dictated the use of leisure in both productive and destructive ways. Industrialization and the rise of mandatory schooling (at least for boys) contributed to growing concern over the use of leisure during the 19th century. Both of these developments helped to reduce the influence and control of the family over its members' behavior.

Those concerned with the moral well-being of society were consumed with the impact of commercialized recreational activity on the community, particularly the youth. Reformers established myriad organizations to combat commercial entertainment and offer positive alternatives. Public recreational service has its roots in their attempts to offer physically and spiritually healthful leisure opportunities to the masses. The introduction of religious organizations, scout activities, community events, and cultural activities did indeed improve the leisure choices made. The leisure market in a rapidly growing, industrially based, mobile society created challenges for those who sought to protect long-held values and a cherished way of life.

The Market and Economics. The seasonally available leisure of the preindustrial era was replaced by predictable segments of free time on a daily and weekly basis. Seasonal activities, fairs, festivals, and pilgrimages were replaced by commercial entertainment available to the masses conveniently close to home. During the 19th century, a genuine leisure market developed, with the goal of providing diversion, novelty, entertainment, and pleasure for financial gain.

The wealthy were the first to enjoy the fruits of marketed leisure through their involvement in spectator sports, travel, fine dining, and cultural events. The emulation of these behaviors by the working class led to a marketing of fads and fashions that followed the interests and whims of the so-called leisure class.

Thorstein Veblen, in his classic work *The Theory of the Leisure Class,* analyzed the practices of a particular segment of the upper class and how their activities shaped the behavior of the middle and lower strata of society. Working-class people sought leisure activities that allowed them to vicariously experience the pleasures of the wealthy. Conspicuous consumption was thought to be a sign of self-definition and importance.

> *Articles are to an extent preferred for use on account of their being conspicuously wasteful; they are felt to be serviceable somewhat in proportion as they are wasteful and ill-adapted to their ostensible use.[15]*

Veblen's sharp criticism of society offers a pragmatist's view of the standards of acceptable behavior and the often twisted logic of decisions about leisure activities. The working class, through its perceived need for leisure experiences, helped to launch the entertainment industry in the United States.

> *The revolution in transportation and communications resulted in both new leisure opportunities and in the homogenization of its experience.[16]*

Modern Leisure

The population at large became consumers of leisure. The entertainment and travel industries, in their infancy, began to realize the importance and potential of this growing market. The growth of circuses, exhibition halls, dance halls, and other amusements initiated what would become an immense economic and cultural force in the 20th century. The use of leisure, in both positive and negative ways, affected the economic well-being of the society.

> *Through the developing period of industrialization, entrepreneurs discovered that there are limits to the ability of men, women, and children to work productively. Owners and*

managers often saw leisure from a different perspective, as a time for recuperation for higher productivity on the job.[17]

Whether fueled by altruism, paternalism, or the desire to create a more productive workforce, organized recreational activities became a fact of urban life during the era of industrialization. Over time, it became the responsibility of government to oversee and regulate the leisure activities of its citizens.

Many forms of recreational experience and leisure were now sponsored by municipal parks and recreational service departments, by volunteer organizations devoted to special leisure interests, and by an array of commercial leisure service organizations.[18]

While commercial recreational service continued to flourish in most urban and many suburban areas, it was the growth of municipal, club, and religiously based recreational

© Richard B. Levine

The growth of circuses and other amusements initiated an economic and cultural force in the 20th Century.

organizations that led to the establishment of government agencies to ensure the availability of meaningful leisure experiences for the modern family.

Industrialization changed leisure dramatically. Discretionary time had become segmented, rationed, and predictable in the life of the working family. It was because of this temporal redefinition of available leisure that the leisure industry was seen to have great potential for making a profit.

The postwar environment in the United States provided the missing ingredients for unprecedented growth in the leisure market. The mass media (television, radio, newspapers, and magazines) impressed consumers with new standards for personal fulfillment and meaning. Marketing developed in the masses a shared consciousness of the desired goals of leisure pursuits. A homogenized version of culture emerged that focused on consumption and gratification. Consumerism infected the average individual's way of life. Half a century later, the leisure industry continues to ride this trend.

What had been for centuries a natural event in the annual cycle of human life became the fastest-growing segment of commercial enterprise. Travel and tourism, the manufacture and sale of recreational wares, entertainment, various forms of educational and cultural experiences, and spectator events became the mainstay of many cities' economies.

De Grazia states that rather than using leisure as a liberating force to improve self-understanding, Americans have settled for ease and abundance.[19]

Commodification of leisure is understood as a necessary element in the subordination of the entire social system to the reproduction of capitalism and its institutional structure. The consequence to the worker is surrendering to forms of leisure which turn away from self-defining, creative experience and instead, consume vast quantities of market-produced goods and services.[20]

Leisure's most pervasive influence on the market is in the area of consumptive behavior. While the argument continues regarding the exact meaning of leisure, most observers agree that leisure behavior, recreational activities, and discretionary pursuits have created one of the largest and most influential markets in the world.

LEISURE AND MARKETING

Given the extent of consumer activity directly related to leisure, it is important for leisure professionals in both the public and private sectors to have a thorough understanding of marketing. Determining the economic impact of leisure is a somewhat elusive goal, since it is difficult to identify all the various aspects of leisure spending.

Do retail markets today follow the same growth pattern as in ancient Rome? What do you think the practical limits of travel are today for someone to frequent a marketplace (i.e., how far would you regularly travel to shop for food and other necessities? How far would you travel to shop for special purchases?) Do you agree with Veblen's statement that the working class prefers throwaway goods because they are conspicuously wasteful? Do you think the statement was true of people in the industrial revolution? Do you think it's true today?

A third of our time is leisure. Americans spend about a third of their income on leisure pursuits. One-third of our land is devoted to leisure and recreational places. A set of activities that accounts for a third of our land, labor, and capital must be central to our economy.[21]

Americans spent $290 billion in 1993 on recreational activities alone. This does not include leisure activities such as travel and tourism, which is a $3 trillion a year industry with revenues of over $600 billion in the United States.[22] The leisure professional is competing for a critical segment of the massive amount of money spent in the pursuit of pleasure. Cultural events, dining, travel, participating and viewing sporting events, the pursuit of fitness and health, recreational vehicle purchases, reading, hobbies, crafts, audio and video components, educational programs, and relaxation and stress reduction are all part of the mix of the leisure market.

Elements of Marketing

The science of product marketing continues to change as we learn more about the sociological implications of leisure. There are, however, some concepts that are constant and provide a basis for developing a marketing plan. Important elements of marketing include consumer psychology, market segmentation, and pricing.

Central to marketing is the product or service being offered to the consumer. The viability of the product depends on the quality of its production or delivery and the existence of a real or perceived usefulness. One may question the utility of basketball shoes that can be pumped up (for greater support) or light up when pressure is exerted on the heels (for night play?). Nevertheless, the sport shoe market has experienced phenomenal growth over the past decade and shows no sign of slowing down.

Product quality is the best marketing tool a product or service can have. Conversely, defective products can erode consumers' confidence, which inevitably leads to a decrease in market share. Defective products can even result in multimillion-dollar lawsuits against the manufacturer.

Recently a class action suit was brought against a leading manufacturer of inflatable boats. Zodiac of North America and its French parent company, Zodiac SA, are being sued by eight boat owners for allegedly selling defective boats. The boats were manufactured with polyvinyl chloride, which reportedly breaks down under sunlight leading to the failure of the boats. The owners filed a very broad-based suit that would affect as many as 65,000 consumers. The suit is now being reduced in scope, and Zodiac has changed its manufacturing process. But it will feel the impact of the lawsuit and the negative press associated with it for a long time to come.

The method of distribution greatly affects the marketability of any product. Current retailing strategies include specialty shops and mass merchandising. Specialty shops aim for a particular niche within a greater market. Mass merchandising includes retail chains and national and international marketing strategies. Why and where customers choose to spend their money is of great importance to retailer and leisure service professionals. Reasons for shopping may be personal or social in nature.

Marketing and Consumer Psychology. Personal motives for shopping include role-playing and learned behaviors for particular members of a family or group. Shopping can be recreational in nature, a diversion from the routine of daily life. The buying process can be a source of gratification for consumers in need of a psychological boost. Since products reflect social trends, shoppers can learn about these trends by visiting a store or purchasing a service.

Personal benefits also include the physical lift shoppers can experience from a walk through a mall or shopping center. Many malls offer early-morning walking programs in conjunction with municipal recreational service departments, taking advantage of the indoor facilities. Urban malls also offer skating rinks that provide a healthy outlet for children during the shopping trip. The increasing ban on smoking in public areas should help promote the healthy image many retailers seek. Shopping also provides a variety of sensory stimuli for shoppers.

Social motives for shopping are critical to understanding the reasons for choosing a particular place to shop. The agora, forum, and fair all gave people the opportunity to socialize outside their homes within the context of buying, selling, and trading goods. This aspect of shopping has universal appeal. Whether it is a gathering of women at an open-air market in the Middle East or a group of ranchers at a cattle auction in the American West, there is a satisfying interplay between trade and social exchange.

Market Segmentation. Sharing knowledge and an interest in a particular product or activity is another example of the social rewards of shopping. The success of trade shows points up consumers' desire to learn more about a product through gatherings of manufacturers, representatives, and other consumers, often annually or even quarterly. Trade shows give manufacturers a chance to feature new products, conduct special sales events, and get a feel for the mood of consumers in the coming sales year. In the highly competitive market for recreational watercraft, the boat show and exposition circuit has been subdivided into shows for sailboats, motorboats, wooden boats, small boats, fishing craft, personal watercraft, and large yachts.

By segmenting the market in this manner, manufacturers are more likely to attract the type of consumer interested in their particular product. This also creates many more boat shows, which has a positive effect on arenas, civic centers, and the supporting industries of hotels and food services.

Pricing. Pricing includes the actual cost of a product or service as well as its perceived value. Perceived value includes such factors as name-brand identification, convenience and availability, and the promotional strategies employed by the retailer.

Warehouse stores, with their glaring absence of design amenities, suggest bargain prices. This is often reinforced by the placement of drastically reduced items in central areas of the store. The payment of a nominal annual membership fee lends further support to the consumer's feelings of having access to goods at a special reduced price. It would once have been inconceivable for shoppers to pay a fee for the privilege of spending their money in a retail outlet. The fact that these stores lack the traditional environment of comfort and personal services makes their current success even more remarkable.

The promotional strategy of a retailer, on either the local or the national level, is yet another critical factor in overall marketing. Promotional activities are closely related to advertising, but they bring particular attention to a product or service at a time or location that is seen to be critical to its success. Promotions often seek to introduce a product to new customers or those without a particular brand loyalty.

Price reductions, two-for-one offers (pizza, pizza at Little Caesar's) or premiums of additional goods or services unrelated to the product are common approaches to promotion. Coupons have been used on a large scale for decades to promote products to the masses. Over 375 billion coupons are distributed to consumers annually; about 4 percent of them are actually used.[23] So many inserts fall out of the Sunday paper each week that most people ignore them. This overabundance has diminished the promotional impact of coupons.

Many retailers now offer coupons at the point of purchase, eliminating much of the wasted effort of mass promotions. It also increases the odds that intended users will continue to purchase the product because of the attention they get. The more precise the target of such promotions, the more expensive they are to support.

Marketing Through Advertising

Commercial recreational enterprises operate with the same opportunities and constraints as other agents in an open market. The actual cost of a leisure product, service, or opportunity is influenced by both the cost of its production or presentation and its perceived value.

For example, compare the cost of a round of golf at a municipal course ($12 to $25) and the cost of the same experience at an exclusive private course (where prices can exceed $150 per round). The actual game of golf is the same in both venues. The price difference is heavily dependent on the quality of the experience, which is a perceived value. Lovely views, manicured fairways, and greens can be found at both courses. The perceived value may be based on a feeling of exclusivity, association with golf's legends who have competed at classic events at the exclusive courses, and the general decorum of the clientele.

In the past decade, public recreational service delivery has taken on many traits of market-driven pricing. Many services are now fee-based; participants are assessed for the proximate cost of their participation in a program or use of a service. Public services are priced according to the philosophy of the organization or department regarding the percentage of actual costs to be recovered through fees. This has forced many municipal agencies to provide services in a more businesslike, responsible fashion. To assess the market value of a product or service, municipal recreational professionals must know the local competition and the economic and demographic characteristics of the customers to be served. Many fee-based municipal departments collect more than half of their needed revenue from user fees, reducing their reliance on taxes and other tariffs.

Again, this change in marketing strategies defies previously accepted notions of advertising. Who would have thought viewers would watch 30-minute commercials? But today's consumer uses information that will ensure an intelligent purchase and values the convenience of previewing products before buying.

Advertising also aims to enhance the image of the product or service being offered. This is accomplished in a variety of ways. Giving the product a personality helps to shape consumers' opinions. This image allows consumers to identify with the product and creates brand loyalty. Some markets describe this phenomenon as a friendship between the buyer and the product. Agencies often define this relationship before developing ads. Jell-O, according to Young & Rubicam, the product's ad agency,

is that very nice lady who lives next door. She's not too old-fashioned, loves children and dogs, and has a little streak of creativity but is not avant-garde.[24]

And all along you probably thought Jell-O was just sugar water and a little gelatin! Bill Cosby took the product to the next level through his association with Jell-O pudding. The message: It's a fun food for kids. To fight the competition of numerous brands of essentially the same product, advertisers invest their product with a personality. Developed through the use of carefully chosen celebrities and the creation of a product environment, such an identity has become the focus of many successful advertising campaigns.

Finally, advertising helps to close the sale. Often the successful sale is influenced by such intangibles as perceived value, product recognition and loyalty, and the prestige associated with the product. These peripheral attributes are the result of carefully planned advertising. Emotional issues, especially those orchestrated and controlled by the retailer or ad agency, provide the momentum that allows a consumer to choose among similar products. Advertising has an enormous effect on the market economy in our consumer-oriented society.

Advertising is critical to the successful marketing of leisure opportunities in both the commercial and public sectors. Whether it is the distribution of flyers through the local school system for an upcoming youth activity or the mass market appeal of an industry like Disney World, organizations need a well-planned advertising campaign. When one considers the number of cultural, athletic, and recreational activities available to consumers, the amount of time and money spent on advertising becomes understandable.

Marketing in the Public Sector

While the Madison Avenue approach to marketing is crucial to the successful life of a consumer product, the needs of municipal, public, and nonprofit entities differ from the competitive demands of commercial enterprise. The long-term health of a service or program depends primarily on its quality and the satis-

Where you play determines what you pay.

faction experienced by participants. Issues that affect quality in the delivery of recreational services are specific to the programs being offered but share many characteristics with commercial enterprise. This is why nonprofits will benefit from using the basic marketing concepts and developing a marketing plan.

Most recreational service organizations involve direct contact with the participants. This includes talking to office staffers on the telephone and registering for programs. The impressions made during initial contact with the public become part of the personality of the organization. As in the commercial setting, the personality of the product or service can be designed to create a bond of friendship with the consumer. Public relations must encompass all facets of the organization.

Organizational Goals. Strategic planning helps to define the mission and goals of the organization. All public relations efforts will be more effective if staff members share a mission and vision that they convey to the public during every interaction.

While each agency operates in unique circumstances, there are some universal issues for recreational services. The manager must make sure that all instructors hired to represent the organization are familiar with its mission and goals. Through individual training and preparation, the instructors must present their product, class material, or programming in a professional manner. They must care about the safety of participants, punctuality, sound teaching methods, ongoing recertification and training, and presenting the agency in a positive, enthusiastic manner. Quality control in the delivery of recreational services depends greatly on an ability to control the consistency of the program or service offered to the public.

In recent years, public recreational managers have begun to embrace the idea of fee-based service delivery. Participants in recreational programs and users of public facilities have become accustomed to paying fees for these activities. While this was not the original intent of public recreational service, it has become a necessity for many municipalities faced with low- or no-growth budgets. By charging fees, the departments can continue to expand, meeting the demand for increased services without needing an increase in taxes.

The pricing of these services in the public sector is an inexact science due to the lack of similar operations in the area. It is the responsibility of the public administrator to make these services financially accessible to all, yet they are often required to be self-sufficient in terms of funding. In order to reconcile accessibility with self-sufficiency, it may be necessary for administrators to inaugurate fees for popular adult recreational activities and let these activities carry or promote greater access to children's services or provide reduced or no fees to needy individuals.

Commercialism and Professionalism. The recreational services professional may face the challenge of operating a department in a business environment but being told not to be too aggressive. Programs offered by a municipal department, such as aerobics and other health-related classes, may be in direct competition with privately run health and fitness clubs. It is not the goal of municipal recreational services to take unfair advantage in the open marketplace due to their tax-based funding. Many of the administrative costs of offering recreational classes may be absorbed in the department's general accounting. By contrast, private clubs must charge high enough fees to amortize their overhead costs.

This can be an awkward position for the municipal service provider. It is best to communicate openly with the perceived competition and look for ways the public programs can augment those offered by private business. The department should also continue outreach to residents who can't afford private clubs.

Like private clubs, public recreational services must stage effective promotions to bring attention to the services they offer. Often a municipal agency offers quality programs, but only a small percentage of the community takes advantage of them. It is inevitable fact that certain segments of the population, generally on either extreme of the economic scale, are unlikely to take advantage of public recre-

Parks and Profits: Survival in the 90s

As funding is reduced at all levels of government, municipal parks and recreational departments are faced with the task of either reducing services or finding alternative ways to finance the operating costs of parks, community centers, and open space.

New York City has recognized the value of public parks as a potential marketplace. In just over one year, the city parks and recreational department has negotiated the rights to special events held in the parks earning over $1.7 million. This new revenue will remain within the parks department rather than being returned to the city general fund. The special events have included dinner theaters, volleyball tournaments, a toy fair, test drives of the newest BMW, and the world premiere of the Disney movie *Pocahontas.*[25]

Corporations have also made many physical improvements as in-kind trades for product/name exposure to park users. For example, Modell Sporting Goods replaced basketball backboards in many neighborhood parks free in exchange for its logo on the backboard. The department also renegotiated concession contracts, allowing it to replace $9 million in lost municipal funding in the past year.

While the corporate partnership is a successful, creative solution to funding needs, it does have the potential to destroy the nature of the park experience. Frederick Law Olmsted, the architect of Central Park and of Bushnell Park in Hartford, Connecticut, saw the parks as places of refuge in a disordered environment. "We want the greatest possible contrast with the streets and shops and rooms of the town which will be consistent with the convenience and the preservation of good order and neatness," he said.[26]

Billboards and other intense forms of marketing will undoubtedly bring the marketplace into the parks. Such efforts to create additional revenue for a park system that operates in the environmentally challenging confines of New York City have been praised by many as a way to maintain the parks system infrastructure.

When does the need for funds override the purpose and integrity of the park system?
How does a public entity choose appropriate advertisers, and how are inappropriate advertisers denied access to this developing market in the parks?
The city's guidelines will be challenged by companies that are denied space, and lawsuits are inevitable. If you were hired by the parks division for its new marketing department, what guidelines would you recommend?

ational services. However, for the vast majority in the middle, lack of participation is often due to unawareness of the programs being offered.

Planning and Responsiveness. Public administrators, like business owners, must allocate a certain amount of planning, time, and resources to promoting their product. Most recreational departments are identified with the general stock of programs: swimming lessons, sport activities, summer programs, and the occasional dance class. This becomes the personality of the department, and the general public looks elsewhere for other leisure services.

Do you think that most people consider shopping a leisure activity or simply a necessary way to get what they need? How important is perceived value to a recreational experience? If money was no object, would you pay more to swim at a private club than at a public pool, given pools that were exactly alike? What dictates how much you'll spend for perceived value? What is more important to the continued success of a recreational program: advertising, providing good service, appropriate pricing, or something else?

An expansion of activities must be accompanied by a marketing strategy that includes special promotions, advertising, public service announcements (PSAs), and sponsorships that not only bring attention to the program being offered but also help to redefine the department in the eyes of consumers. By expanding the boundaries of recreational service through special events and sound marketing, a department can open new market segments that will benefit the department on many levels.

A department that responds to the changing leisure market and keeps an eye on trends in the field will usually be a relevant force in the leisure service matrix of the community. Over time, these new programs and events become part of the expected level of service provided by the department. The new market segments can justify programs that would have been considered too expensive before the expansion. It is critical to continue to offer the old programs that the public expects. The new, adventurous programs may even begin to subsidize them.

SELECTED REFERENCES

Berk, R.A., and S. F. Berk. *Labor and Leisure at Home.* Beverly Hills, Calif.: Sage, 1979.

Bird, C. *The Two-Paycheck Marriage.* New York: Rawson-Wade, 1979.

Harriman, A. *The Work / Leisure Trade-Off: Reduced Work Time for Managers and Professionals.* New York: Praeger, 1982.

Howard, D., and J. Crompton. *Financing, Managing, and Marketing Recreation and Park Resources.* Dubuque, Iowa: Brown, 1980.

Kotler, P. *Marketing Management.* 6th ed. Englewood Cliffs, New Jersey: Prentice Hall, 1988.

Martin, D. "This Time Parks Mean Business," *New York Times,* February 16, 1996.

Miller, D. *Material Culture and Mass Consumption.* New York: Blackwell, 1987.

Osgood, N., ed. *Life After Work: Retirement, Leisure, Recreation and the Elderly.* New York: Praeger, 1982.

Runyon, K. E. *The Practice of Marketing.* London: Merrill, 1982.

Schiffman, L. G., and L. L. Kanuk. *Consumer Behavior.* 3d ed. Englewood Cliffs, New Jersey: Prentice Hall, 1987.

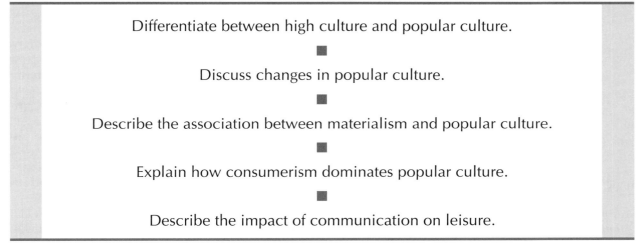

Chapter 12

LEISURE AND POPULAR CULTURE

Objectives

After reading this chapter, the student will be able to do the following:

Differentiate between high culture and popular culture.

■

Discuss changes in popular culture.

■

Describe the association between materialism and popular culture.

■

Explain how consumerism dominates popular culture.

■

Describe the impact of communication on leisure.

Leisure has been available to some class of individuals almost as long as there have been human beings. In the long course of history, certain people have had a great deal of leisure and others have had very little. Over time, class division and cultural level became crystallized. Popular culture, however, has become increasingly identified with consumerism and rapid change. Faddism seems to underlie much that is perceived as popular culture.

Much of popular culture appears to be based on crassness or poor taste. It therefore behooves recreationists to provide an environment where leisure offers opportunities for mind-stretching activities and exploration of ideas beyond the pap that pours from television and movie screens. Surely, technological invention can be oriented to something of value, to ideas of cultural refinement that are enjoyable, and to the expectations of an uplifted, nontrivialized leisure.

The relationship between leisure and culture has been documented in the previous chapters. It has also become evident that there are numerous ways that people may choose to enjoy leisure. A society or culture is defined in part by how the general public, as well as relevant subgroups, uses leisure.

CULTURAL LEVELS

From earliest recorded times, there have been distinctions among the privileged (leisure) class, the working class, and the class of servants, serfs, or slaves. It is convenient to analyze culture in any given society based on these three levels. There is an elite class, typified through the ages by rulers, merchants, and the well-educated. Thorstein Veblen's work *The Theory of the Leisure Class* identifies this group, describes its inclinations concerning the use of leisure, and relates its impact on the masses.

The ordinary class of people, from salespeople to soldiers, from factory workers to service employees, is what we call the middle class in modern society. Most people are in this group, and much of organized leisure, whether municipal or commercial, is directed toward them. The third division within this oversimplified stratification of society is the lower class, which historically included indentured servants, serfs, and other marginal members of society. The people of this group are often too busy making ends meet to worry about using their leisure well.

This framework of class divisions has evolved into a two-tiered system of culture. High culture, or the culture of the well-to-do, is concerned with music and literature and the support of the fine arts. Self-enrichment, education, travel, and an appreciation of nature are considered worthy of this class of individual. Popular culture describes the middle-class way of life. This includes the knowledge, beliefs, art, morals, customs, and leisure pursuits of the most visible segment of society. To borrow an analogy from the massest of mass media, TV sitcoms, high culture is *Frasier* and popular culture is *Roseanne*.

> *This division in the tastes of the populace is evident in the high and low comedy in Greece, the drama and circuses of Rome, the medieval cathedral plays and street fairs, the Renaissance court drama and the tavern farce.[1]*

The history of popular culture and its relationship to leisure have been described in many books. Academics have studied culture for several centuries, and pop culture has been a fertile ground for analysis by sociologists for several decades. Asking someone to define popular culture has

What do you think of the two-tier classification of culture? Do you agree that high culture refers to things that are unique, expensive, exclusive, and within the domain of the upper class, whereas pop culture "appears to be based on crassness or poor taste" and is the domain of the middle and lower classes? If you don't agree, how would you distinguish high culture from pop culture?

been compared to asking a fish to analyze water.[2] Especially in the United States, pop culture is so prevalent that it is difficult to separate or to identify what is not part of it.

CHANGE AND POPULAR CULTURE

Throughout the centuries, societies have been identified with their use of leisure. The interplay of the cultural aspects of a society—including religious beliefs, class divisions, and socioeconomic realities—and their relationship to free time together form the popular culture of the era. The major attribute of popular culture is the fact that, because it depends on so many societal variables, it is constantly changing.

Popular culture changes over time within the context of an individual country. It also differs greatly from one nation to another. In western society, the historical framework for studying changes in popular culture is frequently divided into three categories: preindustrial society, industrial society, and postindustrial (consumer) society. Due to the symbiotic relationship between work and leisure, it is easy to understand how leisure and popular culture can be studied within the context of the industrialization of the workforce.

Prior to the Industrial Revolution, from the 15th to the 18th centuries, Western Europe experienced dramatic changes due to forces that, at the time, went unnoticed by most inhabitants. Most critical was the population growth from approximately 80 million people in 1500 to over 190 million in 1800. By 1800 London had more than a million residents.[3]

Increasing numbers of peasants left the countryside, moving to towns and cities in search of work. Their demand for food caused dramatic increases in food prices, which led to economic polarization. The rich, who controlled the production of goods and services, became richer as increasing prices outpaced the pay rates of the typical worker.[4] But workers, especially tradespeople and crafters, began to move beyond subsistence level and to collect material goods beyond the bare necessities of life.

> *In the past, a peasant and his family slept on the floor, and a mazer and a pan or two comprised all his substance, but in the late*

High culture contributes to the support of the fine arts.

© Jack Vartoogian

*16th century, a farmer might have a fair gar-
nish of pewter in his cupboard . . . three or
four feather beds, so many coverlets and car-
pets of tapestry, a silver salt, a bowl for wine
(if not a whole nest), and a dozen spoons to
furnish up the suit.[5]*

As the demand for material goods increased,
there was a movement toward standardized
production, which created uniformity in the
material aspects of popular culture. The similarity of most material goods stood in contrast
to the exclusivity of design favored by the aristocratic class. While the common folk contented
themselves with surroundings that were becoming mundane and commonplace, the rich
bemoaned the cultural poverty associated with
the lower classes of society.

*By 1800 . . . the clergy, the nobility, the mer-
chants, the professional men—and their
wives—had abandoned popular culture to the
lower classes. . . .[6]*

The middle class sought to imitate the culture of the nobility; this was reflected in the
manners, language, education, and leisure pursuits of upwardly mobile merchants, lawyers,
and local officials. Local dialects and popular
literature, theater, and musical performances
were shunned by the nobility, further creating
a culture of the common people. Yet it is interesting to note that, by the latter part of the 18th
century, it had become acceptable for the well-
educated and culturally curious to study and
collect the folk traditions of the common people.

*When I travelled, I took particular delight in
hearing the songs and fables that are come
from father to son, and are most in vogue
among the common people of the countries
through which I passed; for it is impossible
that anything should be universally tasted
and approved by a multitude, though they
are only a rabble of a nation, which hath not
in it some peculiar aptness to please and
gratify the mind of man.[7]*

The simple culture of the peasants became a source of study for the well-educated. Perhaps the nobles felt a nostalgic longing to return, at least vicariously, to a simpler way of life. While change was evident in the societal order of Western Europe in this preindustrial era, future events would have a far greater effect on nascent societies.

MATERIALISM AND POPULAR CULTURE

The dawn of a factory-based world led to an unparalleled redefinition of society. The time, place, and character of leisure activities were permanently altered by the factory schedule. Gender differences as a determining factor in the availability and use of leisure were magnified by the demands of industrial society. One's place in society relative to the work cycle also primed the changes in popular culture. Those too young, too old, or too disabled to work occupied the periphery of the emerging culture. By contrast, in the United States today, the youth culture often sets precedents for the general population. This will be explored in greater detail later in this chapter.

John Kelly outlines popular culture through the life cycle by identifying five generational subgroups in American society: children, youth, adult singles, parents, and older people. Each cohort is viewed in terms of predominantly materialistic orientation or typical purchases made for amusement and some sense of self or lifestyle.[8]

Several interesting conclusions may be drawn from our interpretation of popular culture. The emphasis seems to be on the electronic media (computers, TV, recorded music, movies) and the ways they affect the commodities associated with popular culture. Certainly technology has an enormous impact on popular culture. In fact, relevant examples of pop culture are hard to give, not because there aren't any but because they will be outdated so quickly.

There was a time when changes in popular culture did not take place as rapidly as they do today. Not that long ago, all television shows ran on an annual basis; changes occurred only in the summer with reruns or replacement shows. Likewise, new cars arrived in the fall, coinciding with the new TV shows and the end-of-summer activities. Now new cars come out in a sequence that best suits the needs of the manufacturer, and TV shows are pulled from production after a few weeks if they don't get big ratings. These seemingly insignificant examples typify the increasingly rapid rate of change in the icons of popular culture. The changes in media-generated popular culture between the writing of these words and their publication will be such that more specific examples will be outdated before they are ever made public.

Cite some examples of pop culture on your campus today. How long do you think these fads will last?

CONSUMERISM AND POPULAR CULTURE

The postindustrial era has been referred to as the age of the consumer. The competition for dollars associated is at the foundation of much popular culture today. Consumerism dominates the lifestyles of most people. Their choices concerning the personal use of leisure are heavily influenced by the impressions cast by the consumer-based marketing efforts of business, industry, and government. As Herbert Gans puts it:

> *The criticism of the process by which popular culture is created consists of three related charges: that mass culture is an industry organized for profit; that in order to be profitable, it must create a homogeneous and standardized product that appeals to a mass audience; and that this requires a process in which the industry transforms the creator into a worker on a mass production assembly line, requiring him or her to give up the individual expression of his own skill and values.[9]*

Dwight MacDonald, one of the first to legitimize the study of popular culture, says:

> *Mass culture is imposed from above. It is fabricated by technicians hired by businessmen; its audience are passive consumers, their participation limited to the choice between buying and not buying.[10]*

Such criticisms are not surprising. Popular culture has become a commodity in modern America. This situation can be partially explained by the evolution of culture that has taken place in the United States during the past two centuries.

The immigrants who came to this country sought a better life and a chance to pursue their dreams in a land of manifest destiny and new opportunities. They were not wealthy entrepreneurs but generally simple folk who may have had a few possessions and a marketable trade. While the diversity of customs, languages, and skills certainly made the United States a melting pot, a mosaic of the working-class populations of the world, this country lacks an aristocratic cultural history. This raises a question: Is there a basis for high culture in the United States, or does high culture here simply mean a higher level of consumption, as Veblen and others would argue?

In the eyes of many western European nations, American culture is immature, lacking a foundation in the more established ways of the older western societies. American culture, based on a very competitive market economy, values such notions as convenience, availability, immediate gratification, and being first. These elements are present in most western cultures, but not to the extent found in the United States. Our culture fosters people's desire for items and experiences that satisfy present needs, are easy to attain, and are fashionably acceptable.

These elements of our consumer society largely define the limits of popular culture. The essence of pop culture in the United States is change. This change comes about for two equally important reasons. Consumers seek the new and unique for a variety of reasons, ranging from psychological needs for relevance to a penchant for conspicuous consumption. The manufacturers of goods and services, including public recreational services, have identified these and other traits of consumers and capitalize on the opportunity for sales. Consumers are trained almost from infancy to seek new goods and experiences. While this is a necessary part of a market economy, it has eroded our sense of culture.

Webster's Dictionary defines *classic* as:

Of the highest quality or rank. Having recognized or permanent value; of enduring interest and appeal. Forming part of the permanent culture of mankind. Felt to be among the great works.[11]

It is mind-boggling to imagine how this word, once reserved for the very finest elements of western society, came to be emblazoned on the side of soft-drink cans thanks to a massive marketing miscalculation. This is not to say that all that was once held in highest esteem is now forgotten; perhaps it has merely been misplaced.

Can you think of any examples of modern American high culture? Is it true that Americans are too concerned with convenience and immediate gratification to develop high culture and classic elements?

POPULAR CULTURE AND TASTE

Our popular culture has produced a multitude of products that are regarded by most discerning observers as lacking good taste and appropriateness. In *The Encyclopedia of Bad Taste*, Jane and Michael Stern state in no uncertain terms that:

Despite phalanxes of eager lifestyle experts who write books and articles to tell us what to wear, how to decorate, and what to eat in order to prove we are not slobs, bad taste does not go away. It clings like a barnacle, multiplying like some deranged cell, filling the corners of the planet with wall tapestries of dogs playing poker, gift-shop garden gnomes, rubber dog poops, fuzzy dice, and souvenir plaques that say "God bless our mobile home." The strange thing is that although bad taste is ubiquitous, no one has ever paid it much serious attention.[12]

The Encyclopedia of Bad Taste explores the world of popular culture by focusing on the more bizarre fads and trends of the past 30 years. While explaining the history of everything from ant farms to zoot suits, the authors provide insight into our insatiable desire for new merchandise. For example, during the late 1960s, artificial grass made of nylon was used around pools and gardens throughout America.

It never needed mowing and was virtually indestructible.

This material was first used as a playing surface at the Moses Brown School in Providence, Rhode Island, in 1964. Its use was then extended to other fields. The Houston Astrodome and other professional sport venues took it up with a vengeance. Despite problems, including excessive heat (as high as 160°F) and difficulty cleaning the playing surface, the product was retained and refined. It has now made a significant impact on sports participation at all levels of competition.[14] For the average consumer, who may have envisioned his or her half-acre lot carpeted with never-fading green, the idea was somewhat far-fetched. But for professional athletics, the product has offered a marketable alternative

That's Entertainment

In the past, guilds, churches, and educational centers had influenced popular culture, but by the early 20th century commercial institutions began to exert more of an effect. Culture had become a materialistic measure of an individual's success, of taste, and of a sense of one's place in society. This evolution of culture from the classical sense to a more materialistic meaning resulted in new cultural icons that characterized the post–World War II American experience.

While most fads of the past 50 years have been curious and harmless, some trends are of concern. In *Hollywood vs. America: Popular Culture and the War on Traditional Values,* Michael Medved describes what he believes are the underlying themes of the entertainment industry. Many of these themes undermine what have traditionally been considered American values. The entertainment industry, offering the prurient lyrics of gangster rappers and displaying an evident urge to offend television viewers, is promoting values and behaviors that are questionable at best, according to screen writer and notable film critic Medved. He cites the following as examples of his concerns. Prime-time television has more violence and murder in one night than the actual police log of any major city has for an entire week. In 1965 the Oscar for best picture went to the *Sound of Music;* four years later it went to the X-rated *Midnight Cowboy.*

Frank Capra, a well-respected and successful film director of such classics as *It's a Wonderful Life* and *It Happened One Night,* wrote in his 1991 autobiography of his displeasure with the film industry:

The winds of change blew through the dream factories of make believe. . . . The hedonists, the homosexuals, the hemophiliac bleeding hearts, the God haters, the quick buck artists who substituted shock for talent all cried: Shake 'em! Rattle 'em! God is dead. . . . Emancipate our films from morality! . . . To hell with the good in man. Dredge up his evil.[13]

Mr. Capra retired from the film industry disillusioned by the industry's erosion of values.

One may question the relationship between freedom of expression, artistic license, the societal acceptance of abhorrent behavior as depicted in popular entertainment, and the effect of this acceptance on the values of society. The ever-present tension between free speech and censorship from within or outside the industry has once again intensified in recent years.

The solution to the continual degradation of values by the entertainment industry, by default, lies in the economic viability of entertainment. The most effective censorship, ultimately, is the will and interest of consumers. If customers avoid entertainment that attacks or denigrates their sensibilities, then the industry will necessarily adjust to the changing interests of and feelings expressed by these consumers.

to the rigors and expense of traditional groundskeeping.

Trolls, gnomes, flamingos, fountains, and religious shrines to various saints and the Blessed Virgin pointed to the common need for individuality in an increasingly uniform environment. Along with these icons to suburbia came plastic flowers, used to decorate the shrines and other "natural" settings created by lawn ornaments. The two most infamous were perhaps the pink flamingo and the black jockey hitching post.

The flamingo conjures up images of senior citizens moving into the newly conceived retirement communities of Florida. The flamingo became a symbol of bad taste in the 1970s but has experienced a resurgence of popularity lately. For the first time since the 50s, flamingos are outselling plastic ducks as a staple of tongue-in-cheek popular culture.[15]

The hitching post jockey, sometimes seen holding a lamp, was also popular in the late 50s. As the civil rights movement raised the level of consciousness regarding institutional racism in our country, many jockeys were whitewashed by their politically sensitive owners. Many others disappeared altogether. Curiously, collecting such mass-produced commercial items with obvious racial implications has become a lucrative hobby for those who have moved beyond the collective guilt of the 1970s and 80s. African-American collectors of these artifacts point to their historical and cultural importance. The items are becoming valuable collectibles in the antique market as well.

Another symbol of bad taste of the 70s was the leisure suit. Originally made of wool and costing four times as much as a traditional suit, the leisure suit was created for wealthy socialites who wanted informal vacation wear. Like so many other symbols of the leisure class, the suit was copied for the mass consumer market—and underwent many mutations along the way.

The preferred fabric of the 1970s was polyester (a substance curiously similar to that used in artificial grass). A feature of this material was its ability to accept dyes and colors that went well beyond the boundaries of traditional clothing. Leisure suits came in lime green, burnt orange, yellow, and the more traditional navy blue. They expressed the need for a certain level of nonconformity that grew out of the unrest of the 60s. Simultaneously, the business and academic worlds embraced the four-day workweek and the culture of leisure. Inexpensive to produce, the leisure suit became the uniform of the misplaced middle-class socialite, the lounge lizard, and the street hustler of the 1980s.

Why should energy be spent studying the articles of popular culture, including leisure suits, lawn ornaments, and everything from Twinkies to tattoos and taxidermy? While fads come and go, they have a cumulative impact on popular culture. In every society, there is a tendency for culture to descend slowly into more profane forms of merchandising and entertainment. It is rare to experience a genuine renaissance of previously valued cultural artifacts in modern times. The truly classical elements of culture are rendered inaccessible and unimportant to the masses by popular culture's proclivity toward fad and fashion.

© F-Stock/Steve Bly

An icon of popular culture.

RECREATIONAL SERVICE: *QUO VADIS?*

The field of recreational service must come to terms with the level of amusement the public wants. Children in particular are passive recipients of popular culture. Schools and recreational service providers must determine whether children should be given what they want or encouraged to explore other leisure opportunities. Our society places such high value on individualism and deconstructionism that we tend to avoid imposing or even suggesting standards of taste and culture. This leaves the youngest members of our society to be educated in their leisure choices by the often questionable, commercial motives of the merchants of contemporary culture.

A friend, recently returned from a trip to Europe, recounted watching a group of young German boys in a small Bavarian town in a friendly snowball fight. One boy rushed his opponents with a fistful of snow, slammed it down on another's head, and triumphantly declared himself to be Michael Jordan. My friend was shocked that amidst the undecipherable banter of the snowball fight, someone would yell the name of an American sports figure. There are many other examples of cross-cultural impact due to the new global economy. Central to this economy is the role of technology, in particular communications technology.

We have seen how new technologies, from the improved tools and weapons of prehistoric humans to the agricultural improvements of ancient times to the machines of the Industrial Revolution, have had major effects on society and leisure. While advances continue to be made in the fields of manufacturing and agricultural productivity, it is in communications that we are experiencing the newest revolution.

The impact of communication on leisure and popular culture has been evident since ancient times, when the mercantile routes across Europe and the East were a major source of communication for people living near of these roads. Gutenberg's invention of the printing press in the 15th century allowed the dissemination of sacred and secular thought for the literate few. Advancements in transportation, including the steam and internal combustion engines, increased the speed and frequency of communication. For almost the entire span of human existence, people could travel only as far in three hours as they could walk, perhaps 10 or 12 miles. After learning to ride a horse, a person could travel 20 or 30 miles in three hours. When the railroad came into being, people could travel 150 to 200 miles. Now the Concorde crosses the Atlantic—3,000 miles—in three hours. The space shuttle travels some 75,000 miles in the same time span.

Is the role of a recreational service provider to meet the public's demand for amusement or to lead others into new and rewarding areas of leisure activity? Is formal culture beyond the grasp of most people? Is high culture only for the wealthy? Do bad taste and a poor selection of leisure activities result from a faulty educational system?

COMMUNICATION, LEISURE, AND POPULAR CULTURE

What is evident in the field of transportation is far more dramatic, but perhaps not as well understood, in the field of communications. The invention of the radio and eventually the cathode tube (television) greatly expanded the impact of communication and entertainment on popular culture.

This century has seen a decrease in the time between the invention of a new technology and its implementation in society. In the past, many new technologies were the result of research and development on the part of government agencies. Their practical implications were often ignored. Today technological advancements, regardless of their source, become part of the consumer market very quickly. It took 56 years from the invention to the use of the telephone. Television was available approximately 12 years after its invention. Recent advances in computer technology are on the market within months.[16] This is certainly the case in communications, where the commercial profits from product development often help to underwrite emerging technologies.

Television has become a major source of home entertainment. While it does not necessarily foster communication among family members, it does provide a communication link between the home and the outside world. Interactive video and home shopping channels have made the communication between viewer and broadcaster somewhat bilateral. Computers and the network of cyberspace are already bringing millions of people into contact to exchange ideas.[17] This, too, will have a tremendous effect on popular culture during leisure activity.

The average family member is estimated to watch 2 1/2 hours of television a day. At that rate, a 70-year-old would have spent over seven waking years in front of the TV set.[18] Television is cheaper than many other forms of commercial entertainment. It is available in most homes, and it offers a wide variety of subjects, from the banal to the dramatic. Television is the most pervasive feature of current popular culture. Televised events become cause for national holidays; major sporting events attract advertisers paying up to $900,000 for 30 seconds of air time. Natural disasters, war, and a wide range of human tragedies are played out, often live, to the viewing audience. The immediacy of satellite hookups allows the viewer to be there as news is happening anywhere in the world.

Television also promotes the consumerism that has come to identify our culture. The images it brings into homes across the country dictate acceptable language, dress, and actions, including violent and sexual behavior, for many audience members. It is imperative that the producers of such entertainment come to terms with the enormous impact television imagery has on society. Its impact on the evolution of popular culture can be tracked in various age groups.

It is certain that the debate on the value of television as a use of leisure will continue for years to come. Recreational professionals must monitor the impact of television on the needs and interest of the public. Television often creates new fads, both positive and negative,

How influential is television in the development of culture?

which can provide useful ideas for the recreationists in planning relevant, appealing programs for their constituencies.

SELECTED REFERENCES

Arnold, M. *Culture and Anarchy.* New Haven, Conn: Yale University Press, 1994.

Bourdieu, P. *Distinction: A Social Critique of the Judgment of Taste.* Cambridge, Mass: Harvard University Press, 1984.

Calagione, J., D. Francis, and W. Nugent, eds. *Workers' Expressions: Beyond Accommodation and Resistance.* Albany: State University of New York Press, 1984.

Gans, H. *Popular Culture and High Culture: An Analysis and Evaluation of Taste.* New York: Basic Books, 1974.

Giametti, A. B. *Take Time for Paradise: Americans and Their Games.* New York: Summit Books, 1989.

Grover, K., ed. *Hard at Play: Leisure in America 1840-1940.* Amherst: University of Massachusetts Press, 1992.

Krippendorff, J. *The Holiday Makers.* London: Heinemann, 1987.

Larrabee, E., and R. Meyersohn, eds. *Mass Leisure.* Glencoe, Ill: Free Press, 1958.

Levine, L. *Highbrow/Lowbrow: The Emergence of Cultural Hierarchy in America.* Cambridge, Mass: Harvard University Press, 1986.

Lynes, R. *The Tastemakers: The Shaping of American Popular Taste.* New York: Rover, 1980.

Nasaw, D. *Going Out: The Rise and Fall of Public Amusements.* New York: Basic Books, 1993.

Oldenburg, R. *The Great Good Place.* New York: Paragon House, 1991.

Twitchell, J. B. *Carnival Culture.* New York: Columbia University Press, 1994.

TRENDS IN LEISURE

Objectives

After reading this chapter, the student will be able to do the following:

Differentiate between current leisure definitions and theories.

■

Understand the residual time aspect of leisure.

■

Describe a number of leisure trends.

The whole concept of trends indicates a movement toward some point or emerging thrust from a body of knowledge. In leisure scholarship, a number of theoretical views have been put forward in an attempt to define or explain this phenomenon. Semi-leisure, flow, experience, state of mind or being are some of the terms currently used. Unfortunately, these attempts have been less than satisfying from either a theoretical or a pragmatic standpoint.

Semi-leisure is probably not possible. It's like being a little pregnant. Either leisure is present or it isn't; there's no halfway. Flow suggests that leisure is total absorption in some activity. Since total absorption can occur during obligatory efforts, it is not necessarily free time. The attempt to define leisure as some positive experience fails to specify what experiences are to be considered leisure. A state of mind or state of being plays to perceived freedom or even a pathological perception on one hand, while being at hard labor or otherwise gainfully employed is contradictory, because obligatory experiences cannot be free time regardless of the individual's perception.

The most commonly accepted definition of leisure is free or unobligated time. Leisure is "that portion of time which remains when time for work and the basic requirements for existence have been satisfied."[1]

There is a general agreement among authors that leisure is in some way connected to time at one's disposal or discretionary time. It is interesting, however, to examine the multifaceted definitions of leisure that scholars have offered over the past 50 years. Each definition embellishes the basic understanding of leisure as unobligated time, yet many go far beyond this simple but practical definition to include assorted subjective and value-laden characteristics. To understand the current trends in defining leisure and assigning subjective qualities to it, we must first examine the basis for the accepted use of the term.

CLASSICAL LEISURE

Most scholars agree that the Greek word *schole* was used to describe the state of being free from obligation. Schole meant literally to stop or cease. Leisure in the classical sense can still be described as unobligated time. Leisure activities for the Greeks included everything from recreational activity to contemplation, peripatetic dialogue and, in the case of the Spartans, preparation for war.

It is clear that those seeking wisdom, the philosophers, saw the best use of leisure as the pursuit of self-development and appreciation of the Ideal. The Ideal refers to the perfect model of a concept or being that exists outside our imperfect world. Beauty, for example, is experienced in many different ways in this world. Plato suggested that worldly beauty reflects the ideal of Beauty existing as a complete and perfect concept. Human beings are also a reflection of a more Perfect Being that religions refer to as God, Yahweh, and Allah. To contemplate this perfection is, for Plato, the best of leisure. Happiness, then, is achieved through coming closer to the Ideal. In terms of human existence, and from an appreciation of the pure or ideal sense of truth, beauty and grace exist imperfectly in our lives.

While these aspirations are admirable and worth pursuing, they were not available to the average citizen in Greek culture. The contemplative life was reserved for the men of the aristocracy at the expense of women, the lower classes, and slaves.

If one accepts the position of many modern authors that leisure is not simply freedom from labor (as stated by Aristotle in *Politics*), then it becomes difficult to categorize the free time of women, workers, and slaves. There were certainly periods of time when average citizens and slaves were not required to work, and these times were filled with public amusements like festivals, theater, and sport. These activities took place in a segment of time best described as leisure. These leisure activities may not have met the lofty standards of the philosophers, but they represented the culture of the society.

Surely, self-development is greatly enhanced by an understanding of basic philosophical schools of thought, as well as an appreciation of art, music, theater, politics, and religion. This does not preclude participation in the leisure activities that are popular with the masses. To define leisure as participation in what is referred to as high culture is to misinterpret the intent of the great philosophers and assign to them a message of elitism.

It is critical for the student to understand the many theories of leisure that have developed through earnest scholarship in the fields of recreational service, sociology, history, economics, and business administration. These definitions, or more correctly theories, of leisure are represented by the following summaries of relevant scholarship, including the work of Sebastian de Grazia, John Neulinger, Gary Cross, James Murphy, and Karla Henderson.

MODERN DEFINITIONS

The essence of modern scholarship in the field of leisure may be characterized by a statement made by John Neulinger in *The Psychology of Leisure*. He writes, "What is leisure? Perhaps it is best to realize that there is no correct answer. . . . Definitions are what people make of them."[2] The ambiguity of this statement reflects the subjectivity that has influenced the study of leisure in various academic disciplines.

Sebastian de Grazia

In his significant text *Of Time, Work and Leisure*, Sebastian de Grazia became the fountainhead for many scholars and students in their study of leisure. He describes leisure as a state of being in which activity is performed for its own sake:

> *In its title this study carries three words— time, work and leisure. Time is a major element, since today's leisure is measured in units of time—hours, days, weeks. Work is included because today's time is considered free when not at grips with work. Work is the antonym of free time. But not of leisure. Leisure and free time live in two different worlds. We have got in the habit of thinking them the same. Anybody can have free time. Not everybody can have leisure. Free time is a realizable idea of democracy. Leisure is not fully realizable, and hence an ideal not alone an idea. Free time refers to a special way of calculating a special kind of time. Leisure refers to a state of being, a condition of man, which few desire and fewer achieve.[3]*

De Grazia uses the common interpretation of schole to mean spare or free time. This is supported by Artistotle's statement that the Spartans used their leisure unwisely in their preparation for war. De Grazia extrapolates the meaning of schole, to halt or cease, to also include peace or quiet.[4] He adds more to his interpretation: "But one senses a different element, an ethical note, a hint that spare time when misused is not leisure."[5] De Grazia details the development of leisure, its relationship to changes in labor practices, and the ways time has been regarded throughout the centuries.

While admitting that there has not been much serious study of the ancient concept of leisure, we find in de Grazia's theory an initial attempt to create a value-laden definition for leisure. While the use of leisure for ethical and positive purposes was certainly a goal for the ancient Greeks, as it is for many in modern society, the use of unobligated time should be distinct from the recognition that this time is available for whatever purpose chosen.

Gary Cross

Gary Cross examines leisure as free time. Free time is determined by the amount of time allocated for work. He studied leisure over the course of three centuries and observed changes in response to the demands of a changing work environment. Leisure was first experienced as a seasonal or cyclical time during the agricultural seasons of the year. As cottage industries grew, home-based, family-centered leisure was experienced. Industrialization created daily and weekly segments of leisure that were predictable based on one's relationship to the factory. The description of leisure and its relationship to the obligations of the workforce provide clear insight into the changes technology brought to bear on leisure as we understand it today.[6]

John Neulinger

After reviewing several theories of leisure, John Neulinger concludes that the only proper definition of leisure is a very subjective one. He relies on de Grazia for a basic understanding of leisure and proceeds to identify two trends, leisure as free time and leisure as a state of being or human condition. Both of these concepts are evident in de Grazia.

Neulinger concludes that there is an objective definition of leisure—residual time—and a subjective or psychological definition. His psychological definition of leisure highlights the condition of perceived freedom. For Neulinger, to leisure is to engage in activity freely and at one's discretion. Psychological study then centers on the examination of this experience of freedom of choice and activity.[7]

James Murphy

James Murphy provides a thorough investigation of many of the concepts and definitions of leisure. His book features 20 authors, each supplying a different perspective on leisure. They take into account the generally accepted definition of leisure as unobligated time, though most see this as too simplistic to account for the importance of leisure in society. The author categorizes these various concepts into six dimensions as follows:

1. Discretionary time
2. Social instrument
3. Social class, race, occupation
4. Classical
5. Anti-utilitarian
6. Holistic[8]

The book is valuable to the student of leisure because it presents the contributors' theories in enough detail that the reader may draw conclusions. A more recent edition of this work provides additional contemporary study of various theories of leisure.

Karla Henderson

Karla Henderson, Susan M. Shaw, M. Deborah Bialeschki, and Valeria J. Freysinger review several definitions and dimensions of leisure in *A Leisure of One's Own: A Feminist Perspective on Women's Leisure.* "Recreation, leisure and free time are words that are often used interchangeably. The terms are not mutually exclusive but each has a distinct meaning."[9]

The text defines leisure as a perceived freedom, giving it a social psychological definition.

Freedom, in some form at least, is essential to the leisure experience. Leisure is time so free from obligation that the individual can choose how to use it; time that allows one to realize a sense of freedom, choice, and enjoyment or pleasure, whether through relaxation and contemplation or activity.[10]

Henderson and colleagues document the historical development of women's relationship to leisure. They identify the Industrial Revolution in particular as a critical event shaping the perceived value of women's labor, both in the factory and at home. The long-term effects of these perceptions are relevant to one's understanding of the feminist perspective on leisure. Freedom and choice are two concepts embraced by the feminist philosophy that offer insight into the difficulties women experience concerning leisure. Leisure is seen to have the potential to facilitate self-development, liberation, and behavior change in many aspects of women's lives.

> *In other words, leisure would imply a positive dimension as well as simply the absence of constraint. This positive dimension may be thought of as enjoyment, personal involvement, self-expression, or intrinsic motivation.*[11]

This valuable feminist approach to leisure study reflects current issues that have long gone unrecognized by scholars and leisure service providers.

Boundaries of Leisure

The works cited so far present diverse opinions and theories regarding the essence of leisure. The authors, guided by their own fields of academic study, view leisure as an integral part of their development of theories of social, psychological, and historical concepts that aid in the understanding of human behaviors and social interactions.

It is curious that many authors acknowledge an objective relationship between leisure and free time. Beginning with de Grazia, a trend develops whereby leisure takes on a series of cultural and personal qualities, opposition to work, and the positive enhancement of self and society. While it is true that there are a number of activities that can be engaged in that permit these things to occur, leisure in its most objective sense is unobligated time that provides the opportunity for an individual to realize these and other goals.

The use of the word *leisure* in other languages lends some credence to the definition of free or unobligated time. *Lazer,* the Portuguese equivalent, is often interchanged with the word *folga,* a rest time, and *horas vagas,* meaning spare time. In Spanish, *ocio* means idleness and denotes free time. The French equivalent of leisure is *loisir*. The German term, *freizeit,* is literally free time. The point of all of this is that leisure is closely related to the idea of free time in many Western languages. These definitions do not refer to particular activities or experiences, nor are they juxtaposed with work. It is true that work is not free time, but there are other obligatory activities that also reduce the amount of leisure available in society.

With the understanding that leisure is a period of unobligated time free from the demands of survival and moral obligation, we must determine its parameters. The finite reality of human existence requires that each individual meet survival demands on a daily basis. In the Judeo-Christian tradition, these demands could be attributed to original sin and the loss of paradise by man (and woman). This could suggest that paradise is a place of leisure. The role of leisure in eschatological terms has not yet been the subject of much scholarship.

While survival activities might be more readily identified in primitive societies when there were beasts to be tamed and enemies to be conquered, real and perceived threats to survival continue to exist. Modern people, having created a plan for survival through shared societal responsibilities and specialized labor, have also created new obligations that limit the boundaries of leisure.

These ancillary obligations of a moral or societal nature make it more difficult to set the limits of our understanding of leisure. When a commitment is made to an individual or a group, a type of contract exists between the two parties. With the establishment of a contract (social, legal, religious, or otherwise), a certain level of obligation is created. While people are operating within the implicit confines of such a contract, their time is obligated. So leisure and the opportunities that avail themselves during free time are disallowed.

A social contract requires a different level of involvement from the demands of survival. It may be terminated by mutual or unilateral action. When it is, the individual may experience an increase in leisure, affording opportunities for enjoyment, self-development, or detrimental behaviors. This time, objectively speaking, is available to provide the venue for any type of activity or a complete lack of activity. The choices made by the individual do not alter the basic meaning of leisure. Leisure is a period of time when a person may explore the realms beyond those of routine daily living.

To fully understand the complexity of modern leisure theory, it is important for the student to critically examine as many examples of this type of scholarship as possible. It is also important to remember that theories are intended to expand and clarify one's thinking on a particular topic and foster an interest in generating new theories.

After considering the topics covered in this book and especially the theories of leisure discussed in this chapter, what is your philosophy of leisure? How do you see the relationship between leisure and contemplation?

TRENDS IN LEISURE SERVICE

Several recent trends in leisure service show promise for improving the lives of individuals and society. They are workplace wellness programs, sponsorships and privatization, and volunteerism.

Wellness and the Workplace

An interesting development in the workplace has significant implications for leisure activities and the provision of leisure services. In the late 1970s, major corporations began to study the relationship between the relative health of their employees and the productivity of the workplace. Corporate fitness programs grew out of the recognition that healthy workers in a healthful work environment are more productive. The focus originally was on fitness, and a fitness center on the premises was a sign of a responsible, progressive company.

In the early 90s, the emphasis gradually broadened to a concern for wellness. Wellness extends beyond mere physical fitness by seeking to reduce health risks in one's life as well as to accentuate positive behaviors that lead to a healthier lifestyle. Companies have studied the effects of wellness programs and have found favorable results.

The Travelers Corporation claims a $3.40 return for every $1 invested in health promotion, yielding total corporate savings of $7.8 million in benefit costs in 1990. Besides improving the overall health of Travelers' employees by reducing poor health habits and increasing good ones, the company realized cost savings by decreasing the number of unnecessary visits to doctors and emergency

© F-Stock/Caroline Wood

Workplace wellness center.

rooms. Smoking rates decreased, as did drinking rates, and employee participants increased their physical activity.[12]

The behavioral changes that take place when individuals are educated about the positive outcome of making healthy decisions will certainly carry over to the home and to their view of leisure. Wellness program participants may replace sedentary behaviors with newfound physical activities. Recreational activities will become more appealing as participants realize their benefits. Reducing negative behaviors may provide additional discretionary income to pursue healthy leisure activities. Leisure can very well take a new and more important role in the lives of participants.

As employers become convinced of the benefits of wellness programs for their businesses and participants discover the positive effects of their involvement, recreational service providers will find an expanded and motivated group of potential customers for programs and services.

Sponsorships and Privatization

The provision of recreational services has been a facet of national, state, and local governments for well over a century. From the Boston playground movement of the 19th century to the modern recreational center found in many towns and cities at the close of the 20th century, there has been continued public support for services and facilities funded through government agencies.

During difficult financial times, government agencies have turned to the private sector to support public recreational service. Many national forests and parks have been established through the generosity of private foundations and altruistic families.

Corporate involvement in the sponsorship of local events is usually the responsibility of a public relations officer, who is charged with budgeting and disbursing funds for worthy causes in the community. The value of such activity is measured in goodwill between the company and the community. The activity is unilateral; the company officer weighs the needs of the soliciting organization and makes an independent decision regarding the level of funding.

The sports world has led the way as a profitable setting for the marketing of goods and services that may have little to do with the event used as the marketing vehicle.

Increased participation in fitness and sport activities, the value placed on leisure, and a high demand for fitness and sport opportunities all provided sports more visibility and thus gave licensees/sponsors a credible vehicle with which to communicate their commercial message.[13]

Corporate sponsorships like those associated with the major college football bowls grew out of mutually beneficial relationships between sports promoters and commercial sponsors. The objective of this type of relationship is to foster an association and a set of conditions that are beneficial and valuable to both parties.

Promotional licensing is the provision of resources of any kind by an organization in direct support of an event (sports or art) or social concern (educational or environmental) with the purpose of directly associating the organization's name/product with the event. The licensee then uses this relationship to achieve its promotion objectives or to facilitate and support its broad marketing objectives.[14]

It is important for public recreational service providers to learn how to create these types of public/private partnerships in order to supplement the funds available through government appropriation. Sponsorships help to secure the place of existing activities and allow for program expansion and renewal. This strategy of sharing the financial burdens of program management with the private sector is one way privatization can take place in the public sector.

Privatization reduces the involvement of government in the production and delivery of public services. Areas affected by this strategy may include recreational services, trash pickup and recycling, and police protection. The degree and means by which privatization may occur can range from government provision of fee-supported services to the contracting of private companies to offer services. At times the public agency may choose to abandon a service altogether, leaving citizens to choose between competing commercial services.

The benefits of privatization through any of these strategies must be carefully considered

One Man's Dream: Arcadia National Park

About nine hours north of New York City, off Route 1A in downeast Maine, lies Mount Desert Island. The island and much of the surrounding landscape are the result of millions of years of glacial activity resulting in a diverse and breathtaking arrangement of lakes, rocky seashores, and precipitous cliffs crowned by the 1,530-foot Cadillac Mountain. The island also features Somes Sound, the only fjord in North America. The island had been home to native Americans, most notably the Abenaki tribe, for over 6,000 years. In 1604 Samuel de Champlain named the area Iles des Monts Deserts, or Island of Barren Mountains, due to the lack of noticeable vegetation at the heights of the summits.

Many wealthy Americans were drawn to the beauty of the area and established summer colonies in Bar Harbor and Grindstone Point in Winter Harbor.

The efforts of John Dorr to influence his wealthy friends to donate land for preservation of the scenic landscape caused President Wilson to create a national monument and later the first national park east of the Mississippi on Mount Desert Island.

It was, however, the generosity of another man that would have the greatest impact on the character of the park for decades to come. John D. Rockefeller, Jr., whose father had made his fortune in the oil business, donated over 11,000 acres to the park. This enormous donation of real estate greatly increased the size of the park, and it was Rockefeller's wish to preserve the land in a most thoughtful manner.

Between the years 1915 and 1933, Rockefeller had 57 miles of carriage paths constructed in the park so that residents and visitors could escape the continual encroachment of the automobile into their daily lives. It is ironic that a family that made a fortune from the exploitation of oil, so important in the operation of cars, would use this wealth to limit the negative impact of this increasingly pervasive form of transportation in an effort to preserve a simpler, quieter way of life.

Many of those trails provide the most scenic venues within the park and continue to be enjoyed by hikers, horseback riders, and cyclists from all over the United States and many foreign countries. Despite the millions of visitors each year, the character of the park has been retained through thoughtful planning and the realization of one man's dream.

Current national park policies include the leasing of facilities for food, lodging, and various concessions to commercial enterprises. What limitations would you place on these activities?

How would an administrator deal with ADA regulations in the no vehicle zones of Arcadia?

Should benefactors who contribute significant gifts of money or land be permitted to set policy for the use of facilities? How far should this permission be extended?

---

before existing government services are restructured. Local governments are now examining the essential needs of the community and how those needs will be met for the next 5 to 10 years.

The role and size of government have been the source of political debate since the earliest days of U.S. history. Local service providers should explore the possibilities offered by some level of privatization in order to meet their organizational goals more efficiently. The success of many leisure service agencies shows that this approach can in fact enhance the quantity and quality of programs and services provided to the public.

Volunteerism

Volunteerism is both a recreational activity and a way to support the delivery of recreational services. Motives for volunteering include a desire for community service, companionship with one's children, affiliation, achievement and recognition, a change from the demands of the working world, filling unscheduled hours with meaningful activity, fostering social consciousness and change, opportunities for self-expression and personal growth, and a way to satisfy unmet ambitions.

Corporations see volunteerism on the part of their employees as a way to build loyalty and commitment within their workforce. Often a corporation will pick a charity or organization and encourage employees to participate in fund-raisers and other activities that produce social benefits for the group. Employees are sometimes permitted to volunteer during paid working hours or to offer their expertise to a particular worthy cause. The United Way often borrows employees to help in its annual campaign. Community involvement, like corporate giving, creates a meaningful relationship between a faceless corporation and the members of a community.

During the 1980s, President Bush and others saw volunteerism as a viable means to address some of the many problems and deficiencies in our society. The Thousand Points of Light program monitored and publicly recognized the impact of individuals' and agencies' volunteer efforts on their communities. Volunteerism experienced growth during this period, offering many opportunities for meaningful interaction and increased understanding between previously unrelated groups and individuals.

Volunteerism has been a mainstay in the continued ability of public agencies to provide recreational activities to people of all ages. People attracted to this type of service find that they often receive much more than the time and effort they give.

Youth sports coaches, literacy volunteers, hospice visitors, day-care providers, and the many people who offer their time to special events in their community contribute greatly to the welfare of their neighbors. It is estimated that 80 million people volunteer annually in the United States, putting in an average of 4.4 hours per week.[15]

There are, however, certain liabilities to using volunteers. Due to the character of their involvement, the commitment to volunteer must sometimes give way to more critical re-sponsibilities and obligations. The time spent in orientation and training is wasted if the volunteer loses interest in the program or activity. A volunteer who is highly skilled in a particular segment of the operation of an agency but unaware of the larger issues confronting the department may represent the agency in an inaccurate or incomplete manner. On occasion a volunteer doesn't meet the department's standards, and these individuals are often difficult to reassign or dismiss.[16]

Volunteerism offers individuals the opportunity to expand experience and to learn new skills that they may later use on the job. The use of volunteers in public recreational service delivery is certainly worth the planning and continued supervision needed to make the program a success.

Do you consider the sponsorship of recreational activities by corporations a positive trend? Are there any disadvantages in that sort of public-private partnership?

LEISURE AND AGING

Seventy-six million people were born between 1946 and 1964. These baby boomers have shaped the market for goods and services in our nation for the past 40 years and will continue to do so into the next century. Because of their economic impact, much study has been done to define and predict their behaviors. This group will soon become the emerging senior population in the United States and will permanently alter our perceptions held regarding aging.

Besides the value system of this generation, recreational managers must consider many other factors when planning leisure services for the elderly. Older Americans are healthier, wealthier, and more active than their counterparts in previous generations. In the year A.D. 1000, life expectancy was 25 years. By 1900 it was 45 years and by 1995 it was 75 years. By the turn of the century, 28 percent of the population will be over age 50. This group controls more than 70 percent of the household income in America.

The perceptions and myths associated with old age are changing rapidly as individuals seek out meaningful activities and relationships for increasingly longer periods of their lives. In both private and public sectors, the impact of older Americans must be acknowledged and planned for to assure continued relevance and success over the next 25 years.

Aging and Leisure Activities

It is evident that older adults continue to value quality leisure experiences, although they tend to seek them individually before looking to public agencies for support. Senior centers have been established in many communities. They often rely on the expertise and energy of retired professionals and committed volunteers to make their programs a success. These centers frequently operate as separate public agencies, but they may come under the auspices of a parks and recreational or leisure services department.

Activities at senior centers frequently include sedentary board and card games, exercise and walking programs, trips and special events, and health-related talks and seminars. The goal of such activities is to keep older adults active physically, mentally, and socially. The basic needs of this group must be supported if the goals of the organization are to be achieved.

Significant Problems

An important issue facing senior citizens is proper nutrition, since many are living alone for the first time. It is wise to include provisions for well-balanced, interesting meals to accompany programs and special events. Mealtimes can be lonely and depressing, leading to poor eating habits and neglect.

Another big issue is transportation. The loss of the use of a car for financial or health reasons can be harmful to an elderly person's health. Providing transportation for these individuals goes beyond mere convenience; it may be their only means of making contact with people outside their residence. Transportation services are paramount to providing quality leisure opportunities as well as addressing the necessities of shopping, doctor's appointments, and other basic needs. An organized transportation system can also provide for trips and outings that elders could not otherwise attempt due to financial or logistical difficulties.

A variety of activities reflecting the interests and abilities of community residents should be offered. As the population continues to shift toward an older median age, leisure demands will reflect the diverse socio-economic makeup of this emerging segment of the population.

© Terry Wild Studio

Older adults continue to seek leisure experiences.

What should a community's responsibility be in providing leisure services for its older citizens? Should the responsibility be a public one or do private individuals and families bear that responsibility?

Leisure service providers should establish ways to educate people approaching retirement about the many opportunities available to make those years meaningful and enjoyable.

SUMMARY

The various trends cited in this book describe current thinking about the definitions and use of leisure. We have attempted to trace the historical development of leisure concepts from ancient times to current events. We have shown how leisure is conceived by contemporary thinkers as well as those from distant eras. We have demonstrated the need to recognize how subjective encrustations have become attached to the leisure definition. Unfortunately, the less objective and precise a definition is, the more vague and idiosyncratic it becomes—until it is worthless.

We have also cited trends regarding leisure use. Obviously, as opportunities for learning grow, there will be increased possibilities for the use of free time. There is no last word on that subject.

ENDNOTES

PART I

1. J. M. Roberts, *History of the World* (New York: Oxford University Press, 1993), 8-9.

CHAPTER 1. THE DAWN OF LEISURE

1. Donald C. Johanson and M.A. Edey, *Lucy: The Beginning of Humankind* (New York: Simon & Schuster, 1981), 327-40.

2. Donald C. Johanson and James Shreeve, *Lucy's Child: The Discovery of a Human Ancestor* (New York: Morrow, 1989), 19, 21, 83.

3. John N. Wilford, "Skull in Ethiopia Linked to Earliest Man," *New York Times* (March 31, 1994), 1, A8.

4. G. E. Chick, "Leisure and the Development of Culture," *Annals of Tourism Research,* vol. II (1984), 623-26.

5. Johanson and Shreeve, *Lucy's Child,* 258-66.

6. W. E. Stevens, "Neanderthal: Dead End or Ancestors?" *New York Times* (February 4, 1992), 9, C1.

7. John N. Wilford, "A Jawbone Could Smite Ideas About Prehumans," *New York Times* (February 3, 1992), B7.

8. "Science and Technology," *The Economist* (August 13, 1988), 72.

9. Johanson to Jay Shivers, personal letter, May 10, 1990.

10. Johanson and Shreeve, *Lucy's Child,* 252.

11. Johanson and Shreeve, *Lucy's Child,* 259, 265.

12. Phillip Tobias, *The Brain in Hominid Evolution* (New York: Columbia University Press, 1971). See also Frank E. Poirier, *Fossil Man: An Evolutionary Journey* (St. Louis: Mosby, 1973), 153.

13. Sherwood Washburn, ed., *Social Life of Early Man* (Chicago: Aldine, 1961), 176-93.

14. C. Loring Brace, "Environment, Tooth Form and Size in the Pleistocene," *Journal of Dental Research* 46 (September/October 1967), 809.

15. John Pfeiffer, "When Homo Erectus Tamed Fire He Tamed Himself," *Human Variations,* ed. M. Bleibtreu and J. Downs (Beverly Hills, CA: Glencoe, 1971), 193-203.

16. James F. Murphy, *Concepts of Leisure: Philosophical Implications* (Englewood Cliffs, NJ: Prentice Hall, 1974), 6.

17. Alexander Marshack, "Exploring the Mind of Ice Age Man," *National Geographic* 147 (January 1975), 74-81.

18. Grahame Clark, *The Stone Age Hunters* (New York: McGraw-Hill, 1967).

19. David Rodnick, *An Introduction to Man and His Development* (New York: Appleton-Century-Crofts, 1966), 29.

20. Marshack, "Ice Age Man," 65-89.

21. Pfeiffer, "The First Food Crisis, *Horizon* XVII (Autumn 1975), 33. Copyright 1975 by American Heritage Publishing Co., Inc. Reprinted by permission.

22. Julius Lippert, *The Evolution of Culture,* ed. George P. Murdock (New York: Macmillan, 1931), 415.

23. George R. Stewart, *Man: An Autobiography* (New York: Random House, 1946), 118.

CHAPTER 2. ANCIENT NEAR EASTERN CIVILIZATIONS AND LEISURE

1. Franz Oppenheimer, *The State: Its History and Development Viewed Sociologically*, translated by John M. Getterman (Indianapolis: Bobbs-Merrill, 1914), 16.

2. G. Renard, *Life and Work in Prehistoric Times* (New York: Knopf, 1929), 65.

3. Sabatino Moscati, *Ancient Semite Civilizations* (New York: G. P. Putnam's Sons, 1957), 55-66.

4. Edward B. Tylor, *Religion in Primitive Culture* (New York: Harper & Brothers, 1958), passim.

5. Johan Huizinga, *Homo Ludens: A Study of the Play Element in Culture* (Boston: Beacon Press, 1955), 15. Copyright 1950 by Roy Publishers.

6. Robert R. Marett, *The Threshold of Religion* (London: Methuen, 1914), 42-68.

7. Wilfred D. Hambly, *Tribal Dancing and Social Development* (London: Witherby, 1926), 133-35.

8. Robert H. Lowie, *An Introduction to Cultural Anthropology* (New York: Rinehart, 1947), 171-74.

9. B. Meissner, *Babylonian and Assyrian*, vol. I (Heidleberg: Carl Winters Universitatsbuchhandlung, 1910), 420.

10. C. Leonard Woolley, *The Development of Sumerian Art* (New York: Scribner's, 1935), 126-30.

11. Herodotus, *Histories*, vol. II, translated by Henry Cary (London: 1901), ch. 14.

12. H. G. Spearing, *Childhood of Art*, 2d revised edition (London: E. Benn, 1930), 230.

13. Herodotus, *Histories*, vol. II (New York: Harper & Brothers, 1868), 117-18.

14. Z. Zaba, *Les Maximes de Ptah-hotep* (Prague: Czecholovakian Academy of Sciences, 1956), 176.

15. C.H.W. Johns, *Hastings' Dictionary of the Bible*, extra vol. (New York: Scribner's, 1906), 584.

16. Excerpts from "Akkadian Myths and Epics," translated by E. A. Speiser in *The Ancient Near East—An Anthology of Texts and Pictures*, ed. James B. Pritchard (Princeton, NJ: Princeton University Press, 1958), 64. Reprinted by permission of Princeton University Press.

17. Archibald H. Sayce, *Babylonians and Assyrians, Life and Customs* (New York: Scribner's, 1900), 64.

18. G. Rawlinson, *Five Great Monarchies of the Ancient Eastern World*, vol. II (New York: G. P. Putnam's Sons, 1887), 510.

19. G. Maspero, *The Passing of Empires* (London: Society for Promoting Christianity, 1900), 564, 782.

20. J. B. Bury (ed.), Cambridge, *Ancient History*, vol. III (London: Cambridge University Press, 1925), 208.

21. Elie Faure, *History of Art*, vol. I, translated by W. Pauch (New York: Harper & Brothers, 1921), 90.

22. J. H. Breasted, *Ancient Times* (Boston: Ginn, 1916), 161.

23. G. Rawlinson, *Five Great Monarchies of the Ancient Eastern World*, vol. II (New York: G. P. Putnam's Sons, 1887), 277.

24. Meissner, *Babylonian and Assyrian*, 429 and plates 217-18.

25. Hugo Winckler, *The History of Babylonia and Assyria* (New York: Charles H. Scribner & Sons, 1907), 7.

26. 1 Sam. 8.

27. Abba Eban, *Heritage: Civilization and the Jews* (New York: Summit Books, 1984), 51-56.

28. H. G. Wells, *The Outline of History* (New York: Garden City, 1921), 230-31.

29. R. Briffault, *The Mothers*, vol. II (Chicago: Macmillan, 1927), 433.

30. Psalms 46:10.

31. S. Reinach, *Orpheus: A History of Religions* (New York: Liveright, 1935), 195. See also C. Potok, *Wanderings* (New York: Knopf, 1978), 28, 97, 133, 141.

32. T. Carlyle, *Complete Works, Heroes and Hero-Worship*, vol. I (Philadelphia: H. Altemus, 1899).

33. Job 7:9-10, 14:12.

34. Job 14:1-2.

35. Eccles. 2:24, 9:7.

36. Gen. 32:24-25.

37. 2 Sam. 6:5, 6:14-16, 6:21.

CHAPTER 3. ANCIENT WESTERN CIVILIZATIONS AND LEISURE

1. A. Glotz, *The Aegean Civilization* (New York: Knopf, 1925), 42-48.

2. Helen Gardner, *Art Through the Ages*, 6th ed. (New York: Harcourt, Brace, 1975), 101-20.

3. M. I. Finley, "The Rediscovery of Crete," *Horizon* VII (Summer 1965), 65-75.

4. C. M. Bowra, "Homer's Age of Heroes," in *The Light of the Past,* Joseph J. Thorndike (ed.) (New York: Simon & Schuster, 1965), 17.

5. V. Olivova, *Sports and Games in the Ancient World* (New York: St. Martin's Press, 1984), 63-75.

6. Harry R. Hall, *The Ancient History of the Near East* (New York: Macmillan, 1935), 56-67.

7. Werner Jaeger, *Paideia: The Ideals of Greek Culture*, vol. I (New York: Oxford University Press, 1943), 5.

8. H.D.F. Kitto, *The Greeks*, rev. ed. (London: Penguin Books, 1957), 174. Copyright 1951, 1957 by H.D.F. Kitto. Reprinted by permission of Penguin Books Ltd.

9. V. Berard, *Did Homer Live?*, translated by B. Rhys (New York: Dutton, 1931), 10, 17-18.

10. Homer, *The Odyssey,* translated by S. Butler (New York: Walter J. Black, 1944), 185.

11. G. M. Calhoun, *Business Life of Ancient Athens* (Chicago: University of Chicago Press, 1926), 13.

12. Homer, *The Odyssey,* translated by S. Butler, 97.

13. *The Odyssey,* 91-94. See also Homer, *The Iliad,* translated by S. Butler (New York: Walter J. Black, 1942), 352-71.

14. Kitto, *The Greeks,* 134-35.

15. Bernard Bosanquet, *The Education of the Young in the Republic of Plato* (New York: Macmillan, 1904), 12.

16. Plato, *The Republic,* vol. IV, translated by Benjamin Jowett (New York: Random House, 1956), 135.

17. Jaeger, *Paideia,* vol. II, 315.

18. Plato, *The Laws,* translated by A. E. Taylor (London: J. M. Dent & Sons, 1934), 34.

19. Plato, *The Republic,* vol. IV, translated by Benjamin Jowett, 253-59.

20. Plato, *The Dialogues of Plato,* vol. IV: Laws, 4th ed., translated by Benjamin Jowett (Oxford: Clarendon Press, 1953), 371.

21. Aristotle, *The Basic Works of Artistotle,* vol. I: Magna Moralia, ed. W. D. Ross (Oxford: Clarendon Press, 1915), 4.

22. Aristotle, *The Basic Works of Aristotle,* vol. VIII: Politics, ed. Richard McKeon (New York: Random House, 1941), 1306-07.

23. Aristotle, *The Basic Works of Aristotle,* vol. VIII: Poetics, ed. Richard McKeon (New York: Random House, 1941), 1460.

24. Edith Hamilton, *The Greek Way* (New York: Norton, 1930, 1942), 31-32.

25. A. D. Kahn, *The Education of Julius Caesar* (New York: Schocken Books, 1986), 7ff.

26. Virgil, *The Aeneid,* vol. VII, translated by H. H. Ballard (New York: Scribner's, 1930), 378-83.

27. W. W. Fowler, *The Roman Festivals of the Period of the Republic* (New York: Macmillan, 1925), 206ff.

28. E. N. Gardiner, *Athletics of the Ancient World* (Oxford: Clarendon Press, 1930), 119.

29. V. Chapot, *The Roman World,* translated by E. A. Parker (New York: Knopf, 1928), 261.

30. C. E. Van Sickle, *A Political and Cultural History of the Ancient World From Prehistoric Times to the Dissolution of the Roman Empire in the West* (New York: Houghton Mifflin, 1948), 341-42.

31. Van Sickle, 523.

32. Johan Huizinga, *Homo Ludens: A Study of the Play Element in Culture* (Boston: Beacon Press, 1955), 174-76.

CHAPTER 4. LEISURE DURING THE MIDDLE AGES

1. H. W. Davis, *Medieval England* (Oxford: Oxford University Press, 1928), 266.

2. George G. Coulton, *Medieval Village, Manor, and Monastery* (New York: Harper & Row, 1960), 307.

3. Carl Stephenson, *Medieval Feudalism* (Ithaca, NY: Cornell University Press, 1942), 18-38.

4. Edgar Prestage, ed., *Chivalry* (New York: Knopf, 1928), 37-55.

5. Jeffrey B. Russell, *Medieval Civilization* (New York: Wiley, 1968), 245-50.

6. Henri Pirenne, *Medieval Cities* (Princeton: Princeton University Press, 1925), 70, 73-77.

7. John Ciardi, "Lesson Plan for Today—The Mother Tongue," *Saturday Review* vol. II (October 18, 1975), 6.

8. Francis Oakley, *The Medieval Experience—Foundations of Western Culture Singularity* (New York: Scribner's, 1974), 106-21.

9. Dorothy G. Spicer, *The Book of Festivals* (New York: Woman's Press, 1937), 81, 90, 171, 221-22, 263-64.

10. Nellie Neilson, *Medieval Agrarian Economy* (New York: Henry Holt and Company, 1936), 38-39. See also J. H. Mundy and P. Riesenbert, *The Medieval Town* (Princeton: Van Nostrand, 1967), 43.

11. Howard L. Adelson, *Medieval Commerce* (New York: Van Nostrand, 1962), 28-29, 32-34, 55-58. See also Pirenne, *Medieval Cities,* 85.

12. Phillippe Wolff, *The Cultural Awakening* (New York: Pantheon Books, 1968), 197-203.

13. J. J. Norwich, *A History of Venice* (New York: Vintage Books, 1989), 275, 280-82.

14. Norwich, *Venice,* 55.

15. Norwich, *Venice,* 275, 280-82.

16. Norwich, *Venice,* 318.

17. Norwich, *Venice,* 412.

18. Frederick Heer, *The Medieval World: Europe 1100 to 1350* (London: Weidenfeld & Nicolson, 1961), 59-60.

19. Maude V. Clarke, *The Medieval City State* (New York: Barnes & Noble, 1928), 1-18.

20. Pirenne, *Medieval Cities,* 175-220.

21. Georges Renard, *Guilds in the Middle Ages,* translated by Dorothy Terry (London: G. Bell and Sons, 1919), 42-45. See also George Unwin, *The Guilds and Companies of London* (London: George Allen & Unwin, 1938), 116-24, 176-215, 267-92.

22. Robert J. Blackham, *London's Livery Companies* (London: Sampson Low, Marston, 1940), 40-41. See also Herbert F. Westlake, *The Parish Guilds of Medieval England* (New York: Macmillan, 1919), 49-59.

23. William E. Mead, *The English Medieval Feast* (New York: Houghton Mifflin, 1931), 15-31.

24. J. Gies and F. Gies, *Life in a Medieval Castle* (New York: Harper & Row, 1974), 111.

25. Gies and Gies, *Life in a Medieval Castle,* 117-22.

26. Prestage, ed., *Chivalry,* 17-18. See also Frederic V. Grunfeld, "The Troubled Troubadours," *Horizon* vol. XII (Summer 1970), 16-26.

27. Thomas Bulfinch, *The Age of Chivalry* (New York: Airmont Publishing, 1965), 71-72.

28. J. B. Russell, *Medieval Civilization* (New York: Wiley, 1968), 438.

29. Norman Zacour, *An Introduction to Medieval Institutions* (New York: St. Martin's Press, 1969), 129-32.

30. Herman H. Horne, *The Democratic Philosophy of Education* (New York: Macmillan, 1960), 414.

31. G. G. Coulton, *Medieval Panorama* (New York: Macmillan, 1944), 95.

32. James J. Walsh, *High Points of Medieval Culture* (New York: Books for Libraries Press, 1969), 83-99.

33. Samuel Dresden, *Humanism in the Renaissance* (New York: McGraw-Hill, 1968), 12, 83-91.

34. Ladislav Reti, ed., *The Unknown Leonardo* (New York: McGraw-Hill, 1974), passim.

35. Norwich, *Venice,* 456-57.

36. Walsh, *High Points,* 135-45.

37. Roy McMullen, "Italy's Other Eternal City, Siena," *Horizon* vol. XV (Spring 1973), 16-31.

38. Baldassare Castiglione, *The Book of the Courtier,* translated by Sir Thomas Hoby (New York: Dutton/Everyman's Library, 1948), 41-42.

39. Castiglione, *The Book of the Courtier,* 42.

40. Johan Huizinga, *Homo Ludens: A Study of the Play Element in Culture* (Boston: Beacon Press, 1955), 180. Copyright 1950 by Roy Publishers. Reprinted by permission of Beacon Press.

41. P. Malmenti, *Venice* (London: J. Murray, 1906), 231.

42. E. Gibbon, *Decline and Fall of the Roman Empire* (London: Methuen, 1914), 331.

43. Castiglione, *The Courtier,* 76.

44. Oxford, *The History of Music,* vol. I (Oxford: Oxford University Press, 1929), 215.

45. Thomas M. Lindsay, *Luther and the German Reformation* (New York: Books for Libraries Press, 1970), 64-65.

46. J. Lortz, *The Reformation in Germany,* translated by R. Walls (New York: Herder and Herder, 1968), 259-83. See also G. Freytag, *Martin Luther,* translated by H.E.O. Heinemann (Chicago: Open Court, 1972), 60-68.

47. John M. Todd, *Reformation* (New York: Doubleday, 1972), 154-239.

48. Williston Walker, *John Calvin: The Organizer of Reformed Protestantism* (New York: Schocken Books, 1969), 181.

49. John Calvin, *On God and Political Duty* (New York: Bobbs-Merrill, 1956), 72-73.

50. Geogia E. Harkness, *John Calvin: The Man and His Ethics* (New York: Henry Holt, 1931), 163.

51. Henry Cowan, *John Knox, The Hero of the Scottish Reformation* (New York: Anos Press, 1970), 379-83. See also W. Stanford Reid, *Trumpeter of God* (New York: Scribner's, 1974), passim.

52. John Wood, "The World of Edmund Spenser," *Horizon* vol. XVII (Winter 1974), 78.

53. R. K. Massie, *Peter the Great: His Life and World* (New York: Knopf, 1980), 617.

CHAPTER 5. THE AMERICAN EXPERIMENT

1. Foster Rhea Dulles, *A History of Recreation: America Learns to Play* (New York: Meredith, 1965), 5-6.

2. J. I. Robertson, Jr., *General A. P. Hill: The Story of a Confederate Warrior* (New York: Random House, 1987), 176, 248.

3. R. M. McMurry, *John Bell Hood and the War for Southern Independence* (Lexington: University Press of Kentucky, 1982), 67.

4. Robertson, *A. P. Hill,* 248.

5. B. Catton, *Civil War* (New York: The Fairfax Press, 1984), 26.

6. James A. Baley and Jay S. Shivers, "Recreational Activity and Family Health," *The American Recreational Society Bulletin* vol. XII (February 1960), 8-9.

7. E. Culen, ed. "Leisure," *Road Maps of Industry* no. 1815 (New York: The Conference Board, September 1977).

8. Josef Pieper, *The Basis of Culture,* translated by A. Dru (New York: Pantheon Books, 1952), 26.

9. C. E. Rainwater, *The Play Movement in the United States* (Chicago: The University of Chicago Press, 1922), 192.

10. G. Hjelte, *The Administration of Public Recreation* (New York: Macmillan, 1940), 16.

CHAPTER 6. UNDERSTANDING LEISURE AND THE RECREATIONAL EXPERIENCE

1. Jay S. Shivers, "The Metaphysics of Leisure," *World Leisure & Recreation* 31:2 (Summer 1989), 28-31.

2. *Oxford English Dictionary* (Oxford: Clarendon Press, 1991), 821.

3. Juliet B. Schor, *The Overworked American* (New York: Basic Books, 1991), 8, 83-85.

4. Otto Friedrich et al., "The Robot Revolution," *Time* (December 8, 1980), 72-78, 83.

5. John R. Kelly, *Leisure,* 2d ed. (Englewood Cliffs, NJ: Prentice-Hall, 1990), 2.

6. M. Csikszentmihalyi, *Beyond Boredom and Anxiety* (San Francisco: Jossey-Bass, 1975), 36.

7. Foster Rhea Dulles, *A History of Recreation: America Learns to Play* (New York: Meredith, 1965), 5-6.

8. John Neulinger, *To Leisure: An Introduction* (Boston: Allyn & Bacon, 1981), 29-33.

9. Johan Huizinga, *Homo Ludens: A Study of the Play Element in Culture* (Boston: Beacon Press, 1955), 88-103.

10. Schor, *The Overworked American,* 136, 165.

CHAPTER 8. THE ECONOMICS OF LEISURE

1. United States Bureau of the Census, *Statistical Abstract of the United States, 1995*, 115th ed. (Washington, DC: Bureau of the Census, 1995).

2. "Driven into the Ground," *The Economist* (January 20, 1996), 64-67.

3. "Las Vegas: The Sky's the Limit," *The Economist* (January 20, 1996), 27-28.

4. Emory Thomas, Jr., "Neigh-Sayers," *Wall Street Journal* (May 21, 1996), A1, A6.

5. Michael de Courcy Hinds, "Cash-Strapped Cities Turn to Companies to Do What Government Once Did," *New York Times* (May 14, 1991), A8.

6. "Holtzman Wants Sewer Contracts Cancelled," *New York Times* (February 27, 1992), B3.

CHAPTER 9. LEISURE THREATS TO THE ENVIRONMENT

1. Editorial, "Beware the Auction Mentality," *The Hartford Courant* (Wednesday, October 9, 1996), A16.

2. R. H. Nelson, "Tom Hayden, Meet Adam Smith and Thomas Aquinas," *Forbes* 146:10 (October 29, 1990), 94-97.

3. J. B. Leigh and W. Cissel, "The U.S. Forest Service: Issues and Answers," *Parks and Recreation* 25:9 (September, 1990), 74-77.

4. Douglas M. Knudson, *Outdoor Recreation* (New York: Macmillan, 1980), 19.

5. David Shribman, "Unnatural Foes, Backpackers and the Disabled Battle Over 'Upgrading' Access to Remote Pond," *Wall Street Journal* (July 26, 1990), A18.

6. Betsy Carpenter, "Redwood Radicals," *U.S. News and World Report* (September 17, 1990), 50-51.

7. D. H. Meadows, "Mankind's Impact on a Tough Planet," *Hartford Courant* (September 23, 1990), E1, E4.

8. L. B. Williams and E. H. Williams, "Global Assault on Coral Reefs," *Natural History* (April 1990), 46-54.

9. Peter B. Pack, "The Sound Has Absorbed Far Too Much," *The Hartford Courant* (Wednesday, September 19, 1990), B1.

10. David Stippe, "Toxic Turpitude," *The Wall Street Journal* (September 10, 1990), A1, A5.

11. W. Von Eckardt, *The Challenge of Megalopolis* (New York: Macmillan, 1964), 53.

12. Von Eckhardt, *Megalopolis,* 228, 229.

13. Editorial, "To End the Legacy of Poison," *New York Times* (February 3, 1981), A18.

14. Paul Frisman, "Green Snow Becomes Waste Plant Symbol," *Hartford Courant* (February 22, 1981), 1, A24

CHAPTER 10. SOCIAL PRESSURES AND LEISURE

1. Richard Bernstein, "Judge Halts Publication of Pamphlet," *New York Times* (June 26, 1990),

C20. See also Andy Grundberg, "Art Under Attack: Who Dares Say That It's No Good?" *New York Times* (November 25, 1990), sec. 2, pp, 1, 39. See also David Broder, "Kill the Cuts and You Kill the Soul," *San Jose Mercury News* (March 11, 1992), 7B.

2. Editorial, "Mr. Bush's Artless Surrender," *New York Times* (February 26, 1992), A20. See also "Bum Rap," *The Economist* (February 29, 1992), 96.

3. J. P. Zane, "Teacher, Doctor, Counselor in One," *New York Times* (February 26, 1992), B1-B2.

4. Arthur Schlesinger, Jr., "Toward a Divisive Diversity," *Wall Street Journal* (June 25, 1991), A22. See also Schlesinger, *The Disuniting of America: Reflections of a Multicultural Society* (New York: Norton Books, 1991), 160.

5. Mary Lefkowitz, "Not Out of Africa," *New Republic* (February 10, 1992), 26-29.

6. Robert Goldber, "Bill Moyers' Doubleheader," *Wall Street Journal* (November 26, 1990), A8. See also Clifford Kraus, "Bank Overdrafts Split Republicans," *New York Times* (March 11, 1992), A13, and Editorial, "Come Clean on the House Bank," *New York Times* (March 11, 1992), A22.

7. John Sullivan, "Mayor's Aide in Newark Is Indicted," *New York Times* (January 26, 1996), B1, B5.

8. Amy Dorker Marcus, "Thievery by Lawyers Is on the Increase, with Duped Clients Losing Bigger Sums," *Wall Street Journal* (November 26, 1990), B1-B6. See also Peter Kerr, "Centers for Head Injury Accused of Earning Millions for Neglect," *New York Times* (March 16, 1992), A1, D4, and Matthew Kaufman, "Grievance Committe Disciplines 15 Lawyers Accused of Misconduct," *Hartford Courant* (January 27, 1996), B5.

9. The Editors, "Notebook," *New Republic* (November 19, 1990). See also Associated Press, "Federal Judge Convicted of Bribery," *Hartford Courant* (June 30, 1991), A11.

10. Jonathon Rieder, "Adventure Capitalism," *New Republic* (November 19, 1996), 36-40.

11. Jack Rosenthal, "A Surer Way to Control Crime," *New York Times* (November 23, 1990), A14.

12. Leonard Buder, "Police to Form New Unit to Combat Robberies in City, Now at a Record," *New York Times* (March 5, 1981), A1.

13. Nation, "Second Park Jogger Case Goes to Jury," *Los Angeles Times* (December 1, 1990), A24.

14. A. M. Rosenthal, "Park Avenue Lady," *New York Times* (November 23, 1990), A37.

15. Richard Levine, "A Little Lonelier in the 70s, New York Faces Fiscal Crisis," *New York Times* (October 14, 1990), 21.

CHAPTER 11. LEISURE AND THE MARKET

1. Editorial Advisory Board, *Leisure Today* (Fall 1972), 15.

2. James Pritchard, *The Ancient Near East,* vol. 1 (Princeton, NJ: Princeton University Press, 1958), 149.

3. Pritchard, *Near East,* 149.

4. John Boardman, Jasper Griffin, and Oswyn Murray, *The Oxford History of the Classical World* (Oxford: Oxford University Press, 1986), 205-07.

5. Anthony Pereirra, *Rome* (New York: Hastings House, 1974), 20.

6. Joan Frayn, *Markets and Fairs in Italy* (New York: Clarendon Press/Oxford University Press, 1993), 2.

7. Juvenal and Persius, *Satires,* translated by A. C. Ramsey (Cambridge, MA: Harvard University Press, 1969), 278.

8. Frayn, *Markets,* 9.

9. Frayn, *Markets,* 17.

10. Martial, *Epigrams,* edited and translated by Dr. Schacketon Bailey (Cambridge, MA: Harvard University Press, 1993), 7.61, 9-10.

11. Shepard Clough and Richard T. Rapp, *European Economic History* (New York: McGraw-Hill, 1975), 35.

12. Frayn, *Markets,* 9.

13. Gary Cross, *A Social History of Leisure* (State College, PA: Venture, 1990), 11.

14. Cross, *Leisure,* 70.

15. Thorstein Veblen, *The Theory of the Leisure Class: An Economic Study of Institutions* (New York: Macmillan, 1899), 94.

16. Cross, *Leisure,* 125.

17. John R. Kelly and G. Godbey, *The Sociology of Leisure* (State College, PA: Venture, 1992), 171.

18. Kelly and Godbey, *Sociology,* 70.

19. Sebastian de Grazia, *Of Time, Work, and Leisure* (New York: Doubleday, 1964), 394, 401, 402, 405, 413.

20. Kelly and Godbey, *Sociology,* 96.

21. Academy of Leisure Sciences, 1.

22. *Predicast Forecast 1993,* issue 132, various pages.

23. Ronald Alsop and B. Abrams, *The Wall Street Journal on Marketing* (Homewood, IL: Irwin, 1986), 149.

24. Alsop and Abrams, 76.

25. D. Martin, "This Time Parks Mean Business," *New York Times* (February 16, 1996), B1.

26. L. Levine, *Highbrow/Lowbrow: The Emergence of Cultural Hierarchy in America* (Cambridge, MA: Harvard University Press, 1986), 202.

CHAPTER 12. LEISURE AND POPULAR CULTURE

1. R. Nye, "The Popular Arts and the Popular Audience," in D. M. White and J. Pendleton, eds., *Popular Culture: Mirror of American Life* (Del Mar, CA: Publishers, Inc., 1977), 22.

2. Nye, "The Popular Arts," 2.

3. Peter Burke, *Popular Culture in Early Modern Europe* (New York: New York University Press, 1978), 244.

4. Burke, *Popular Culture,* 245.

5. Burke, *Popular Culture,* 246.

6. Burke, *Popular Culture,* 270.

7. Burke, *Popular Culture,* 285.

8. John Kelly, *Leisure* (Englewood Cliffs, NJ: Prentice Hall, 1990), 244-45.

9. Herbert Gans, "Popular Cultures Defects as a Commercial Enterprise," in Pendleton and White, 31.

10. Gans, 31.

11. Gove, ed., *Webster's Third New International Dictionary* (Springfield, MA: Merriam, 1976), 416.

12. Jane Stern and Michael Stern, *The Encyclopedia of Bad Taste* (NY: HarperCollins, 1990), 8.

13. Michael Medved, *Hollywood vs. America: Popular Culture and the War on Traditional Values* (New York: Harper Collins, 1992), 279.

14. Stern and Stern, 24.

15. Stern and Stern, 182.

16. John Kelly and G. Godbey, *The Sociology of Leisure* (State College, PA: Venture, 1992), 75.

17. Peter H. Lewis, "Strangers, Not Their Computers, Build a Network in Time of Grief," *New York Times* (March 8, 1994), 1.

18. Kelly, *Leisure,* 454, 460.

CHAPTER 13. TRENDS IN LEISURE

1. John Kelly, *Leisure* (Englewood Cliffs, NJ: Prentice Hall, 1990), 77.

2. John Neulinger, *Psychology of Leisure* (Springfield, IL: Charles C. Thomas, 1974), 3.

3. Sebastian de Grazia, *Of Time, Work and Leisure* (Garden City, NY: Doubleday, 1964), 5.

4. De Grazia, *Of Time,* 10.

5. De Grazia, *Of Time,* 1.

6. Gary Cross, *A Social History of Leisure* (State College, PA: Venture, 1990).

7. Neulinger, *Psychology,* 8.

8. James Murphy, *Concepts of Leisure* (Englewood Cliffs, NJ: Prentice Hall, 1974), 42-47, 77, 91-100, 133, 145-50, 213-28.

9. K. Henderson, M. D. Bialeschi, S. M. Shaw, and V. J. Freysinger, *A Leisure of One's Own: A Feminist Perspective on Women's Leisure* (State College, PA: Venture, 1989), 9.

10. Henderson et al., *Feminist Perspective,* 11.

11. Henderson et al., *Feminist Perspective,* 61.

12. Wellness Council of America, *Healthy, Wealthy and Wise* (Omaha, NE: Wellness Council of America, 1993), 25.

13. Bernard Mullin, Stephen Hardy, and William Sutton, *Sport Marketing* (Champaign, IL: Human Kinetics, 1993), 211-12.

14. Mullin et al., *Sport Marketing,* 208.

15. Mary K. Kouri, *Volunteerism and Older Americans* (Santa Barbara, CA: ABC-Clio, 1990), 22.

16. Kouri, *Volunteerism,* 363.

INDEX

A

Abu Simbel, 26
Advertising, 175-176
Aelfric, 52, 73
Agememnon, 37, 48
Aging, 198-200
    leisure and, 199
Air pollution, 141-142
Akkad, 22, 24, 25, 31
Alexander, 28
American revolution, 80
Animal domestication, 13, 15
Anglo-Saxon, 73
Arcadia, 37, 47
Arété, 37, 40, 42
Aristocratic leisure, 71-72
Aristotle, 38, 40, 47, 97, 192
    and play, 40
    on happiness, 41
    and catharsis, 41
    on leisure, 41
Art, 12
    as chattle, 12-13
    as magic, 11, 12
    and toys, 23
Aesceticism, 89
Aschole, 40
Association, 19
Assyria, 22, 29-30
    leisure in, 29-30
Athletics, 123
Attica, 37, 47
Augustus, 45
Australopithicus afarensis, 5, 18

B

Babylon, 22, 28-29, 30, 31
Bacon, Roger, 62
Barcelona, 56

Beijing, China, 5
Bipedalism, 5
Bougeois, 54
Bronze age, 32
Brueghel, Pieter, 70
Bubonic plague, 62, 63, 64, 68
Burg, 54
Burgesses, 54
Burghers, 54
Byzantium, 51

C

Caesar Augustus, 36
Caesar, Gaius Julius, 45
Calvin, John, 69-70, 97
    leisure belief of, 70
    recreational view of, 70
Calvinism, 77, 78, 79
Campus Martius, 47
Canaan, 30
Capra, Frank, 186
Carthage, 44, 47, 148
Castiglione, Baldassarre, 65
Chalcolithic culture, 42-43
Chaldea, 22, 30
Charlemagne, 51, 54
Charles V, 64, 66, 69
Chartres Cathedral, 59-60
Chaucer, Geoffrey, 67
Chivalry, 53, 61
Cicero, Marcus Tullus, 63
Circadian rhythm, 1, 10
Civil War, 82, 83
    soldiers' leisure during, 82
Colonial life, 77
    Jamestown, Virginia, 77
    leisure in, 77-79
    Plymouth Bay, 77
    shift to humanism, 79, 80

Columbus, Christoopher, 77
Commune, 58
Communication, 14, 21
Community, 14
  involvement in, 163-164
Conservation, 138
Constantinople, 56, 57
Coordination, 107-118
  cooperation and, 107
  councils for, 108-113
  efforts for, 114
  leisure and, 107
  shared executive and, 117-118
Coordinator, 117
Copper, 15
Crete, 36
  slavery in, 36
Crime, 162
  recreational activity and, 162-163
Cro-magnon, 10
  art of, 11, 12
  culture of, 11, 12
  rituals of, 12
  tools of, 1, 11
Cross, Gary, 192, 193
Cotters, 51
Courtesy, 62
Csikszentmihalyi, Mihalyi, 97
Cyrus, 30-31

D

Dark ages, 51
David, 31
Deconstructionism, 18, 188
de Grazia, Sebastian, 98, 173, 192,
  194, 195
Disney Corporation, 120
Doge, 73
Dorians, 36, 38, 42, 48
Durer, Albrecht, 67

E

Easter, 55
Eck, John, 69
Economics of leisure, 119-135
Egalitarianism, 80
Egypt, 22, 23-24, 25-27

architecture of, 25-26
art in, 25-26
culture in, 25
leisure in, 26-27
trade in, 25
Elam, 24
Elizabeth I, 67, 71, 72
Empiricism, 47
Enlightenment, 79, 89
Environmental issues, 137-149
Environmental Protection Agency
  (EPA), 144
Eridu, 22, 30
Erigina, John, 51
Etruscans, 42, 43, 48
Eudaemonism, 41, 48
Euphrates river, 22, 28

F

Family recreational activity, 160-161
Famine, 13, 52
Farming, 13, 14
Feudalism, 51, 53, 60, 61
Fire, 9
  human development and, 9
  leisure and, 9, 10
  social organization and, 9
Florence, Italy, 63, 66, 67
Food surplus, 16
Forum, 170
France, 51, 54, 61, 62, 67, 171
Francis I, 67
Frayn, Joan, 170
Frontier movement, 80-82
  attitude toward leisure, 80, 82
  recreational activities and, 82

G

Gans, Herbert, 184
Genoa, Italy, 56, 63, 66
Gilgamesh, 28
Giza, Egypt, 26
Greek culture, 37-38
Greek games, 37-38
  Isthmian, 38
  Menean, 38
  Olympic, 38

Panhellenic, 38
Pythean, 38
Greek leisure, 38, 39-40
Greek slavery, 37, 38
Greeks, 35
Gregory VII, 51
Guilds, 58
Gymnasium, 43
Gymnastics, 39

H

Hamilton, Edith, 42
Hammurabi, 28, 168
Hanging gardens, 28, 29
Hebrew, 32
Hedonism, 41
Hellenic age, 37, 38
Henderson, Karla, 192, 193
Heresy, 73
Herodotus, 27
Hittites, 30
Hjelte, George, 87
Homer, 37, 38, 48
Hominid, 18
Homo erectus, 6, 9, 10
Homo habilis, 5, 7, 8, 9, 18
Homo neanderthalensis, 6, 18
Homo sapiens, 10, 18
Horace, 45
Huizinga, Johan, 44, 66
Humanism, 63, 67, 73, 79
Hunting, 13, 25, 62
Hyksos, 27, 32

I

Idealism, 40, 48
Idleness, 70, 78, 97
The Iliad, 48
Individualism, 104-105
Industrial pollution, 147
Industrialization, 80, 83
  leisure outcome of, 83
Institutes of the Christian Religion, 69
Instruction, 131
Invention, 15
Islam, 31, 51, 53
Israel, 30-32

J

Jacob, 30, 32
Jaeger, Werner, 37
Jefferson, Thomas, 82
Jeffersonian, 21
Jehovah, 31
Jericho, 15
Jews, 31-32
Johanson, Donald C., 5, 7
Josephus, 31
Joshua, 31
Judah, 31
Judea, 30
Julius II, 68
Juvenal, 170

K

Kassites, 28
Kelly, John, 97, 184
King-priests, 22-23
Kish, 22
Kitto, H.D.F., 37, 38
Knossos, 36
Knox, John, 70

L

Labor, division of, 5-6
Lagash, 22, 30
Lake Baringo, Kenya, 4
Larsa, 22, 30
Lascaux, France, 12
Leisure
  acceptance of, 86-87
  aging and, 198-200
  art and, 12-13
  as activity, 97
  as pleasure, 97
  as state of being, 98
  as work, 97-98
  attitude toward, 80
  boundaries of, 194-195
  classical sense of, 191
  completion and, 96
  communication and, 189
  concepts of, 97-98
  defined, 93-94
  direct expenditures on, 122

Leisure (continued)
economic ownership and, 94
economics of, 85, 119-135
environmental threat by, 137-149
evolution and, 17
free time as, 7
functions of, 98-100
growth of, 83-87
human development and, 1, 5-7, 10
hunting during, 149
indirect expenditures on, 120
industrialization and, 171
marketing and, 167-168, 172-173, 174
market economics and, 172
market mortality and, 172
modern definitions of, 192-194
nature of, 98
planning and, 163
popular culture and, 186-189
poverty and, 161-162
procrastination and, 95
recreational service and, 85-88
restriction and, 95-96
retirement and, 96
Sabbath and, 31-32
school and, 156-157
sectarian agencies and, 158-159
social context of, 91-92
social movement and, 156
social pressures and, 151
specialization and, 12
survival and, 16
technological advances and, 94-95
trends in, 191-200
vacation homes and threat to, 148
workplace and, 195-196
Leisure class, 22-23, 25
Leo III, 54
Leo IX, 51
Leo X, 67, 69
Leonardo da Vinci, 64, 65, 66, 67
Livy, 45
Luther, Martin, 68, 69

M

McGuire, Robert J., 162
MacDonald, Dwight, 184

Magdalenian period, 11, 18
Magna Carta, 61, 73
Manorialism, 53, 60
Mapplethorpe, Robert, 152, 153
Market culture, 169-172
agrarian society and, 174-177
consumptive behavior and, 173-174
industrialization and, 171-172
leisure and, 174-177
morality and, 171-172
Market segmentation, 175
Marketing, 167-179
Markets, 43
Marseilles, 56
Martel, Charles, 54
Mass leisure, 70
Mass media, 157-158
May Day, 55, 62
Mazzoth, 31
Medes, 30
Menes I, 25
Mesolithic era, 13-14
Mesopotamia, 22, 24, 25, 30
Metropolitan area, 86
Michelangelo, 66
Middle ages, 51-63
agriculture in, 52, 55
aristocracy in, 60, 61, 62
fairs in, 58, 59
leisure in, 51, 52, 55, 59, 61
manners in, 62
specialization in, 62
town life in, 54-56, 59
Milan, Italy, 63, 66, 67
Mohammed, 53
Moses, 30
Mount Gilboa, 30
Municipal government, problems of, 154
Murphy, James, 192, 193
Music, 25, 27, 39, 67
Mycenae, 36, 38, 48

N

Nabopolassar, 28
Nature-oriented activities, 126-127
Nebuchadrezzar II, 28, 30
Neolithic era, 14-17

Neulinger, John, 98, 192, 193
New York City, 134
Nile river, 25, 26, 27
Nineveh, 30
Nippur, 22
Noise, 142-143
Norwich, John Julius, 64
Nubia, 25

O

Octavian, 36
The Oddyssey, 48
Odysseus, 37
Olduvai Gorge, 8
Olympics, 35
Oppenheimer, Franz, 21
Otto I, 51, 54
Overcrowding, 145-147

P

Paleolithic era, 10, 11, 12, 13
Palio, 64-65, 73
Pantheism, 48
Paris, France, 61
Passover, 31
Pax Romana, 73
Pebble culture, 8
Peloponnesian War, 48
Pentateuch, 30
Pentecost, 31
Penelope, 37
Percolation, 121-122
Pereirra, Anthony, 169
Pharaoh, 25
Pharaoh Sheshnle, 31
Pfeiffer, John, 14
Philistines, 30
Phoenicians, 30
Pisa, Italy, 65
Plato, 37, 38, 39, 40, 42, 48, 192
    on arétè, 40
    on gymnastics, 39
    on music, 39
    on play, 38-39, 40
Poitiers, France, 54
Pompey, 45
Polo, Marco, 57

Popular culture, 181-189
    change and, 182-184
    communication and, 188
    consumerism and, 184-185
    materialism and, 184
    taste and, 185-188
Popular recreational activities, 123-130
Poverty, 161-162
Pritchard, James, 169
Privatization, 133, 196-197
Ptah-hotep, 27
Public planning, 163
Public sector marketing, 176-179
Publications, 128
Punic wars, 48
Puritanism, 72, 74, 77
    leisure attitude of, 78

R

Rabelais, Francois, 67
Rainwater, Clarence E., 87
Recreational experience, 102-105
    as a positive act, 103-104
    choice and, 102
    fun in, 105
    leisure and, 103
    pleasure and, 102-103
    self-fulfillment and, 104, 105
Recreational service, 130-135, 163-166
    as a movement, 87-88
    business and, 130-131
    community involvement and, 163-164
    economic impacts on, 132-133
    employment opportunities in, 131
    local government and, 164-166
Recuperation, 100
Reformation, 68-70, 78
    Calvin and, 69-70
    Luther and, 68-69
Release, 100
Renaissance, 63-68
    Italy and, 63, 66, 67
    Humanism in, 67
    leisure in, 64, 65, 66
    spectacles in, 64-65, 67
    spread of, 66

Rialto, 74
Risk activities, 126
Rome, 35, 36, 42-46, 51, 63, 67, 169, 170
  art in, 43
  games in, 43
  leisure in, 43
  markets in, 43
  slavery in, 43
Roman domination, 43-46
Rosh Hashana, 31

S

Sabbath, 31-32
  free time and, 31
Saint Augustine, 46
Sargon, 24
Saul, 30-31
Savonarola, 66, 74
Schole, 40, 41, 191, 192
Schools, 156-157
Schor, Juliet B., 106
Self-fulfillment, 104
Serfdom, 51, 53
Settlement, 14
Shabouth, 31
Shakespeare, William, 67
Shalmaneser, 31
Siena, Italy, 65, 66
Slavery, 21, 45, 87
Social development, 152-153
Social disorganization, 159-160
Social institutions, 153-154
Social problem resolution, 163-166
Social pressure, 151-166
Socialization, 151
Socrates, 37, 48
Solomon, 30
Spain, 48
Spectator sports, 123-124
Sporting goods, 130
Sports, 62, 64-66
Spectacles, 62, 64-65
Spinoza, Baruch, 48
State, rise of the, 119

Stein, Jane, 185
Stein, Michael, 185
Stoicism, 89
Sumer, 22, 23, 24, 25, 36
Superficiality, 155
Survival, 5, 6, 9, 14, 15, 16, 29-30
  leisure and, 16
Susa, 22
Syrians, 30

T

Technology, 129-130
Television, 189
Tiglath Pileser I, 29
Tigris river, 22
Tools, 7-8
  free time and, 8
Travel and touring, 125-126, 130
  destination for, 126
  dining needs, 125-126
  lodging for, 125

U

Ucello, Paola, 65
United States Supreme Court, 46
Ur, 22, 30
Urk, 22, 30
Urban living, 154-156
Urbanization, 85-86, 144-147
  public recreational service and, 86
Utilitarianism, 79, 80, 82

V

Van Sickle, C.E., 145
Veblen, Thorstein, 172, 181
Vehicle manufacturing, 131
Vehicular threats, 147-148
Venice, Italy, 56-58, 63, 64, 65, 66, 67
  domain of, 57
  leisure in, 57
  trade of, 57-58
Venus of Willendorf, 12
Villeins, 51, 74

Virgil, 45
Volunteerism, 197-198
Von Eckardt, Wolff, 145

W

Water pollution, 143-144
Wellness, 195
Wells, H.G., 31
Winckler, Hugo, 30
Work, 97, 100-102
   and leisure, 100

as leisure, 101
for leisure, 101
leisure as, 101
leisure for, 101-102
Writing, 25

Y

Yahweh, 31, 192

Z

Zeus, 35

ABOUT THE AUTHORS

Dr. Jay Shivers has been a college instructor of professional courses in recreational service education since 1955. During this time, he has systematically studied leisure and culture and gathered historical data. His travels around the world have allowed him to observe different cultures, examine how people behave during their leisure, and gain insight into the value that people place on their leisure.

He has written 23 books, 70 articles, and numerous studies, reports, plans, and analyses that address topics within the field of recreational service. A member of the National Recreation and Park Association, Dr. Shivers was presented with its National Literary Award in 1996.

Dr. Shivers earned his doctorate in education from the University of Wisconsin in 1958. He is a senior professor in the Department of Sport, Leisure, and Exercise Sciences and the coordinator of leisure science at The University of Connecticut. His favorite leisure activities include reading, traveling, and stamp collecting.

Lee J. deLisle is the director of parks and recreational service in Groton, Connecticut. He has more than 25 years' experience in the field of leisure services, including public and private management experience in the leisure industry.

A student of many disciplines, deLisle holds degrees in education, philosophy, and theology. In 1997, he will earn his PhD in leisure service administration from The University of Connecticut. But deLisle hasn't always played the role of student; he has also taught undergraduate course in leisure services at The University of Connecticut and at Mitchell College.

As a member of the Noank Fun Arts Council in the village of Noank, Connecticut, where he lives, deLisle works to bring social and cultural events to the town. He enjoys sailing, traveling, and participating in a variety of sports.

A classic text for Recreation & Leisure Studies

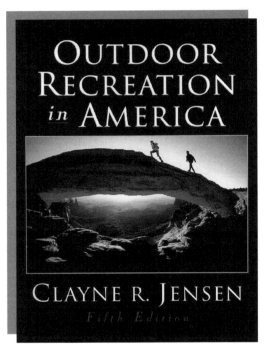

Outdoor Recreation in America
(Fifth Edition)
Clayne R. Jensen, EdD

1995 • Cloth • 288 pp
Item BJEN0496 • ISBN 0-87322-496-5
$35.00 ($52.50 Canadian)

Prices subject to change.

"No other text compares to Outdoor Recreation in America. *I have used earlier versions of this book over a period of 12 years, and I am intensely satisfied with this fifth edition. The pictures, graphs, and other materials are remarkably complete and accurate."*

Clemeus M. Brigl, ReD
Professor Emeritus, Physical Education, Health, and Recreation
Metropolitan State College, Denver

This fifth edition of the classic text has been revised and updated to provide comprehensive coverage of the development, regulation, and management of outdoor recreation in America. It presents practical information including

- common recreation objectives;
- the history and development of outdoor recreation in America;
- factors and trends that influence participation;
- the current and future resource base for recreation;
- resource management philosophies;
- the role and impact of governmental agencies and the private sector;
- financial, legal, and educational considerations in resource management; and
- future trends and needs.

Written in a friendly style, the book includes more than 150 photos, maps, charts, graphs, diagrams, and tables. Discussion questions at the end of each chapter help students grasp key concepts.